AGRARIAN WARLORD

AGRARIAN WARLORD

SATURNINO CEDILLO AND THE MEXICAN REVOLUTION IN SAN LUIS POTOSÍ

DUDLEY ANKERSON

NORTHERN ILLINOIS UNIVERSITY PRESS

On the frontispiece: Saturnino Cedillo, in July 1938, is shown reading a newspaper account of the federal army's efforts to capture him. This photograph, taken by a journalist from the magazine *Hoy*, was one of the last ever taken of Cedillo. Courtesy of the Archivo General de la Nación, México.

Library of Congress Cataloging in Publication Data

Ankerson, Dudley.
  Agrarian warlord.

  Bibliography: p.
  Includes index.
  1. San Luis Potosí (Mexico: State)—History.
2. Mexico—History—1910-1946.   3. Cedillo, Saturnino.
4. Land reform—Mexico—San Luis Potosí—History—
20th century. 5. Peasantry—Mexico—San Luis Potosí—
History—20th century.   6. Revolutionists—Mexico—
San Luis Potosí—Biography.   I. Title.
F1336.A64   1984   972'.44   84-20683
ISBN 0-87580-101-3

Copyright © 1984 by Northern Illinois University Press
Published by the Northern Illinois University Press, DeKalb, Illinois 60115
Manufactured in the United States of America

CONTENTS

LIST OF APPENDICES   VIII
LIST OF MAPS   IX
LIST OF ABBREVIATIONS   X
PREFACE   XI
ACKNOWLEDGMENTS   XV

CHAPTER 1   THE BACKGROUND   1

CHAPTER 2   THE REVOLUTION   31

CHAPTER 3   THE REBEL CHIEF   59

CHAPTER 4   THE RISE OF CEDILLO   92

CHAPTER 5   THE CRISTERO INTERLUDE   120

CHAPTER 6   THE CEDILLISTA REGIME   132

CHAPTER 7   CEDILLO AND CÁRDENAS   146

CHAPTER 8   THE OVERTHROW OF CEDILLO   165

CHAPTER 9   CONCLUSION   192

APPENDICES   201
GLOSSARY   219
NOTES   223
BIBLIOGRAPHY   269
INDEX   291

APPENDICES

Appendix 1.   Some of the Leading *Haciendas* in San Luis Potosí   201

Appendix 2.   The Prices of Several Leading Products on the *Haciendas* of Montebello (1889–1911) and Bledos (1884–1911)   205

Appendix 3.   The Profits of the *Haciendas* of Montebello (1889–1910) and Bledos (1883–1935)   208

Appendix 4.   The Market Price of Selected Basic Foodstuffs in San Luis Potosí, 1931–1940   209

Appendix 5.   The Official Rate of Exchange between the Mexican Peso and the U.S. Dollar, 1900–1940   210

Appendix 6.   Mexican Agricultural Production: Selected Crops, 1900–1907 and 1925–1940   211

Appendix 7.   Translations of Cedillo's Manifestos to the Nation in 1938   212

MAPS

Map 1.   The State of San Luis Potosí   2

Map 2.   México   6

Map 3.   The Location of Some of the Leading *Haciendas* in the Municipality of Ciudad del Maíz in 1910   19

Map 4.   The Municipality of Ciudad del Maíz   54

Map 5.   The Location of the Agrarian Military Colonies Founded by Saturnino Cedillo in the Municipality of Ciudad del Maíz   96

ABBREVIATIONS

ARM	Acción Revolucionaria Mexicana
ASRC	American Smelting and Refining Company
CCM	Confederación de la Clase Media
CCM	Confederación Campesina Mexicana
CGOCM	Confederación General de Obreros y Campesinos de México
CNA	Comisión Nacional Agraria
CNC	Confederación Nacional Campesina
CNOM	Confederación Nacional de Organizaciones Magisteriales
CPRM	Confederación Patronal de la República Mexicana
CTM	Confederación de Trabajadores Mexicanos
CROM	Confederación Regional Obrera Mexicana
DAAC	Departamento de Asuntos Agrarios y Colonización
FROC	Federación Regional de Obreros y Campesinos
LNC	Liga Nacional Campesina
LNDLR	Liga Nacional de la Defensa de la Libertad Religiosa
PCN	Partido Cooperatista Nacional
PLM	Partido Liberal Mexicano
PNR	Partido Nacional Revolucionario
PRI	Partido Revolucionario Institucional
PRM	Partido de la Revolución Mexicana
UNVR	Unión Nacional de Veteranos de la Revolución

PREFACE

U ntil recently, historians of modern Mexico tended to neglect the years 1920 to 1940 and to concentrate upon the more dramatic decade of the Maderista revolution and the subsequent civil wars (1910–1920) or upon Mexico's spectacular—albeit uneven—economic growth since the 1940s. During the last few years, however, an attempt has been made to rectify this imbalance. The most important contribution has been the outstanding account by Jean Meyer of the Cristero revolt; other examples are Anatol Shulgovski's provocative history of the Cárdenas period, and volumes III to VI of the *Historia de la Revolución Mexicana,* produced by a team of historians from the Colegio de México. In addition to these more general works there have been several regional studies. Good examples of these are Heather Fowler Salamini's and Romana Falcón's accounts of the agrarian movement in Veracruz, Ian Jacobs's work on the Figueroa brothers, Carlos Martínez Assad's analysis of the regime of Tomás Garrido Canabal in Tabasco, and Gil Joseph's history of the early years of the Revolution in Yucatán. In a country as geographically and culturally diverse as Mexico, such studies have proved of particular value and contributed greatly to our understanding of the period.[1]

This book is the by-product of one such regional study, which I prepared for presentation as a doctoral thesis at Cambridge University. When I planned the research for my dissertation I decided to consider the relationship at a state level between political stabilization and agrarian reform in Mexico in the years 1920 to 1940. I chose San Luis Potosí as the region in which to analyze this relationship, since this was the setting for one of the more important agrarian movements of the period. This movement was led by Saturnino Cedillo, a local guerrilla leader turned revolutionary general. Cedillo's dominance of the state after 1920 was so dramatic that I was drawn into combining my regional study with an account of his life. In so doing I became aware of another tradition within the historiography of the Mexican Revolution, exemplified by

John Womack's study of Zapata, Michael Meyer's work on Orozco and Huerta, and Linda Hall's portrayal of the rise of Obregón. And thus, these two threads of local history and political biography also run through this book. It is impossible to understand Cedillo's initial revolt and rise to prominence without close reference to the economic and social conditions that prevailed in San Luis Potosí in the late Porfiriato, and the development of the state from 1920 onwards was inextricably linked to Cedillo's political career. In fact, it is probably true to say that for the last decade of his life the government of the state was synonymous with his name.

An additional benefit to be derived from studying the career of an important agrarian leader such as Cedillo is that it allows the historian to address one of the central problems of the Revolution: the role of the peasantry. Was the Mexican Revolution the first successful peasant revolt of the twentieth century, which through the subsequent agrarian reform provided the rural masses with substantial material gains? Or were those masses simply mobilized by the national bourgeoisie to overthrow the Porfirian oligarchy, only to be brought under the tight control of the new ruling class once they aspired to goals of their own? The former view was common among contemporary observers such as Tannenbaum or Gruening. Highly critical of the *hacienda* system which dominated Porfirian agriculture and which they considered economically backward and socially oppressive, they stressed both the role of the peasantry in the overthrow of Díaz and the benefits that the rural masses derived from the agrarian reform. More recent commentators, however, such as Córdova, Fowler, and Meyer, have tended toward the latter viewpoint. They have emphasized the manipulation of the peasantry in post-Porfirian Mexico, popular resistance to the regime which found expression in the Cristero revolt in the 1920s and the Sinarquista movement in the 1940s, and the relatively slow rise in living standards in the rural sector since 1920.

I do not pretend that this study even begins to resolve the above questions, which more learned historians than I will doubtless continue to debate for years to come, but I hope that it sheds some light upon them in the context of San Luis Potosí. There, as I trust will become clear, popular agitation for agrarian reform as personified by Cedillo did play an important role in the continuing political violence from 1910 to 1920. Similarly, the land redistribution carried out during the following two decades, much of it under Cedillo's own aegis, did have a profound effect upon rural society. Also, and this I believe is the crucial point, the beneficiaries of the agrarian reform, both in San Luis Potosí and elsewhere, never freed themselves from their subordination to the interests of the country's post-revolutionary rulers.

Initially this subordination took the form of political support for a number of regional *caudillos* and provincial politicians who had sponsored land reform, such as Saturnino Cedillo in San Luis Potosí and Adalberto Tejeda in Veracruz. More importantly, it also involved military service. During the 1920s the government mobilized large number of *ejidatarios* and other recipients of land—known collectively as *"agraristas"*—in order to overcome a series of armed uprisings. Sometimes these two expressions of clientship merged, as when Cedillo raised eight thousand *agraristas* from San Luis Potosí to help to quell the Cristero revolt. (This insurrection, which was provoked by the government's persecution of the Church and developed into a three-year civil war, was perhaps the most dramatic illustration of the dependent status of the *agraristas*. As the price for their land, they were obliged to participate in a gratuitous and bitter armed conflict with their fellow *campesinos*). Gradually, however, the patronage of individual military commanders and state governors was absorbed into that of an all-embracing agrarian bureaucracy, which, by the end of the 1920s, had effectively assumed the functions of the vanquished *hacendados*. To the *ejidatarios,* this development did not always appear to be to their obvious advantage. Cedillo was not alone in pointing out that the emerging class of agrarian bureaucrats and politicians could be as parasitical and tyrannical as the *hacendados*. The files of the Agrarian Department contain many such complaints from *ejidatarios* throughout the country. Nevertheless, the government's control over the *ejidatarios* was to have important consequences for Mexico's subsequent political stability and economic development. It assisted successive administrations in maintaining low prices for agricultural products during the early stages of the country's industrialization without fear of provoking unrest as a result of the imbalance between rural and urban living standards.

This book, however, is above all a political biography: the history of one man and the role he played in the events of his time. It is an account of how, in the circumstances of the Revolution, Saturnino Cedillo, the humble son of a *ranchero,* could rise to govern San Luis Potosí like a private fief and be considered a candidate for the country's presidency. It also seeks to explain why his power crumbled and how he came to die a fugitive in the mountains near his birthplace. Chapter 1 describes the political and economic development of San Luis Potosí during the Porfiriato and thus provides the background for what follows. Chapters 2 and 3 are an account of the Maderista revolt in San Luis Potosí, the entry of Saturnino Cedillo and his brothers into the Revolution, and the years of civil war that followed Madero's overthrow. Chapter 4 traces the rise of Cedillo through the De la Huerta revolt of 1923–1924 and ends with his ousting of Aurelio Manrique as governor of San Luis Potosí in 1925. Chapter 5 is a brief history of the religious conflict in San Luis Potosí from 1926–1929 and of Cedillo's own role in combating the Cristeros. Chapter 6 is an analysis of his regime in San Luis Potosí, and chapters 7 and 8 trace the course of his relations with the central government under Cárdenas, ending with Cedillo's abortive rebellion in 1938. This is followed by a short conclusion.

Such is the outline of the story I have attempted to reconstruct. Readers may find that it has some of the attributes of a tragic drama; and certainly for Cedillo and many of his associates it ended upon such a note. In the eyes of most of his fellow countrymen Cedillo died a traitor and a renegade, and he was recorded in the annals of the time as a tool of foreign interests and a friend of Fascists. Even now, when his name is largely forgotten outside San Luis Potosí, it still evokes scorn from most of those few of his compatriots who recognize it. But only rarely does history deal kindly with those who seek to detain its progress. Zapata, perhaps Cedillo's closest counterpart among the major revolutionary leaders, died young enough to be enshrined as a hero in the Revolution's mythology. Cedillo's real tragedy was that he outlived the first violent years of the Revolution and proved unable to adapt to the new world of state bureaucracy and machine politics in which he found himself enmeshed toward the end of his life. Now, over forty years after his doomed revolt, we can perhaps look at his career more dispassionately. That, for better or for worse, is what I have sought to do here.

ACKNOWLEDGMENTS

In the course of preparing this book I received help and encouragement from many people. They include the staffs of the libraries and archives where I worked, as well as friends and colleagues. I do not have the space to mention them all here, but there are some to whom I am particularly indebted. Any errors of fact or interpretation in the book are, of course, my own sole responsibility.

I would like to thank Dr. John Street and Professor David Rock, who first encouraged me to take an interest in Latin American history. Dr. David Brading was the supervisor of my doctoral dissertation. Without his guidance, patience, and wisdom I would never have completed either the dissertation or, in consequence, this book. Dr. Peter Calvert and Mr. Malcolm Deas were sympathetic examiners of the dissertation. Professor Christopher Platt made a number of constructive suggestions about how I might improve the manuscript for publication. Professor John Lynch helped me raise my head above the parapet of the Mexican Revolution and see it in a wider Latin American context, and Dr. James Murray greatly increased my understanding of the development of the Mexican political system since 1910. Jonathan Hill, Tim Connell, and Robin Lloyd shared with me numerous insights into contemporary Mexican society and politics.

I would also like to thank those colleagues who attended the seminar on "Caudillo and Peasant in the Mexican Revolution," which Dr. David Brading organized at Cambridge in 1977. Their comments on the paper I gave there helped to clarify my thoughts on Cedillo's role in the Revolution. Particularly useful were the views of Professor Gil Joseph, Dr. Hector Aguilar Camín, Professor Raymond Buve, Dr. Hans Werner Tobler, Mr. Malcolm Deas, Dr. Ian Jacobs, and Dr. Alan Knight. The latter two are long-standing friends to whom I am particularly indebted. I have spent many hours discussing the Mexican Revolution with Alan Knight and profited greatly from his extensive knowledge and deep understanding of the subject. The same is true of Ian Jacobs, whose recently published account of the Revolution in Guerrero is a model of its kind. The staffs of Cambridge University library, the Public Record Office in London, and the Library of Congress in Washington were as courteous as they were efficient.

While in Mexico City, I was greatly assisted by the staffs of the National Archive, the archives of the Ministry of Defense and Agrarian Reform, the Hemeroteca Nacional, the library of the Colegio de México, and the National Library. The late former president Emilio Portes Gil not only gave me several hours of his time to discuss his role in the Revolution but also obtained the permission of the then defense minister, General Hermenegildo Cuenca Díaz, for me to have access to the Ministry's archive. Sr. Jorge Prieto Laurens was kind enough to spend an hour with me discussing his political career and relationship with Cedillo, and Sr. José Valades gave me a vivid account of the labor movement in the 1920s. The late Dr. Prodyot Mukherjee gave me early encouragement to persevere with my research, and Professor Jean Meyer freely offered me advice on possible sources on the Revolution in San Luis Potosí. Dr. Romana Falcón broadened my understanding of Cedillo's regime in San Luis Potosí and of the Cárdenas presidency, and Dr. Alfonso Campos clarified a number of points relating to the general history of the Porfiriato. Others to whom I am indebted for the benefit of their knowledge of the Revolution include Dr. Enrique Semo, Dr. Arnaldo Córdova, Dr. Beatriz Rojas, Professor Jan Bazant, Professor Lorenzo Meyer, Dr. Malcolm Hoodless, and Professor Robert Quirk. Although we only met briefly in Morelia in 1981, I would also like to express my debt to Professor James Cockroft. Anyone studying the Porfiriato in San Luis Potosí must begin by acknowledging his pioneer work. His book is important not only in itself but also as a valuable guide to future researchers.

In San Luis Potosí I received help in many ways. Sr. Octaviano Cabrera Ipiña allowed me free access to his valuable family archive and shared with me his encyclopedic knowledge of the history and traditions of the state. The hospitality which he and his wife Doña Carmen showed me made my stay there unforgettable. Sr. Ernesto Cabrera Ipiña, Octaviano's brother, described to me the exciting, if hazardous, life of an *hacendado* in San Luis Potosí during the 1920s and 1930s. The late Sr. Nereo Rodríguez Barragán, who made such an important contribution to the historiography of the state, happily allowed me to tap his immense store of knowledge of the Revolution and obtained permission for me to visit the state archive. Father Rafael Montejano y Aguiñaga, another noted local historian, gave me free access to the University library and archive in San Luis Potosí. Sr. Alejandro Espinosa y Pitman kindly provided me with information on the Espinosa y Cuevas family estates. Licenciada Ruth Arvide, the restorer and custodian of the municipal archive in San Luis Potosí, authorized me to have the use of a room there for the duration of my stay. She also introduced me to her father, Colonel José Arvide, who was Saturnino Cedillo's secretary for over ten years until 1938. The colonel kindly lent me his manuscript biography of Cedillo and showed me a number of interesting documents in his possession. He also clarified certain questions I had concerning Cedillo's later career. Other Cedillistas who were happy to share their reminiscences with me were Sr. Salvador Muñiz and Colonel Manuel Fuentes. In 1979 I was Colonel Fuentes's guest at Palomas for the annual lunch that Cedillo's followers hold in his honor on the anniversary of his death. It was a memorable occasion in true *ranchero* style. Sr. Juan Ochoa Vázquez, the Agrarian Department official in charge of Cedillo's colonies during my time in San Luis Potosí, provided me with much information about them. Licenciado José Perogordo y Lazo, who was Cedillo's defense lawyer when Cedillo was tried for rebellion in 1913, described to me Cedillo's early life. Sr. José Martínez and Sr. Manuel Mata, veteran *agraristas,* recounted for me their experiences in the Cristero war, including the battle of Tepatitlán. Finally, on a more personal note, I will always be grateful to that honorary Potosina, the late Fiona Alexander, for helping me with introductions in San Luis Potosí. She is badly missed by all her many friends both there and elsewhere.

For financial support during the period in which I researched and wrote this book I am grateful to the British Council, the National University of Mexico, and the Social Science Research Council in London. I would like to thank Miss Jill Biddington, Miss Helen Wilson, and Mrs. Rae Browne for typing the manuscript at various stages; Mr. John Childs for the preparation of the maps; and the staff of the Northern Illinois University Press for all their guidance and help in the editing and production of the book.

I am also grateful to Mr. Graham Greene for permission to quote from his book, *The Lawless Roads,* one of the most illuminating contemporary accounts of life in Mexico during the presidency of Lázaro Cárdenas.

My greatest debts are to my parents, for their early encouragement to me in my studies and research, and, above all, to my wife Silvia. She has seen this book grow from the hesitant first chapter of a doctoral dissertation into its present form. Without her constant support and understanding I would certainly never have completed it.

CHAPTER 1

THE BACKGROUND

THE COUNTRY AROUND SAN LUIS POTOSÍ IS WONDERFULLY PRODUCTIVE, AND THIS HAS DONE MUCH TO INCREASE THE CITY'S PROSPERITY.

AFTER DÍAZ WHAT? THAT IS THE QUESTION WHICH IN THESE YEARS HAS BEEN ASKED AGAIN AND AGAIN IN MEXICO.——W. E. Carson, *Mexico: The Wonderland of the South*

The state of San Luis Potosí is situated on the southeastern fringe of the Mesa del Norte, the vast expanse of arid plains and mountains which extends from central Mexico into the United States. It lies across the mountain ranges of the Sierra Madre Oriental which run parallel to the Gulf Coast and form a series of steppes falling away from a height of 2,200 meters above sea level in the west to about 100 meters above sea level in the east.

The nature of the climate and terrain divides the state into five well-defined sectors. The north and west are hot and dry and suitable for cattle and sheep farming; the northeast is similar, but it contains an abundance of fiber plants which extends into Nuevo León and Tamaulipas. The southwest is divided into a series of valleys separated by rocky hills. San Luis Potosí shares the same climate as the adjacent states of Guanajuato and Querétaro and forms the northeastern edge of the Bajío. More abundant rainfall than further north permits the production of large quantities of arable crops. Sheep find adequate pasture on the hillsides, and vines and prickly pear are successfully cultivated in this area. Eastward, through the mountains beyond Santa María del Río and at 1,000 meters above sea level is the plain of Río Verde. Lying in the shadow of the Sierra Madre Oriental but with greater rainfall than the corresponding zone to the north, the region is rich in agriculture—crop and fruit farming, cattle raising, and sugar production. Dividing this region from the tropical Huasteca is the Sierra Madre, a confusion of tree-covered mountains

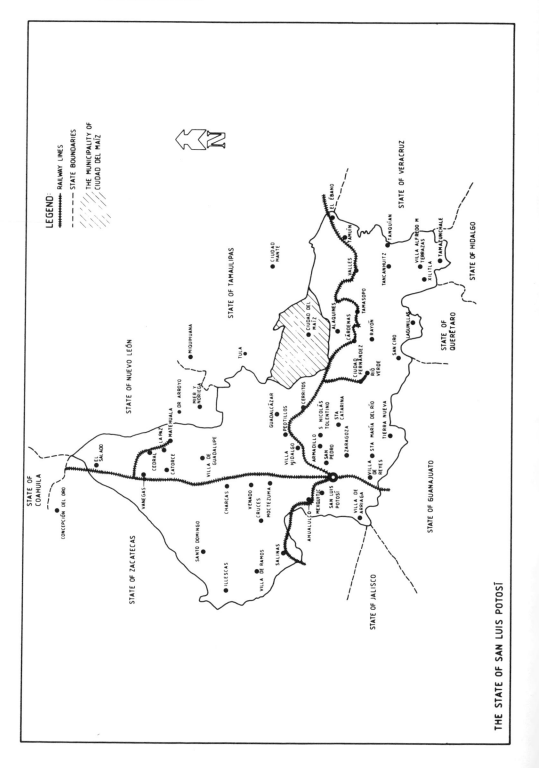

LEGEND:

~~~~~~ RAILWAY LINES

- - - - STATE BOUNDARIES

///// THE MUNICIPALITY OF
///// CIUDAD DEL MAÍZ

THE STATE OF SAN LUIS POTOSÍ

and narrow fertile valleys. The Huasteca itself is totally different from the west of the state and falls into two parts: the coastal plain in the north and the hilly jungles in the south, both of which are very humid and hot. Although the two areas are jointly called the Huasteca Potosina, the north belongs to the strip of flat, low-lying land that runs along the whole of the Gulf Coast, while the south is a small section of the Huasteca proper which extends into the states of Veracruz, Hidalgo, and Querétaro.

In the colonial period the city of San Luis Potosí was famous for the wealth of the surrounding mines, and following the reforms of Charles III, it became the administrative center for an intendancy that covered the present-day states of Coahuila, Nuevo León, Tamaulipas, and Texas, as well as San Luis Potosí itself. Compared with neighboring states, it was relatively unscathed by the wars of independence, and when the British emissary H. G. Ward visited the region in 1827, he commented upon the prosperity of San Luis Potosí and nearby towns such as Catorce. In the following decades, however, the state entered a period of decline. The war with the United States in 1847 and the subsequent years of civil strife caused serious economic disruption and checked demographic growth. The state was afflicted by serious disorders in 1869–1870 as local political leaders vied for power following the rule of Maximilian and again five years later during the successful revolt against the central government led by Porfirio Díaz. When Díaz assumed the presidency in 1876, commerce, mining, and agriculture were all at a low ebb. In San Luis Potosí, as in the country as a whole, there was a general longing for an end to the constant political strife and for a prolonged period of more orderly government.[1]

Such wishes were to be granted in Díaz's thirty-five-year rule (1876–1911), commonly known as the Porfiriato. At the cost of freedom he provided Mexico with its longest period of political stability since independence. Through a shrewd blend of repression and bribery he induced the majority of those elite groups who had contributed to the former unrest—the regional *caudillos,* the leaders of the army and the church, foreign merchants and bankers, and even intellectuals—to collaborate with the new regime. The small minority who opposed him were excluded from positions of power and patronage. Political stability encouraged economic development, which in turn increased the president's ability to reward obedience. Gradually, Díaz tightened his grip upon the country, creating an effective, if highly personalized, political machine through which he exercised patronage and coercion.

Probably the president's most important step in this process of political consolidation was to create the office of *jefe político* (district commissioner) in 1885. These officials, who were responsible for executive control and minor judicial authority in their districts, occupied a peculiar place within the system. Although they were technically subordinate to the state governors, who appointed them in close consultation with Díaz, they also acted as Díaz's agents and could report to him directly. By 1910 they numbered some three hundred in the country as a whole. For law enforcement the *jefes políticos* depended upon another Porfirian creation, the federal mounted police known as the *rurales,* reinforced if necessary by local units of the federal army. With the assistance of the *rurales*, the *jefes políticos* significantly increased the authority of the central government in the hinterland of the country and helped to create the conditions for the increase in trade and investment which was one of the features of the period. Needless to say, however, their activities won them little affection, and among the masses they were often held responsible for the regime's shortcomings.[2]

At the beginning of the Porfiriato the population of San Luis Potosí stood at approximately half a million, the vast majority being mestizos. The only region where there was a large number of Indian language speakers was the Huasteca. Prior to the Spanish Conquest, the north and west of the state had been inhabited by the fierce and nomadic Chichimecas, but they had been exterminated or absorbed into the mestizo population as early as the seventeenth century. The plain of Río Verde, inhabited by more sedentary tribes in pre-Hispanic times, was also almost totally mestizo by the nineteenth century.[3]

As may be observed in Table 1, the majority of the population lived in small settlements, usually near mines or *haciendas*. The sixteen centers with more than 2,500 inhabitants accounted for only about one fifth of the population. The wealthiest and most populated *partidos* were San Luis Potosí, Catorce, Santa María del Río, and Río Verde, the value of whose real estate was over 70% of the total in the state. These *partidos* also contained over half of the *haciendas* and *ranchos* in the state. In contrast, the population of the three *partidos* of the Huasteca was only just over 10% of the state total, and the value of the real estate there was only about 4%. The Huasteca also accounted for a disproportionately high percentage of *congregaciones*, as was to be expected in view of the long-standing Indian settlements in the region.[4]

The reason for these imbalances in the geographical distribution of wealth and population at the beginning of the Porfiriato is evident. As in neighboring Guanajuato, the economy of the region was based upon mining and supporting agriculture. The oldest mines were situated near San Luis Potosí itself, which owed its existence to the presence of nearby silver deposits and was named after Potosí in the area known at that time as Upper Peru. The subsequent discovery of more silver in the north led to the founding of the towns of Charcas and Catorce in the eighteenth century. Smelting took place both at the mines and on nearby *haciendas*.

The mines and mining communities created a market for both staple foods and raw materials, which then stimulated local agriculture. The districts of San Luis Potosí and Santa María del Río produced beans and corn in large quantities, and the cattle and sheep *haciendas* of the north and west supplied the mines with wood, leather, and candle wax. Agriculture also prospered further to the east, in the plain of Río Verde and around Ciudad del Maíz, where a variety of goods was produced, including sugar. Ciudad del Maíz was the home of many landowners whose estates lay in the insalubrious coastal plains, and it vied with Río Verde for control of the trade between the coast and the central zone. The hot, unhealthy, and inaccessible Huasteca remained largely

TABLE I: DISTRIBUTION OF POPULATION AND RURAL PROPERTIES BY
PARTIDO IN THE STATE OF SAN LUIS POTOSÍ, 1878

Partido[a]	Population	Towns with More than 2,500 Inhabitants	Haciendas	Ranchos	Congregaciones
San Luis Potosí	116,712	San Luis Potosí 39,522	28	389	61
		Soledad 4,549			
		Pozos 3,000			
Santa María del Río	45,205	Santa María del Río 7,546	15	242	32
		Villa de Reyes 5,972			
		Tierra Nueva 3,989			
Salinas	9,576	Salinas 3,110	1	49	0[b]
Venado	31,792	Venado 3,500	14	173	12
Catorce	47,642	Catorce 2,872	12	180	18
		Matehuala 10,034			
Guadalcázar	33,151	Guadalcázar 2,987	13	95	13
Cerritos	25,626	San Nicolás Tolentino 2,507	10	105	20
Río Verde	38,138	Río Verde 4,283	16	37	13
		Fernández 3,200			
Ciudad del Maíz	29,143	Ciudad del Maíz 3,986	6	80	8
Hidalgo	33,405	Rayón 3,779	10	98	7
		Alaquines 3,251			
Valles	8,454	—	8	58	4
Tancanhuitz	24,719	—	7	36	27
Tamazunchale	18,379	—	2	35	8

Source: F. Macías Valadez, *Apuntes geográficos y estadísticos sobre el estado de San Luis Potosí* (San Luis Potosí, 1878), 25–129.

[a]Macías Valadez added to the above properties 45 *congregaciones*, 184 *ranchos*, and 26 *haciendas* that he did not record under any particular *partido*, making a grand total for the state of 168 *haciendas*, 1,767 *ranchos*, and 254 *congregaciones*. Unfortunately, he did not define the difference between a *hacienda* and a *rancho*, but presumably he accepted the usual classification of a *rancho* as a small property that could be worked by family labor with hired seasonal assistance if necessary.

undeveloped. In 1871 a visitor to Valles wrote of the town, "The appearance of the place is very miserable, for everything bears the stamp of a ruin and decadence which inspires sadness in the heart of anyone who sees it; there is no commerce, nor industry, not any of those things that contribute to the pleasures of life." Such comment was appropriate for any of the municipal centers of the region.[5]

The major barrier to economic growth in the state was poor communications, both internal and external. According to a report on Tamazunchale drawn up by a representative of the finance ministry in 1877, all agricultural products were consumed locally except coffee and sugar cane, which were taken to Tampico in canoes, "a difficult journey along the narrow course of the Río Moctezuma, a distance of sixty leagues at a cost of four *reales* the *arroba*." Roads out of the *partido* were notoriously difficult—some were impassible even for pack animals—and fruit rotted before it reached the coast or markets of the interior. "For the production of agricultural goods to take place

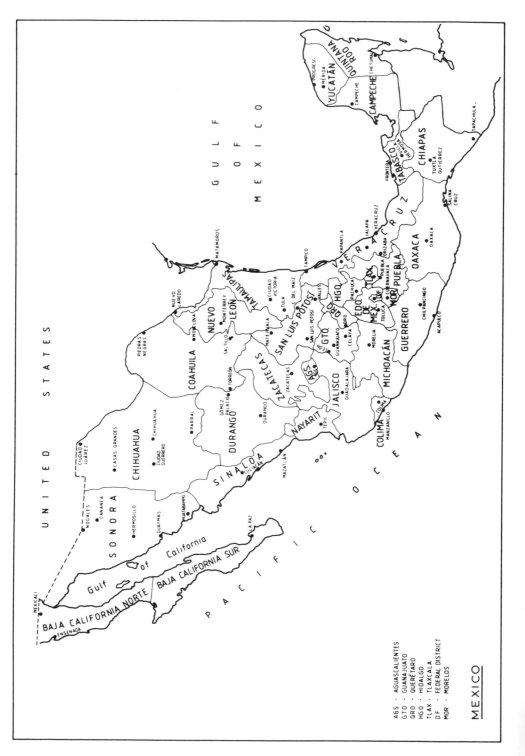

AGS · AGUASCALIENTES
GTO · GUANAJUATO
QRO · QUERÉTARO
HGO · HIDALGO
TLAX · TLAXCALA
D F · FEDERAL DISTRICT
MOR · MORELOS

MEXICO

on a larger scale than at present," he concluded, "more and better means of communication must be found." His counterpart in Cerritos recorded a similar situation: "Since there are few elements of transport in the municipality, products are sold here at a relatively low price for they cannot be carried to nearby markets." Conditions elsewhere were only marginally better, and with such barriers to commerce, agricultural production was generally limited to local markets. Only nonperishable goods could be dispatched outside the state, and then at great expense.[6]

The problem of poor communications was not confined to San Luis Potosí but was common to Mexico as a whole. It was partly resolved during the Porfiriato by the construction of the country's railway network. Between 1876 and 1898 the length of track in the country increased from 650 to 12,800 kilometers, and by 1910 there were over 19,000 kilometers linking all the main centers of industry and commerce. The financing of the railroads reflected the regime's general approach to economic development and foreign investment. The federal government granted or sold concessions to individuals or consortia for the construction of specific lines. Such concessions, which could later be sold at a profit, were, of course, an important form of patronage which allowed Díaz to reward his supporters and confirm the loyalty of regional *caudillos*. Not surprisingly, in view of the heavy capital outlay involved, American and British investors ultimately occupied a dominant role in the funding of construction, but Mexican public and private finance was also involved. One important consequence of the primacy of the Americans and British in the industry was the employment of their nationals in all of the more responsible jobs in the leading companies. This caused great resentment in their Mexican fellow-workers and contributed to labor unrest at the end of the period.[7]

The construction of the railways had a marked effect upon mining and agriculture, as well as increasing the domestic market for the country's relatively few manufactured goods. The stimulus that the railways gave to trade and economic development led in turn to urbanization and the rapid growth of a number of towns and cities, especially in the north and on the Gulf Coast. For example, between 1892 and 1910 the populations of Ciudad Chihuahua and Torreón rose from about 13,500 to 40,000 and from 200 to 34,000, respectively; between 1891 and 1910 that of Cananea rose from 100 to 14,800; and between 1876 and 1910 those of Guaymas and Monterrey rose from 3,400 and 14,000 to 31,900 and 78,500, respectively. On the other hand, as John Coatsworth has shown, land speculation connected with railway development caused or exacerbated property disputes. Such disagreements were usually between politically influential landlords and neighboring villages, although some were between railway companies and local landowners, or between rival villages. A number of these conflicts led to violent incidents of agrarian unrest, such as the prolonged disturbances in the Tamazunchale district of San Luis Potosí between 1877 and 1881.[8]

The location of San Luis Potosí gave it a strategic position within the country's railway network. Two of Mexico's main rail arteries crossed the state:

Mexican National Railroad, which was opened in 1888, ran from Mexico City to Laredo on the United States border; and the Mexican Central Railroad, begun in 1879 but not completed until 1890, ran from Aguascalientes to Tampico, the country's second port and the future outlet for the burgeoning oil industry. The city of San Luis Potosí, where these two lines crossed, thus became one of the country's most important railway junctions. Two branch lines were subsequently built in the state, one linking the mining center of Matehuala with the Mexican National Railroad at Vanegas, and another the town of Río Verde with the San Luis Potosí–Tampico line at San Bartolo. As might be expected, the local authorities were active in promoting this development. In the years 1878 to 1880, for example, the state government issued new paper currency for the payment of a special tax surcharge levied in order to assist the financing of the San Luis Potosí-to-Tampico line. It also gave generous assistance to the companies building the line, such as tax concessions and the grant of free land for stations in the towns along the route. San Luis Potosí also provides a good example of how important regional *caudillos* loyal to Díaz managed to enrich themselves through railway development. Carlos Díez Gutiérrez had been one of Díaz's most active supporters in his seizure of power in 1876. He was rewarded with the state governorship, a position which he held from 1877 until his death in 1898 (except for one four-year term when it was held by his brother), and also with a railway concession for a line from Matehuala to Río Verde, which he later sold to the Mexican National Railroad for 5,500 pesos per kilometer. Moreover, the San Luis Potosí–Tampico line was routed through Díez Gutiérrez's *hacienda* of Cárdenas, which then became a center of extensive marshalling yards and railway repair shops.[9]

In spite of the advantages bestowed by these railway connections, the economic development of San Luis Potosí during the Porfiriato did not match that of most other northern states. The manufacturing industry failed to attract major investment even in the state capital. The city of San Luis Potosí possessed a number of small factories, such as a nail factory, a brewery, and a woolen mill, but it remained essentially a center of government and commerce, servicing the local mines and *haciendas*. Its population increased relatively slowly by the standards of other major cities in the north, rising during the period from 40,000 to 68,000. With the exception of smelting, the growth of the local mining industry was also fairly modest. In terms of the value of production, mining and smelting formed the leading sector of the local economy; and among the minerals exploited were gold, silver, lead, copper, antimony, iron, zinc, and sulfur. By far the most important of these was silver, and the sharp fall in its price at the end of the nineteenth century caused a crisis in local business circles. There was considerable speculation in mining shares, and several of the wealthiest families in San Luis Potosí suffered serious financial loss. Recovery came eventually with a stabilization of silver prices and with foreign investment in the state's mines and smelters, but the industry in San Luis Potosí never regained its former preeminence. As in neighboring Zacatecas, it fell victim to the reduced demand for silver and the increased de-

TABLE 2: AVERAGE ANNUAL PRODUCTION OF SELECTED CROPS IN THE
STATE OF SAN LUIS POTOSÍ, 1893–1895 AND 1905–1907 (IN TONS)

Crop	1893–1895	1905–1907
Cotton	18,000	38,500
Sugar	1,100,000	2,350,000
Coffee	20,000	30,000
Tobacco	9,350	12,000
Henequén	64,275	104,600

Source: El Colegio de México, Seminario de Historia Moderna de México, *Estadísticas económicas del Porfiriato. Fuerza de trabajo y actividad económica por sectores* (México, n.d.), 71–75.

mand for other metals such as copper and lead, which were more cheaply and easily obtained in Sonora, Chihuahua, and Coahuila.

Smelting, the most dynamic sector of the local mining industry, was largely controlled by foreign investors. Their dominance became a virtual monopoly in 1911 when the Guggenheims, who already had a majority holding in the Compañía Metalúrgica Mexicana, acquired the American National Metallurgical Company and were in a position to dictate smelting charges throughout the region. Local mining interests were not entirely happy about this situation; moreover, like other employers, they were irritated by the high wages paid by the Americans, who thus attracted the most skilled local labor. As Roberto Ipiña, a local *hacendado,* wrote to an American mining entrepreneur who wished to construct a smelter on his property, "The proximity of an industrial center always does serious harm to agricultural concerns, since the latter can never pay the wages offered by the former." However, no one took action about these grievances since they were of little account compared with the overall advantages which the local bourgeoisie derived from cooperation with foreign investors.[10]

The sector that benefited most from the arrival of the railways in San Luis Potosí was agriculture, particularly the production of cash crops. The development of large-scale commercial farming throughout the country was a feature of the Porfiriato, as landowners sought to exploit the opportunities offered to them by the new transport system. Many of them assumed the role of agricultural entrepreneurs, importing the latest technology from abroad and investing in irrigation schemes and other improvements to their estates. Notable examples of this trend were: in the north, the cotton *haciendas* in the Laguna region on the Durango-Coahuila border and the farms of the Yaqui Valley in Sonora; and further south, the sugar estates of Morelos, the tobacco *haciendas* of the Valle Nacional in Oaxaca, the *henequén* plantations of Yucatán, and the coffee *fincas* in Veracruz. The results of the endeavors of these commercially minded landowners can be observed in Table 2.[11]

The landowners in San Luis Potosí were no exception to this trend toward taking a more businesslike approach to their estates. The Espinosa y Cuevas brothers increased the number of goats on their 178,000-hectare *hacienda,* Angostura, to some two hundred thousand and exported their hides to New York for the manufacture of gloves. They began to grow cotton in 1905 and two years later installed machinery to treat the raw material. There were two stations on the San Luis Potosí–Tampico railway line within the estate, San Bartolo and Las Tablas, and the brothers had a further fourteen kilometers of track built so that ox-drawn wagons could take the *hacienda*'s produce to them. When the railroad arrived in the town of Río Verde, José Encarnación Ipiña invested 35,000 pesos in sugar milling machinery on his nearby *hacienda* of San Diego, and an additional 10,000 pesos in railway track to move the sugar from the *hacienda* to the town. He also inquired about the possibilities of selling chile in Texas, but it is not clear whether he ever did so. Hoping to boost maize production, Felipe Muriedas, another well-known local landowner, made considerable investments in artesian wells on his *hacienda* of Gogorrón, which lay close to the railway line to Mexico City. He also established a factory on the estate for making cashmere coats from the wool of his sheep.[12]

Among those who profited from the growth in commerce were the owners of *haciendas* that produced hard fibers used for making brushes. These fibers were extracted from a variety of plants growing wild in the state, notably *lechuguilla* and *palma,* and were sold both in Mexico and in the United States. As new markets became available, there was a minor fiber boom, comparable on a smaller scale to that taking place in *henequén* production in Yucatán. In 1892 the *hacienda* of Montebello produced 3,500 *arrobas* of *lechuguilla* fibers (approximately 41,250 kilograms); ten years later, in 1902, it produced 29,000 kilograms of *lechuguilla,* 50,000 kilograms of *palma,* and 70,000 kilograms of *zamandoque.* For the years 1892 to 1895 the average annual production of fibers in the state was 1,828,500 kilograms, whereas for the years 1903 to 1906, it was 3,184,000 kilograms. The state of San Luis Potosí regularly produced between a quarter and a fifth of the country's total output, with most of the remainder coming from the states of Coahuila, Tamaulipas, and Nuevo León.[13]

The most marked effect of this growth in commercial agriculture was, however, in the Huasteca, where the construction of the railway from San Luis Potosí to Tampico, which passed through the region, led to a boom in the production of cash crops and tropical fruits. For example, the average annual production of tobacco and coffee in San Luis Potosí for the years 1893–1896 and 1903–1906 is as follows: tobacco, 27,500 kilograms (1893–1896), 124,000 kilograms (1903–1906); coffee, 538,000 kilograms (1893–1896), 906,000 kilograms (1903–1906). By 1904 the state was fourth in national coffee production, and in the following year it was second in the output of bananas and third in that of oranges.[14]

The discovery of oil in the Huasteca brought a further stimulus to the region. The search for oil there began in 1901 when agents of Waters Pierce Oil Company acquired oil exploration rights to 30,000 hectares of land in the municipality of Valles. However, oil was not struck until April 1904, when Edward Doheny, an American entrepreneur, discovered a well which was soon producing 1,000 barrels a day in the district of El Ébano. Doheny's original capital had already been exhausted in previous unsuccessful attempts to find oil in the

TABLE 3: POPULATION INCREASE IN THE STATE OF SAN LUIS POTOSÍ BY
PARTIDO BETWEEN 1895 AND 1910

Partido	Population, 1895	Population, 1910	Percentage Increase
Valles	18,087	30,084	+66%
Tamazunchale	31,602	43,618	+38%
Tancanhuitz	34,790	44,563	+28%
Cerritos	26,694	34,015	+27%
Hidalgo	41,472	49,740	+20%
Río Verde	45,406	50,565	+11%
Guadalcázar	30,797	33,745	+9%
Ciudad del Maíz	33,656	35,979	+6%
San Luis Potosí	141,691	149,168	+5.5%
Catorce	70,162	71,631	+2%
Santa María del Río	40,483	40,817	+1%
Salinas	11,333	10,699	-6%
Venado	36,022	33,176	-8%

Source: Secretaría de Fomento, Colonización e Industria, Dirección General de Estadística, *Primer censo de población de los Estados Unidos Mexicanos 1895*, p. 9; *Tercer censo de población de los Estados Unidos Mexicanos*, p. 21.

area, and his final triumph was made possible only by a timely loan of 50,000 pesos from the Banco de San Luis Potosí, a typical example of an alliance for mutual benefit between local businessmen and foreign interests.[15] As a result of these developments, the population of this region rose more sharply than elsewhere in the state.[16] (See Table 3.)

During the Porfiriato the development of commercial agriculture in the country was assisted by legislation which reflected the Liberalism then predominant in Mexican economic thought and which was designed to encourage an individualist and entrepreneurial approach to farming. Already in 1857 the new constitution had provided for the division of all corporately held land into individual properties. Laws in 1863 and 1894 permitted private citizens to "denounce" and claim *tierras baldías* (land to which no legal title existed), and legislation in 1883 authorized the establishment of companies to survey and acquire public land for agricultural purposes. There is no complete record of the effect of these laws upon land tenure, but it is probable that individual titles were given to half a million hectares of community lands, that approximately ten million hectares of land were appropriated under the Laws of 1863 and 1894, and that an additional one to two million were given to railway companies and to agricultural colonists, some of whom were foreigners. The survey companies, most of whose work was carried out in the more remote regions of the north and far south of the country, received approximately twenty million hectares.[17]

These laws often proved socially divisive, particularly those of 1857 and 1894, and apparently their abuse was not uncommon in the country as a whole. Village *caciques* appropriated community landholdings; *hacendados* such as the sugar plantation owners of Morelos and the cattle barons of Chihuahua exploited the laws to increase their estates at the expense of neighboring smallholders; and the survey companies sometimes clashed with local interests in the more populated districts. Such disputes easily led to violence, sometimes prolonged and on a major scale, such as occurred around Papantla in Veracruz between 1891 and 1896, and in the Yaqui Valley in Sonora from 1880 onwards. In San Luis Potosí, however, the effect of this agrarian legislation upon land tenure appears to have been relatively slight. Much of the north and west of the state was suitable only for large-scale cattle farming, and its sparse population put little pressure on the land. In the more fertile and densely populated regions such as Santa Maria del Río and Río Verde, the boundaries of *haciendas* and other properties were, with one or two important exceptions, well defined and generally accepted, so that there was little room for conflict. Such changes as took place were usually the result of a competitive market.[18]

Under the agrarian laws, between 1867 and 1906, 285 title deeds were made out in San Luis Potosí covering 172,263 hectares of land, but only a few cases provoked friction. These figures refer to the whole spectrum of agrarian legislation, including the dissolution of *ejidos* and colonization, and most of the titles were issued before 1895, the year in which the most notorious of the Porfirian land laws, the Colonization Law, began to take effect. The survey companies, which received 78,948 hectares of land in eight titles in 1894 and 1895, were not awarded any further grants of land. In the period from 1894 to 1906 there were only two "denunciations" of *tierras baldías*, one of which covered only two hectares; and six title deeds of public land totaling 3,848 hectares were granted. The remaining 11,657 hectares of land affected by the agrarian laws in those years came under four acts of *composiciones hechas* (the registration of land already held), and all were passed in 1894 or 1895. No titles of land were recorded as a result of the dissolution of *ejidos*, a process which continued only in states with a high proportion of landowning villages, such as Yucatán or Oaxaca. Most of the balance of land affected by the agrarian laws changed hands in the following ways: as a result of the early work of the survey companies, through efforts at colonization such as the Díez Gutiérrez colony of Italian immigrants near Ciudad del Maíz, and through the dissolution of *ejidos* and the formal registration of land already held without a title. Only the interference with *ejidos* caused serious disturbances, and this practice ceased quite early in the period. The land obtained by the survey companies was mainly on the Zacatecas border and in the Huasteca, both regions that were then undeveloped and sparsely populated.[19]

Changes in agriculture were particularly important because, as in the rest of Mexico, society in San Luis Potosí had a strong rural bias. According to the 1900 census, there were in the state 18 *ciudades* (cities), 41 *villas* (towns), 13 *pueblos* (villages), 156 *haciendas*, 2,071 *ranchos*, 12 *congregaciones* (settlements), 1 colony, and 1 mining camp. However, over 75% of the population still lived in communities of less than 2,500, and over half of the economically active population was agricultural laborers.[20]

Unfortunately, the compilers of the census referred to in Table 4 did not define the categories that they used so their figures are as vague as those of Ma-

TABLE 4: SAN LUIS POTOSÍ: THE POPULATION IN 1900 (BY OCCUPATION)

Occupation	Total Number	Occupation	Total Number
Peones de campo	134,122	Teachers	456
Agricultores	4,248	Smelting workers	437
Jardineros	453	Hatmakers	382
Ganadores	147	Tanners	377
Administradores y dependientes		Mechanics	362
de campo	151	Slaughterhouse workers	252
Total working in agriculture	139,138	Military personnel	238
Servants	29,183	Barbers	222
Corngrinders	11,877	Water carriers	219
Schoolchildren	9,092	Dressmakers	178
Merchants	8,682	Tinsmiths	159
Miners	5,367	Police	142
Seamstresses	2,729	Fireworks makers	142
Carpenters	2,182	Weavers (palm fiber)	134
Shoemakers	1,756	Porters (carriers)	128
Launderers	1,535	Beltmakers	126
Bricklayers	1,500	Silversmiths	113
Private employees	1,490	Travelling salesmen	113
Industrial workers	1,403	Sweetmakers	111
Muleteers	1,056	Lawyers	108
Tailors	998	Decorators	107
Rentiers	902	Chauffeurs	107
Musicians	766	Chandlers	106
Tortilla makers	692	Doctors	101
Blacksmiths	662	Priests	88
Bakers	653	Telegraphists	62
Students	596	Children	167,030
Weavers (wool and cotton)	590	Unemployed	113,298
Public employees	577	Housewives	43,732
Cigarette makers	510	Unknown	17,358
Shop assistants	473		
		Total population	575,432

Source: Secretaría de Fomento, Colonización e Industria. Dirección General de Estadística. *Censo general de la República Mexicana. Estado de San Luis Potosí.* 1900. (México, 1903), 227-51.

cías Valadez in 1877. Nevertheless, certain conclusions can be drawn from their findings. The rise in the number of *ranchos* and the decline in that of *congregaciones* were a result of the legislation that converted corporate village landholdings into small properties. The large number of *administradores de campo* suggests that many *hacendados* were either absentee landlords or owned more than one estate. The *ganaderos* were presumably cattle ranchers, since the term is too specific to refer to the owners or administrators of *haciendas,* who usually supervised a variety of agricultural pursuits. Those workers classed as *agricultores* who were not *hacendados* included a wide spectrum of small landowners, from the prosperous owners of two to three thousand hectares of arable land and pasture to the possessors of a few hectares of land near a village or on the edge of a *hacienda,* who augmented the income from their property with other work. Within the group called *peones de campo* were both laborers domiciled within the estates where they worked *(peones acasillados)* and those lacking access to land who lived in villages outside the boundaries of any property. The latter could have worked either as sharecroppers or as day laborers. There is no mention in the 1900 census of those renting land, who were presumably included among either the *agricultores* or the *peones de campo.*

At the turn of the century, therefore, the vast majority of the rural population in San Luis Potosí was landless, although in many cases they had access to land for their own use either as sharecroppers or as resident *peones.* Above them was a small but growing middle class of cattle ranchers and smallholders and a declining number of those with rights to corporate village land, especially in the eastern part of the state. Also, above the first group was the hierarchy of the *haciendas*—the foremen and administrators—whose positions depended upon the affluence of the estates where they worked, and who were usually allowed the use of some *hacienda* land. Finally, there was the small number of large landowners whose estates dominated the rural economy, giving them powers of patronage over the landless majority of the population, whether in the form of land and credit to sharecroppers and renters or in the form of wages and food rations to their employees. Among this group of landowners was an elite of interrelated families, whose ownership of very extensive estates made them into a local landed aristocracy that controlled wage rates and basic food prices in many municipalities. In 1921 the state governor reported that of the 7,200 owners of rural real estate in San Luis Potosí, twenty-two possessed a third of the whole state, and sixty-eight owned half of it. The most important landowning families were the Ipiña, Díez Gutiérrez, Toranzo, Rascón, Verástegui, Rodríguez Cabo, Barragán, Hernández Ceballos, Soberón, Arguinzóniz, Gordoa, Cabrera, Espinosa y Cuevas, Meade, Muriedas, De la Maza, and Barrenechea.[21]

Most of these families had interests in other fields, such as mining or urban real estate, and only encountered serious business difficulties in periods of general depression such as 1892–1893 and 1907–1908. The majority of them were descended from merchants who had accumulated capital in the late colonial and early independence period through commerce and usury and who then invested it in land and mining. They were, therefore, wealthy when Porfirio Díaz came to power, and they used the economic expansion during his rule to extend their interests further. The small minority who became rich during the Porfiriato itself usually prospered through partnership with one of the established families, whose control of land, mineral resources, credit, and local government allowed them to gain a share in any new enterprise. The leaders of the local oligarchy were keenly attuned to commercial opportunities in all sectors of the economy, and toward the end of the period they were concerned by the failure of San Luis Potosí to match the growth of the other northern states. In 1905 they therefore founded an organization designed to promote investment in the state, the Centro Industrial y Agrícola Potosino. José María Es-

pinosa y Cuevas, the state governor and an important landowner, obtained
15,000 pesos from the state treasury to further the work of the new organization, but it achieved little before the upheavals of 1910–1911.[22]

Generally speaking, the growth in the power and prosperity of this oligarchy
in the rural sector went unchallenged during the Porfiriato, but there were a
few important exceptions. There was a serious revolt beginning a year after
Díaz first assumed the presidency and one subsequent minor uprising in 1905.
There were also several instances of friction between large landowners and
neighboring villagers and smallholders. None of these cases of rural unrest
threatened the position of the state authorities, but they are, nevertheless,
worth examining in some detail. Such incidents, more common in certain
other states than in San Luis Potosí, provide an insight into the grievances of
the rural population and do much to explain the widespread peasant *jacquerie*
that contributed so greatly to the collapse of Porfirian rule and to the subsequent years of political violence.

The unrest at the beginning of the Porfiriato first broke out in Tamazunchale in 1877 and continued intermittently until 1883, by which time it had
spread north and west as far as Ciudad del Maíz. The trouble began after the
government authorized the construction of a railway line from San Luis Potosí
to Tampico. This decision led to considerable property speculation in the east
of the state, during which outsiders acquired a number of properties near Tamazunchale on land which the local Indian communities claimed as their own.
In 1877 the Indians concerned sent representatives to Mexico City to obtain
copies of the titles to their land from the National Archive. Before this delegation returned, however, their more impetuous brethren, influenced by the inflammatory sermons of the radical parish priest of Tamazunchale, Father
Mauricio Zavala, took the law into their own hands. Under the leadership of a
local chief, Juan Santiago, they seized land on several nearby *haciendas*. The
state authorities thereupon sent troops to the region to disperse the Indians.

Sporadic unrest continued in the district for the next two years until, in July
1879, the Indians' delegates returned from Mexico City with the copies of the
relevant title deeds. When, in spite of this, the *jefe político* of Tamazunchale,
José Peña, prevented the Indians from reoccupying the disputed land, Santiago again resorted to force. He first produced a forged document in which
President Díaz named him governor of the district; and then, armed with this
mandate, he and his men attacked Tamazunchale, which they captured to
cries of "death to all who wear trousers" (i.e., all who were not Indians). The
rebels drove out the small local garrison and killed Peña. After attempts by the
local authorities to retake the town had failed, the government sent an expedition there under Colonel Bernardo Reyes, later a famous figure in national
politics. After some negotiation Santiago surrendered with his men and was
pardoned. Peace was, however, shortlived, since the local officials still sanctioned what the Indians considered to be encroachments upon their land. After numerous further incidents of friction, Santiago again took up arms in
December 1881, when at the head of 2,000 men he once more occupied Tama-

zunchale. Determined to stamp out the revolt before it could spread, the government moved troops into the area who scattered the rebels and eventually captured Santiago. This time he was not pardoned but sent to jail in Ciudad del Maíz.[23]

Santiago's imprisonment did not, however, mark the end of the unrest in the region, for his intellectual mentor, the fifty-year-old Zavala, took up the banner of agrarian revolt in his place. Father Zavala, who had been transferred to Ciudad del Maíz shortly before, remained convinced that social justice demanded land redistribution, by force, if necessary. Therefore, he gave encouragement to those rebels who remained active, and in February 1883 he drew up an agrarian manifesto known locally as "The Plan of Father Zavala." Then, in July, he and a former army sergeant, Felipe Cortina, organized an uprising in the district. Cortina took charge of the military side of the revolt, and having led attacks upon three local *haciendas,* during which his men killed two of the *hacienda* administrators and severely wounded the third, he established a base in his home village of Platanito. There he issued an agrarian manifesto that, among other demands, called for representative municipal and village government and for the conversion of *haciendas* and *ranchos* into communities of smallholders. The authorities reacted quickly to this new threat to the social order. The commander of the military zone was Bernardo Reyes, now a general, who had campaigned against Juan Santiago four years previously. Reyes sent both state and federal troops into the area, and on 15 July they defeated Cortina and his men in an engagement near their camp. Cortina fled into the mountains but was captured soon afterward. Zavala also went into hiding and eventually escaped to Guatemala. Realizing that more than repression was needed to pacify the region, the state governor, Pedro Díez Gutiérrez, replaced the civil administrator of the area, Jesús González, with Mariano Moctezuma, a local man who was well known and liked by the local Indian communities. Moctezuma's conciliatory administration, which obtained at least partial governmental recognition of the Indians' property claims, restored peace to the region.[24]

The second revolt in the state during the Porfiriato—if such a minor event can be so described—also took place near Ciudad del Maíz. Vicente Cedillo attempted this uprising in 1905. Cedillo, who was not related to the famous Saturnino and his brothers, was a member of the *Partido Liberal Mexicano* (PLM), and his movement was one of the PLM-inspired revolts during the last decade of the period. He conspired to seize the American-owned *hacienda* of Minas Viejas with some of the *hacienda*'s peons, but the authorities learned of his plans and sent a troop of *rurales* to the property who dispersed Cedillo's men without bloodshed. This insignificant disturbance made little impression in the area.[25]

Apart from these revolts, there were several incidents of unrest over property disputes during the period. When, for example, the communal land of Xilitla was divided up under the 1857 Constitution, the town mayor expropriated it and sold it to the state governor; and in Santa María Acapulco, neighboring *hacendados* seized village property in similar circumstances. In Tampate a survey company, the Compañía Deslindadora Eisman Urista, "denounced" a plot of village land as *baldío* and sold it to a consortium of local entrepreneurs interested in using it for fiber production. In all three cases the protests of the villagers were overcome without bloodshed, but many of them remained dissatisfied and reclaimed the land after the fall of Díaz in 1911.[26]

Two other cases were of greater political significance because they both involved the *hacienda* of Angostura, which was the focus of considerable violence from 1912 onward. The first case concerned the village of Villa de Carbonera, whose inhabitants held a *sitio de ganado mayor* (approximately 1,755 hectares) through the right of their descent from one Juan Reyes who had received the land from the Spanish crown in 1741. They added to it during the reign of the ill-fated emperor Maximilian but lost the extra property when his decrees were cancelled in 1868. In 1879 Antonio Espinosa y Cervantes, the owner of Angostura, which bordered upon the village, had a survey made of his estate and subsequently enclosed within its boundaries 350 hectares of the land claimed by the villagers. He later obtained official recognition of the new boundary line from the Ministry of Development and from the local district judge, José Moctezuma. At this time the villagers made no protest at their loss; but in 1889 the Compañía Deslindadora de Tierras Baldías came to work in the area, and the villagers requested the company's legal secretary to arrange for a survey of the land in the locality with the judge of Río Verde. With the judge's consent the company's engineer measured the village's landholding according to the original titles, placed boundary stones in accordance with his findings, and declared the district free of unclaimed land *(tierras demasiadas)*. Espinosa y Cervantes decided that the company and the villagers were conspiring to steal his property. He ordered the removal of the boundary stones and even accused the legal secretary of calling for a "distribution of lands." In order to protect his estate from this supposed threat, he then entered into an agreement with the Ministry of Development to draw up plans to all his properties, thus preventing the company from completing its work on Angostura. He had this survey made in May 1889, and his plan of the estate was approved by the Ministry in January 1891. The following November, Espinosa y Cervantes marked off the property accordingly, with the assistance of state troops who intimidated the local population.

The case is of interest for several reasons. It illustrates how one of the functions of the survey companies, that of arbiter in long-standing boundary disputes, could bring it into conflict with a local elite on behalf of other less powerful interests. The case also reveals how successfully the local *hacendado* elite could defend itself against such a threat, using its control over the local judiciary and municipal authorities. More specifically, this case is a good example of the high-handed way in which the successive owners of Angostura, first Espinosa y Cervantes and then his heirs, the brothers José María and Alejandro Espinosa y Cuevas, behaved toward their poorer neighbors. Among the latter were the Cedillo brothers, who, as we will see, later exacted a terrible retribution for the wrongs which they and others felt that they had suffered at the hands of the Espinosa family.[27]

The second major conflict involving Angostura, and the most important agrarian dispute in the state, concerned the property of the Moctezumas, a group of families who claimed descent from a daughter of the Aztec ruler Moctezuma. Early in the seventeenth century a series of viceregal decrees granted them extensive estates in the municipality of Alaquines, which lay to the southwest of Ciudad del Maíz on the fertile slopes of the Sierra Gorda. They were given the land in the form of a *condueñazgo* (i.e., the heads of the families and their descendents were the joint owners of the property), and in 1810 they possessed 28,116 hectares. This was about a quarter of their original grant, the remainder having been absorbed into neighboring estates. Since they wanted the government of the newly independent Mexico to recognize the titles to the land that they still held, they had it surveyed by federal officials in 1824 and again in 1835. On both occasions they were confirmed as owners of the property, which they held intact until the Porfiriato.

With the construction of the railway from San Luis Potosí to Tampico, which passed close to Alaquines, the properties in the area increased in value, particularly that of the Moctezumas, which was suitable for the production of various cash crops. At this time the Moctezumas' holdings were surrounded by estates belonging to some of the most powerful families, not only of the district but also of the state. They bordered upon *ranchos* belonging to the Barragán and the de la Torre families and upon several important *haciendas:* Angostura of the Espinosa y Cuevas brothers, Martínez and Cárdenas of the state governor Carlos Díez Gutiérrez, and Lagunillas and Santa Gertrudis, which were owned by Díez Gutiérrez's cousins, the brothers Joaquin and Mariano Arguinzóniz, whose properties virtually encircled the town of Ciudad del Maíz. With the connivance of most of these landowners a group of politicians in the state government conspired to seize the Moctezumas' property through abuse of the agrarian laws. In June 1898, Francisco Galván, a local state deputy and former *jefe político* of the nearby town of Cerritos, "denounced" the estate to the authorities as *baldío.* The secretary of the state government, Emilio Ortiz, registered the denunciation and set in motion the legal process for Galván to acquire the rights to the property. But in the same year, Díez Gutiérrez died, and Galván, having lost his patron, passed on his rights to the denunciation to another local politician, Agustín Ortiz, who had survived the change of governor unscathed. Galván had cited Genaro de la Torre as the Moctezumas' representative, but they angrily rejected him, claiming that he was "a man generally feared in the region for the abuses he had committed and for the arbitrary use of power by which he purchased various portions of his properties." Instead, they sought help from Mariano Arguinzóniz; but Arguinzóniz, who also stood to benefit from a successful denunciation, did nothing for them, and in a decree of 1 October 1901, the state authorities awarded the property to Ortiz. Ortiz thereupon took possession of the estate under police protection. The Moctezumas then held a demonstration of pro-

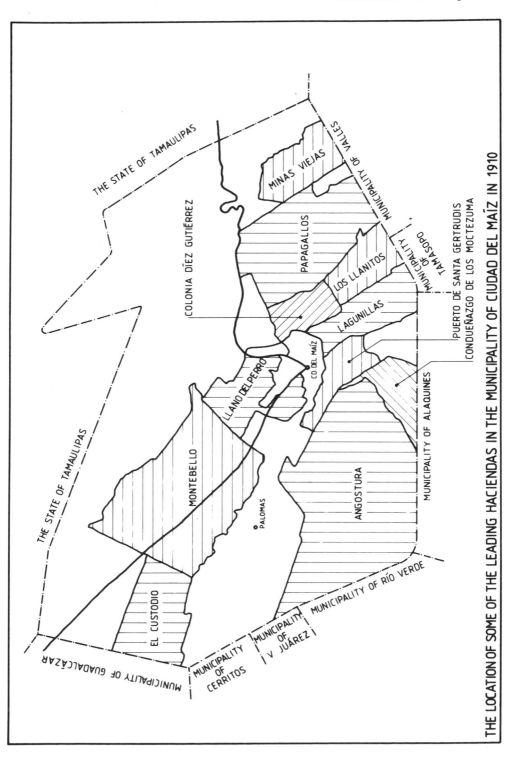

THE LOCATION OF SOME OF THE LEADING HACIENDAS IN THE MUNICIPALITY OF CIUDAD DEL MAÍZ IN 1910

test in Ciudad del Maíz, which ended in the arrest of their leaders, followed by the detention of some of their companions who had cut wood on a portion of the property which Ortiz had leased to the Espinosa y Cuevas brothers. However, in the meantime the Moctezumas had hired Wistano Orozco, an eminent lawyer from Guadalajara. A man of humble origins, who had been born into a family of *rancheros* in Jalisco, Orozco had long been concerned with the incidents of injustice arising from the agrarian laws and he willingly took action on the Moctezumas' behalf. Eventually, after a year of strenuous efforts, he obtained a supreme court ruling in November 1902, which declared the denunciation to be illegal and restored the property to the Moctezumas. Even then the troubles of the Moctezumas were not over, for in May 1908 the president's nephew, Félix Díaz, obtained the right to rent their land from the Ministry of Agriculture, in an act which again asserted that the property belonged to the state. Another court case followed, and the Moctezumas' leaders were again arrested by the authorities. But the government of Porfirio Díaz was overthrown before a judgment was given, and Félix Díaz did not attempt to enforce his claim to the property.[28]

The case of the Moctezumas is a good illustration of the struggle between smallholders and politically influential *hacendados* that took place throughout Mexico at this time. The municipalities of Ciudad del Maíz, Alaquines, Cárdenas, and Cerritos were dominated by *haciendas* belonging to some of the state's elite families, and their attempt to rob the Moctezumas showed that they were quite prepared to use all their political influence to extend their landholdings at the expense of their less powerful neighbors. Although the Moctezumas won their case in 1902, the maneuvers of Félix Díaz suggested that they would eventually lose the property, and other *rancheros* in the district, such as the Cedillo family, could draw little comfort from their example. When José María Espinosa y Cuevas became state governor in 1906, his appointment underlined the alliance between the state authorities and the landowners of the region. In 1910 the *jefes políticos* of Ciudad del Maíz and Alaquines were both members of the landowning class that had been involved in the Moctezumas' case. In Ciudad del Maíz, Genaro de la Torre was boss, and in Alaquines, Mariano Zuñiga had held the post for fourteen years, "doing nothing in the place except to antagonize the local priest and treat the local people in an arbitrary way." The district of Ciudad del Maíz was one of the few in San Luis Potosí where conditions prevailed similar to those which provoked Zapatista unrest in Morelos and the uprising of Calixto Contreras in the Laguna region. Apart from minor revolts in the Huasteca, Ciudad del Maíz was the only region that produced open support for Madero in the early months of 1911, and it was the scene of continuing violence from 1912 onward. Most significantly, Ciudad del Maíz was the home of the most notorious of all the revolutionaries from San Luis Potosí, the Cedillo brothers, whose differences with the local landowning elite, as we shall see, dated from shortly before the end of the Porfiriato.[29]

But, in spite of these hints of future unrest, the prevalent mood in the rural sector during the last decade of the Porfiriato was one of social stability, even in the face of rising food prices and a serious agricultural crisis in 1908 and 1909. Such changes as there were in the structure of rural society may be observed from the following table.[30]

	1900	1910
Peones de campo	134,122	148,048
Agricultores	4,268	10,856
Ranchos	2,071	1,540
Haciendas	156	211

The most noteworthy aspect of these figures is the decline in the number of *ranchos* and the increase in *agricultores*. In Mexico as a whole, the number of *ranchos* rose sharply during the Porfiriato, from approximately fifteen thousand in 1876 to almost fifty thousand in 1910. This increase was also the pattern in San Luis Potosí between 1876 and 1900, during which time, as we have seen, the number rose from 1,767 to 2,071. The subsequent fall in their numbers was probably due to the agricultural crisis of 1908–1909, when drought and frost may have caused many *rancheros* to abandon or sell their properties to wealthier neighbors, either to *hacendados* or even to their more prosperous fellow *rancheros*. Instances of such changes may have contributed to the rise in the number of *haciendas*, although this was probably also the result of large *haciendas* being subdivided among the heirs to the property. The decline in the number of *ranchos* may also explain in part the increase in *agricultores*, many of whom presumably rented land on larger properties. The fact that their numbers more than doubled suggests that the practice of renting became more widespread. Naturally the problems of the years 1908–1909 tended to benefit the landed oligarchy who were better placed to survive and more able—with the storage facilities on their estates—to take advantage of years of bad harvests.[31]

The growth in the number of *peones de campo* by over 10% meant that rural labor remained cheap. As Jan Bazant has shown, this increase enabled employers to hold down agricultural wages at a time when food prices were rising sharply, and the average daily wage of a farm laborer remained at twenty-five cents throughout the decade. In this context those whose wages were augmented by a food ration of fixed quantity regardless of price were in a relatively privileged position. It is impossible to say how widespread this practice was in San Luis Potosí. Apart from their wages, the *peones acasillados* on the thirteen *ranchos* and *haciendas* of José Encarnación Ipiña received a food ration or small plot of arable land, and free pasture and corrals for their animals. On the other hand, there was no food ration given on the Bocas *hacienda* despite the poor wages there, and on nearby Cerro Prieto, wages were paid in vouchers exchangeable only at the *hacienda* store, a system employed with slight variations on Angostura.[32] The problems caused by stagnant wages and rising food prices led to a movement away from the countryside. Between 1900 and 1910 the number of settlements of less than 2,500 persons fell from 2,299 to 1,719, and the percentage of the population living in them dropped from 75% to 71%. Many laborers were forced to leave the area in search of work, some going as far as the United States. José Encarnación Ipiña took note of this exodus as early as 1906. Writing to Luis Toranzo, the owner of Cerro Prieto, he predicted that it could have dire political consequences:

> I am thinking of selling all my haciendas, not because they are not profitable or cause me any losses, but I already hear the approaching steps of the commune. . . . you cannot imagine how the countryside is here in San Luis. . .it is like a desert and the people are departing in droves for the north.[33]

Such pessimism was, however, rare among the state's *hacendados* for whom the early years of the decade 1900–1910 were a period of great prosperity. They were able to take advantage of improved communications, increased prices for their products, a labor surplus, and a decline in real wages. Not only did *haciendas* bring social status, but if well-managed, they also offered a good return on the capital invested in their purchase and administration. It was a time of growing confidence among landowners, symbolized by the large number of agricultural journals on sale in the state, the interest in farming matters in the local press, and the influence of the *hacendados* in the Centro Industrial y Agrícola Potosino. Suggestions that large estates should be divided up into small farms in order to absorb surplus labor, increase the domestic market for the country's consumer industries, and relieve social tension were ignored. Even those like José Encarnación Ipiña who advocated such measures didn't put them into practice on their own estates, perhaps through a lack of prospective purchasers for the planned smallholdings, or perhaps discouraged by the profits they were making from their *haciendas* in their existing form. In 1905 the prospects for the progressive-minded *hacendado* appeared brighter than they had ever been.[34]

The optimism of the *hacendados* was soon checked, however, by a decline in the prices of agricultural exports, which affected coffee, sugar, cotton, tobacco, and fibers. The *hacienda* of Montebello, for example, which had made profits averaging 25,500 pesos per year between 1902 and 1907, made a loss in both 1908 and 1909, the result, according to the administrator, "of an unusual mortality among the cattle and lower fiber prices." The *hacendados'* problems were compounded by a credit squeeze which the government imposed following a crisis on Wall Street in 1907—a move which reflected the degree to which Mexico under Díaz had become incorporated into the world economy. The restriction on credit made it more difficult for the *hacendados* to obtain or increase the mortgages on their estates, a traditional refuge in times of financial hardship. The Espinosa y Cuevas brothers, for example, preferred to seek a loan on the security of Angostura, not from a bank but from another more businesslike *hacendado* who was in a position to help them. Other groups, such as *rancheros* or even sharecroppers, who often borrowed from the *hacendados,* were also affected, just at a time when they had to meet a rise in food prices. The increase in the cost of food was a national phenomenon, resulting from stagnant production and an inadequate system of distribution.[35]

The problems caused by the decline in agricultural export prices and the rise in food prices became increasingly acute, particularly for the lower classes, during the period from 1907 to 1909, when two years of bad droughts were followed by a year of even more disastrous frosts. This last calamity destroyed almost all the harvest in San Luis Potosí in 1909 and caused losses to producers throughout the state calculated at almost fourteen million pesos. The more wealthy landowners were able to draw upon their financial reserves to help them over the crisis, but most people were in a more precarious position. The families of miners and industrial workers made what economies they could and tightened their belts for the lean months ahead, but for many families in the countryside the agricultural crisis meant absolute shortages and physical deprivation. Those most vulnerable were free laborers, sharecroppers, and the poorer of the *rancheros* and renters. Many of them were forced to sell their possessions and move away. In Villa de Arriaga, for example, the sharecroppers faced the total loss of their crops and income, and the local landowners were unable or unwilling to help them. They had no means of paying the high municipal taxes, which included a tax on the right to sow, and were forced to sell their animals and move away from the district. As a result the municipality faced depopulation. The wealthier *rancheros* survived on their reserves, although sorely pressed. In contrast, the resident laborers were in a relatively advantageous position, since they received part of their wages in the form of food and, at a risk of falling into debt, they could expect to obtain short-term credit from their employers. [36]

The sufferings of the agricultural laborers did not, however, lead to political unrest or acts of violence. The failure of the harvest was a periodical event in the life of rural Mexico. Most of those affected survived as well as they could and hoped for better things the following year. Those who found their position impossible did not stay and protest but followed the tendency of surplus laborers elsewhere in Mexico and sought employment in nearby towns or further afield. *El Estandarte*, the leading local newspaper, noted a sharp rise in the numbers of vagrants and beggars on the streets of the state capital. There were, of course, pockets of tension, such as Rascón, where the Mexican workers of the large American-owned sugar plantation committed acts of arson in protest against their employer's discrimination in favor of the American staff, or such as Ciudad del Maíz, where there was friction between the Espinosa y Cuevas brothers and some of the other local *hacendados* and the neighboring smallholders, such as the Moctezumas and recently the Cedillos. But such cases were fairly exceptional and never led to any open challenge to the authorities. On the other hand, the agricultural crisis from 1907 to 1909 was to have important political consequences later. For when, in the spring of 1911, Madero's followers turned to the countryside in search of support for their revolt against the government, the rural lower classes were far more receptive as a result of their recent troubles than they would otherwise have been.[37]

The problems of agriculture coincided with a national recession in mining and industry, which resulted from a fall in the price of raw material exports, particularly metals, the credit squeeze of 1907, and a drop in the demand for industrial products on the domestic market. Employment was affected in both sectors, declining between 1900 and 1910 by 3% in mining and in manufacturing by 2%, in spite of having risen earlier in the decade. In San Luis Potosí the picture was slightly better: the manufacturing industries there escaped the worst effects of the depression, and including workers in the smelters in Matehuala and San Luis Potosí, employment in the sector rose by over 13% during the decade. Mining, on the other hand, suffered badly. Between 1908 and 1910 the number of mines in the state paying taxes fell from 599 to 570, and between 1905 and 1910 tax revenue from mining fell from 52,946 pesos to 41,179 pesos. There was also growing unemployment among mine workers, whose numbers fell by 40% between 1900 and 1910.[38]

As in the countryside, these developments were not associated with much labor unrest or political agitation. Miners went on strike in Matehuala in 1901 but returned to work soon afterward, following an agreement with their employers. Two years later there was a stoppage at the smelter in San Luis Potosí. This was a more serious affair and several workers were injured in clashes with the police at a protest meeting. But such repression had its desired effect, and shortly afterward the workers returned to their jobs on management's terms. In any case, unskilled miners and industrial workers were in a weak position because their wages were higher than those paid in agriculture, and there was a surplus of labor moving from the rural to the urban sector. Partly as a result of this shift, the only subsequent labor disturbances in the state were among the railwaymen, who, among their other grievances, resented their employers' policy of using Americans rather than Mexicans for all responsible posts. There were strikes by the Mexican railway workers in 1906 and 1908, and a violent clash between Mexican and American railroad operatives at Cárdenas in 1907. The 1908 strike was the culmination of these tensions and paralyzed the Mexico City–to–Laredo railroad for nearly a week. It ended only when the state governor of San Luis Potosí, José María Espinosa y Cuevas, threatened the strikers with imprisonment and their leaders advised them to give in. The strike's organizers were subsequently discharged and the railway unions were severely weakened. The failure of local labor to organize effectively in these years strengthened the position of the state authorities and made it easier for them to quell the initial Maderista movement in the autumn of 1910.[39]

The authorities' ruthless attitude toward strikes was due in part to their belief that strikes were connected with the activities of the *Partido Liberal Mexicano* (PLM), the only serious political opposition to Díaz. The PLM was founded in San Luis Potosí in 1900 by a group of local anticlericals led by Camilo Arriaga, a former member of the national congress, as a revival of the old Liberal Party of Juárez and Lerdo de Tejada. They were concerned by the government's toleration of recent breaches of the 1857 Constitution by the church, and anticlericalism was the dominant theme of the party's first congress in February 1901. Originally the PLM had close links with the local elite; apart from Arriaga himself, among the signatories of the party's founding document were members of the Ipiña, the Cabrera, and the Escontría families. But as the party's policy statements became more radical and anti-Díaz in tone, it faced severe repression, and many of these supporters fell away. The police broke up the PLM's second congress in January 1902 and imprisoned many of its leaders. Thereafter, the PLM went underground, and under the influence of younger members such as Ricardo Flores Magón, it became even more radical and militant. In 1906 the leaders of the party launched a manifesto that advocated wide-ranging reforms, including compulsory education, land redistribution, and improvements in the conditions of industrial workers, as well as prohibition of reelection to political office. But by this time the PLM had lost its momentum. It never achieved broad working-class support and its activists were limited to a small number of industrial workers and petit bourgeois. Efforts by the party's leaders to organize revolts in September 1906 and June 1908 were conspicuously unsuccessful, and thereafter the party declined—the victim of ideological divisions, government repression, and defections to other movements. By the time of the elections in 1910 its support was insignificant in comparison with that of other opposition groups.[40]

The government's success in repressing the PLM may have contributed to the false sense of security which so many senior officials seem to have felt in the late Porfiriato and which blinded the authorities to their own growing unpopularity. The last years of Díaz's rule were marked not only by economic problems but also by growing middle-class resentment of Porfirian rule. As the U.S. ambassador noted at the very end of the Porfiriato:

> The growing middle class. This class, while not an evil, is a danger. Its existence springs from the better things which the government has done....All over the Republic a class of sturdy tradesmen, usually of Indian blood, has developed. This class is industrious, intelligent, takes an acute interest in public affairs, is impatient of existing conditions and is constantly exerting a stronger and wider influence. Usually this class is opposed to the present Government and bitterly hostile to the group of men supposed to be its moving force.[41]

By 1910 the regime appeared increasingly decrepit and immobile. The senior level of the administration was a gerontocracy; of the eight members of the cabinet, two were over eighty years old and the youngest was fifty-five, and of the thirty state governors, two were over eighty, six over seventy, and seventeen over sixty. Several of them had been in office for over twenty years, and the regime as a whole suffered from exclusiveness and stultification. As the editor of El Estandarte complained, "Many senior officials are no longer able to carry out their duties actively and can be seen staggering half deaf and half blind along the corridors of public buildings..., and there are governors who are cordially hated but who are reelected after six, ten or twelve years of oppressing the people under their charge." In the context of a growing urban middle class, such political rigidity caused great resentment; ambitious young men, embittered because they were denied access to responsible government posts, were drawn into opposition to the regime both in Mexico City and in the provinces.[42]

Local government was also unpopular, to a certain extent because of its increasing intrusion into people's daily lives. This process manifested itself in various ways: higher taxation, enforced military service, the suppression of banditry—an achievement which probably enjoyed widespread support only among the wealthier classes—the help given to outside mining or commercial enterprises whose activities were prejudicial to the local community, and the protection of hacendados who abused the agrarian laws to further their own interests. The key figures in local government, the jefes políticos, became the focus of all the vague popular hostility provoked by such developments. According to the American consul in Tapachula, Chiapas, "Almost all of the departments of the state have their grievances against the jefes políticos. They have confiscated property for personal ends, perpetrated abuses, and exploit the poor and well-to-do alike by means of what the complainants set forth as unjust fines, contributions and punishment." The British consul in Durango echoed these sentiments, "Such men, badly paid and with almost absolute power, have established a traditional caciquismo." Criticisms such as these, sometimes by men generally well disposed toward the regime, were far from isolated.[43]

San Luis Potosí was not immune to such abuses, particularly in the countryside. The state governor, José María Espinosa y Cuevas, was generally considered able and energetic enough, and being only forty-five years of age when he first took office in 1906, he was the youngest governor in the country. But to the urban middle classes he personified the grip which the landed oligarchy held upon the state, and his reputation as the co-owner of Angostura hardly endeared him to the majority of the rural population. As for his administration, it exemplified many of the vices of Porfirian rule. The congress was a tame and self-perpetuating oligarchy, while local government was increasingly exclusive and despotic, tending toward incompetence and the protection of vested interests. The municipal presidencies of Armadillo, Villa de Arriaga, Alaquines, and Villa de Reyes were held by the same men for lengthy periods of up to twenty years; and the local authorities in other municipalities such as Ciudad del Maíz, Valles, and Río Verde were infamous for their arbitrary and oppressive rule. Complaints ranged from the absence of a school (Alaquines) and the failure to establish a public graveyard (Armadillo) to the victimization of smallholders in the interests of hacendados (Ciudad del Maíz) and arbitrary arrest (Valles). None of these grievances provoked more than muted protest or occasional minor disorders, but they laid the foundations for the widespread unrest in the state which began in the spring of 1911. If the crisis in mining and agriculture provided recruits for the revolt, their local leaders were, more often than not, the victims of the inadequacy and despotism of Porfirian local government.[44]

There is no better illustration of this fact than the background of the most famous revolutionary leader from San Luis Potosí, Saturnino Cedillo. Like his counterpart in Morelos, Emiliano Zapata, Saturnino Cedillo was of rural, petit bourgeois stock. He came from a family of *rancheros*, thus belonging to what Frans Schryer, in his study of a *ranchero* community in neighboring Hidalgo, has aptly called "the peasant bourgeoisie."[45] Saturnino's father, Amado Cedillo, was born in 1851 and began his working life as a peddler, selling his wares between Ciudad del Maíz and Guadalcázar. When he was about thirty years old, Amado married Pantaleona Martínez, the daughter of a *ranchero* from Palomas near Ciudad del Maíz. They first settled in Portezuelos, where Amado purchased a store and small property and where their first child, Elena, was born in 1886. But in that same year Amado sold out and bought land in Palomas, where he opened another store. Palomas was originally an *estancita*, or fraction of the *hacienda* of Angostura, and covered over thirteen thousand hectares. In the middle of the nineteenth century it was divided into smallholdings which were sold as individual plots but retained the collective name of the *estancita*. The property lay in the arid region that falls in the rain shadow of the Sierra Madre Oriental. To the north it bordered upon the *hacienda* of Montebello, to the west on that of San Rafael, and to the south and the east on the *hacienda* of Angostura. Further to the east, across the foothills of the Sierra, was the property of the Moctezumas and the fertile Valle de Maíz. When Amado arrived, there were about one hundred heads of families on Palomas. A few of the occupants were smallholders like himself; the remainder rented land from their more prosperous neighbors. He and his children thus enjoyed a status above the majority of the community but well below that of the neighboring large landowners. The basis of the Palomas community's subsistence was the exploitation of fibers and the raising of cattle and goats, but some of its members also cut fibers and provided seasonal labor on neighboring *haciendas*.[46]

Shortly after Amado and Pantaleona settled at Palomas, their first son, Homobono, was born. Thereafter, they had five other children: Magdaleno, Saturnino, Cleofas, Engracia, and Higinia. Amado's farming and commercial interests prospered, and he became a leader of the community. Both of the parents were religious; they had all of their children baptized, and when there was an appeal for a new bell for the parish church of Ciudad del Maíz, Amado gave generously to the fund, an indication of his relative wealth and standing in the community. Amado also employed someone to teach his children to read and write, skills which he did not possess himself. As they grew older, the boys took up farm work, tending to their father's cattle and cutting *ixtle* on Palomas or nearby *haciendas*. Later they also worked as peddlers, moving between *ranchos* and settlements in the district. The four sons differed greatly in character. Homobono was a dissolute character with a reputation for drunkenness. He kept aloof from his brothers and, when quite young, married into the Salas family, the second most prosperous family on Palomas after the Cedillos themselves. Magdaleno, the most imposing physically, was a somber man with an almost instinctive resentment of officialdom. Saturnino was the most intelligent and articulate of the four and acquired a modicum of primary education. He soon began to act as the family's spokesman in any dealings with government officials, and his experiences in this respect led him to share Magdaleno's prejudices about the local authorities. Cleofas, the youngest brother, was an extrovert with a wide circle of friends in the district. Saturnino and Elena followed Homobono's example and married into the Salas family, but Magdaleno and Cleofas remained unmarried.[47]

About a decade after Amado and Pantaleona arrived at Palomas, the tranquility of the surrounding area was disturbed by the boom in the fiber market. This development was to have important social and political consequences, for the resulting rise in the value of real estate and the demand for a pool of cheap labor induced the local *hacendados* to seek greater control over the nearby resources of land and manpower. This in turn brought them into conflict with neighboring smallholders such as the Moctezumas and the Cedillos. In order to keep agricultural wages stable at their current low level, the *hacendados* agreed to pay laborers sixty centavos per *arroba* for fibers cut on their properties, regardless of the market price of the product. The normal quantity of fiber that a man could cut in six twelve-hour days was two *arrobas* (approximately twenty-three kilograms), thus giving the fiber cutters an average daily wage of twenty centavos, which was approximately that of the *peones acasillados* in the area. But Amado Cedillo and the other important *rancheros* on Palomas offered more favorable terms. They simply charged an annual rent of four and one-half pesos for the right to cut fibers on Palomas, allowing those who did so to sell their produce directly to the local merchants at the market price of two pesos per *arroba*. The abundance of fibers in the region made this proposition attractive, and some of the peons from nearby *haciendas* moved there. As a result, relations between the inhabitants of Palomas and the neighboring *hacendados* became increasingly strained. To the *hacendados*, Palomas appeared to be a "subversive influence" in the district. They claimed that conditions there encouraged demands for wage increases on their own properties and that the movement of workers to Palomas disrupted the work cycle on the *haciendas*, which depended upon a regular supply of labor. In fact such claims were ill-founded; despite the low wages paid on local *haciendas*, they did not suffer from a labor shortage. Nevertheless, the *hacendados* had some grounds for their distrust of the community on Palomas, and of the Cedillos in particular. They suspected, probably with good reason, that some of their sharecroppers and laborers were selling part of their produce on Palomas. And on more than one occasion the Cedillo brothers bribed the watchmen of Montebello and Angostura to allow them to pilfer fibers from the *hacienda*'s stocks. Moreover, the Cedillos rented pasture on San Rafael and Montebello, and the administrators of both properties believed that they incorporated *hacienda* animals into their own herd whenever they could. On the other hand, the Cedillos also had their grievances. With equally good cause Amado and his sons believed that the *hacendados* aspired to total control over all the resources of the local economy and that, like other smallholders in the district, their family stood in the way of this ambition. In consequence they saw their relations with the Arguinzóniz, the Espinosa y Cuevas brothers, and other landowners with large estates in the area as a war of attrition against powerful and ruthless opponents who enjoyed the full backing of local officialdom.[48]

The Cedillos' suspicion and resentment of their *hacendado* neighbors were shared by other smallholders in the district and also by many *hacienda* laborers. They came to regard Palomas as something of a bulwark against the *hacendados*' ambitions and the Cedillos as the natural champions of all who fell afoul of them. The Cedillos' poorer neighbors' faith in them was not unjustified. For example, when on one occasion some of the *hacendados* in the district persuaded the local *jefe político* to arrest certain of their former laborers who had settled on Palomas for stealing fibers from them, Saturnino, the Cedillo family spokesman, traveled to San Luis Potosí to complain to the governor and to protest the innocence of the detained men. In fact, Saturnino received scant satisfaction, being told by officials that the governor had received bad reports of his family and would hold them personally responsible for any disorders in the district. But his intervention was not forgotten either by the grateful laborers or by the *hacendados* who were angered by his initiative.[49]

The Cedillos' war of attrition with the *hacendados* seemed likely to become a struggle for survival when in 1910 José Encarnación Ipiña sold Montebello to Zeferino Martínez, a merchant from San Luis Potosí. Martínez had a reputation for ruthlessness in business matters and, unlike Ipiña, could not be expected to tolerate the slightest infringement of his property rights. Moreover, in any clash with the Cedillos, Martínez could be confident of the full support of the *jefe político* of Ciudad del Maíz, Genaro de la Torre, who was both his relative and, as he had shown in his dealings with the Moctezumas, a strong ally of the *hacendados*. The Cedillos' fears about Martínez were soon confirmed. Shortly after he acquired the *hacienda*, some of his men seized fifteen head of cattle belonging to the Cedillos and put them into the municipal compound on the grounds that they had strayed onto the *hacienda*'s arable land. De la Torre, happy to oblige Martínez, charged Amado Cedillo five pesos per head to redeem them. A few weeks later some of the cowboys from Angostura followed the example of their counterparts on Montebello. On this occasion de la Torre demanded ten pesos per head for the cattle, and Cedillo left them to the municipality.[50] At this point the local landowners and government officials eased their harrassment of the Cedillos, since they wanted to avoid any disorders during the presidential elections. However, their high-handed treatment of the Cedillos had already left its mark. For, despairing of ever obtaining justice from a state administration that seemed committed to furthering the landowners' interests, the Cedillos were drawn into the growing political opposition to the regime—the anti-reelectionist movement. No matter that the leading figure in the movement, Francisco Madero, was himself a *hacendado*

from Coahuila or that he counted *hacendados* among his sympathizers in San
Luis Potosí. Like Emiliano Zapata and his fellow villagers in Morelos, locked
in conflict with the state's sugar barons, the Cedillos saw the anti-reelectionist
cause as the last possible channel for obtaining the peaceful satisfaction of their
grievances.

CHAPTER 2

THE REVOLUTION

IT SEEMS AS IF MADERO HAD STARTED SOMETHING THAT HE IS UNABLE TO HANDLE, AND HAS CREATED A CONDITION THAT ALLOWS THE DISORDERLY TO PLUNDER THE LAW ABIDING ELEMENT.——American Consul William E. Alger in Mazatlán, 30 March 1911

In retrospect it is easy to see that the economic and social tensions of the late Porfiriato were a potential threat to the stability of the regime. Bad harvests and rising food prices; land hunger and rural unemployment; conflicts between expansionist *hacendados* and their politically vulnerable *ranchero* neighbors; a decline in metal prices leading to a depression and unemployment in the mining industry; an expanding middle class frustrated by the exclusiveness and rigidity of the regime; and young bureaucrats embittered by the lack of upward mobility within the administration—such a combination of circumstances hardly favored political stability. Indeed this catalog of problems may lead one to believe that the regime's overthrow was inevitable and that the presidential elections of 1910 merely served as a catalyst to convert widespread discontent into an invincible popular uprising. Such a conclusion, however, would be premature, for if Díaz had carried out even limited political reforms during his last term in office, he would probably have averted the revolt that led to his downfall. It was the president's stubborn rejection of such measures, his refusal even to replace unpopular senior officials, that drove his electoral opponents into an uprising which heralded a decade of political violence and eventually caused the disintegration of the whole Porfirian system.

This system was, as U.S. Ambassador Henry Lane Wilson observed, autocratic government in republican form.[1] While respecting the letter of the constitution, Díaz thoroughly abused its spirit, demanding unswerving loyalty to himself from all members of the administration. But such a personalized style of rule did not lend itself to promoting political stability once the pivotal figure was removed, and concern for the regime's long-term survival preoccupied the more far-sighted members of the administration from the beginning of the century onward. The most important faction in the government during the last decade of the Porfiriato was the *científicos,* a small group of politicians and businessmen whose collective name derived from their adherence to the philosophy of positivism and their belief in applying the methods of science to politics. Led by the finance minister, José Limantour, their solution to the problem was for Díaz to form an official party that could act as a mechanism for political continuity. Opponents of the *científicos* argued that this would produce political wrangling and urged that Díaz should simply name a successor. Their favorite candidate for this privilege was General Bernardo Reyes, the governor of Nuevo León and the same man who crushed the revolt in Tamazunchale in 1882. Reyes had support in both business and labor circles in Monterrey, the state capital, and was also popular with the leaders of the federal army. Díaz, however, like so many absolute rulers before and since, refused to cooperate in reducing his own power in this way. He made his views on the subject clear in 1904 by appointing to the newly created post of vice-president the notoriously corrupt and dissolute governor of Sonora, Ramón Corral.[2]

Even Díaz, however, was eventually obliged to acknowledge the passing of the years, and in 1908 he indicated to an American journalist that he would not seek reelection at the end of his term of office in 1910, when he would be eighty. Few were convinced that he was serious, but his remarks caused renewed public discussion about the country's future. The most important product of this debate was a book entitled *La Sucesión Presidencial en 1910* by Francisco Madero, an affluent and progressive *hacendado* from the northern state of Coahuila. Madero was a firm believer in democratic government following the American model. Earlier he had corresponded with several leaders of the Liberal party, the *Partido Liberal Mexicano* (PLM), but had broken with them in 1906 over their decision to organize a revolt. His book, which appeared in 1909, analyzed the record of the Porfirian regime and recommended that Corral, the vice-president, be replaced by someone committed to more open government.[3]

Madero's concern with the vice-presidency was shared by other respectable upper-class elements who had prospered under the regime but who wished to see it reformed and rejuvenated. Correctly assuming that Díaz would eventually stand for reelection, they formed a number of political clubs in 1909, both in the capital and in the provinces, to press him to choose one of their number as his running mate. Support for these clubs grew quickly, particularly among two sectors of society: the urban middle classes, whose expansion had been one of the features of the Porfiriato, and the industrial workers, who were being driven into increasingly open opposition to the regime by the persistent refusal of their employers and of the authorities to respond to their grievances. The city of San Luis Potosí, for example, boasted several anti-reelectionist clubs by the summer of 1909, at least one of which was run by local industrial workers. In the rural sector, in contrast, the anti-reelectionist cause made much less of an impression. Apart from a number of *rancheros* and a few *hacen-*

dados, its support there was confined to the inhabitants of the small towns and centers of municipal government. Typical among the leading anti-reelectionists in rural San Luis Potosí were Leopoldo Vega in Lagunillas, described by *El Estandarte* as a "rico," Gregorio Sáinz, a prosperous Tamazunchale merchant, and the Lárraga family from near Valles, who were sufficiently wealthy to send one of their sons to the exclusive Instituto Científico y Literario in San Luis Potosí. Most country dwellers, however, were largely unmoved by the anti-reelectionists' message. The inhabitants of the remaining landowning villages, which tended to be in the more remote areas of the country, such as the relatively inaccessible Huasteca of San Luis Potosí, were more preoccupied with local issues. They had no reason to believe that the opposition leaders would help to defend their property from speculators and large landholders any more than would the established authorities. And as for the landless agricultural workers who formed the vast majority of the rural population, they were, if anything, even more indifferent to the movement. Dependent for their livelihood upon the country's *hacendados,* who remained committed to the regime in spite of the recent government-inspired credit squeeze that damaged their interests, the hapless and mainly illiterate *peones de campo* would have found the anti-reelectionist message of free elections irrelevant to their problems.[4]

Among the possible candidates for vice-president the most popular choice was not Madero but instead the better-known General Bernardo Reyes. If Díaz had picked Reyes as his running mate, he would have appeased many of the anti-reelectionists and probably preserved his regime. But he had lost his customary feel for the country's political pulse. He was old and stubborn, and long since unaccustomed to facing open opposition. Perhaps, too, after so many years in office surrounded by time-servers, he had come to believe his own government's propaganda. For whatever reason, he opted to confront the anti-reelectionists rather than undermine them. He announced that he would seek reelection for president with Ramón Corral as his running mate, and the machinery of government was put into operation to generate support for them. As if to emphasize the president's intransigence, "official" candidates were imposed over more popular rivals in elections for state governorships in Morelos, Coahuila, Sinaloa, and Yucatán. If Reyes had persisted with his candidacy, he might still have forced Díaz to pursue a less provocative course, but he proved inadequate to the challenge, accepting an official mission to Europe in September 1909.[5]

The departure of Reyes marked the failure of the reformist strategy aimed at securing the election of an enlightened vice-president who could renovate the administration and smooth the transition to post-Porfirian politics. Henceforth, anti-reelectionism ceased to be a movement of reform within the regime and gradually became a challenge to the whole Porfirian system, including Díaz's own position as president. The man who presided over this transformation was Francisco Madero, the author of *La Sucesión Presidencial en 1910.* He had recently campaigned in the gubernatorial elections in his home state of

Coahuila on behalf of the unsuccessful opposition candidate, Venustiano Carranza. Thereafter, while Reyismo declined in the absence of its leader, Madero assumed a central role in the whole anti-reelectionist movement, embarking upon a full-scale campaign to convert it into a coherent and organized political force. Madero's program was essentially political; his main theme was the need for free elections at every level of government. He had little to say on economic matters and saw no need to put forward any specific social or economic reforms. A successful businessman and convinced supporter of capitalism, he believed, in the tradition of nineteeth-century liberalism, that a freely elected government would respond to working-class demands and that a free market economy would provide an increasingly better standard of living for all classes.[6]

In the winter of 1909–1910 Madero visited several states in the north and west of the country to rally support for his cause. As he traveled around, he began to encounter the official harassment which was to become increasingly marked as the elections approached. When, for example, he visited San Luis Potosí in March, he found that the authorities had just arrested Dr. Rafael Cepeda, his foremost supporter in the city. Cepeda had organized a meeting for Madero to address, and the local officials claimed that the wording on the invitations was subversive. However, their attempt at intimidation was a failure. Over five hundred people attended the meeting, formed an anti-reelectionist club, and promptly elected the absent Cepeda as president.[7]

Madero's emphasis upon the need for more democracy in government naturally had a considerable appeal to the middle-class elements who formed the mainstay of the anti-reelectionist clubs, and it was no surprise, therefore, when the delegates to a national anti-reelectionist congress in Mexico City in April 1910 elected him as their presidential candidate. For his running mate they chose Francisco Vázquez Gómez, a member of an oligarchical family and former personal physician to Díaz. The choice of Vázquez Gómez underlined the close links which still existed between the anti-reelectionist leadership at the national level and the country's elite, even though many upper-class supporters of the movement were already beginning to melt away rather than face defying the fearsome Don Porfirio. Local Maderista leaders, in contrast, tended to be solidly middle class in background—lawyers, merchants, doctors, engineers, etc. In the city of San Luis Potosí, for example, the leading Maderistas in November 1910, as listed in *El Estandarte,* were a doctor, a merchant, a cattle dealer, two teachers in a Wesleyan college, two butchers, three tailors, two tinsmiths, an owner of urban real estate, a scrap iron dealer, and several students. At a grass roots level Madero inherited the support for the anti-reelectionist cause among the urban middle classes and industrial workers. This support was particularly strong in the boom towns in the north, such as Torreón, Ciudad Chihuahua, and even Reyes's own stronghold of Monterrey, and around Orizaba, where some of the country's leading textile factories were located. In contrast, his movement made relatively little headway in the countryside, which was not surprising in view of his apparent indifference to the need for social or economic reform.[8]

Following his nomination, Madero made a campaign tour of the country, drawing large and enthusiastic crowds even in cities outside the north, such as Puebla and Guadalajara. The authorities became concerned at his popularity and attempted to disrupt his itinerary. They harassed and persecuted his leading supporters and obstructed the work of Maderista activists in a number of cities. For example, when Madero visited San Luis Potosí on 5 June, the police attempted to prevent a crowd from gathering at the station by announcing that his train was delayed. (In fact, the ploy proved unsuccessful, since about two thousand persons were waiting to greet him when he arrived, but it was typical of the government's maneuvers and its determination to sabotage his campaign.) The authorities' efforts in this regard were, however, generally in vain, and frustrated by Madero's growing popularity, they eventually resorted to more direct action. They began to detain large numbers of Madero's supporters, including, in San Luis Potosí, the recently liberated Rafael Cepeda and the student leader, Pedro Antonio de los Santos. Then on 7 June Madero himself was arrested in Monterrey with one of his aides, Roque Estrada, accused of having preached rebellion during their recent visit to San Luis Potosí. On 21 June they were transferred to prison in San Luis Potosí on the grounds that their "crime" had been committed there. Five days later the elections were held in an atmosphere of repression and fraud unprecedented since the early days of the Porfiriato. Five thousand Maderistas were in jail, and the government machine ensured a victory for Díaz and Corral, which was confirmed by the electoral college on 10 July.[9]

Confined to his prison quarters in San Luis Potosí, Madero discussed his next step with close advisers such as his brother Gustavo and Rafael Cepeda. Driven to extremes by the government's intransigence, he began to consider launching an armed insurrection. As he knew, however, such a move required careful planning and his own escape from detention. While the appropriate preparations were being made, he sought a last peaceful means of reaching a compromise with the government by ordering his followers to petition congress to have the elections annulled. If, as was probable, the congress rejected their appeal, he intended to lead a revolt. In the meantime Madero remained in close touch with his family and supporters. His conditions of detention were not particularly arduous—*El Estandarte* described him as occupying a "suite" in the jail—and he was able to receive visitors quite freely. Among them, on 19 July, was Saturnino Cedillo.[10]

Initially the Cedillos had shown only slight interest in the anti-reelectionist movement, which seemed to offer them little succor in their parochial problems with their *hacendado* neighbors. Gradually, however, they changed their views, concluding that if the anti-reelectionists' promise of free municipal elections was implemented, it would produce changes in the local administration favorable to their interests. They therefore made contact with the leaders of anti-reelectionist groups in the region, among them a schoolmaster from Tula, Tamaulipas, Alberto Carrera Torres, whom Magdaleno Cedillo already knew from his visits there on business. Although only twenty-three years old, Carrera Torres was already a long-time opponent of the regime, having been arrested three years previously for disseminating anti-Porfirian propaganda. Largely self-taught, he was something of a radical ideologue. With his encouragement the Cedillos became active anti-reelectionist, and in due course Saturnino, who was the electoral representative for the inhabitants of Palomas, cast his vote on their behalf for Madero and Vázquez Gómez. When the Cedillos heard that Madero had been transferred to San Luis Potosí, they dispatched Saturnino to see him. The two men must have seemed improbable associates: the one, the scion of one of Mexico's leading families, a wealthy young *hacendado* educated in the United States and Europe; the other, a twenty-year-old *ranchero* with the most rudimentary education, for whom a trip to San Luis Potosí was an event in itself. Unfortunately there is no record of what transpired at their meeting, but Saturnino apparently returned to Palomas convinced that however gloomy the prospects for Madero's cause, it was still worth supporting.[11]

On 22 July Madero was released on bail after several influential figures had interceded with the authorities on his behalf. They included the Bishop of San Luis Potosí, Ignacio Montes de Oca y Obregón, and Madero's fellow director in a mining company near Matehuala, Pedro Barrenechea, who provided his bond. One of the conditions of Madero's release was that he should not leave the confines of the city of San Luis Potosí, and after getting out of prison he went to stay in the town house of Federico Meade, another member of the state's elite. The respectability of Madero's helpers reflects the continuing connection of his movement with the country's ruling class. All three men assumed that Madero's cause was lost and simply wanted to help him recover from his excursion into politics.[12]

In September the congress rejected the anti-reelectionists' petition for fresh elections, and Madero therefore went ahead with his plans for a revolt. His intention was to flee to the United States and then return to lead a coordinated uprising in all the major cities. His plan was based upon the location of his political strength (i.e., the urban middle classes and industrial workers), and he hoped to overthrow the government in a swift coup d'état. He seems largely to have ignored the potential for revolt in the countryside, and for the moment his followers made little effort to harness incidents of rural unrest to his cause. When, for example, the Huasteca Indians near Tancanhuitz took up arms against the oppression of their local government officials, the Maderistas made no effort to exploit the uprising, which was quickly crushed. Madero set 20 November as the date for his uprising and escaped to the United States in early October with the assistance of a railroad employee sympathetic to his cause. There he published his Plan of San Luis Potosí, a revolutionary manifesto in which he outlined the nation's problems and assumed the leadership of a revolt. In keeping with Madero's campaign it was almost wholly political in content, making no mention of the problems of industrial labor and only one reference to agrarian matters.[13]

The authorities heard of Madero's plans and took appropriate countermeasures. In San Luis Potosí they arrested a large number of local Maderistas in the days immediately prior to 20 November, and by the twenty-fifth of that month there were 700 prisoners in the state penitentiary, or about 200 more than normally. Madero's local supporters were easily cowed by these measures. There was no political movement in the city itself, and as *El Estandarte* commented, "Here is where a revolt is least in danger of erupting." The only uprising elsewhere in the state was led by Leopoldo Lárraga in the Huasteca, but it was quickly suppressed and Lárraga was imprisoned in San Luis Potosí.[14] It was much the same story throughout the country. Aquiles Serdán, a shoemaker in Puebla, provided the revolt with its first martyr when he resisted arrest on 18 November, and there were a number of small uprisings during the next few days, most of which, however, soon fizzled out. The majority of Madero's leading supporters waited upon events, reluctant to commit themselves, or were detained without incident. Their inaction was commented upon by the British vice-consul in Guadalajara, who attributed it to the ambivalent position of the revolutionary property owner:

> ...in fact, a middle class, hitherto lacking, has sprung into being. It may be that this suddenly created class menaces the present order of things since it thinks: it may even be the very cause of much of the present trouble. On the other hand this very class is made up of individuals who have acquired a stake, who have something to lose, to whom self-interest invariably applies.[15]

The only uprising which was not immediately suppressed was in western Chihuahua, a district notorious for its defense of traditional local liberties against any infringement by the state authorities. By the beginning of December observers concluded that the rebellion had failed, and even Madero, who was obliged to remain in the United States, began to despair.[16]

Contrary to general expectation, however, the movement in Chihuahua survived and spread. This was due to the particular circumstances of the state at that time. In the nineteenth century the municipalities in Chihuahua had enjoyed a large degree of independence. During the Porfiriato, however, the Terrazas family built up an impressive political machine through which it came to control both the central administration of the state and also local government. In 1904 Enrique Creel, the son-in-law of Luis Terrazas, the leader of the clan, became governor and strengthened the powers and patronage of the state government even further. Since Chihuahua was one of the states most affected by the economic depression of the late Porfiriato, there was considerable potential in the region for popular unrest. Madero's campaign acted as a catalyst for local grievances and his call for revolt found a ready response. Within a few weeks the government had lost control of the west of the state.[17]

The survival of the uprising in Chihuahua encouraged Maderista leaders in other areas to emerge from hiding and to renew their challenge to the government. The movement they now led differed from the abortive insurrection in November. Rejecting the towns and cities, where the respectable men of property who formed the backbone of political Maderismo remained cowed by government repression, they turned instead to the countryside, where they exploited the popular reaction against the recent growth of local government and against the expansion of large-scale commercial farming. The participants in this armed phase of Maderismo, unlike many of those who had been active in Madero's political campaign, shared his concern with democracy only in the context of their local grievances. Their aims were parochial: the removal of an inefficient or corrupt town mayor; vengeance against a tyrannical chief of police; or the recovery of a smallholding or plot of community land which had been dubiously acquired by a neighboring *hacendado* with the connivance of the local *jefe político*. They were led by men of some standing in their community whose occupations gave them both an awareness of local grievances and contact with neighboring districts. They included three prosperous *rancheros* (Luis Moya and the brothers Ambrosio and Rómulo Figueroa), two muleteers (Domingo Arrieta and Pascual Orozco), a cowboy (Toribio Ortega), a saloonkeeper (Jesús Morales), a tinsmith (Orestes Pereyra), four schoolteachers (Manuel Chao, Cesario Castro, Francisco Figueroa and Alberto Carrera Torres), a Protestant preacher (José Ruiz), a merchant (Ignacio Gutiérrez), a village notary (Severiano Ceniceros), a bandit (Francisco Villa), a tramway conductor (Agustín Castro), a saddler (Rafael Tapia), a dispossessed smallholder (Calixto Contreras), and a *hacendado* (José Maytorena). As a result the rebellion in the spring of 1911 was only loosely coordinated, and yet it developed because of the wide geographical spread of the unrest, the inertia of the central government, and the inadequate forces available to the authorities in any one area.[18]

There were three main regions of revolt outside Chihuahua: southern Sonora, Sinaloa, Durango and the Laguna, where the Maderistas were active as early as January 1911; a belt of territory from Tabasco and Veracruz on the Gulf Coast through Puebla and Morelos to Guerrero, where the movement developed soon afterward; and, finally, Yucatán. Several regions, notably the northeast (Nuevo León and northern Tamaulipas), Jalisco and the Bajío, Chiapas and the bulk of Oaxaca, were free of unrest. Although all the revolutionary bands acted in Madero's name, only a few, such as those of Luis Moya in Durango and Pascual Orozco in Chihuahua, operated under his orders. Most of the uprisings were directed against the local authorities and in many cases had an agrarian element. For example, the British chargé d'affaires considered that by March the chief center of unrest was the Laguna, where, according to his local vice-consul, "the immediate cause of the outbreak was a bad land grab from the Oqui Indians by some wealthy neighboring landowners." The British official was referring to the uprising in the area led by Calixto Contreras, a smallholder from San Pedro de Ocuila. For several years Contreras had been leading his fellow villagers in their efforts to regain some land stolen from them by the owners of the neighboring *hacienda* of Sombreretillo, and he had already suffered a term of forced enlistment as a result.[19] The revolutionary movement in Morelos under Emiliano Zapata, another smallholder, was a reaction against the expansion of the state's sugar *haciendas* at the expense of neighboring villages; and much of the unrest in Sinaloa, Puebla, and Veracruz was also connected with disputes over land. In Yucatán, however, the typically Maderista phenomenon of urban middle class agitation sparked off revolts by the workers on several of the local *henequén* plantations, and in the face of this threat to the social order the upper classes closed ranks. Several unpopular officials resigned, including, eventually, the governor, and many of Madero's followers and sympathizers helped to suppress the revolts. Similar disturbances on the tobacco plantations of the Valle Nacional in Oaxaca were also soon crushed.[20]

In San Luis Potosí the authorities succeeded in maintaining control of the situation throughout the winter months. The leading Maderistas both in the state capital and outside it were either detained or kept under surveillance. The *jefe político* of Ciudad del Maíz, for example, maintained a close watch on the Cedillos. As an additional precaution all laborers who passed through San Luis Potosí en route for the United States without any written contract of employment were drafted into the army or imprisoned. By March 1911 the American consul, Wilbert Bonney, reported that the state penitentiary was "overflowing." The police also confiscated all guns other than side arms and forbade further sales of high caliber weapons. As a result of such measures the rebellion continued to make no impression in the state, and many Maderistas either went into hiding or fled to join Orozco in Chihuahua. At the beginning of 1911 the state government felt sufficiently confident to transfer the majority of the federal garrison to the north, leaving just over a hundred federal soldiers, in addition to the normal contingents of police and *rurales,* to deal with the few remaining Maderistas still at large.[21]

As news of the success of the northern revolt filtered back to San Luis Potosí in the spring, however, Madero's sympathizers in the more remote municipalities were encouraged to take up arms on his behalf. Although their position was still weak, the unpopularity of many local officials and, in some districts, agrarian discontent, facilitated their task. This was the case in the region between the Huasteca and Río Verde where the authorities were believed to have been forced to rig the recent elections in order to prevent Madero and Vázquez Gómez from winning by an overwhelming margin.[22] Violence erupted there as early as January, when Leopoldo Vega attempted to assassinate the unpopular municipal president of Lagunillas. He failed—killing the man's nephew instead—and was arrested, but later he escaped from detention with the help of the local townsmen led by Francisco Robledo, who was also, like Vega, a man of some standing in the community. In February there were reports of Maderistas on the borders of neighboring Zacatecas and Guanajuato, and at the end of the month a religious fanatic, calling himself "Padre Zavala" after the former priest of Ciudad del Maíz, recruited 100 men to attack Atotinalco. (The local *jefe político* heard of "Padre Zavala's" plans in advance and prevented any trouble by making a number of pre-emptive arrests.) In March there were said to be three separate groups of rebels active in the Huasteca, the most important of which was operating near Valles under Leopoldo Lárraga's brother, Manuel. The authorities tried to raise auxiliary forces to meet the threat posed by such bands, but with little success. The *jefe político* of San Luis Potosí, for example, failed to attract volunteers from the *partido* despite an offer of one and a half pesos per day, or five times the average wage of local farm workers. In Río Verde and Villa de Arriaga the municipal presidents requested weapons to form a defense force, but were similarly unable to obtain recruits. As a result, local officials in the state were forced to rely upon any available units of *rurales* or federal soldiers for the maintenance of law and order.[23]

In spite of these stirrings of unrest, however, as Easter approached, the Maderista rebellion in the state was little more than an irritant as far as the government was concerned, and it certainly presented no serious threat to the political order. The authorities calculated that there were only 150 rebels in the whole state, and although this was probably an underestimate, the majority was concentrated in the Huasteca where they contented themselves with attacks upon *haciendas* and with disrupting communications. The inhabitants of the state capital enjoyed their usual vacation activities. Employees of the Mexican Metallurgical Company organized an excursion to the Sierra de Alvarez, and a group of cycling enthusiasts went on a trip to Río Verde and San Ciro. And Manuel Ugalde, the *jefe político* of San Luis Potosí, accompanied the Arguinzóniz and other landowning families to the health resort of Taninul in the Huasteca. Most government supporters believed that the Maderista uprising would soon die out.[24]

Elsewhere in the country, however, the revolt was gaining an unstoppable momentum. The government's main instruments for maintaining order—the army and the *rurales*—were too ill-equipped in either numbers or organization to suppress widespread social unrest. According to Paul J. Vanderwood, not one of the country's ten military zones contained sufficient forces in the autumn of 1910 to quell a determined guerrilla movement. There was poor coordination between the military and civilian authorities, and too many decisions were referred to Díaz, even, on occasion, by subordinate officers who were in disagreement with their superiors. Militarily, Díaz's only hope of success was to win a conclusive victory over the main body of rebel forces. He almost achieved this when Madero made a rash and unsuccessful assault on Casas Grandes, Chihuahua, in early March, but the opportunity was never repeated. At the political level the government was paralyzed by illness and old age, a fact which Díaz recognized when in March he belatedly summoned Bernardo Reyes from Europe to lead the government's military campaign. On April 1 the president attempted to conciliate the rebels by putting a number of reforms before congress, including a law prohibiting reelection to political office and a proposal on agrarian reform. But his opponents regarded this move as a sign of weakness and pressed for his resignation. Throughout April the rebels continued to make progress, undermining the government's authority with a series of small victories, particularly in the north of the country and on the Gulf Coast.[25]

The rebels' success brought new life to the movement in San Luis Potosí. On 17 April, two separate bands, both well disciplined and organized, requisitioned goods from the *haciendas* of El Salado and Illescas in the northwest of the state. The force near Matehuala consisted of almost four hundred well-armed cavalry under a retired army colonel and included members of the richest families in Saltillo. The other band was much smaller and failed in an attack upon Salinas at the beginning of May. The troubles around Valles caused the replacement of the *jefe político* on 22 March. His successor reacted vigorously to the growing unrest and ordered the arrest of numerous Maderista sympathizers. Two of these cases led to the first deaths in the state under the act suspending constitutional guarantees: a servant of the Lárraga family, shot when troops were searching for the father of Manuel and Leopoldo Lárraga, and a rancher named Ahumada, killed while resisting arrest.

In spite of such measures, however, unrest continued to spread throughout the region. On 29 April there was an uprising in Lagunillas organized by Miguel Acosta, the nephew of one of Madero's closest collaborators. Acosta had observed the strong support for Madero in the district during a visit earlier in the year and returned there with a consignment of arms that he had acquired in the United States. With thirty followers he attacked and captured San Ciro, killing the municipal president and imprisoning the town council. There they were joined by eighty more rebels under Isauro Verástegui, a local rancher related to one of the state's most prestigious families. The whole party then moved to Arroyo Seco, which was held by another Maderista, Andrés Flores. On 3 May the *jefe político* of Río Verde, Manuel Parente, reoccupied San Ciro but then had to withdraw to Río Verde, which was likewise threatened by another force under Pedro Montoya, a wealthy local rancher and cattle dealer. Rebels also menaced Santa María de Río and Villa de Reyes from the south. Some belonged to forces that Dr. Rafael Cepeda had raised in Guanajuato after returning from the United States, and the remainder were led by Cándido Navarro, a local schoolteacher.[26]

On 4 May Manuel Ugalde, the *jefe político* of San Luis Potosí, was replaced and given the task of coordinating the operations of the other *jefes políticos* in the state, but there was little he or they could do to contain the revolt. The small number of troops available to the state government, which had been sufficient to meet the original Maderista threat in the capital and main towns in the autumn of 1910, were unable to cope with the growing number of guerrilla bands that confronted them in late April. Local *hacendados,* who could have given significant material assistance to the authorities, generally kept apart from the struggle. Moreover, such steps as they did take to assist the government were often ineffective. When, for example, the administrator of El Jabalí *hacienda,* owned by Pablo Escandón, the governor of Morelos, armed fifty of his men and sent them against the forces of Miguel Acosta, they were unable to prevent him from linking up with Verástegui and subsequently withdrew to the *hacienda* without having achieved anything. In the first two weeks of May, Xilitla, Tamazunchale, and Tancanhuitz all fell to the forces of Acosta and Montoya, leaving Valles as the only sizeable town in the Huasteca still in government hands. In the north there were 1,000 rebels between Matehuala and Saltillo, the state capital of Coahuila, and a further 1,500 on the Guanajuato–San Luis Potosí border. In the week following 11 May, the *jefes políticos* resigned in Cerritos, Río Verde, and Matehuala, and the unpopular Mariano Zuñiga was replaced in Alaquines. On the 16th the authorities in Ciudad del Maíz fled from the town, and four days later the rebels took Rayón.[27]

Apart from the rebels who were under the indirect command of Madero's headquarters, there were other more independent insurgents. Some were bandits, of whom the most important was Nicolás Torres, a former farm hand whose men preyed upon the countryside near Salinas. According to Bonney, his men were "inclined to avenge private grievances, and are not under control, act with unnecessary violence and combine robbery with revolt." Others were villagers who joined the rebellion in order to regain land which they claimed had been stolen from their communities in the past. Miguel Acosta, for example, obtained recruits near Santa María de Acapulco in the municipality of Santa Catarina "by exploiting the discontent in the district, and especially in Guayavos, whose inhabitants consider themselves to have been robbed of land they had held for many years." Finally there were those who bore a personal grudge against the authorities or landowners of the district. Apart from the force operating near Matehuala and the men under Cepeda and Cándido Navarro in the south, the other bands in the state were formed from these irregular revolutionaries. This was the case even when their leaders held a commission from Madero's headquarters, as did Acosta.[28]

Several of the younger members of the state's elite also joined the revolt, seeing in this movement the opportunity for political advancement and a means to protect the interests of their families. On 5 May a band began to operate on the Aguascalientes–San Luis Potosí border under the leadership of Miguel Rincón Terrenos, the nephew of a former Mexican ambassador in London, and of José Pérez Castro, the son-in-law of Carlos Díez Gutiérrez, the late governor of San Luis Potosí. Their followers were recruited from the workers on Rincón Terrenos's *hacienda* in Aguascalientes. At the end of the month Pérez Castro captured and executed Nicolás Torres for banditry. For rich Maderistas such as himself the revolt was political, and any social agitation had to be suppressed.[29]

Throughout this period the Cedillos had remained quiet. Although they toyed with the idea of joining the Maderistas, they knew that the local authorities were keeping a close watch upon their movements and, in consequence, feared pre-emptive arrest. Moreover, they were awaiting a lead from Alberto Carrera Torres, who, having eluded detention in November 1910, had begun to operate with a small group early the following year. As the rebellion spread, Carrera Torres's own forces grew, and eventually on 21 May he captured Tula in neighboring Tamaulipas, just over the state line from Ciudad del Maíz. The Cedillos made preparations to join him, but before they could do so, they heard that the revolt was over. On the same day as Carrera Torres's victory, government representatives had signed an armistice with Madero in the northern border town of Ciudad Juárez. This agreement provided for the resignation of Díaz and the holding of fresh elections. Ten days later Díaz departed for Europe, leaving the finance minister in his last cabinet, Francisco León de la Barra, as provisional president with the task of organizing the elections. In San Luis Potosí the governor, José María Espinosa y Cuevas, resigned on 28 May and was replaced on an interim basis by José Encarnacíon Ipiña. As a prominent *hacendado* who had long been an advocate of social and economic reform, Ipiña was considered by *El Estandarte*'s editor to be particularly suitable to preside over the transition to the new regime. The departure of Espinosa y Cuevas was followed by pressure for the removal of other less important officials. To this end there were demonstrations in San Pedro, Villa de Reyes, Ahualulco, and Matehuala. Some of these ended in violence and had to be suppressed by Maderista troops—a forewarning of the problems that the new authorities were to face in maintaining order over a populace unused to freedom. In order to prevent further unrest Cándido Navarro traveled through the west of the state replacing local officials, and Pedro Antonio de los Santos, who arrived in San Luis Potosí from the Huasteca on 1 June, did the same in the east, benefiting his family in the process.[30]

The sudden collapse of the Porfirian regime after thirty-four years surprised both Mexicans and foreigners alike. Because the rebels had avoided any set-piece battle and had applied pressure upon the government through guerrilla warfare, it almost appeared as if Díaz had surrendered without a fight. But the very ease and speed of the Maderistas' triumph was to prove damaging to their cause. Madero himself and his closest associates had rebelled in order to force the resignation of Díaz and to obtain the promise of fresh elections. For them the revolution had achieved its aims. But many of Madero's followers had other goals. Some of them had joined him for personal gain, and they wanted to receive demobilization payments or to be incorporated into the security forces or even, if they were more important, to obtain a post in the local state government. Others had fought for economic reforms, such as changes in the structure of land tenure or higher mining and industrial wages. By resigning so abruptly Díaz deprived his opponents of the long and hard struggle which alone could have forged a bond between Madero and his followers. Madero, obsessed with political issues and a swift return to peace, was never forced to incorporate the precise demands of all those who fought for him into a coherent political program. As a result, many of his followers, frustrated in their particular ambitions, soon became disillusioned with the regime that they had risked their lives to establish.

Even before Madero became president, it was evident that he did not appreciate the importance of consolidating his political position or the seriousness of the rural unrest which had developed under the aegis of his movement. The provisional president, León de la Barra, was an unrepent Porfirista who was determined to prevent Maderismo from growing into a threat to the old social order. He insisted that Madero's troops be either paid off or brought under the control of the federal army. Bent upon promoting national reconciliation, Madero bowed to his wishes and thus alienated some of his foremost supporters. In the same spirit Madero opposed unilateral action to resolve social and economic grievances, believing that parliamentary democracy was the appropriate channel for eventual social change. However, by appeasing the diehard Porfiristas in this way he became enmeshed in their efforts to prevent reform.

This entanglement was most clearly seen in Madero's dealings with Emiliano Zapata, the rebel chief in Morelos. During the Porfiriato a number of villages in the state lost land to neighboring sugar plantations whose owners used their political influence to further their business interests. Protests by the villagers were unavailing, and finally, in early 1911, they revolted. The man who emerged as their leader was Emiliano Zapata, a smallholder from the village of Anenecuilco, whose inhabitants were threatened with the loss of their land to a neighboring *hacienda*. Impressed by the reference to the restoration of village lands in the Plan of San Luis Potosí, the Zapatistas, as the Morelos rebels came to be called, subscribed to the Maderista revolt. When Madero triumphed, they were reluctant to surrender their weapons until, as they expected, their village lands were restored. The authorities in Mexico City insisted that they demobilize, withdraw from the *hacienda* property they had occupied, and then take their complaints to court. Madero visited Zapata and persuaded him to allow his men to be disarmed in return for an investigation into their case. But León de la Barra regarded the Zapatistas as bandits, and with the collaboration of General Victoriano Huerta, the army commander charged with disarming them, he sabotaged Madero's efforts to reach a settlement. Rather than defy the provisional president who had betrayed him, Madero abandoned Zapata to his fate and left for Yucatán on an election tour. Zapata and his men remained in revolt, a constant irritant to the new regime, which they considered to be no better than its predecessor.[31]

There were similar, if less dramatic, developments in San Luis Potosí. The first problems for the interim Maderista administration were with industrial workers and miners. Between the beginning of June and the end of August there were strikes for higher wages and better working conditions in the smelters at Wadley and Matehuala, the mines at Catorce, Charcas, Guadalcázar, and Matehuala, and the nail factory in San Luis Potosí. The most serious unrest was in Catorce, where the workers of the nearby Santa Ana mine went on strike in the middle of June. When the manager of the mine, who was also the municipal president of Catorce, delayed in meeting the strikers' demands, the miners seized arms and dynamite from the company store and pillaged Catorce and neighboring settlements. Order was restored only the following day when Maderista troops arrived from Cedral, disarmed the strikers, and hung four of their leaders. Troops were also used on three other occasions to prevent violence from erupting during strikes, but without resulting bloodshed. After Cepeda became governor in September, however, the authorities became more conciliatory toward strikers and mediated in a number of disputes. As a result, labor relations in the mines and in industry improved, and there were no serious conflicts during the following winter.[32]

Agrarian unrest was a more persistent problem. The fighting in the spring of 1911 had provided an outlet for the rural unemployed, and those who were not absorbed into the security forces were reluctant to return to the countryside without an improvement in conditions there. Furthermore, a number of villagers and smallholders in the east of the state began to agitate for the restoration of land which they claimed had been stolen from them in the Porfiriato. And finally the *peones acasillados* on at least two of the *haciendas* where working conditions were particularly arduous started to press for higher wages. As Consul Bonney commented shortly before the end of the fighting:

> It is feared here that neither party may be able to control the people who have abandoned civil occupations and taken up arms. It is said here that poverty and bad crops have much to do with the present conditions and also that the grievances of many years will not be promptly quieted. The fact that the state of San Luis Potosí, which has been comparatively quiet and neutral, is beginning to report disturbances, is significant; the discontent here is only partially political. The opposition to the Federal Government is not sufficient alone to lead to action; they have no grievance against their state government. It seems to the most intelligent observers here that the repression of many years has led to a reaction, hastened by the disturbed conditions elsewhere, that no ordinary terms of peace can stop, and that there is a danger of a prolonged period of reprisal and accounting . . . . The sympathizers with the revolution make one large distinct class; disorders are feared from an entirely different and lower class and from the young men who know and care little for the merits of the revolutionary movement and who have little to lose.[33]

The first attempt to meet the demands of rural labor came from José Encarnación Ipiña. Appreciating that without economic reform the overthrow of the old Porfirian political machine would lead to further disturbances, he sought to implement his long-held belief that the state's larger *haciendas* should be divided up and sold off as small farms. Shortly after taking office he put an agrarian law before the congress that established a 2,000 hectare limit on the size of any rural estate. The owner of any larger property was required by law to sell the excess at its fiscal value to a land company which the government would establish for the purpose, and which would then, in turn, divide and sell the land in small plots. Ipiña's proposal was probably too radical to be accepted by the cautious Madero administration, but if more Maderista governors had taken steps to implement land reform, movements such as those led by Contreras, Zapata, and the Cedillo brothers might well have been avoided. In fact, Ipiña's law was never passed since he resigned after only two weeks in office in protest at the interference in the appointment of government officials by Pedro Antonio de los Santos, whom Madero had named secretary to the state government with the rank of brigadier-general. He arrived in San Luis Potosí from Mexico City on 10 June, and shortly afterward he forced Ipiña's resignation. At the instigation of De los Santos, Dr. Rafael Cepeda was then appointed governor, a choice acceptable to the majority of Maderistas.[34]

Unfortunately, Cepeda's administration was soon troubled by factional strife among the local Maderista chiefs, a problem common to several of the new state governments. In San Luis Potosí the two main factions involved were the Santos family and the Lárraga family, who were competing for political control of the Huasteca where they both had property interests. In late June, when Leopoldo Lárraga replaced Santos Pérez as *jefe político* of Valles, the Lárraga faction appeared to have triumphed, but their victory was short-lived. In August, Madero broke with Francisco Vázquez Gómez and his brother Emilio, also a leading anti-reelectionist, who were critical of his conciliatory attitude toward members of the former regime, and ensured the selection of José María Pino Suárez, a lawyer from Yucatán, as his party's vice-presidential candidate. Cepeda and the Santos family remained loyal to Madero, but the Lárraga family, supported by another leading Maderista, Ponciano Navarro, were partisans of the Vázquez Gómez brothers. In the August elections Cepeda was returned as governor and filled the local administration with loyal followers of Madero, leaving the Vazquistas out in the cold. Soon afterward Navarro exploited agrarian discontent in certain villages in the Huasteca to stage a Vazquista uprising there. The state authorities moved quickly to prevent the revolt from spreading; they detained many well-known sympathizers of the Vázquez Gómez brothers, including Leopoldo Lárraga and Miguel Acosta, and soon captured and imprisoned Navarro himself. By late September most of the more prominent Maderista military chiefs were in detention for anti-government plotting, either on behalf of the Vázquez Gómez brothers or in favor of General Bernardo Reyes, who had just withdrawn from the presidential elections on the grounds that they were being rigged in Madero's favor. As an additional precaution the state government increased the federal army garrison to 450 men, or over twice the number of Maderista militiamen who had remained under arms to act as a local police force. This last move was, however, of only limited value, since the militiamen were unwilling to cooperate with their recent enemies—particularly if it meant persecuting their own former leaders—and friction between the two groups was common. Such widespread dissension in the Maderista ranks, combined with the various outbreaks of social unrest, was hardly a good augury for Cepeda's forthcoming term of office.[35]

Madero assumed the presidency in November 1911 with Pino Suárez as his vice-president after an overwhelming victory in Mexico's first free election in living memory. His government lasted only fifteen months, during which time his popularity and prestige gradually declined. The reason for his failure was that Madero lacked the political skills necessary to make a liberal democracy work in the conditions of social and political polarization that resulted from the economic policies of his predecessor's regime and his own violent seizure of power. An idealist with an interest in spiritism, he was an inept and unhappy practitioner of the arts of political wheeling and dealing. Too often he was weak when he should have been resolute and stubborn when he should have been conciliatory. Even before he assumed office, he seriously damaged the unity of his movement by breaking with the Vázquez Gómez brothers. Later, as president, he failed to impose his authority upon several of the more important leaders of the federal army and thus failed to prevent their subsequent insubordination. Most important of all, he underestimated the pressure for social and economic change among the lower classes. He was prepared to tackle rural and urban discontent, but only after careful study. For a man who had assumed power through revolution, such a cautious attitude to government was misplaced.

Perhaps the best illustration of the inadequacy of Madero's gradualist approach to reform was the agrarian question. Rural unrest continued unabated in many areas and threatened the credibility of his government. But instead of ordering state executives to take immediate measures to resolve the causes of local discontent, Madero set up a commission to study the whole agrarian issue. In February 1912 the commission made three major recommendations: that remaining national land be surveyed in order to be divided into small properties; that the authorities purchase private land for the same purpose; and that villagers who claimed to have been illegally deprived of their communal land be able to regain it through the Ministry of Agriculture without recourse to the courts. These recommendations, whose purpose was to encourage small-scale farming, were in the tradition of nineteenth-century liberalism, and Madero accepted the commission's report. Survey teams were sent out and villages were invited to reclaim their *ejidos* (communal land). Attempts to purchase private land for the creation of small properties were, however, abandoned since landowners offered their worst land at inflated prices, and Madero rejected compulsory purchase on principle. Unfortunately, Madero's policy did little to appease rural discontent, to a great extent because many of the problems of the countryside were precisely due to similar attempts to stimulate small-scale private farming in the past. More drastic measures were needed, and in December 1912 a Maderista congressman, Luis Cabrera, proposed the restoration or creation of *ejidos* through compulsory purchase for those villages that lacked them. Although Cabrera's suggestion was a retrograde step in the eyes of liberal economists, it received support from many members of Madero's party, and in early 1913, the government appeared ready to accept it. But Madero's overthrow, which was partly due to his failure to tackle the agrarian problem more energetically, ended such hopes.[36]

Madero's government followed a similar reformist line in other sectors. While the president was prepared to sanction the use of force to end strikes, he recognized that repression offered no long-term solution to labor unrest. In December 1911 he established the National Labor Office in the Ministry of Development (Fomento), which carried out studies on labor questions and arbitrated in disputes. This department settled over seventy strikes and drew up a labor agreement for the important textile industry. He also allowed a workers' center to be founded in Mexico City, the Casa del Obrero Mundial, where labor leaders met to discuss their common problems, although he showed his distrust of the more radical among them by having them arrested or deported. Nevertheless, the prospects for Mexico's workers were better than they had been under the old regime. In the field of education Madero increased government spending and commissioned a young engineer, Alberto Pani, to make a study of education needs in the federal district. Reforms such as these ended with Madero's government, but several of his collaborators resumed similar activities in more propitious circumstances several years later.[37]

To be successful, Madero's cautious reformist strategy required patience from the protagonists of change and tolerance from conservatives, but neither was forthcoming. On the contrary, it was precisely because of continuing agitation for agrarian reform on the one hand and the unrelenting hostility of certain diehard Porfiristas, including several senior army officers, on the other, that Madero's government eventually fell. Associated with both groups was the leader of the most important uprising against Madero, Pascual Orozco, Jr., who had been the president's foremost military commander during the spring of 1911. Disillusioned by Madero's failure to satisfy the hopes and aspirations of many of his followers—he considered in his own case, for example, that his appointment as head of the *rurales* in Chihuahua was an inadequate reward for his services—and encouraged by the old Porfirian elite in the state, whose interests were threatened by the policies of the reformist governor, Abraham González, Orozco rebelled in March 1912. He still had a considerable following among his veterans and at first his revolt prospered. Gradually, however, he was forced upon the defensive and by the late summer the federal general Huerta had driven him back into the mountains of Chihuahua.[38]

In spite of Orozco's connection with the most reactionary elements in Chihuahua, his movement became a rallying point for other disgruntled Maderistas. During the summer of 1912 bands of "Orozquistas" appeared in Zacatecas, San Luis Potosí, Sinaloa, Guanajuato, Veracruz, Oaxaca, and the Laguna. Some were criminals who took advantage of the confusion by pillaging indiscriminately, but the majority saw in support for Orozco the opportunity to press for the solution of specific local grievances. Among those who associated themselves with him were the Zapatistas. In November 1911 they had issued the Plan of Ayala, which called for the restoration of village lands in Morelos and a limited program of land redistribution, and they continued their armed resistance throughout Madero's administration.[39]

Members of the former regime blamed the prevalent social unrest upon Madero's weakness rather than upon their own earlier policies. They aired their criticisms in the press and found an echo among many senior army officers whose confidence had been restored by the defeat of their old enemy Orozco. These prejudices were shared by several influential diplomats. Both the American and German ambassadors, Henry Lane Wilson and Paul Von

Hintze, believed that Madero's overthrow was indispensable for the protection of their countries' interests. Both men were prepared to support such a move, although they differed upon who should succeed him; Wilson preferred Félix Díaz, Porfirio's nephew, and Hintze opted for General Victoriano Huerta, the victor against Orozco and army commander in the capital, whom he considered to be the "strong man" that Mexico needed. Even some of Madero's most loyal followers became concerned at the possible consequences of the administration's inability to pacify the country. In December 1912 Rafael Cepeda traveled to Saltillo to discuss the general deterioration in law and order with Venustiano Carranza, the governor of neighboring Coahuila, and to consider what additional measures the administration might take to improve the situation. Nothing emerged from their meeting, but such actions, innocent enough in themselves perhaps, contributed to the growing climate of uncertainty in the country, provoking rumors of a possible move by the president's colleagues to unseat him. Unfortunately for Madero, his failure to consolidate his earlier support (e.g., by satisfying the aspirations of Orozco or the Zapatistas) and to create a strong personal power base meant that his political survival was largely dependent upon the goodwill of the federal army. This enforced reliance upon his former opponents in war was to prove fatal to him. After several false starts General Bernardo Reyes, Madero's former presidential rival, led a revolt against him in February 1913. Reyes was killed in the initial uprising, but his followers then made common cause with General Victoriano Huerta. The latter had Madero arrested, and after the president's murder under suspicious circumstances, he assumed control of the country.[40]

In San Luis Potosí the Maderista government of Rafael Cepeda passed through the same cycle of excessive optimism, disillusionment, revolt, and repression as its national counterpart. Cepeda's administration was drawn from the same middle-class sectors that supported Madero in his 1910 campaign—merchants, teachers, journalists, lawyers, etc. The new authorities did not have a program for social reform but offered their electoral promises of freedom of speech and efficient administration. They abolished the unpopular office of *jefe político* in October 1912 but did not pass any labor legislation or follow up Ipiña's initiative in agrarian matters. They intended to increase government spending, particularly on education, but could not raise the necessary revenue. They had to borrow money in December 1911, and although their projected budget for 1913 was twice the budget of the last Porfirian administration in 1910, they were not even able to pay their employees at the end of 1912. The lack of government funds for social expenditure resulted from a business depression in 1912, the need to allocate additional resources to the security forces, and a fall in the output of the local mines. (Mining production was affected by slack demand and a shortage of dynamite, which was needed for military purposes.) The government also faced the implacable hostility of the old Porfirian ruling class. Having failed to regain power in the elections of August 1911—their candidate was the same Pedro Barrenechea who had earlier helped

Madero—the state's economic elite refused to cooperate with Cepeda's administration. They contributed to the business depression through a lack of investment and tried to avoid paying taxes.[41]

Cepeda's first months in government continued to be troubled by armed revolts led by former Maderista chiefs. The first disturbance was in the Huasteca, where in December 1911 Miguel Acosta was arrested after he raised a band to support an abortive uprising of General Bernardo Reyes. At the same time, Ponciano Navarro escaped from prison and fled to the Valles region, where he recruited some of his former soldiers and began to disrupt communications. In the same month two other groups attacked the railway station at Río Verde and the *hacienda* of La Parada on the road from San Luis Potosí to Zacatecas. In response the authorities introduced conscription, but they never seriously enforced what proved to be an unpopular measure, and there were still only 300 federal soldiers and 100 *rurales* in the state in January. Reports of fresh rebel activity continued throughout the spring: José Pérez Castro took up arms again and began to operate west of Salinas; Pedro Pesquera, Cándido Navarro's second-in-command in the spring of 1911, also rebelled, gathering together over a hundred men on the Guanajuato–San Luis Potosí border; further east a previously unknown rebel chief called Daniel Becerra started a Vazquista uprising near Río Verde with about fifty followers and actually captured the town in early March before being driven off into the mountains by federal reinforcements; and finally a number of small bands were active in the Huasteca, the most important of which was commanded by a local landowner, Dionisio Hernández. The unrest eventually affected the rural economy. Work was disrupted on several *haciendas* and at least one administrator, the manager of Rascón, asked for federal army protection. Furthermore, in March the sulfur mines at Cerritos closed down, leaving 700 men unemployed, and in April the Cinco Estrellas Mining Company closed its mine at Pinos, just over the state line in Zacatecas, putting 350 men out of work.[42]

At this point the government's fortunes improved. The number of *rurales* was increased to 500 and they began to gain some success. Pérez Castro was captured at the beginning of April, and in mid-May Ponciano Navarro was killed in a skirmish near Tancanhuitz. Faced with a more vigorous enemy, Pedro Pesquera retreated into Guanajuato, and Dionisio Hernández went on the defensive on the Veracruz border. Shortly afterward Cepeda toured the Huasteca and promised to withdraw the *rurales* from country areas if the rebels accepted an offer of amnesty. At the same time the federal army garrison was raised to 1,000 men, and this combination of force and conciliation undermined Cepeda's opponents. Most of the rebels remaining within the state accepted the amnesty, including all those in the Huasteca, and in the middle of August 1912, Bonney reported that communications were uninterrupted and that all banditry had ceased.[43]

The authorities could, however, only ensure lasting peace by tackling the question of agrarian reform, and Cepeda's administration took no initiatives either to raise wages or to redistribute land. Although sympathetic to the plight of the rural poor, Cepeda held a view common within the government that wages should be fixed by the law of supply and demand. As he once told a friend: "I cannot force the landowners to pay more or the laborers to work for less."[44]

The governor's attitude strengthened the resolve of the majority of *hacendados* not to make concessions to their laborers; in their view the recent political upheaval should have no social or economic consequences. Only a few progressive landowners such as José Encarnación Ipiña responded to the climate of the time and raised the wages of their workers; most revealed a stubbornness worthy of the more obdurate members of the *ancién regime* in prerevolutionary France. When, for example, in the late summer of 1912 the agricultural laborers on the *hacienda* of Gogorrón sought parity of pay with the workers in the cashmere coat factory attached to the property, the owner responded by moving the factory to nearby San Luis Potosí. This kind of intransigence could sometimes lead to violence, as was shown during a labor dispute on Cerro Prieto *hacienda*. Labor conditions on the property were relatively poor: the *peones acasillados* were paid 0.25 pesos per day in tickets exchangeable only at the *hacienda* store, where prices where abnormally high. Their families were expected to provide unpaid domestic service. In December they sought a pay raise. The response of the owner of the property, Luis Toranzo, to this move was to actually lower their wages to 0.18 pesos per day. The administrator of the *hacienda* at once resigned, and after a short delay Toranzo appointed a young Spaniard to the post. The latter lived up to his countrymen's reputation for harshness in their treatment of native labor by enforcing the new wage levels and having the workers' spokesmen arrested. Enraged by his action, some of the *hacienda* peons seized and killed him, mutilating his body in the process. Following this incident there was an informal truce on the *hacienda;* the laborers returned to work and the new administrator, whom Toranzo provided with a bodyguard, restored wages to their former level.[45]

The landowners' determination to maintain low wages even at the risk of labor unrest was not motivated solely by a desire to maximize profits. It also formed part of the conflict between the old economic elite which had formerly governed the state and the Maderista administration of Cepeda; for lower wages were prejudicial to the interests of the local merchants who were among the government's most loyal supporters and who wanted them raised in order to stimulate demand. As Bonney commented in early November 1912:

> The middle class of people are now nominally in control in this district and it is believed impossible to go completely back to the feudal conditions or to develop further along that line. . . .
>
> Everything has been done in the past to favor the land owner at the expense of trade and labor. Low wages have deprived the laborer of purchasing power and hampered trade; trade has languished and has been further burdened with direct taxes. The land owner has been a large producer of alcohol, and therefore that industry has not been adequately taxed nor the consumption of alcohol discouraged. Import duties on grain have operated entirely in favor of the land owner.

The problem of the expansion of trade in this district is the same problem con-
fronting the middle classes in their political contest—the overcoming of the feu-
dal system and giving the people proper purchasing power. Fair wages would
result in solving most of the political difficulties and result in an enormous expansion of trade. The chief difficulty underlying the trade situation, the labor
situation, and political situation in this district is the same.

With violence in the district practically suppressed, the problems remain
much the same as before; any attempt at reform or improvement encounters the
obstacle of limited purchasing power of the people as well as the obstruction of
the land owning class.[46]

The government's failure to improve working conditions in the countryside
brought a renewal of unrest in the autumn of 1912. Between September and
December there were reports of rebel activity from the Coahuila border, where
one of Pascual Orozco's lieutenants, Benjamín Argumedo, commanded over
five hundred men, and also the regions of Salinas, Charcas, the Guanajuato
border, Rayón, Ciudad del Maíz, and the Huasteca. The widespread nature
of the unrest made it extremely difficult to contain, even though the federal
troops in the state were by then augmented by 4,000 volunteer police and
rurales. The security forces were confronted by small and mobile groups of
armed men who were thoroughly acquainted with the terrain in which they
operated and who disbanded in the face of superior numbers only to regroup
once the danger had passed.[47] The grievances of these rebel bands were largely
economic, and their anger was directed as much against property as against
agents of the government. A clear analysis of their motives was given by Bonney in a report in September 1912:

> The whole revolutionary activity of the past two years is now considered primar-
> ily as an attempt on the part of laborers, and especially farm laborers, to better
> their conditions. This is indicated by the fact that revolutionary leaders have re-
> sorted to plantation labor for recruits, certain to find discontent there. It is indi-
> cated further by the fact that local violence has been directed chiefly against
> property and only incidentally against government.
>
> The violence was accompanied and followed by labor strikes, and by the for-
> mation of labor unions in the towns, and by a successful attempt to replace
> American skilled labor on the railroads.
>
> There is not now and has not at any time been enough political feeling of any
> kind in this district to cause laborers to resort to violence against the government
> nor to organize into raiding bands, and not enough patriotism to cause them to
> enlist in the army. They have been ready to rise against their employers on the
> plantations, and a considerable number have been induced to enlist by the offer
> of 52½ cents per day.
>
> The belief that the revolutionary activity has been fundamentally a labor
> movement explains also the surprising lack of interest in politics displayed by the
> successful party in this State. They do not vote in large numbers, nor even
> present candidates in some cases. It is true the revolution in its early stages took
> a political color and was directed against President Díaz; but it is generally rec-
> ognized now that this was a mistake and that the real grievances were economic.

The Madero revolution succeeded in this district because it promised economic relief to farm laborers. Every subsequent political proposal has been met with suspicion and dissatisfaction because such proposals did not reach to grievance of the laborers. Laborers have lost their faith in government measures for their relief and have consequently lost their interest in political conditions. They have resorted to other means to accomplish their object. These means are as follows:

1. Labor strikes
2. Emigration to the United States
3. Enlistment in the army
4. Joining lawless bands of marauders.

It is to be noted that in adopting any of these four means of relief their object is the same—economic betterment—and it is the same which led them to join the revolution of 1910. . . .

The native laborer has shown all the faults ascribed to him, but he has been the victim of a system of labor which was inherited from past generations and which gave him no hope of betterment in his private relations. Under such a system the labor of the peon has yielded a large profit to his employer. Land owners cultivating, by their agents, from two to four thousand acres of their holdings, without rotation of crops, without modern machinery, seed selection or roads, after paying for all supervision have drawn very large revenues from their estates, which must be considered proof that native labor has been efficient under most difficult circumstances. There are few countries were farming could be carried on at all in this manner. It is not believed that any agricultural labor in the world would have produced much better results in the same conditions. It cannot be surprising that when age-long restraints have been relaxed the laborer appears occasionally as the enemy of property. . . . There is no purely political revolution on the part of the common people; the discontent is local, and economic, and the danger spots are usually where there are large numbers of agricultural laborers. It is not believed that miners and railroad men have furnished many recurits [sic] to the disorderly bands. Stories of soldiers deserting in bodies have been accompanied by the information that they had not been paid.[48]

It was in the midst of this peasant *jacquerie* that Saturnino Cedillo and his brothers first took up arms against the government. Their motives were the same as those of many of the other rebels in San Luis Potosí: frustration at the administration's failure to offer them and other members of the rural lower and lower middle classes the prospects of a better life. Ever since the fall of Díaz, the *hacendados* around Ciudad del Maíz, like most of their counterparts elsewhere in the state, had been determined to prevent Madero's political revolution from leading to social and economic change in their locality. They had two general aims, which they pursued as single-mindedly as if Díaz were still president: to extend their control over more of the natural resources of the region and to keep labor as cheap and docile as before Madero's rebellion. In pursuit of the first goal, the Espinosa y Cuevas brothers reopened the question of the Moctezumas' property. They took their case to the commissioners whom the Ministry of Development had sent to the state as part of its survey of

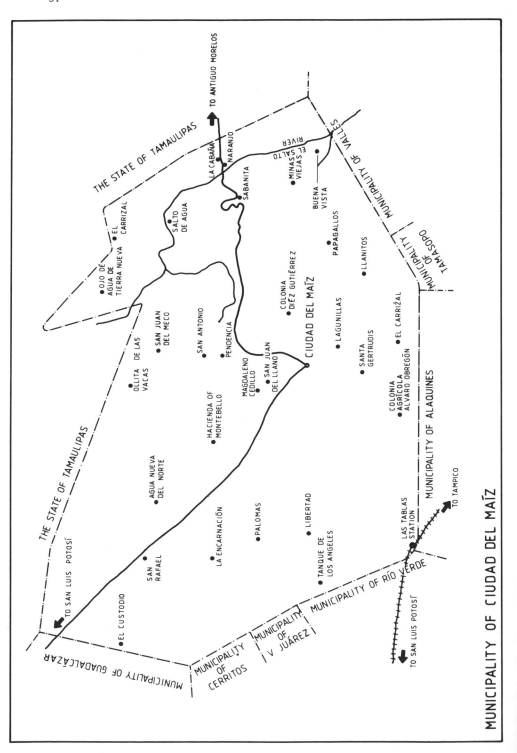

MUNICIPALITY OF CIUDAD DEL MAÍZ

all remaining national land. The brothers claimed that the woods on the Moctezumas' land belonged to the nation and asked the commissioners to measure
the area that they covered. According to the Moctezumas, the survey team
soon became an instrument for the ambitions not only of the Espinosa y
Cuevas brothers but of all the neighboring *hacendados:*

> The very government of Madero sent a commission of engineers body and soul
> committed to the cause of the hacendados nearby, and especially to the Espinosa
> y Cuevas who were thirsting to do evil through their particular idiosyncratic
> kind of hatred and scorn for the poor, and the commissioners set about fixing it
> all. They traced arbitrary lines, reduced our special possessions as heads of fami-
> lies, recognized as legal landholders those who were merely renting from us, ren-
> dered false reports about us, and handed over great portions of our land to the
> Espinosa y Cuevas brothers and smaller sections to the owners of Sabino and
> Carrizal haciendas and to anyone else who wished us harm. In the middle of this
> travesty created by the aforementioned engineers who were ingratiating them-
> selves with the great landowners, who were more interested in robbing us,
> knowing as they did the lack of definite directions and lack of great energy which
> characterized Don Francisco I Madero's government, we had to take up the
> fight again.[49]

The Moctezumas therefore sent representatives to Rafael Hernández, the
Minister of Development, and asked him to reverse the commissioners' findings. Hernández suspended the survey and ordered an investigation of the
case, but the Madero government fell before it could be completed. The Moctezumas remained in possession of all but about 1,900 hectares of their property which the Espinosa y Cuevas brothers incorporated into Angostura.[50]

The *hacendados* were equally intransigent in their treatment of native labor.
They refused to raise wages or accept back any of their workers who had
fought for Madero. As a result, some former rebels went to live on Palomas.
Later, in the summer of 1912, there were difficulties between the *hacendados* and
ixtle cutters of the region. Sharecroppers on one of the *haciendas* requested an
increase from sixty cents to a peso for each *arroba* of fiber they produced and
threatened to sell it directly to merchants if this was refused. The owner of the
hacienda asked the local *jefe político,* Manuel Buentello, to send *rurales* to keep order.

Buentello provided him with a detachment of former Maderistas who arrested the men, hanged two of their leaders, and sent the rest to San Luis Potosí under guard. Friends of the prisoners asked the sons of Amado Cedillo for
help. The brothers accompanied the captives to San Luis Potosí and interceded with Cepeda on their behalf. The governor ordered the release of the
men and promised to persuade the *hacendados* to improve working conditions.[51]

Cepeda's offer was quite inadequate. The Cedillos knew that the *hacendados*
were in no mood for compromise and that only coercion, not persuasion,
would make them change their attitude. As they saw it, the governor's refusal
to pass legislation to force higher wages was tantamount to supporting the *hacendados'* intransigence. And what of Madero's promise of land reform in the

Plan of San Luis Potosí? He may have been referring only to the restitution of *ejidos* rather than the expropriation of *haciendas,* but even on that score precious little had been done by his government. Were the Zapatistas not right to distrust the president? Hadn't Orozco perhaps been correct to call for more sweeping land redistribution in his revolutionary proclamation the previous March? While the Cedillos were pondering these and similar questions, they received a visit on 15 September from a delegation of sixty fiber cutters from the *haciendas* of Montebello and San Rafael. The visitors told the brothers that they had always looked to them to defend their interests, that the new regime had done nothing to improve their working conditions or to protect them from arbitrary abuse at the hands of the *hacendados,* and that they wanted the Cedillos to lead them in a revolt against the state authorities. The Cedillos hesitated, reluctant to take such a decisive step, and persuaded the men to be patient a little longer in the hope that Cepeda might still intervene. They added, however, that if matters did not improve, then they would accede to their request. The men agreed to this, but as they departed, they advised Saturnino that if their sufferings continued and if he and his brothers persisted in their refusal to rebel, they would hold them responsible for the situation.[52]

The Cedillos were in an awkward position, for when news of the meeting spread, they came under the suspicion of Buentello. Furthermore, the local oligarchy wanted to drive them to revolt in order to see them eliminated. This became clear when Zeferino Martínez raised the Cedillos' rent for pasturing their animals on Montebello to a prohibitive level. As Martínez knew, the pasture on Palomas was inadequate. Without all their animals the Cedillos would be more reliant upon obtaining work on neighboring *haciendas;* they would lose their position as independent *rancheros* and would have to accept the semi-dependent status of sharecroppers. Short of direct intervention by Cepeda, the *hacendados'* control over land, wage levels, and the local authorities made their position unassailable, and it was evident to the Cedillos that, for whatever reason, Cepeda was unwilling or unable to intervene. As if to emphasize the balance of power within the district, the *hacendados* persuaded Buentello to order the Cedillos' detention. Without hope that the governor would intervene, the Cedillos decided to act before Buentello could arrest them.[53]

Circumstances favored the Cedillos' enterprise. The national government was preoccupied with the rebellions of Orozco and Zapata and with combating the widespread unrest elsewhere in the country; it had few troops to spare to quell any new movement. Furthermore, the Cedillos expected to cooperate with the other rebels in the state, such as Daniel Becerra near Río Verde or Benjamín Argumedo further to the northwest. The brothers were joined in their enterprise by Paulino García and Sidronio Méndez, each with a small band. As a prosperous merchant and orange grower from Río Verde, Méndez gave the movement an air of respectability. The conspirators planned simultaneous attacks for 17 November on Tula, led by García, on Río Verde, by Méndez, and on Ciudad del Maíz, by the Cedillos. Early that day Magdaleno Cedillo took a small group to Montebello to seize the stock of weapons and ammunition there, while Saturnino and Cleofas took the remainder of their men to Ciudad del Maíz. After a short fight they captured and sacked the Municipal Palace, burning the property register there with its copies of the title deeds of the local *haciendas*. They then addressed a crowd of *campesinos*, explaining the reasons for their revolt and declaring their adherence to the Zapatistas' Plan of Ayala, a copy of which they read out. Manuel Buentello had meanwhile escaped for help to the nearby Colonia Díez Gutiérrez, whose inhabitants enjoyed a basic form of government patronage and might be expected to assist him. There he recruited a band of well-armed volunteers, returned to the town, and drove out the rebels. Cleofas and Saturnino returned to Palomas where they met up with Magdaleno. He had succeeded in his mission after a sharp struggle in which the *hacienda* administrator and several guards had been killed. Hearing that the force of Méndez had failed to take Río Verde, the Cedillos moved toward Tula, depositing weapons and money at *ranchos* en route where they had sympathizers. Near Tula a messenger from García informed them that he had abandoned his plan because the town was too well guarded. Fearful of pursuit, the Cedillos decided to leave for Texas until the situation quieted down.[54]

In company with several companions they arrived in Nuevo Laredo at the end of November. For two weeks they worked in a brick factory near Raíces but left after Cleofas had a disagreement with the foreman. They were then recruited by agents of Pascual Orozco's father, Pascual Orozco, Sr., and the Vázquez Gómez brothers, and moved to San Antonio. Saturnino then quarreled with one of their companions, Gregorio Martínez, over what he considered the latter's excessive drinking, and Martínez left for Mexico accompanied by Cleofas. Magdaleno soon joined them, and together they went into hiding in the hills near Ciudad del Maíz. Saturnino had meanwhile purchased fresh arms and ammunition and followed Magdaleno south. He was, however, arrested on the border and sent to prison in San Luis Potosí. Although the state authorities had consistently treated captured rebels with leniency, Magdaleno and Cleofas expected Saturnino to be executed and thus renewed their guerrilla activities. They enlisted the help of both relatives and friends, such as the Turrubiartes brothers, Ildefonso and Apolonio, and the Tapia brothers, Juan and Catarino, fellow *rancheros* from Cerrito Colorado and Rancho Nuevo near Palomas. On 10 February they robbed a train near the Las Tablas station of 700,000 pesos. Three days later they raided Angostura, seized such arms and provisions as they needed, and retired to the hills. The "Cedillista" movement had begun in earnest.[55]

The Cedillo brothers were, however, far from being the only preoccupation of the Cepeda government at the beginning of 1913. Benjamín Argumedo was still active in the north and west of the state. Pérez Castro escaped from jail in December 1912 and began to operate again in his old hunting ground west of the state capital, and there were other rebel groups near Charcas, Catorce, Salinas, and in the Huasteca. On account of their activity the train service between San Luis Potosí and Saltillo was suspended on 13 February, and the trains to Tampico were subject to long delays. This led to the closure of the smelter near Matehuala, and both the smelter at San Luis Potosí and the rubber factory at Cedral were forced to operate at half their capacity. The widespread guerrilla activity challenged the authority of the government, while the unemployment it caused provided the rebels with more recruits allowing them to extend their operations even further. The government lacked the necessary forces to combat the growing unrest: the *rurales* could not be relied upon; the contingents of the federal army which were available were insufficient for the task; and it was difficult to raise additional troops when banditry appeared a more profitable occupation to potential recruits. In response to the mounting threat to the credibility of his administration Cepeda took a number of repressive measures reminiscent of the rule of Díaz. He established press censorship and closed down *El Estandarte,* the city's leading newspaper. He also planned to exact a forced loan from local businessmen in order to spend more on the security forces.[56]

At this point any further developments in San Luis Potosí were overtaken by Huerta's coup d'état in Mexico City. Madero's experiment in the politics of persuasion and consensus had been brought to an abrupt and bloody end, and Hintze's "strong man" had emerged from the shadows to claim power. Taken by surprise, the Cedillos and the other rebels in the state waited to see how Mexico's new ruler intended to govern the country.

CHAPTER 3

THE REBEL CHIEF

THEIR [THE CEDILLOS'] INFLUENCE IN THE COUNTRY IS ACCENTUATED BY THE FRIENDLY ATTITUDE OF THE CIVIL POPULATION.——Consul Claude Dawson in Tampico, 7 December 1917

Huerta's seizure of power was greeted with relief by most of the upper classes, who assumed that he would establish a regime similar to that of Díaz. Even some of Madero's former supporters welcomed the change, believing that a more energetic administration was needed to tackle the country's problems. But such hopes for "firm government" soon proved illusory, for within weeks of taking office Huerta was faced with an armed resistance movement that forced him to concentrate his energies upon maintaining himself in power. The importance of meeting this threat led to the federal army's playing a prominent role in the administration of the country: Huerta's government became, in essence, military rule under his leadership, supported by elements from the old Porfirian bureaucracy. As time went on, he faced growing opposition both from within Mexico and from the United States. After seventeen months in power his regime collapsed and Huerta himself went into exile. That he lasted so long in such adverse circumstances was a tribute to his skills as a politician and to the brutal methods employed by his security forces.[1]

The internal opposition to Huerta had been two-fold in origin. First, the state governments of Coahuila and Sonora rejected Huerta's usurpation of power. After some hesitation the governor of Coahuila, Venustiano Carranza, refused to recognize the new president. He issued the "Plan of Guadalupe" in which he proclaimed himself First Chief of the Constitutionalist Army and undertook to call fresh elections as soon as Huerta was defeated. In a similar vein the state congress of Sonora also defied Huerta—the governor, José María Maytorena, had avoided the issue of recognition by taking a leave of absence in the United States—and in April sent representatives to confer with Carranza in Monclova. At their meeting they accepted the Plan of Guadalupe as the basis for their operations, and the rudiments of an alternative administration were established.[2]

The second source of opposition to Huerta was more informal and came from those who were agitating for social and economic reforms, usually of an agrarian nature. Some of these rebels were already under arms when Huerta seized power and, having no illusions about the new government, simply remained in revolt. Foremost among them were the Zapatistas, but many other lesser bands reacted in the same way, including the Cedillos in San Luis Potosí. These forces were soon joined by several revolutionary chiefs who had fought for Madero in 1911 and had remained loyal to him thereafter: Calixto Contreras in the Laguna; the Arrieta brothers, Domingo and Mariano, in Durango; Alberto Carrera Torres in San Luis Potosí; Rómulo Figueroa in Guerrero; Manuel Chao in Chihuahua; and, most famous of all, Francisco Villa, who crossed into Mexico from Texas in early March. By exploiting local grievances, again often of an agrarian nature, these men soon mobilized a large following, and restricting their operations to familiar terrain, they defied the government with great success.[3] The only important revolutionary leader to recognize Huerta was his former antagonist Pascual Orozco, who, with his subordinates such as Cheche Campos, was well rewarded for doing so.[4]

The importance of agrarian discontent in the opposition to Huerta was clear to all contemporary observers. William Canada, the American consul in Veracruz, summarized its importance three months after Huerta took power. Canada's remarks, which could have been applied equally well to many states, do much to explain why it was so easy for local rebel leaders such as the Cedillos to mobilize support and why, after the breakdown of the *Pax Porfiriana,* neither Madero nor Huerta succeeded in restoring order in the rural areas of the country:

> For many centuries the Indians had been accustomed to use the ground around their villages without molestation and had looked upon it as common property. In case of disputes they appealed to some one of their number upon whom they looked as their chief and rarely asked the services of the mayor of the town, who represented the Government.
>
> Later, however, the Government declared part of these lands public property and put them up for sale through legal notices so that gradually people who knew the necessary formalities acquired large tracts. As a consequence, these Indians suddenly found they could no longer use the lands which they had believed their own, and discovered that they would be punished by law if they attempted to do so. Deprived of this means of gaining a living, they had no recourse left but to work for the new landlords, and finally their improvidence, involving them in debts to their employers, enslaved them.
>
> This agrarian question, in fact, has always been the cause of most of the unrest in this State. Tradition has taught these peasants to consider this acquisition of lands as an ineffable injustice to themselves. Agitators may gain their ears, and they may call themselves Zapatistas or Carrancistas; yet in the State of Veracruz the uprisings are purely local in their significance. The Indians do not

bother themselves as to who may be in the presidential chair, if only they can regain the liberties their ancestors enjoyed. Sometimes, even, they cannot tell for what principle they are fighting. Nevertheless, their raids are not made in a spirit of lawlessness; abuses exist and the realization that they have suffered them too long makes a reaction in such an extreme form seem lawful to this people. No changes in the administrators of the central government will satisfy them, whatever promises are made, and until reforms have fundamentally altered the whole economic situation, this discontent will continue to prevail.[5]

In time the leaders of various opposition groups began to coordinate their operations, and to a greater or lesser extent they associated themselves with the Constitutionalist movement under Carranza. An important exception to this was the Zapatistas, whose leaders pursued their own agrarian revolution independently of the other resistance to Huerta's rule and never acknowledged Carranza's authority. In July 1913 Carranza imposed a loose organization upon the Constitutionalist forces by creating seven army commands, of which the only meaningful ones were the Division of the Northeast under Pablo González, a former miller's assistant who had risen through the ranks of the Maderistas to head one of the two regiments of the Coahuila state troops under Carranza; the Division of the Center theoretically under Pánfilo Natera, but in fact dominated by Francisco Villa's troops; and the Division of the Northwest under Álvaro Obregón. These commands covered the northern states, and with the exception of Morelos, which remained under the domination of the Zapatistas, Huerta controlled the rest of the country. Of the three commanders, Obregón was the most talented. He was distantly related to the families who had formed the Porfirian elite in Sonora, and before the Revolution he was a successful small-scale businessman and *ranchero*. He first became involved in any fighting when, as the municipal president of Huatabampo, he raised a force to fight the Orozquistas in March 1912. He proved a very able commander, and when the Sonora state congress decided to oppose Huerta, the interim governor appointed him to lead the state troops. The soldiers that he commanded in the summer of 1913 were mainly drawn from the Sonoran militia and had a strong sense of regional identity.[6]

San Luis Potosí remained outside the Constitutionalists' main sphere of operations during the spring and summer of 1913, although several guerrilla groups were very active. Cepeda had recognized the new administration on 24 February, a week after Madero's deposition, but the authorities in Mexico City distrusted him. His statement of recognition lacked conviction, and he was known to be in contact with Carranza, a close personal friend of his. When Carranza finally stated his rejection of the new regime, the federal authorities moved to prevent Cepeda from joining him. He was arrested on 6 March and sent to prison in Mexico City.[7]

The new government of San Luis Potosí was representative of the old Porfirian elite and the federal army. There was a complete change in the personnel of the local federal and state bureaucracies; many who had held office under Díaz returned to their former positions, and they were in no mood to conciliate the fallen Maderistas. The commander of the local federal army garrison became interim governor, and the new state congress that was elected under official supervision included the former governor, José María Espinosa y Cuevas. Pedro Barrenechea later became the mayor of the state capital. The hated office of *jefe político,* which had just been abolished, was restored, and several other reforms of the previous administration were also annulled. Their predecessors in government, mainly middle class and new to political office, strongly resented this violent recovery of power by the old elite and its clients. Neither they nor their supporters wanted a return to the old order. Many Maderistas might have been disappointed with Cepeda's achievements, but they knew that he had faced the unrelenting opposition of the local industrial and landowning elite. Under his administration the state had enjoyed a degree of freedom unknown under Díaz and unlikely to exist under Huerta. The new authorities were wise not to court popularity, for they could not expect it.[8]

Most of the rebel chiefs were also distrustful of the new regime. None of them wanted a return to a government that protected the interests of expansionist landlords like the Espinosa y Cuevas brothers. The majority were fighting for social and economic goals that were as unacceptable to the Huerta regime as they had been to that of Díaz: the restoration of the village lands, fair competition for *rancheros* against *hacendados,* and even, in some cases, a redistribution of land within *haciendas.* As a result the only important leaders who recognized the new regime were Benjamín Argumedo and José Pérez Castro, both of whom were influenced by the decision of their nominal commander, Pascual Orozco, to do so. The others remained in revolt. They were joined by new bands under disillusioned Maderista politicians who declared allegiance to Venustiano Carranza. Of these the most important were Pedro Antonio de los Santos and José Rodríguez Cabo, both based in the Huasteca. In the disturbed conditions of the rural economy there was no shortage of recruits, even if most *peones acasillados* remained on their estates. Six weeks after Cepeda's arrest there were more rebels active than at any other time during his term of office.[9]

Among the main beneficiaries of this new wave of recruits to the guerrillas' ranks were Magdaleno and Cleofas Cedillo. Initially they had shown an interest in negotiating with the regime in order to obtain the release of the still-imprisoned Saturnino. But when the authorities refused to release Saturnino, whom they probably intended to use as a hostage for his brothers' good behavior, Magdaleno and Cleofas came out against them. The brothers would in any case have found it hard to collaborate with an administration so closely identified with the local *hacendados.* Because of their growing reputation as guerrilla leaders they soon attracted a large following, and within weeks their band had swelled to several hundred men. Shortly afterward they joined forces with Alberto Carrera Torres, who was once again operating on the Tamaulipas border.[10]

The Cedillos chose to work with Carrera Torres because of his commitment to land reform, the issue over which they had originally revolted against

Cepeda. Shortly before, on 4 March, Carrera Torres had published a revolutionary proclamation entitled "An Executive Law for Land Redistribution," which embodied the ideals for which the Cedillos were fighting. Article 1 of the decree was a refusal to recognize Huerta's government. Articles 2 and 3 called for the abolition of all newspapers favorable to that administration and the death penalty for all journalists who "denigrated the Revolution." Articles 4 and 5 ordered the expropriation of the property of Huerta and his followers. Article 6 stated that no debts incurred by Huerta's administration would be honored. Article 7 established a First Agrarian Junta consisting of Carrera Torres, his brother Francisco, and his other leading companions. Article 8 stated that all the *haciendas* belonging to Díaz, Huerta, and their more prominent supporters, such as the Terrazas, Creel, or Noriega families, should be confiscated as soon as they were overrun by the Constitutionalist armies and then partitioned into ten hectare plots for distribution to the landless and, on condition that they abstained from fighting against the Constitutionalists, to soldiers of the federal army. (This latter point was a recognition of the problem presented by the large numbers of men mobilized during the recent fighting.) Article 9 cancelled any debts owed to those mentioned in Article 8; Articles 10–15 dealt with matters such as the reorganization of the federal army and government-sponsored irrigation schemes. Articles 16–18 specified the conditions for receiving land under the decree, including a prohibition on its subsequent resale or mortgage, a measure designed to prevent a reconcentration of landholdings. Article 19 gave all settlements, from towns to *ranchos,* the right to appoint a representative to obtain land for them under the decree. Finally Article 20 promised to villages or smallholders the return of land that had been stolen from them during the Porfiriato through abuse of the agrarian laws. When the Cedillos joined Carrera Torres, they at once declared their adherence to the plan.[11]

Owing to the scale of the guerrilla warfare in San Luis Potosí, the Huertista authorities were never in a position to govern it effectively. In the early summer of 1913 the rebels occupied most of the north of the state. Matehuala, Catorce, and Cedral all fell to Carrancistas under Santos Coy at the end of April, and Guadalcázar and Charcas fell to other bands. They were also active elsewhere; besides the Cedillo brothers, four other guerrilla bands were operating in the Huasteca, raiding towns and disrupting the San Luis Potosí–Tampico railway line. There were only 700 federal soldiers in the state, and outside the capital the majority were stationed in the east to guard the approaches to the oil fields. The security situation was becoming critical, and in a dispatch on 29 April, Bonney concluded, "The government is entirely helpless. The garrison of the state is entirely inadequate."[12]

It was clear that drastic security measures were needed urgently if the rebels were not to overrun the whole state. In May, therefore, the federal authorities increased the troops in San Luis Potosí to 1,500, and in June they introduced military service. Following this, the local military commander began a fresh campaign of pacification. His plan was to secure the railway lines and larger towns first and then to move against the rebels in the countryside. The initial stage of the campaign was successful, and during the summer the federals held most of the towns, including all the more important ones. There was only one passenger train on the San Luis Potosí–Saltillo line between mid-May and the beginning of September, but under heavy protection limited goods traffic ran to both Saltillo and Tampico. In July the government received further encouragement when Pedro Antonio de los Santos was betrayed and shot at Tampamolón. But this was the limit of their success, for the federal commanders were never able simultaneously to protect the railway lines, garrison the towns, and take the offensive in the rural sector. The two main reasons for their weakness were a lack of reliable troops and the government's widespread unpopularity. Since the conscription law was discriminatory, affecting only those earning less than an army private, the loyalty of those enlisted was therefore doubtful, and desertions among them were frequent. Of the fifty-man contingent sent to Charcas at the beginning of May, over thirty deserted within a week of arrival. The rebels encouraged this tendency; when they captured federal soldiers, they usually punished only the officers and invited the lower ranks to join them. Government efforts to persuade the middle classes to volunteer for service were notoriously unsuccessful. According to Bonney, they, like the lower classes in the state, remained Maderista in sympathy. The general antagonism toward the new government was underlined by the reaction to the reintroduction of the office *jefe político:* the new *jefe político* in Matehuala was murdered, and five of his colleagues in other towns were forced to flee for safety to the state capital.[13]

Apart from the difficulties of the federal army in finding reliable recruits, the rebels enjoyed a further advantage in a regular supply of food. The harvest of 1913 was excellent, and abundant stocks of grain and other produce accumulated on *haciendas*. The rebels either pillaged the *hacienda* granaries directly or, as often happened, when landowners dispatched their reserves to nearby towns for immediate sale. Thus lowering the price on local markets, they purchased it cheaply through intermediaries. In this way they were able to stay in the field for long periods and sustain a prolonged campaign against the government.[14]

Early in September 1913 Bonney calculated that there were thirty-four separate bands of rebels in or near the state numbering over five thousand combatants, as shown in Table 5.[15] Not all these guerrilla units were active simultaneously, and many only operated during slack periods in the agricultural cycle. Furthermore, the list is somewhat misleading: Magdaleno and Cleofas Cedillo, for example, worked in unison, and both Enrique Salas and José Castillo operated on the Cedillos' orders. But probably some three thousand men were available for operations at any one time. A few of the rebel leaders held commissions from Carranza; they included Santos Coy and Eulalio Gutiérrez, both active near Matehuala, Cándido Aguilar near the Zacatecas border, and the Carrera Torres brothers near Tula. Most of the remainder

TABLE 5: REBEL GROUPS ACTIVE IN AND AROUND THE STATE OF SAN LUIS
POTOSÍ IN SEPTEMBER 1913, ACCORDING TO A LIST COMPILED BY
WILBERT L. BONNEY, THE LOCAL U.S. CONSUL

Rebel Chief	Area of Operations	Number of Followers
Enríque Salas	Near Valles	40
Eugenio Olivo	Near Tanchachín	40
Pedro Carrera	Near Alaquines	40
Francisco Oyarbide	Near Valles	50
Gonzalo Aldape	Near San Ciro	50
Magdaleno Cedillo	East of Ciudad del Maíz	100
Cleofas Cedillo	East of Ciudad del Maíz	150
J. A. Castro	South of Tamaulipas	250
Alberto Dávila	Near Cerritos	50
Julio Castillo	Near San Ciro or Rayón	40
Zacarías Castillo	Near Guadalcázar	20
Ramón Coronado and Jesús Contreras[a]	Sierra Manzano	150
Antonio Torres	Near Dr. Arroyo, Nuevo León	150
Nicolás Flores	Huasteca Potosina	50
Antonio Noriega López	Unknown	50
Julián Medrano	From Nuevo León	200
José Rodríguez Cabo	Near Rodríguez	300
Samuel Santos, Trinidad Santos, Fulgencio Santos, and Francisco Santos	Near Huasteca Potosina	150
Francisco Cosío Robledo	Huasteca Potosina	200
Manuel Lárraga	Huasteca Potosina	120
Manuel Santos Alonso	Huasteca Potosina	40
Ramón Acosta, Timoteo Acosta, and Lorenzo Acosta	Huasteca Potosina	100
Alberto Carrera Torres and Franciso Carrera Torres	East of Ciudad del Maíz	300
Simplicio Torres	Unknown	150
Eulalio Gutiérrez	East of Matehuala	400
Cándido Aguilar	El Oro, Zacatecas	300
Jesús Sánchez Dávila	San Tiburcio, Zacatecas	200
Pedro García and Justina Cervantes	Salinas	150
Mariano Flores	San Tiburcio, Zacatecas	100
Ernesto Santos Coy	Near Salado	400
Idelfonso Pérez	Near Dr. Arroyo, Nuevo León	200
Ismael Alardín	Near Dr. Arroyo, Nuevo León	50
New leader[b]	North of Salinas, leader uncertain	600
Total number		5,190

[a]Coronado and Contreras were operating with Cándido Navarro's force in Sierra Manzano.
[b]Bonney stated that the leader of this band was said to be Raúl Madero but that he found the report unlikely.

were local men who acted independently and rarely strayed far from their home districts: Manuel Lárraga and five members of the Santos family in the Huasteca, Alberto Dávila near Cerritos, and Magdaleno and Cleofas Cedillo around Ciudad del Maíz. Saturnino Cedillo does not feature on the list because, at the time, he was still languishing in detention in San Luis Potosí. Three months later, however, in December, he escaped and rejoined his brothers. The previous month, in an effort to win over Cleofas and Magdaleno, the authorities had released him on parole within the city boundaries. Magdaleno then went there, ostensibly to negotiate terms with the federal army, but in fact to finalize plans for Saturnino's escape. Shortly afterward Saturnino fled from the city. Following his return, the Cedillos began to work more closely with Alberto Carrera Torres, with whom they formed a unified command. Together they incorporated a number of smaller bands into their forces, with the result that by January 1914 Bonney calculated that over three thousand men acknowledged their leadership in different districts.[16]

Because many of the rebel chiefs had a grudge against local landowners, their targets were often *haciendas* or even mines. As Bonney commented shortly before the end of the year:

> The wealthier class supports the military and despotic method of government, and would support any administration which would continue that method and would oppose any administration favorable to representative Government. They fear the social effect of the revolution as much as the political effect...the revolution in this district is aimed instinctively at the caste system of society and the feudal system of production, rather than at purely political ends. While the agrarian question is often referred to as behind the revolution it is believed rather a revolt against the feudal system of production, which system includes land tenure, and which determines the markets, wages and transportation and pervades the whole commercial and social stratification. The revolutionists know of no method of attack except the crude method of destroying the physical property of the landowners; a few propose to attack titles and rights. The wealthy class here fear not so much to lose control of the government: they have already given that up to the army; but they fear to lose the position of a ruling class. The feudal system is very resistant, it presents many problems; the amount of damage that can be done by destroying the surface property of a plantation is small and scarcely affects the system of production which is the real grievance. It is not believed that a political change would reach the basic difficulty.[17]

Between September and December 1913 at least twenty-four *haciendas* within the state were attacked. The properties most affected were, understandably, those where labor conditions had been worst in the past. Rascón, for example, was pillaged in August, and Angostura was sacked by the Cedillos in November. Among foreign landowners the Spaniards suffered most, as they did elsewhere in the country, thus paying for their well-deserved reputation as hard taskmasters of native labor. American properties, on the other hand, with one or two exceptions such as Rascón, were spared the worst depredations, a consequence of the good working conditions and relatively high wages prevailing on most of them.[18] Many rich landowners recruited extra *hacienda* guards, and in September 1913 Agustín Soberón and several other *hacendados* from the north of the state financed a small force of mounted "vigilantes" to defend property there. As late as May 1914 a group of Huasteca landowners led by Eduardo Meade offered to supply the local federal commander with horses if he could raise a similar body in the east of the state, but the projected force was never recruited. However, unless the *haciendas* so defended possessed valuable and easily destructible installations, such measures were often more expensive than they were worth. Furthermore, they were inadequate in the face of a large and determined rebel attack. Angostura was pillaged by the Cedillos, although it was defended by thirty "white guards."[19]

Carrera Torres and the Cedillos never settled in any district long enough for them to carry out the former's program for land redistribution, although they continued to operate under an agrarian banner. On the other hand, within the area under their influence—the strip of land between Tula in the north and Río Verde in the south—there emerged during the years 1913 and 1914 a form of primitive communism:

> In each community of any importance there were stores, shoe-makers, hat-makers, etc. which provided all the inhabitants with basic necessities. The shops supplied all the married men with food rations, while bachelors ate in common dining halls, of which there were several in the villages and even on ranches. The shoe-makers provided sandals (huaraches); the hat-makers, straw hats; the tailors, breeches and cotton shirts, and cotton dresses and shawls for the women.[20]

When the men were not bearing arms, they worked the more fertile sections of abandoned *haciendas* or cut fibers that they sold to merchants for dispatch to the United States. Whenever a federal army column ventured into their district, they concealed their produce and went into hiding. The crops that they grew were consumed locally, and the profits from the fibers were used for the purchase of arms and ammunition, both of which were in short supply.

The Cedillo brothers and Carrera Torres emerged as the leaders of this popular revolution, as tribunes of the local peasantry. And as the political situation within the country polarized, their demands became more radical. They had been driven to revolt against Madero because he had failed to check the ambitions of the *hacendados* and to implement the kinds of reforms—higher wages and better working conditions—which would have raised the standard of living of the local population. They were, at most, reluctant revolutionaries, and a change in the government's agrarian policy might have brought them to accept an amnesty. But Huerta's counter-revolution, which returned political office to members of the Porfirian oligarchy such as José María Espinosa y Cuevas, destroyed any possibility for compromise. From the spring of 1913 onward the Cedillos and their followers were fighting for land of their own and, in consequence, for freedom from domination by the local *hacendados*.

By early 1914 the economy of San Luis Potosí was in desperate straits. All important mining and industrial enterprises were closed or working at very low levels of output, and agriculture was in a perilous state. There was an abundance of maize and beans in local markets, but this was due to the good harvest of 1913 and the consumption of existing stocks, and the increasingly disturbed conditions in the rural sector meant that the state's *haciendas* would be unable to meet local needs the following year. For apart from production difficulties, landowners had little incentive to provide a surplus that was liable to requisition by revolutionaries or federals. The prospects for the future were therefore bleak, and the economic depression encouraged the unemployed to join the revolutionaries.[21]

While this guerrilla war took place in San Luis Potosí, the main Constitutionalist forces further north were consolidating their position and beginning an advance toward the center of the country and Mexico City. Although the federal army often fought bravely, its commanders tended to surrender the countryside in order to barricade themselves in towns from which they were eventually evicted, either by frontal assault or when the rebels cut their lines of communications. Moreover, as we have seen in San Luis Potosí, they suffered badly from desertions among their conscript soldiers. The Constitutionalists, on the other hand, were often fighting in their home territory, and men such as Francisco Villa in Chihuahua and Calixto Contreras in the Laguna enjoyed widespread popularity. In general their armies were composed of men and women who entered the Revolution of their own volition. Villa, a man of considerable charisma, became the best-known Constitutionalist commander after capturing Torreón by storm in October 1913. Described by his enemies as a bandit, which he had once been, Villa was, in Friedrich Katz's words, "a complex mixture of social revolutionary and nineteenth century caudillo." He increased the popularity that he gained through his military successes by promises of long-term land redistribution, which he supported by the immediate confiscation of a number of large estates in the area under his control and by distributing cheap food and other supplies in some of the towns he recaptured.[22]

In February 1914 the American president Woodrow Wilson placed an embargo on arms sales to Mexico. This move was of great help to the rebels, who, unlike Huerta, could easily smuggle arms across the border. But Huerta's apparently inevitable fall was delayed for two reasons: the direct intervention of the United States in Mexico and quarrels among the Constitutionalists. On 21 April American marines occupied Veracruz following an incident between Mexican officials and some visiting American sailors. The move was intended to demonstrate American disapproval of Huerta, but it proved counterproductive. Huerta posed as the champion of Mexican national integrity and called for unity in the face of foreign aggression. Although the main Constitutionalist armies barely paused in their advance, guerrilla activity slackened in the center of the country, and in many cities there were anti-American demonstrations, which Huerta exploited for propaganda purposes. Perhaps the most important impact of the American action was to exacerbate the divisions among the victorious Constitutionalist leaders, which centered upon friction between Carranza and Villa. Since the publication of the Plan of Guadalupe, Carranza had striven to obtain recognition as the head of the country's legitimate government. Many of the Constitutionalist commanders accepted his pretension, either from personal ambition or because they recognized the need to form a new government under an experienced administrator. Villa, however, felt neither respect nor affection for the First Chief, and frequently acted independently of his instructions. Carranza, for his part, disliked the unsophisticated Villa and resented what he considered to be his tendency toward insubordination. When, for example, the U.S. forces occupied Veracruz, Carranza, with his strong sense of national pride, protested vehemently, whereas Villa made no effort to conceal his relative indifference to the move or his belief that Carranza's reaction was dangerously exaggerated. Relations between the two men continued to deteriorate, and by July reached breaking point, according to Zachary Cobb, the customs collector at El Paso who helped to monitor Villa's activities for the State Department. Carranza was even planning to withhold supplies from Villa in order to delay his progress south. Their differences were patched up only in early July when commissioners from Carranza visited Villa with an offer to call a convention of military leaders after the defeat of Huerta in order to decide the country's future, and in response Villa recognized Carranza's position as chief civilian administrative officer of the Constitutionalist movement. This temporary truce between the two men allowed the Constitutionalist advance to continue.[23]

The success of the main Constitutionalist armies encouraged the guerrilla groups operating in San Luis Potosí. By mid-March they had caused the suspension of all railway traffic in the state except that with Mexico City to the south, and they controlled twenty-six small towns and villages and forty-six *haciendas*. The authorities lacked the resources to mount an offensive against them. Ultimately, the security of Huerta's followers depended upon the federal armies further north, and with their defeat the loss of San Luis Potosí became almost inevitable. In a somewhat desperate move they followed Huerta's example in seeking to exploit the American occupation of Veracruz to rouse popular support. The *jefe político* of the state capital harassed the local American community. The railway authorities impeded the free movement of American citizens, and a local businessman, Arturo Martí, organized a demonstration outside the United States consulate, during which the building was stoned. In the face of this officially orchestrated anti-Americanism, Bonney went on indefinite leave; but the authorities' ploy proved a failure, evoking almost no response from the mass of the people. Thereafter, they concentrated upon preparing for the city's defense or their own escape.[24]

The attack on San Luis Potosí was delayed by disrupted communications and by divisions within the Constitutionalists' ranks. The column of Jesús Carranza had to check its drive toward the city from the east in order to repair the railway line from Tampico; while to the north, Venustiano Carranza held back the division under Pablo González for some weeks, through suspicion of Villa's intentions. In early July, however, the Constitutionalists closed in upon the state capital. By this time the whole Huerta regime was crumbling. Huerta himself resigned on 15 July and departed for Europe, leaving the president of the supreme court, Francisco Carbajal, to negotiate with the victorious Constitutionalists. In view of this, the federal army commander in San Luis Potosí, General Romero, abandoned his plans to defend the city, and having plundered the state treasury, he withdrew his men to the southwest on 17 July. On the same afternoon, the first Constitutionalist troops arrived—a small group of the Cedillos' men under Daniel Becerra, who had joined the brothers some months previously. The following day the main Constitutionalist forces entered the city, accompanied by the bands of local chiefs such as Francisco Carrera Torres and the Cedillos.[25]

The first task of the Constitutionalists was to suppress looting, and order was restored only after several shooting incidents. At the same time the Constitutionalists set up a new political administration, and on 20 July Eulalio Gutiérrez assumed office as provisional governor. A former mining employee in Concepción del Oro, Gutiérrez had been elected municipal president of the town under Madero and joined Carranza at the outset of his movement. As a young man whose political thinking was a confused blend of socialism and nineteenth-century, anti-clerical liberalism, he was typical of many Constitutionalist leaders. Gutiérrez immediately showed his anti-clerical colors by attempting to extract a loan of 100,000 pesos from the local church authorities; and when the vicar-general of the diocese refused, he expelled thirty of the forty priests from the state and passed decrees restricting religious practice. He also closed all religious schools and ordered the demolition of a picturesque chapel in the center of the city, "in order to facilitate the movement of traffic." The new governor next turned to labor matters. He permitted a branch of the Casa del Obrero Mundial to be established in the city and passed a decree governing pay and working conditions for local laborers. His law fixed the minimum wages for agricultural workers and miners at 0.75 pesos and 1.25 pesos, respectively, to be paid weekly in cash. He established a nine-hour working day and prohibited the use of company or *hacienda* stores *(tiendas de raya)*. The decree also stated that sharecroppers were to yield up a maximum of only 25% of their produce from unirrigated land and 50% from irrigated, and it controlled the terms on which they could be advanced money. In practice the decree had little effect; most mining and industrial enterprises were closed, and the new administration was not in a position to enforce the measure. But it promised a better future for local labor and thus served to win their political support.[26]

In spite of the bitterness engendered by the fighting, Gutiérrez's government took relatively few reprisals against members of the previous regime or of the local oligarchy, which had of course been largely Huertista in sympathy. It exacted loans from some individuals, and in the case of several absentee landlords, it confiscated their property. Government forces also occupied and pillaged the houses of a number of leading citizens. Finally, the new government carried out about a half dozen executions, the most notorious victims being Arturo Mayo Barrenechea, Jesús del Pozo, and Angel Veral, all well-known Huertista journalists or propagandists, and Javier Espinosa y Cuevas, the brother of the former governor of the state and co-owner of Angostura. Responsibility for the death of Espinosa y Cuevas was widely, and probably correctly, attributed to Saturnino Cedillo. The latter was not known for acts of arbitrary killing and was certainly not bloodthirsty in comparison with the Revolution's more infamous murderers, such as Villa's henchman, the psychopathic killer Rodolfo Fierro. But in view of the Cedillos' past antagonism toward the Espinosa y Cuevas brothers, it would not have been surprising if Saturnino had taken the opportunity to exact a murderous revenge upon them.[27]

In May, the forces of Carrera Torres and the Cedillos had been organized into two brigades, named respectively the Morelos and the Oriente. In late July they were dispatched to the Bajío to suppress Orozquista resistance to the new government. In León, they caught and executed José Pérez Castro, the former guerrilla leader who had put his men at the disposal of Huerta. The Oriente Brigade was then sent to Puebla and Veracruz on similar operations before returning to San Luis Potosí in September. The Morelos Brigade went to Yucatán but also returned at the end of the summer.[28]

The problems that the Constitutionalists faced in San Luis Potosí during the summer of 1914 were manifold. There was a chronic shortage of metallic currency and little confidence in Constitutionalist paper money. Maize and beans were still abundant and therefore cheap—maize costing four pesos per hectoliter—but reserves were dwindling, and the prospects for replacing them remained poor. Some mine owners and the Salinas Salt Company showed confidence in the new government by resuming operations, but there was only slack demand for their products. All the banks were closed, as were many of the large stores that had also functioned as sources of credit in the past. Since government revenues were low, the payment of public employees was irregular; this gave rise to complaints of corruption, not all of which were unfounded. But despite these problems the new government was far more popular than the Huerta regime and was eager to carry out the reforms necessary for the restoration of political stability and subsequent economic recovery. To at least one observer there seemed to be grounds for guarded optimism.[29]

Unfortunately, any hopes for an early peace were shattered by a fresh round of civil strife, this time between the forces of Carranza and Villa. The convention of the victors over Huerta, to whom Carranza had committed himself earlier in the year, was held in Aguascalientes in November. It resolved nothing. Carranza regarded it as a front for Villa's ambitions, and Villa failed to persuade Carranza's most loyal generals to abide by the decisions of the convention against the wishes of their leader. Within a few weeks civil war broke out, and with varying degrees of enthusiasm the country's military leaders committed themselves either to Carranza or to the "Convention" forces under Villa.[30]

The conflict between Villa and Carranza has provoked considerable debate among historians. Was it merely a crude power struggle between the associates of two very different individuals—the one a *hacendado,* the other a former cowboy-turned-bandit—or were deeper issues involved? In analyzing this question one must bear in mind the nature of the Constitutionalist armies. Even the most professional, such as the Division of the Northeast commanded by Obregón, were based upon a strong personal bond between the leader and the led. In many cases the relationship was a simple one of patron and clients. To a large extent, therefore, the alignment of forces hinged upon the choice of individual chiefs, which in turn depended upon the motives of these chiefs for pursuing their hazardous military calling and how they believed they could best satisfy their own personal and political ambitions and those of their followers. The military leaders made their choices partly on what the two protagonists represented to them. Carranza embodied the cause of national unity based upon moderate social reform, fitting in a man who had belonged to the progressive upper-class opposition to Díaz. In spite of rhetoric to the contrary, he had shown little active interest in implementing agrarian reform. Villa, on the other hand, was a more provincial figure, a veritable "man of the people," but of his own people in Chihuahua. He was less concerned than Carranza with questions of national sovereignty or the supremacy of the state and more interested in social change, including, as his recent administration of Chihuahua indicated, some form of land redistribution. In the light of these factors, those whose major interest was in agrarian reform, such as the Zapatistas, were more likely to support Villa. So too were regional *caudillos,* such as Manual Peláez in Veracruz, who were interested in forming an alliance of equals which would leave them relatively undisturbed in their own area of influence. On the other hand, those interested in economic modernization backed by a strong national government or in achieving greater control over foreign, and particularly North American, capital, would incline toward Carranza rather than Villa, who was then regarded as pro-American. Beyond what these two men might seem to represent, other more personal considerations came into play: the loyalty of lesser commanders to one of the more important chiefs; power struggles in certain localities; or the proximity of one of the major military contingents to a smaller band. Such factors could override other considerations: *hacendados* supported Villa and proletarians joined Carranza. Above all, with self-interest playing an important role in dictating which faction the various military leaders joined, the act of changing sides, particularly among the minor chiefs, was to become a frequent occurrence.[31]

In retrospect, the key figure in the alignment of military chiefs between Carranza and Villa was to be Obregón, and he, along with the other leaders of the Division of the Northeast, remained loyal to Carranza. As Katz has recently suggested, his reasons for doing so were probably resentment at Villa's support for his rival in Sonora, Governor José María Maytorena, and his belief that he could exercise more influence upon the civilian Carranza than upon the militarily more powerful, but personally unpredictable, Villa.

Obregón proved to be the most skillful army commander to emerge from the Revolution. Employing those defensive battle tactics which were proving to be so murderously successful in the European war, he defeated Villa in a series of engagements in the first half of 1915 and thus ensured for Carranza control over the main centers of government. By the autumn, Villa and those of this allies who remained loyal to him were forced to resort to guerrilla warfare.[32]

Among Villa's allies were the Cedillos and Carrera Torres, who chose to support him because of his greater commitment to agrarian reform. As the leaders of sizeable revolutionary bands, Alberto Carrera Torres and Magdaleno Cedillo were both invited to attend the Convention of Aguascalientes, but instead they elected to remain in San Luis Potosí and to send Saturnino on their behalf—an indication of their confidence in his judgment. When Saturnino arrived at the Convention, he found that he had been named a delegate in his own right and therein nominated Colonel Manuel García Vigil to represent Magdaleno and Carrera Torres. Whatever the result of the Convention, however, Carrera Torres, at least, had already decided to commit himself to Villa in any conflict with Carranza. While the Convention was still meeting, he rejected Carranza's attempt to win his support with the offer of the state governorship. Furthermore, he and Saturnino's brothers concluded—erroneously—that the president of the Convention, the recent governor of San Luis Potosí Eulalio Gutiérrez, was simply a front man for Carranza and therefore decided to reject his authority. They even instructed Enrique Salas to arrest the local Constitutionalist military commander, Herminio Álvarez, who had publicly declared his loyalty to Gutiérrez and the Convention. Fortunately they informed Saturnino of what they intended to do, and he sent them a telegram asking them not to take any action until he returned. When he arrived, they held an immediate council of war, consisting of Alberto Carrera Torres, his brother Francisco, and the three Cedillo brothers, at which Saturnino persuaded them to accept the Convention government. Shortly afterward, in November, the Convention made its temporary base in San Luis Potosí before moving on to Mexico City, which allowed the others to assess the position for themselves. Following the Convention's departure, the Cedillos and Carrera Torres reissued the latter's agrarian reform decree, noting in a new preface that the Zapatistas' Plan of Ayala had been recognized in the Convention and ought, therefore, to be implemented in all areas under Constitutionalist rule. This restatement of their support for agrarian reform was to be their banner in the forthcoming struggle against Carranza.[33]

Carranza's advisers recognized that Villa had the greater appeal to those military chiefs whose involvement in the Revolution was primarily motivated by agrarian grievances and urged him to make some kind of public commitment to land reform. At their instigation, therefore, Carranza issued a decree on 6 January 1915 that made provision for land redistribution. The most important measures in the decree were the following:

1. All concessions made by government officials under the agrarian laws of 1856 and 1857 and which were proved to have defrauded communities of their land were to be annulled and the land in question returned to the communities as *ejidos*.

2. All divisions of communal land carried out under those laws could be annulled at the request of two-thirds of the members of the community.

3. All sales of public land that similarly defrauded communities were also annulled.

4. In cases of extreme need, i.e., where it was vital for the livelihood of the members of the community, villages could be granted land if they were not eligible for it through restoration.

5. Only agrarian communities outside *hacienda* boundaries could benefit from the decree.

6. Agrarian commissions were to be established on a state and national level to oversee land distribution.

7. In the first instance, petitions for land would go to the state governor or local military commander, who would reach a decision in consultation with the state Agrarian Commission.

8. If they decided in favor of the petitioners, the executive branch of the state Agrarian Commission was to carry out the act of land distribution on a provisional basis.

9. The final decision on definitive land distribution was to be made by the president.

10. Landowners affected by the law had one year to appeal against any decision.[34]

As legislation designed to further agrarian reform, the decree had several intrinsic defects, apart from the fact that when Carranza issued it he controlled well under half the country. It left the initiative for land redistribution with those who wanted land, and potential beneficiaries from the law were often cowed by neighboring landowners or left in ignorance of the opportunities open to them. It excluded from its provisions the majority of the rural labor force, those agricultural workers domiciled on estates *(peones acasillados)*. And finally, the involvement of army commanders in processing petitions proved to be an error; for it provided the less scrupulous of Carranza's military chiefs with the opportunity—which several of them took—for acquiring the land for themselves under the pretext of redistribution. Certainly the decree made little impact upon the Zapatistas or other less important agrarian leaders such as the Cedillos, who continued their opposition to Carranza. Moreover, the legislation had no immediate consequences. Due to weaknesses in the law, Carranza's own lack of zeal for agrarian reform, and the fact that his administration was too preoccupied with maintaining power to concern itself with other issues, no land was formally redistributed under the decree in 1915, and only 1,200 hectares in 1916. In the long term, however, the decree was to prove of greater significance. For in issuing it Carranza implicitly recognized that a stated commitment to agrarian reform was a prerequisite not only for military victory but also for eventual political stability. The latter principle subsequently became an article of faith for his successors and had an important influence upon their policies.[35]

Ten days after Carranza published his decree, Eulalio Gutiérrez and some of the Convention leaders broke with Villa and headed north to establish an independent base in San Luis Potosí. General Eugenio Aguirre Benavides, whom Gutiérrez had made governor of the state, was prepared to support him but was forced to retreat before an advance by Villa's lieutenant, Tomás Urbina, who occupied the city on 1 February. The hapless Gutiérrez then veered eastward into the territory held by the Cedillos. He made contact with Saturnino, who gave him temporary refuge in Ciudad del Maíz but was unwilling to leave his home district and follow Gutiérrez on a campaign against Carranza in Coahuila. This is hardly surprising; in such a fluid situation in which the alignment of the major military chiefs had not yet been fully clarified, it would have been rash of Saturnino to associate himself too closely with the fugitive Gutiérrez, even though he still claimed to recognize his government. Carrera Torres treated Gutiérrez more harshly, refusing to allow him to pass through his territory and forcing him north into Nuevo León.[36]

Following Gutiérrez's departure, Saturnino and his brothers committed themselves wholeheartedly to the Villista cause. In March they and Carrera Torres joined the Villista generals Manuel Chao and Noriega Hernández in an offensive in the east of the state toward the oil town of El Ébano. Not all the revolutionary leaders in the state had joined Villa, and among the Carrancista chiefs facing them were Samuel de los Santos, who had inherited the mantle of the Santos clan from his brother Pedro Antonio, and Manuel Lárraga. It is likely that considerations of geography and regional politics had dictated the two men's choice to support Carranza. Both were vulnerable to attacks from the Carrancista stronghold of Tampico, and both probably saw in support for the First Chief an opportunity to assert their hegemony over their home district in the Huasteca. Similar factors probably influenced César López de Lara from neighboring Tamaulipas, who fought alongside them. The main leaders of the Carrancista forces were Jacinto B. Treviño and Manuel García Vigil, the Cedillos' former ally. When the opposing forces met, the Villistas suffered a serious defeat and were driven back toward San Luis Potosí. Among their casualties was Cleofas Cedillo, who died of wounds received in the battle. His death was a severe blow not only to his brothers but also to their followers. The youngest and most extroverted of the brothers, he had been the most popular among their soldiers, for he was brave in action but always ready to join in any festivities thereafter. During the hard times to come, Magdaleno and Saturnino were sorely to miss his cheerful presence. After the battle Villa summoned the forces of Carrera Torres and the Cedillos to the Bajío to help him in his campaigns against Obregón. Saturnino was given the command of the garrison of Dolores Hidalgo, while Magdaleno and Alberto Carrera Torres fought alongside Villa at León. Following the final rout of Villa and his retreat north in July, the Cedillos and Carrera Torres retired to familiar terrain around Ciudad del Maíz and Tula. Tomás Urbina abandoned San Luis Potosí on 12 July and withdrew northward to join Villa, and a few days later Obregón occupied the city. He offered an amnesty to the Villistas still in the area, which included payment for their equipment and free transport home, but few accepted it. Obregón then established a new administration for the state, appointing General Gabriel Gavira as state governor.[37]

Shortly after the Cedillo brothers retreated to Ciudad del Maíz, they received a welcome and unexpected visitor, Wistano Luis Orozco, the Jalisco lawyer who had assisted the Moctezumas in their litigation with their *hacendado* neighbors some fifteen years previously. Orozco came to them as a fugitive from the Constitutionalists. Although he had not become involved in politics during the years 1913 to 1915, both his two sons had joined Villa's staff when the latter's forces occupied Guadalajara in 1915. When General Manuel Diéguez later captured the city for the Constitutionalists, he held Orozco responsible for his sons' actions and had him arrested. After harsh treatment at the hands of his captors, Orozco was freed when the Villistas reoccupied Guadalajara shortly afterward. However, fearing eventual re-arrest, he fled from the city eastward, finally seeking refuge in Ciudad del Maíz, the home of his wife's family. There he came under the protection of the Cedillos, who welcomed him warmly as both "friend and advisor."[38] While he was with the Cedillos, Orozco drew up a number of plans for agrarian reform in the country. Unfortunately none of these projects survive, and it is therefore impossible to say whether they formed a framework for the program of land redistribution which Saturnino eventually carried out. But for the first time Saturnino had an opportunity to clarify his ideas on agrarian reform with a sympathetic and learned specialist on the subject, and it is likely that Orozco's influence upon him was fairly considerable. After several months, however, the fifty-nine-year-old Orozco found the dangers and rigors of life with the Cedillos too much for him. With much regret on both sides he left for Tampico, escorted by a detachment of troops provided by Alberto Carrera Torres. It is tempting to compare Orozco's sojourn with the Cedillos with the visits that a number of urban intellectuals paid to the Zapatista headquarters in 1914, but the parallel should not be drawn too closely. As far as the Zapatistas were concerned, their visitors were never more than sympathetic outsiders, and the relationship between the two groups always had an artificial air about it. In contrast, Orozco's long contact with the district of Ciudad del Maíz, his local prestige as the Moctezumas' lawyer, and his honorable record in other similar cases caused the Cedillos to view his arrival for what it was—that of a friend in need.[39]

The break between Villa and Carranza led to far more disruption in the economy of San Luis Potosí than the three preceding years of the Revolution. The railways were taken over by the military for troop transportation, and the mines, smelters, and industries that depended upon them were forced to close. The issue of paper currency by various revolutionary chiefs drove hard currency off the market and ruined business confidence. In the rural sector conditions were equally grave. Both *haciendas* and *ranchos* were robbed of their animals and food stocks, and, not surprisingly, their owners made little effort to replace them. In late June, Bonney reported that 30,000 hectoliters of maize were being hidden a day's journey from the city of San Luis Potosí, the owners refusing to release it until the political situation had clarified and until they could be paid for it in hard currency. The majority of the rural population retreated into isolation; few *hacendados* remained on their estates, most leaving their administrators to maintain a minimum of production and to feed their laborers as well as they could. Sharecroppers and casual laborers worked abandoned arable land, and villagers reclaimed communal property. Recognizing that surplus production would be stolen by one or another of the roaming bands of armed men, all sectors of the farming community hoarded and concealed what little they grew. The few economic measures that were taken by the Villista authorities were intended to provide supplies and funds for their armies and did nothing for the local economy. They banned the export of hides and food and levied taxes on other exports. They also made compulsory purchases of *ixtle* at one-sixth of its market price in the United States. As for the supplies they needed, such as dynamite from mines or horses from *haciendas,* they either confiscated them or paid for them with their own paper money. In consequence, the local economy was in a desperate condition when the Villista forces left the state capital, and the mass of population was concerned only with survival.[40]

Although Villa had been forced to yield control of the country's major cities by the end of 1915 as a result of his defeat at the hands of Obregón, he and many of the rebel chiefs allied with him, such as Calixto Contreras in the Laguna, Manuel Peláez in Veracruz, Benjamín Argumedo in Coahuila, and the Cedillos in San Luis Potosí, ignored their enemies' offers of amnesty and fought on in the countryside. There were two main reasons for this continuing resistance. The first was the Villistas' belief that they had less to lose by fighting than by surrender. As Leocadio Parra, a Villista chief in Tepic, commented:

> Wen [*sic*] asked why he and his men did not take advantage of the amnesty proclamations he smiled, and rejoined that if they were to do so, it would only be a short time until they would all be executed, under one pretext or another, and that they could live indefinitely in the mountain fastnesses, and that maybe matters might shape up differently after a while, when they could come out and be received by those who were not so recently their deadly enemies, or join some "opposition" crowd with some hopes of success—that they had no faith whatever in the promises of the Carrancistas as matters now were.[41]

The second reason for the continued unrest was the unpopularity of many Constitutionalist commanders and their men, who were, in effect, an army of occupation in the territory they controlled. Furthermore, although Carranza's generals owed him nominal allegiance, many of them were virtually independent warlords, responsible only to their followers. Some of them, such as Salvador Alvarado in Yucatán and Francisco Múgica in Tabasco, used their authority to carry out reforms that won them popularity. Others, however, were less responsible. They extracted forced loans from merchants and businessmen and pillaged the countryside ruthlessly, stealing cattle and stocks of food. The U.S. consular reports of the time are full of examples of these and other malpractices: General Ramón Iturbe in Sinaloa "seized all manner of goods from the poor and rich to sell in Mexico City"; in Aguascalientes, "Carranza's subordinates prey vulture-like on the helpless peons and wealthier Mexicans"; in Durango and the surrounding district, "the pueblo is entirely against the Carrancistas, that is the military. They have been robbed and robbed and are still being robbed"; in rural Jalisco, "the Carrancistas do nothing but live off the townsmen"; and in Veracruz, detachments of Carrancista soldiers "commit all manner of abuses," while their local commander, General Cándido Aguilar, allowed his family to monopolize the retail trade in cattle and cereals, using his soldiers to extort animals from farmers at a low price. Activities such as these swelled the ranks of their opponents and thus prolonged the unrest. Communications continued to be disrupted, mining and industry operated at reduced levels of output, and agricultural production declined. Disease, and in several districts even starvation, were widespread.[42]

In San Luis Potosí the Carrancistas continued to face fierce opposition not only from the Cedillos and Carrera Torres but also from numerous smaller bands. By the end of 1915 the Carrancistas still controlled only the main towns in the north and west of the state and in the Huasteca and the railway lines which linked San Luis Potosí with Saltillo and Aguascalientes. The center of the state remained in the hands of the Cedillos and Carrera Torres, who together still commanded about one thousand five-hundred troops in various bands and prevented the passage of all but a few heavily guarded trains from San Luis Potosí to Tampico. Conditions overall in the rural sector were chaotic, and all but the largest communities were dependent for their defense upon their own resources. Food supplies remained haphazard and were made worse by a serious drought; there were frequent shortages throughout the state and prices were consequently high.[43]

At the local level the institutions of municipal government had disappeared and were replaced by ad hoc arrangements designed to meet the most pressing needs of each community. Subject to the visitations of bands of armed revolutionaries, anyone who could provide subsistence for the local populace came to exercise political authority. In some cases this applied to the old patron class of hacendados or their administrators. The manager of Bledos, for example, kept the loyalty of the hacienda peons by ensuring them a supply of food in even the most difficult periods. He also sent provisions to the workers on his employer's other estates. And in Cedral, an American called Stackpole, who made his living by recovering ore and quicksilver from unused mines in the region, supplied his laborers and the poor of the town with maize from Zacatecas. Transporting his product by mule and burying it when necessary, he continued his operations throughout the turbulent summer of 1915. Once, when a band of revolutionaries attempted to interfere with his work, they were repulsed by a "protesting posse" of local women who declared that he was the town's support and benefactor.[44] But where the old ruling class had fled, or were otherwise powerless to help their former dependents, local strongmen assumed power, often acting in collaboration with nearby bands of insurgents to whom they offered support in return for protection. In this way, revolutionary leaders such as the Cedillos acquired authority over large areas of the state. Both they and their men worked abandoned *haciendas* and protected the local population from the depredations of all but the largest columns of Constitutionalists; in return they were given logistical and moral support to continue fighting. For outside the Huasteca, where Carranza was supported by several local military *caudillos,* the Carrancista soldiers were almost universally feared and hated. Expected by their commanders to live off the land, they behaved— as in so many areas of the country—like an invading army, robbing *haciendas, ranchos,* and villages indiscriminately.

By the spring of 1916 the military situation had clarified somewhat. The Carrancista administration controlled the city of San Luis Potosí and all the urban centers in the north and west of the state. It also had a loose control over the countryside in the region, which it maintained through mobile columns of soldiers. The Cedillo brothers and Carrera Torres dominated the municipalities between Guadalcázar and Cerritos in the west, and Ciudad del Maíz, Cárdenas, and Rayón in the east. They lived in the countryside but occupied the towns in the area as they wished. They also made raids outside their sphere of influence whenever the opportunity arose, both as a gesture of defiance and in search of munitions that they usually obtained from train robberies or by attacking small detachments of their opponents. Further to the east the Carrancistas held the Huasteca under Manuel Lárraga and Samuel de los Santos. They garrisoned the main towns, controlled the countryside, and made occasional and wholly ineffectual forays against the forces of the Cedillos and Carrera Torres.[45]

General Vicente Dávila, who succeeded General Gavira as state governor after a two-month term in September 1915, was a moderate reformer rather in the mold of his counterpart in neighboring Coahuila, Carranza's former secretary Gustavo Espinosa Mireles. He gave enthusiastic support to improvements in education, introducing co-education in secondary schools and even permitting church schools to reopen in spite of the national government's anticlerical inclinations. He established a Labor Department to act as an arbitrator in industrial disputes and to serve as an employment office. His administration also improved the defense and organization of the railways, both to act as a stimulus to trade and, when necessary, to facilitate the movements of troops. As a result of these and other similar measures, industry and commerce slowly revived. By March 1916 there were thirty-five factories or workshops in operation in the state capital, and shortly afterward the Mexican Crude Rubber Company renewed work in Cedral. Mining was slower to recover because of the dangers of transporting ore to the railways; but several mines reopened during the year, as did the smelter in Matehuala. The smelter in San Luis Potosí, on the other hand, remained closed. Local economic revival was, however, hampered by the national government's financial policy.

The administration continued to issue paper money that rapidly lost its nominal value and drove metal currency off the market. In San Luis Potosí, as elsewhere, merchants and industrialists found their profits eroded by inflation and were therefore unwilling to invest. Many of the workers were reluctant to accept paper money and received their wages in the form of corn or beans.[46]

In the important question of land reform, however, Dávila proved distinctly conservative. He made no effort to implement Carranza's decree of 6 January 1915. Rather than confiscate any *haciendas,* he ordered a revaluation made of all real estate in order to increase tax revenue from it in its existing form. (According to Bonney, 30% of real estate in San Luis Potosí had never been registered for tax purposes.) He was soon on good terms with several local *hacendados* and could frequently be seen wining and dining with them in the state capital. He even authorized the return of land to the *hacienda* of Gogorrón which his predecessor had granted to the adjacent village of Villa de Reyes. Such blatant anti-agrarianism, which was in fact an increasing feature of Carrancista rule throughout the country, naturally reinforced the resistance of rebel chiefs who were fighting under an agrarian banner, such as the Cedillos and Carrera Torres. Throughout 1916 they continued to carry out numerous operations against the government. British businessman H. J. A. Wheeler, who visited Saltillo in October of that year, described the scale and nature of their revolt at this time to William Blocker, the American consul in Piedras Negras:

> Mr. Wheeler states that there has been no trains [*sic*] operating between San Luis Potosí and Tampico for the past two weeks nor is it expected that traffic will be resumed over that line for some time. A certain band of outlaws under the leadership of the Cedillo brothers are [*sic*] said to be creating havoc in that section, destroying bridges, tearing up track, and raiding the outlying ranches near San Luis Potosí. So effective have been their operations that traffic could not be kept open between San Luis Potosí and the gulf ports. De facto [*sic*] government forces are doing all possible to run them down, but without success, on account of the native sentiment in favor of the bandits out in the mountains. When once within their mountain homes, guns are discarded and each member of the band returns to his home, until such an opportune time as when other raids are planned by the leaders. They then assemble and begin their work of devastation as is now going on in that district. Mr. Wheeler says that railroad officials have practically given up all hopes of operating trains on that division until these conditions are done away with.[47]

In the autumn of 1916 Carranza called a constitutional congress to provide a new charter that would take into account the circumstances that had led to the Revolution. The draft which Carranza put forward was prepared by his more conservative advisors and differed little from the Constitution of 1857. During the congressional debates, however, many delegates, supported by several military commanders including Obregón, pressed for a more radical document, particularly with regard to labor and agrarian reform. The final version reflected various influences: nineteenth-century liberalism, anti-clericalism, nationalism, and socialism. Articles 3, 5, 24, 27, and 130 "hedged in the Church to such a degree that it lost all freedom of activity except in the most narrowly defined concept of dogma."[48] Article 123 dealt with labor matters and probably was the most progressive statement of labor principles made by any government in the world at the time. It also represented a reward for the leaders of organized labor who had supported Carranza in his struggle against Villa and who were closely associated with Obregón.[49]

Article 27 dealt with agrarian matters and was a more elaborate version of Carranza's decree of January 1915. It stated that all land was vested in the nation, which could transmit titles to it in accordance with the conditions imposed by the constitution and subsequent legislation. Ownership of land was forbidden to religious bodies, schools, charities, and commercial stock companies, and severely restricted in the case of banks. Foreigners were allowed to own land only if they agreed to be considered as Mexicans under the law. Agrarian communities were permitted to petition for *ejidos* according to a slightly amended version of the 1915 decree, e.g., if they failed to obtain restitution of land, they had an automatic right to petition for a grant (*donación*); and military commanders were excluded from the process of land redistribution. The underlying assumption behind Article 27 was the continuation of private property as the basis of land tenure. There was no provision for wholesale land redistribution or the establishment of a system of collective farming. The limits on the acquisition of real estate imposed upon the church authorities and, to a lesser extent, upon foreigners were in line with the nationalistic and anticlerical tone of the constitution as a whole.[50]

The constitution was promulgated on 5 February 1917. For the moment it remained a dead letter, since the government's authority was still widely challenged. As Charles Parker, the U.S. State Department official covering the congress, reported:

> While the armed opposition to General Carranza's government does not appear to be united it is nevertheless considerable....Villa seems to be practically in control of nearly all of the States of Chihuahua and Durango. The Cedillo Brothers have been for a long time and still are operating in the section to the East of the main line of the National Railways, between San Luis Potosí and Saltillo. They recently cut the line there and stopped through traffic for some days. Farther East, in the coast lands near Tuxpam [*sic*] is Peláez. Practically the whole state of Veracruz is teeming with bandits, whose activities extend to the States of Puebla and Oaxaca. The most notable among these are Higinio Aguilar, who was acquitted of conspiracy against President Madero in 1912, took to the hills around Tehuacán, State of Puebla, and has been there ever since, and the Márquez brothers, the scene of whose operations is the vicinity of Necaxa, where is located the large hydro-electric plant of the Mexican Light and Power Company....The Márquez brothers have at various times received large sums of money from the various authorities in charge of Mexico City as a bribe for the release of the Necaxa plant. Emiliano Zapata and his satellites are still operating in the States of Morelos, Mexico, Michoacan and Guerrero....Still further South are the forces of Félix Díaz, José Isabel Robles and Guillermo Meixuero,

the latter being a chief of the Serrano Indians. In addition to all the bandit or in-
surrectionary leaders mentioned, it must be borne in mind that there are a great
many small bands operating in all parts of the country. As conditions are now a
man may one day be a peaceful laborer in the fields, and the next night, having
recovered his rifle and horse from their hiding places, become a fully fledged
bandit. Many otherwise peacefully inclined men have undoubtedly been driven
to outlawry simply to obtain a livelihood. Others are in it because it is easier for
them to make a living that way than by honest work, and it is this latter class that
offers the greatest obstacle to the pacification of the country.[51]

Much of the continuing unrest was due to the government's failure to employ
land reform as an instrument of pacification. In 1916 Carranza unsuccessfully
urged that the new constitution should include a clause prohibiting land confiscation without first indemnifying the landlords, and his government did not
pass the relevant *reglamento* for Article 27 of the constitution, i.e., convert it
into legislation. According to official figures, Carranza's administration redistributed only 167,000 hectares of land during his four years as President, an
area equivalent to one large *hacienda* in any of the northern states. Moreover,
as recent research has shown, he authorized the return to their owners of numerous *haciendas* that had been seized or confiscated earlier in the Revolution.
Such a negative attitude toward agrarian reform had the same consequences
elsewhere as they did in San Luis Potosí; like the Cedillos, agrarian leaders
such as Calixto Contreras in the Laguna or Emiliano Zapata in Morelos, as
well as numerous lesser chiefs fighting for land redistribution, remained firm
in their opposition to the government.[52]

In the spring of 1917, Carranza issued a decree calling for a return to constitutional rule throughout the Republic as soon as circumstances permitted. In
some states the prevailing conditions required continuation of military rule: in
Oaxaca and Chiapas, for example, where adherents of Félix Díaz were keeping the local Carrancista authorities on the defensive; in Chihuahua, where
the irrepressible Villa remained active; and in Morelos, where the Zapatistas
controlled the countryside. But in most of the country, including San Luis Potosí, elections were held for state governorships and legislatures. Carranza was
determined to install loyal subordinates in the elections for the state governorships and malpractice was widespread. In Tamaulipas and Coahuila, for example, both bordering on San Luis Potosí, the imposition of Carranza's
nominees, López de Lara and Espinosa Mireles, caused their rivals, Generals
Luis Caballero and Luis Gutiérrez, to take up arms against the government.
Without leading to such a violent conclusion, the elections in San Luis Potosí
were similarly controversial. There were two candidates for the post, Juan
Sarabia and Juan Barragán. The former was born into a lower middle-class
family in 1882, and after leaving school at fourteen he found employment first
in a local library and then as a miner and factory worker. He was a founding
member of the PLM and served several terms of imprisonment for his opposition to Díaz before he was finally released in June 1911. He was elected to the
National Congress that same year, where, as a committed socialist, he pressed

for radical social and economic reforms. He was arrested following the Huerta coup but escaped to join Carranza. After an unsuccessful mission to heal the rift between Carranza and Zapata in 1914, he went to the United States. He eventually returned to Mexico City where he became the director of a school for orphans. By contrast, Barragán belonged to one of the most prestigious families in the state, which had important interests in mining and agriculture. As a student he supported General Bernardo Reyes, but he later became friendly with Francisco Madero's brother Gustavo, who sent him on a mission to Japan. When Madero was overthrown, Barragán organized a force from among the laborers on one of his family's *haciendas* and campaigned against the Huertistas in the Huasteca. He subsequently attached himself to Carranza's entourage and soon rose to become his chief of staff. Sarabia's credentials—his social background, long opposition to Díaz, and socialist ideology—should have made him the favorite in the contest for a senior post in a "revolutionary" regime. He had the support of local radicals, such as Antonio Díaz Soto y Gama, and also appears to have been the more popular candidate. But Carranza favored Barragán, thus illustrating the increasing links between his administration and the national bourgeoisie, and Barragán was confirmed the winner in an election marked by repression and chicanery.[53]

Shortly before the elections, Saturnino and Magdaleno Cedillo suffered a severe setback when Enrique Salas, one of their more important lieutenants, deserted with some of his men to the enemy. Salas had been with the Cedillos since the early days of their movement, and his name appeared immediately beneath those of the Cedillo brothers when they subscribed to Carrera Torres' agrarian decree at the end of 1913. His knowledge of the Cedillos' tactics made him a valuable recruit to the Carrancistas and a particularly dangerous opponent for his erstwhile comrades-in-arms. Salas's defection might have led the Cedillos to consider giving up the struggle themselves; but if they had, then the death of Alberto Carrera Torres soon afterward would have certainly decided them against such a course. Carrera Torres had not enjoyed good health since the time he had been badly wounded during the Maderista revolution in 1911, and in late 1916, illness forced him to accept an offer of amnesty from the Carrancista authorities. However, instead of allowing him to go free, they imprisoned him; and in February 1917, the local military commander in Tamaulipas, General Luis Caballero, had him executed, claiming to be acting upon orders from Mexico City. Carrera Torres had never lost his popularity around Tula, and according to Claude Dawson, the U.S. consul in Tampico, his death caused considerable anti-government feeling in the region. It also provoked a series of reprisals by his former companions, Magdaleno and Saturnino Cedillo and Alberto's brother Francisco. Throughout the summer of 1917 they launched numerous attacks upon federal army encampments and railway traffic between San Luis Potosí and Tampico, forcing the line's closure for long periods.[54]

In the autumn, however, the Cedillos and their allies faced new and sterner opposition when General Manuel Diéguez arrived in the area. He had instructions to quell the unrest that had resulted from the recent governmental elections in Tamaulipas and that was to culminate in Caballero's revolt early the following year, and then to conduct a campaign against General Manuel Peláez in the oil fields around Tuxpan, Veracruz. Peláez, a local landowner, had first taken up arms against Huerta but had subsequently carved out what was, in effect, an independent territory covering a large area. He had never recognized Carranza's administration and maintained his well-organized and disciplined forces with arms and supplies provided by the oil companies operating in the area, whose installations he protected in return. Peláez's control of such an economically important zone had long been an irritant to Carranza, who had decided that the time had come to bring him to heel.[55]

In order to protect his flank, Diéguez dispatched a detachment of troops under General Rentería Luviano to combat the Cedillos. Rentería, assisted by local forces under Colonels Marcial Cavazos and Miguel Z. Martínez, captured Ciudad del Maíz from the defending forces of the Cedillos on 17 October. Two weeks later, on 3 November, they caught up with Magdaleno Cedillo and his men in the hills overlooking the *hacienda* of Montebello. Most of the men escaped, but Magdaleno was mortally wounded by an artillery shell. His body was taken to the state capital where it was displayed outside the cathedral as proof of his death.[56]

Following this victory, the Carrancistas laid waste the whole district, concentrating as many civilians as they could find in settlements outside the area. In this way they hoped to deprive the rebels of their logistical support, but their tactics proved counterproductive, and merely alienated their few supporters in the region. Ciudad del Maíz and neighboring municipalities became ghost towns, inhabited by the old and infirm. In the countryside people went into hiding in the mountains, planting corn and beans in remote valleys and in the clearings of woods. Their hatred of the federals increased and with it their support for the rebel leaders. In December, Saturnino Cedillo and his men sacked the railway depot at Cárdenas, seizing stores of food and ammunition, and in the following weeks they launched attacks upon the railway lines from San Luis Potosí to Saltillo and Tampico. In the spring of 1918 the military authorities resigned themselves to the situation and concentrated upon containment. They protected the main towns and the railway lines and dispatched punitive columns into rebel-held areas. Occasionally these columns achieved some success, as when Enrique Salas caught and hanged Homobono Cedillo, who, having shunned any previous involvement in the Revolution, had joined Saturnino shortly after Magdaleno's death, but they failed to establish any lasting authority. Saturnino and his men continued to dominate the countryside between Tula and Río Verde, using hit-and-run tactics against vulnerable targets and making a mockery of government claims concerning their imminent capture or surrender. A typical example of their methods was an attack they made upon Tamasopo in September 1918. Having reconnoitered the area, they captured the town in a lightening assault, stocked up with supplies, cut the nearby railway line to Tampico, and then retired to the hills before Carrancista reinforcements could arrive.[57]

Saturnino Cedillo was only one of many agrarian leaders who still remained active as 1918 drew to a close. Francisco Villa in Chihuahua, Emiliano Zapata in Morelos, and countless other less important chiefs still fought on in pursuit of their ideals or in the belief that surrender would mean humiliation and probably death. Nevertheless, the position of the government gradually improved as physical exhaustion, disease, and improvements in the organization of the Constitutionalist armies slowly reduced the level of unrest. The continuing resistance to the government meant that political power remained firmly and visibly in the hands of Carranza's military commanders. However much the president might have wanted to establish effective constitutional government, circumstances dictated otherwise. The army whose goodwill kept Carranza in power was, of course, very different from its Porfirian predecessor. It was essentially a coalition of warlords for whom the Revolution provided the rapid, upward social and economic mobility denied to most of them under Díaz and who used their military power to further political and commercial ambitions. Beneath them were poorly equipped irregulars, whose loyalty depended upon their leader's ability to grant them material rewards. In the words of Ernest Gruening, one of the most perceptive contemporary observers of Mexico, the generals were "a collection of chieftains, if one wishes to speak in terms of their Indian lineage, or of robber barons, if one prefers the Spanish analogy."[58]

The Constitutionalist forces remained an army of internal occupation and a parasite upon the economy, but as its leaders developed their business interests, the methods of their plunder became more sophisticated and closer to those of many Porfirian politicians. They were gradually absorbed into the national bourgeoisie, and far from threatening the economic system of the country, they acquired a stake in it as employers of rural labor, speculators, and merchants. The classic example of this trend was Alvaro Obregón. Having resigned from his post as war minister in May 1917, he established a highly profitable import-export business in Sonora, and soon acquired a virtual monopoly in the sale of locally produced chickpeas to the United States. He later branched out into other fields, acquiring a cannery and soap factory, banks in Cajeme and Navojoa, automobile and petrol distribution agencies, rice and flour mills, and several large stores.[59] Although perhaps one of the more successful "military entrepreneurs," Obregón was far from unique in this respect. General Manzo occupied an *hacienda* near Guaymas and set his soldiers to work it for him. General Murguía prolonged his campaign against Villa in order to increase his opportunities for graft, and he seized cattle for a ranch he had acquired in Zacatecas. General Heriberto Jara became rich by selling hides that he purchased from rebels he supposedly was fighting. The governor of Sinaloa, General Iturbe, became wealthy through graft. General Luis Gutiérrez obtained possession of extensive landholdings in Coahuila as well as a number of other interests.[60]

One of the foremost exponents of this form of military entrepreneurship was the young governor of San Luis Potosí, General Juan Barragán. As Carranza's chief of staff and effective paymaster-general of the army, Barragán had quickly become a peso millionaire. After his election to the state governorship, he extended his family's already considerable local interests by acquiring further properties and a share in a casino which he permitted an American businessman to establish in the government-owned Teatro de la Paz. Barragán's fellow military officers in San Luis Potosí were no less active in such matters.

> The Generals and other officials devote more time to mercantile pursuits than to combating banditry; they have trains and cars and they attend to their own private business first, and sometimes they arrange with the railroad men to hinder shipments arriving at a point where monopoly prevails and where competition would hurt their business.[61]

Economic revival in the state was slow, which was not surprising under such a parasitic local administration. The transport system in San Luis Potosí was badly disrupted through a lack of rolling stock and poor organization on the railways and continuing interference from rebel bands. (Some mining companies preferred to hire and run their own trains rather than to depend upon local services.) This, combined with the graft among local officials, both civilian and military, meant that the materials needed for mines, factories, and *haciendas* were very costly. Moreover, certain supplies, such as dynamite for the mines, were still subject to diversion to the army. Agriculture was in a poor state as the farms and *haciendas* still in operation frequently suffered from the depredations of both rebels and federals alike. In consequence, food supplies were uncertain and prices were high, as may be observed from Table 6 for the district of Matehuala.[62]

There were, however, signs of slight improvements in some sectors, notably in mining. The high metal prices resulting from the war in Europe enabled mineowners around Matehuala to continue their operations in spite of the many difficulties they had to overcome. According to an official of the ASRC smelter there, they also kept their costs down by paying the same wage rates as in 1910, i.e., one peso per day for unskilled surface workers, 1.50 to 2.00 pesos for ordinary face workers, and 2.00 to 7.00 pesos for skilled workers of various kinds. There was no risk of their provoking strikes or other labor unrest by so doing, partly because of the prevailing unemployment—there were several thousand laborers out of work in the district—but largely because they provided their employees with heavily subsidized corn; each mineworker was allowed to buy three liters of corn per day at 12.50 pesos per hectoliter, when the market price was between 20 and 35 pesos. In view of the disruption in food supplies, this was not a privilege that workers were likely to put at risk very readily.[63]

The prospects of industrial workers in San Luis Potosí and elsewhere in the country were made worse by the unsympathetic attitude of the government. Carranza's relationship with organized labor was, to say the least, ambivalent.[64] In February 1915, through the offices of Obregón, Carranza had made an agreement with a number of labor leaders from the Casa del Obrero Mundial, whereby he offered to pass legislation to meet the "just complaints" of the workers in return for their support against Villa. A deal was struck result-

TABLE 6: A COMPARISON BETWEEN THE PRICES OF SELECTED
FOODSTUFFS IN MATEHUALA IN 1910 AND 1918

Product	1910 Price (in Pesos)	May 1918 Price (in Pesos)
Corn	0.04	0.20 (liter)
Beans	0.12	0.40 (liter)
Rice	0.17	0.56 (kilo)
Sugar	0.19	0.90 (kilo)
Sugar cane	0.20	0.60 (kilo)
Beef	0.20	0.40 (kilo)
Goat meat	0.20	0.60 (kilo)
Eggs	0.02	0.10 (each)

ing in the formation of six regiments of industrial workers, mainly from Mexico City and the Orizaba region. These so-called Red Batallions, each of which contained some seven hundred men, proved a useful addition to Carranza's forces during the heavy fighting in the spring and summer of 1915. Carranza, however, had no intention of permitting an independent labor movement to emerge; when the victory over Villa was assured, he disbanded the Red Batallions and took steps to check the ambitions of the Casa leaders. In 1916 he suppressed a general strike in Mexico City by invoking a treason law of 1862, which carried the death penalty, and subsequently closed down the offices of the Casa throughout the country. In a further move to gain control over organized labor, the government sponsored a new labor grouping in 1918, the *Confederación Regional de Obreros Mexicanos* (CROM). Backed by the authorities, the influence of the CROM spread, and it eventually became the leading labor organization in the country. In dealing with incidents of labor unrest, Carranza's government initially sought a balance between employers and workers, but as time went on, it tended to favor the employers in any disputes. This increasing conservatism was not surprising in view of the influence within the administration of both residual members of the Porfirian ruling class, such as Carranza himself, and the emerging military bourgeoisie, but it caused unease among Carranza's more radical colleagues and subordinates, who would have liked him to be more sympathetic to the problems of labor. The latter group did not, however, include Juan Barragán, who faithfully reflected Carranza's approach to the question. His administration made no effort to pass legislation based upon Article 123 of the constitution, and the few gestures it did make in favor of local workers, such as its half-hearted attempt to enforce an eight-hour working day, invariably ended in failure.[65]

If Barragán was slow to assist local industrial workers, he was even less zealous in promoting reform in the agrarian sector. First of all his administration did not exercise effective control over the region where there had been most agrarian agitation in recent years, i.e., the triangle between Guadalcázar, Ciudad del Maíz, and Cárdenas. In this area it was not the government but Saturnino Cedillo who carried the banner of land reform. Second, even where

TABLE 7: LAND DISTRIBUTION SAN LUIS POTOSÍ, JANUARY 1915–MAY 1920:
PETITIONS FOR LAND CARRANZA'S DECREE OF 6 JANUARY 1915
AND RESOLUTIONS BY THE STATE GOVERNORS AND THE PRESIDENT

Year	Number of Petitions for Land under the Agrarian Laws and Their Classification (R or D)[a]		Resolutions by the State Governor Granting Land on a Provisional Basis (R or D)		Resolutions by the President Granting Land on a Definite Basis (R or D)	
1915	1 (R)	0	1 (R)	0	0	0
1916	4 (R)	3 (D)	1 (R)	2 (D)	0	0
1917	1 (R)	0	2 (R)	0	1 (R)	1 (D)
1918	1 (R)	1 (D)	0	0	0	1 (D)
1919	0	0	0	1 (D)	0	1 (D)
1920 (until May)	2 (R)	2 (D)	0	0	0	0
Total land area affected, 1915–1920			29,197 hectares		20,464 hectares	

[a]A *restitución* (R) was land granted to the petitioners because of their claim that the land had been stolen from their community in the past. A *donación* (D) was a grant of land to which the petitioners had either an unprovable claim under the law or land to which they had no claim at all.

Source: Secretaría de Agricultura, Comisión Nacional Agraria, *Estadística 1915–1927* (México, 1928), 42; Secretaría de Economía Nacional, Departamento de Estadística, *Anuario estadístico 1930* (México, 1932), 376.

Barragán was in a position to authorize widespread land redistribution, he, like Carranza, was reluctant to do so for fear of disrupting production at a time when there was an urgent need to increase food supplies to urban markets. And third, both the governor and several members of his administration had valuable real estate that they wished to protect. But apart from these considerations, there was the nature of the agrarian legislation itself. Since the government had not passed the necessary *reglamento* of Article 27 of the constitution, claims for land still had to be made under Carranza's decree of January 1915. As noted previously, this placed the onus for seeking any land redistribution upon those who wanted the land, and excluded the majority of the rural population, the *peones acasillados,* from the right to petition for it. In the absence of any official encouragement from Barragán, the minority who were eligible to do so were unwilling to risk the wrath of powerful landlords by seeking land they might subsequently lose with a change in administration. In view of these factors it is not surprising that there was so little land redistribution in the state under Carranza's regime, as Table 7 shows.

In May 1919, elections were held to choose a successor to Barragán. The more popular of the two candidates was Rafael Nieto, a local man who was under-secretary in the Ministry of Finance. But Barragán wished to maintain his influence in state politics and ensured the election of Nieto's opponent, Severino Martínez, a figure of no prominence whatsoever but of unswerving loyalty to Barragán. His installation of Martínez in office did nothing to diminish the already widespread popular sympathy for the rebels, and for Saturnino Cedillo in particular, the best-known and most successful guerrilla

leader in the region. At the beginning of 1920 Cedillo and his men still exercised effective authority over the area between Guadalcázar and Ciudad del
Maíz, just as they had for the previous five years. They made frequent attacks
upon federal army outposts and constantly disrupted railway communications
between the state capital and Tampico. Enjoying considerable local support in
their home district, they looked capable of sustaining their revolt for a long
time to come.[66]

The situation was much the same in many other states, in spite of a growing
war-weariness in the country. As Carranza's term in office drew to a close,
several rebel leaders and numerous lesser chiefs continued to defy the authorities. In the north, Francisco Villa was still active in Chihuahua, having eluded
an American expedition sent to capture him, while Esteban Cantú, a former
federal army officer, governed the virtually independent state of Baja California. Further south the Zapatista movement had survived the death of its chief
in an ambush in April 1919 and kept up its resistance under the able leadership
of Gildardo Magaña; Manuel Peláez continued to command the area around
Tuxpan in the pay of the oil companies there; Félix Díaz and his adherents remained active in Veracruz, even if support for his cause was declining; in
Chiapas and Oaxaca, only the main towns and railway lines were under government control—the countryside beyond being prey to numerous rebel
groups that were really local defense forces protecting their districts from the
ravages of the Carrancistas—and finally Alberto Pineda O. led an important
movement on the Tabasco-Chiapas border in conjunction with other chiefs,
which threatened to cut land communications with the Yucatán Peninsula. Together these rebel leaders and their followers presented a formidable obstacle
to the short-term pacification of the country. They believed that they had more
to gain by continuing their fight than by negotiating terms with an untrust-
worthy government and were sustained by the hope that circumstances might
eventually turn against Carranza and favor their own return to power.[67]

That this was not wishful thinking became clear on the eve of the 1920 presidential elections. To many observers Carranza's most natural successor was
Obregón, who had shown that he wanted the job by launching his candidacy
as early as June 1919. Obregón was popular among the commanders of the federal army and had a powerful base in his home state of Sonora. He also enjoyed close links with the leaders of organized labor and in August 1919 signed
a secret pact with representatives of the CROM in which, in exchange for
their support, he promised to make a number of concessions to the unions if he
was elected president. Carranza, however, wished to keep the presidency in civilian hands, thus containing what he considered to be the excessive influence
of the military in politics. He therefore sought to impose as president the Mexican ambassador to the United States, Ignacio Bonillas, whom he believed he
could manipulate once he was in office. In choosing to support Bonillas
against Obregón, Carranza showed serious misjudgment. Power within the
regime resided not with himself, as president, but with the leaders of the Constitutionalist army, whose loyalty remained first and foremost to themselves

and their men, rather than to the president-of-the-day, and who could be expected to favor one of their own kind, Obregón, over the relatively obscure Bonillas. When Obregón persisted in his candidacy, Carranza moved to weaken his power base in Sonora. In late March he ordered large numbers of federal troops to the state, purportedly to deal with unrest among the Yaqui Indians. It was a fatal error. The state governor, Adolfo de la Huerta, supported by the legislature, challenged Carranza's authority to take such measures. Relations between the president and the Sonoran authorities rapidly deteriorated, and on 23 April the latter issued the Plan of Agua Prieta in which they withdrew recognition from both the national government and also from several notoriously Carrancista state administrations, including that of Severino Martínez in San Luis Potosí. Within a few weeks the rebellion became a general army uprising. Carranza retired toward his old base of Veracruz but was murdered en route.[68]

Adolfo de la Huerta became provisional president and energetically pursued a policy of national reconciliation. Several rebels had already been incorporated into the new regime by virtue of having joined the movement of Agua Prieta before it triumphed. Among them was Saturnino Cedillo. Impressed by the Sonorans' break with the authorities in San Luis Potosí, he sent De la Huerta a telegram in May offering his support to the revolt. Many others were now offered amnesty. They included Félix Díaz, who left Veracruz for exile, Pineda O. in Chiapas, and the most famous of all the guerrilla leaders, Francisco Villa in Chihuahua. In Baja California, Esteban Cantú came to terms with the government when De la Huerta ordered an invasion of the state, and in Morelos the Zapatista chiefs also reached agreement with the new authorities, which permitted tranquility finally to return to the area. In order to ensure a lasting peace the government authorized certain rebel leaders to establish agricultural colonies for their veterans. Villa and Cedillo in particular were receptive to this idea and established such colonies in Chihuahua and San Luis Potosí. Presidential elections were held in September which resulted in an overwhelming victory for Obregón. He assumed office in December in a country exhausted by a decade of civil strife, but probably less disturbed than at any other time since the early months of Madero's presidency.[69]

Nowhere was this return to relative order more welcome than in San Luis Potosí. Between 1911 and 1920 this state had suffered some of the most sustained popular unrest in the whole country. The fighting there was comparable both in its intensity and in its origins to that which took place in the Laguna region, Sinaloa, Veracruz, and the states where Zapatistas were most active: Morelos, Puebla, and Mexico. The roots of the prolonged violence in these areas lay in the grievances felt by the rural lower classes since the late Porfiriato, such as rising food prices, the arbitrary behavior of powerful and expansionist *hacendados,* and abuses by local officials, and in their consequent desire to check the power of the local landowning elite by obtaining greater protection for the rights of smallholders, by enforcing more favorable agreements for sharecroppers, or through the defense or recovery of village landholdings. When Madero issued his call for revolt, he provided an opportunity for the expression of these grievances and aspirations. Revolutionary leaders emerged such as Emiliano Zapata in Morelos, Alberto Carrera Torres in San Luis Potosí, and Calixto Contreras in the Laguna, who were spokesmen for the rural discontented and advocates of agrarian reform. Madero's subsequent failure to implement any radical reforms led some of these men to remain in revolt and drove others who had not yet taken up arms, such as the Cedillos, to do so. These leaders came to command a considerable following, even in adverse conditions, because they represented a popular desire for more equity in the relations between wealthy landowners and the remainder of the rural population. They did not necessarily oppose the existence of *haciendas* per se, simply their existence or expansion at the expense of other forms of land tenure. Similarly, they tended to discriminate between "good" and "bad" *hacendados*, i.e., those who either respected or infringed upon what they considered to be the traditional rights of their poorer neighbors, whether smallholders or villagers.[70]

Most of these agrarian rebels joined Villa in his struggle against Carranza. He did not share all their characteristics, such as a close identification with the agrarian unrest in any particular community or district, but his expropriation of a number of large *haciendas* in his home state of Chihuahua and his expression of interest in further land redistribution at a later date made him the more attractive to them of the two contenders for power. Villa's defeat caused his movement to fragment, and these agrarian leaders retired to their home bases. There, in familiar terrain where they enjoyed considerable popular support, they engaged in guerrilla warfare against the Constitutionalists. Like other opponents of the regime—Villista generals, regional *caudillos* such as Peláez, Pineda O., or Esteban Cantú, or the leaders of small local bands driven to revolt by the depredations of the Constitutionalists—they saw little reason to surrender. In time they would probably all have been liquidated—Calixto Contreras was killed in 1916, Carrera Torres in 1917, and Zapata in 1919—but Carranza's overthrow allowed the survivors to make peace on terms that they considered acceptable. In the case of agrarian chiefs such as Genovevo de la O, Zapata's henchman in Morelos, or Saturnino Cedillo in San Luis Potosí, this meant the satisfaction of their demand for agrarian reform in their localities.[71]

And Cedillo himself? What were his thoughts as he concentrated his forces in Ciudad del Maíz for their official demobilization? The twenty-year-old *ranchero* who had visited Madero in jail was now, ten years later, a hardened guerrilla leader scarred by the loss of his three brothers. For the previous four years he had eluded the persistent attempts of the Constitutionalist authorities to hunt him down; for the past two and a half years, following Magdaleno's death, he had been the undisputed leader of the rebels in the east of the state. He must have wondered whether the sacrifices that he and his followers had made in the cause of agrarian reform were to be rewarded. Would the new government keep its word and allow them to return to a life of farming on land of their own? Or would there be further sacrifices in the future?

CHAPTER 4

THE RISE OF CEDILLO

THE RECORD OF GENERAL CEDILLO IS THAT OF AN ILLITERATE OUTLAW WHO HAS SOLD HIS SUPPORT TO THE GOVERNMENT IN RETURN FOR MILITARY COMMAND, HAVING THOROUGHLY INTRENCHED HIMSELF IN THIS STATE BY PLACING HIS FOLLOWERS ON LANDS THAT DO NOT BELONG TO THEM, NOR TO THE GENERAL EITHER, AND PROTECTING THEM IN THE POSSESSION OF PROPERTY AS LONG AS THEY STAND READY TO RENDER HIM MILITARY SERVICE. THE LAND SEIZURES BY THE GENERAL ARE DEFENDED AS HIS EFFORTS TO AID THE DOWNTRODDEN AT THE EXPENSE OF THE WEALTHY LANDOWNERS.——Consul Walter F. Boyle in San Luis Potosí, 6 November 1924

When Obregón assumed the presidency, he took charge of a country devastated by the upheavals of the previous decade. The civil wars had destroyed the system of tight, centralized rule established by Díaz and had unleashed the powerful centrifugal forces then latent in Mexican society. This breakdown in government had led to economic decline. Agricultural production had suffered from the constant pillaging of revolutionary bands, while both mining and industry had been the victims of disrupted communications, arbitrary taxation, and meaningless paper currency. The new government's main task was therefore to restore political stability and promote economic recovery.

Like the provisional regime of De la Huerta, Obregón's administration was a product of the movement of Agua Prieta. In consequence, a disproportionately high percentage of ministers and senior officials shared the president's Sonoran background; and under their influence the new government sought to repeat on a national scale the economic progress that had been the hallmark of the northwest during the Porfiriato. They placed great emphasis upon technical innovation and modern business methods and favored the growth of an entrepreneurial middle class as the instrument for economic development. The power of the central government was, however, circumscribed by the federal army, whose leaders remained the dominant influence within the regime. Apart from the presence of Obregón and other generals in the cabinet, large areas of the country were subject to the mandate of the various regional army commanders. These warlords, whose troops gave them a virtually independent power base, exercised considerable authority within the area under their command and acted as power brokers between the central government and the local population. They tended to share Obregón's perception of the economic and political direction that the country should take, and through their business interests they merged into the expanding post-revolutionary bourgeoisie. In some cases they also encouraged agrarian or labor reform, either for reasons of idealism or in order to strengthen their political base. On the other hand, their personal power made them a potential threat to political stability, and recognizing this, Obregón sought to purchase their goodwill. Through the War Ministry he provided them with ample funds that met their military and business needs. In return they kept the peace, maintained the loyalty of their subordinates, and waxed rich. As Ernest Gruening observed:

> Exceptional was the *jefe de operaciones* who did not carry several side lines— usually the exclusive gambling house concession, forbidden by law, the proceeds of a *hacienda* or two, to which his soldiers would carry the manure of the *jefatura's* horses, or the lucrative task of "protecting" other *hacendados* from agrarians. The fault, in part at least, was Obregón's.[1]

The president's policy of bribing his fellow generals was probably the only course open to him under the circumstances, and as a short-term antidote to further upheavals it proved effective. But it offered no long-term guarantee that they would keep the peace, as he was to discover toward the end of his term in office.

The other major tactic that Obregón employed in ensuring the pacification of the country was land redistribution. The president's approach to the question of agrarian reform was influenced by three main factors: his Sonoran background and that of many of his senior colleagues, his personal experience as a successful *ranchero,* and his appreciation of the potential of land redistribution for promoting political stability. Apart from the rather special claims of the Mayos and Yaquis, both frontier tribes, men like Obregón, Plutarco Elías Calles, his minister of the interior, and Adolfo de la Huerta, his minister of finance, had little experience with the problems of long-established agrarian communities such as those of the center or south of the country, and even less with the collectivist agrarian tradition in states such as Chiapas or Oaxaca. Their aim was to encourage the kind of farming in which Obregón had engaged in Sonora: entrepreneurial, market-oriented, and mechanized. They placed more emphasis upon improvements in land usage, such as irrigation projects, than upon changing the structure of land tenure. (As Linda Hall has observed, the Sonorans' first major initiative in the sphere of agrarian reform was De la Huerta's Law of Unused Lands of June 1920, which was designed to bring unexploited land under production as soon as possible.[2] Neither Obregón nor his colleagues had any objection to large estates in principle, as long as their resources were effectively utilized. When faced with petitions for land from plantations or other large and productive agricultural units, they often sought to meet the request by finding land elsewhere in the neighborhood. They dismissed the collectivization of such estates as irrelevant to the country's needs and as damaging to agricultural production. Their views were summarized in a speech that Obregón gave at Guadalajara in November 1919:

> One of the ways of resolving the agrarian problem is, without doubt, the encouragement of small-scale agriculture. I am a supporter of the development of small-scale agriculture because I support the idea of giving help to anyone who is struggling to escape from a miserable and narrow existence and of giving a hand to anyone making an effort to improve himself; but I do not in any way believe that one should resort to breaking up estates to distribute them among small farmers before small-scale agriculture is further developed.[3]

On the other hand, Obregón knew full well that Mexico was not Sonora and that in many areas a serious program of land redistribution was a prerequisite for any lasting peace. Furthermore, being a shrewd politician, he also appreciated that a commitment to such a program could be a valuable instrument for strengthening the support for his administration among the rural population. As the British chargé d'affaires reported in July 1921:

> Agrarian properties continue to be seized in many states of the Union and without payment of compensation given to the owners. Several "generals" are known to have thus become proprietors of haciendas. . . . When seeking to understand fully the motives of the Government in this connection it should be observed that not only do they consider it necessary to dispel resentment created by the nonfulfilment of earlier promises of land, but, carrying the thought further, it is considered—and from the Government's point of view with some reason— that the persuasive arguments of the new revolutionary agents will meet with no response from the man who has a home and a crop planted by his own hand on land which he considers his personal property.[4]

In the light of these conflicting considerations—the need to offer landowners guarantees in order to boost production and the need to redistribute land in the interests of political stability—Obregón trod a careful path of increased, but controlled, reform. Eight days after taking office he issued an agrarian reform law intended to supercede all earlier legislation on the question. In fact his decree confused rather than clarified the process of land redistribution, making restitution of land, for example, particularly complicated. Nevertheless, his minister of agriculture, the former PLM activist General Antonio Villarreal, used the law to press ahead with the reform, increasing the number of straightforward grants, so that 638,438 hectares had been distributed in this way by September 1922. Villarreal's activities evoked considerable criticism in the press, and after a year in office he resigned. Obregón did nothing to prevent Villarreal's departure, which allowed him to bring the National Agrarian Commission (*Comisión Nacional Agraria* or CNA) more closely under his personal control. To succeed Villarreal he appointed Ramón de Negri, a long-time associate and fellow Sonoran.[5]

In April 1922 the government replaced the unsatisfactory law of 1920 with the *reglamento* of Article 27 of the constitution. This law clarified the bureaucratic procedures for petitioning for land along the lines of former practice: a petition had to be sent from a local *ejidal* committee elected by the villagers to their state agrarian commission; if the commission approved the petition, they passed it to the governor for the provisional grant of the land; once this was awarded, it then had to be confirmed by the CNA, prior to the definitive grant by the president. The law defined the size of *ejidal* plots under different conditions and restricted the rights of agrarian communities to seek land by establishing the inviolability of small property and "agro-industrial" plants, e.g. cotton and sugar plantations with processing machinery installed on them. Small property was defined as an estate not exceeding 150 hectares of irrigated land, 250 of arable land watered by rainfall, and 500 of other land. Finally, *peones acasillados,* who formed the majority of the rural labor force, were still prohibited from petitioning for land. The law made no mention of the internal organization of *ejidos.* This was dealt with later in CNA Circular 51 of October 1922, which advised that they should be run as cooperatives, thus forming the basis of a communal system of agriculture operating alongside the private sector. This provoked fairly considerable opposition from among the *ejidatarios,* and since it also received only lukewarm support from the president and other senior officials, the question remained open when Obregón left office.[6]

The powers granted to the state governors by the agrarian laws gave them control over the pace of land reform. Although many of them did little to further land redistribution, several others encouraged it in order to promote their political careers. During the 1920s ambitious governors such as Emilio Portes Gil in Tamaulipas, Adalberto Tejeda in Veracruz, and José Zuno in Jalisco, created a clientele in the countryside by distributing land and forming agrarian leagues from among its recipients. While the agrarian bureaucracy remained relatively primitive, such men acted as brokers between the central government and the beneficiaries of the land reform. Their position in this respect was, of course, less important initially than that of their military counterparts, the regional chiefs of operations, who still interfered in the process of land redistribution. But their exploitation of the agrarian bureaucracy as a power base, as opposed to the crude force employed by the generals, indicated the shift in political power from the military to the civilian sector and from regional independence to dependence upon the central bureaucracy, which was to take place during the next two decades. In this context Cedillo is particularly interesting because he combined the attributes of both warlord and agrarian politician. Although his predominant power base always remained the

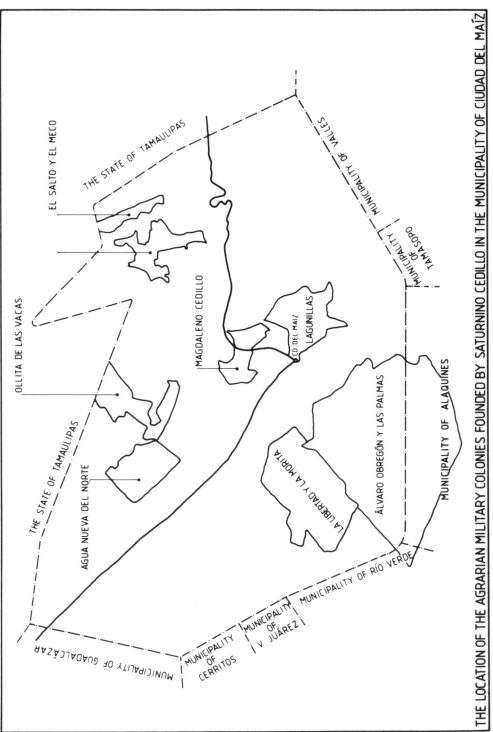

THE LOCATION OF THE AGRARIAN MILITARY COLONIES FOUNDED BY SATURNINO CEDILLO IN THE MUNICIPALITY OF CIUDAD DEL MAÍZ

network of agrarian military colonies that he established around Ciudad del Maíz in 1920–1921, he later extended it by promoting further land redistribution through his control of the state bureaucracy.[7]

The movement of Agua Prieta marked the return of Cedillo and his men to the legitimacy enjoyed by those who join the winning side in civil wars. In return for his support and subsequent loyalty he extracted from De la Huerta demobilization payments for himself and his men, confirmation of their military rank, and land for their resettlement. As he told an American visitor several years later, he informed the new government:

> I want land. I want ammunition so that I can protect my land after I get it in case somebody tries to take it away from me. And I want plows, and I want schools for my children, and I want teachers, and I want books and pencils and blackboards and roads. And I want moving pictures for my people too. And I don't want any Church or any saloon.[8]

In fact Cedillo and his followers, who numbered 583 officers and men, were given two months' demobilization pay, which cost the Ministry of War $96,483.60 pesos, and farm equipment to help them get started in their new life. The authorities also endorsed Cedillo's seizure of large tracts of land for the establishment of ten agrarian colonies in which to resettle his men. Finally, after lengthy correspondence, Cedillo was confirmed as chief of military operations for the 28th zone (Ciudad del Maíz), with the rank of *General de Brigada* and a salary of twenty-eight pesos per day. His followers were also confirmed in their respective ranks. Ten of them remained in active service to form Cedillo's staff and twenty-five acted as his escort.[9]

These arrangements were satisfactory to both Cedillo and the central government. Unlike many other military leaders in the various revolutionary armies, Cedillo did not aspire to establish himself in politics or business. He wanted to enjoy the untroubled use of Palomas and to reward his followers with land. Through war he had achieved the upward social mobility that was the aspiration of all smallholders but that had been denied to his family during the Porfiriato. His followers, many of whom were former *hacienda* peons or sharecroppers, also moved up in the world. They acquired land of their own, and their status as colonists was popularly considered superior to that of the *ejidatarios*. From the central government's point of view, the settlement ensured tranquility and support in a previously troubled region. It established a chain of patronage—in which Cedillo was the central link—between themselves and the rural population of San Luis Potosí. Cedillo's colonists were, in effect, an army reserve.[10]

Cedillo founded his colonies mainly on land from the largest *haciendas* in the district and from those landowners most identified with the Porfirian political elite. Of the ten original colonies, seven were on land formerly belonging to the *haciendas* of Angostura (Espinosa y Cuevas), Cárdenas (Díez Gutiérrez), Lagunillas and Llano del Perro (Arguinzóniz), and Montebello (Martínez). Apart from the woods and pasture, each colony contained 100 six-hectare plots of arable land, half of which were reserved for Cedillo's veterans and the other half for the widows and orphans of his followers who had died in the fighting. Although the colonies were generally well endowed with arable land of reasonable quality, they lacked many other facilities such as adequate water supplies or electricity and suffered from poor communications with the outside world.[11] A good idea of the conditions in which the colonies were established may be deduced from the following statement that Cedillo made about one of them, San José, for the Ministry of War in November 1921:

> A questionnaire answering the enquiries made by the Department of the First Reserve, Agrarian-Military Colonies section, concerning the colony of San José located on land belonging to Pozo de Acuña.
>
> 1) In January of this year my subordinates moved into a military colony which had been established in a locality known as San José belonging to the Hacienda of "Pozo de Acuña."
>
> 2) The colony covers 618 hectares altogether, of which 200 are of unirrigated arable land. The 200 hectares had been abandoned for six years, and it was only at great sacrifice that the colonists converted them back into arable land. They are at present making strenuous efforts to open up the other 418 hectares for the same purpose.
>
> 3) When the colonists took possession of their respective lots, there were no houses or buildings on the site, nor were there any cisterns, only an old abandoned well and a low stone wall along one side of the 200 hectares of arable land.
>
> 4) The following personnel at present occupy the colony: 1 Lieutenant Colonel; 1 Major, 4 Captains, first rank; 1 Captain, second rank; 3 Lieutenants and 45 troopers.
>
> 5) The colony was established on the following basis: a hundred plots of 6 hectares to provide a parcel of land for both soldiers as well as widows and orphans; a hundred allotments of 50 square meters each for dwellings or other domestic purposes; and an area of 100 square meters for public use.
>
> 6) The land was officially handed over to the colonists by Samuel O. Yúdico, who was the special envoy of the then Minister of War, Divisional General Plutarco Elías Calles, and by Engineer Genaro Arzabe, on behalf of the Ministry of Agriculture.
>
> 7) On the orders of General Calles no agreement or arrangement was made with the owner of the land, since the said owner should come to an understanding directly with the government.
>
> 8) The measurements of the various plots occupied was carried out by the commissioner of the Ministry of Agriculture, Engineer Genaro Arzabe.
>
> 9) 100 plots of land each measuring 6 hectares were partitioned off, and with them 100 allotments for domestic use.
>
> 10) The relevant documents and plans are in the Central Office of the Ministry of Agriculture.
>
> 11) Those in charge of the estate have been consistently obstructive; they have constantly told the colonists that they are to be deprived of the land which they have been awarded, and that they should therefore not make any improvements to it.
>
> 12) No reply was obtained to this question.
>
> 13) For the colony of San José to be a success, it should be given pasture land;

this can be taken from the same estate without affecting any other kind of land or buildings there.

14) When the colonists took over the land they were not given any tractors, and as far as equipment is concerned they only received twenty ploughs with their respective harnesses. The reason for this is that the undersigned was only given 200 ploughs for the 10 colonies which he established in the region, all of which are in the same condition as the subject of this questionnaire.

EFFECTIVE SUFFRAGE. NO REELECTION.—Ciudad del Maíz, November 10, 1921.

Brigade General Saturnino Cedillo.[12]

Theoretically the colonies were initially the responsibility of the Ministry of War and later of the Ministry of Agriculture. In practice, of course, Cedillo kept them under his close personal control. He was in constant contact with their respective leaders, who in turn considered themselves answerable to Cedillo alone. As for the colonists themselves, there was no question whom they regarded as their patron. It was through Cedillo that they had obtained their land and the means to work it. He was also the guarantee that they could keep it, and not only with regard to its former owners, the vanquished *hacendados:* in October 1921, for example, he prevented some former peons from the *hacienda* of Cárdenas from taking 137 hectares of land occupied by the colony of El Naranjo for their *ejido* of El Labor. Furthermore, the colonists turned to Cedillo in times of trouble. When there was a temporary food shortage in some of the colonies in the autumn of 1921, Cedillo obtained a grant of no less than 5,000 pesos from Obregón to purchase maize for them.[13]

The development of the individual colonies varied greatly and depended to a large extent upon the initiative and energy of the man in charge. The largest colony was Álvaro Obregón, over which Ildefonso Turrubiartes presided until his election to the state governorship. Although Turrubiartes behaved in some ways like a landlord—he expected the colonists to provide unpaid work on his own plot—he did much to improve facilities in the colony. In 1927 a visitor from the CNA commented favorably on conditions there, stating that it possessed two schools, an electric light plant, and a small cinema, was connected by road with all the other settlements in the district, and was also linked to Ciudad del Maíz by telephone. Conditions were also good for the ninety-five colonists and their families on Magdaleno Cedillo, where by 1930 they were cultivating 800 hectares of maize, wheat, beans, and chickpeas, as well as cutting fibers on the less fertile ground. In contrast another CNA official who visited El Naranjo in 1929, in order to measure its boundaries with the Moctezumas' property, claimed that the colonel in charge there was little better than a drunken despot. He recommended that its administration be linked to that of the more successful colonies, such as Álvaro Obregón, which he also praised. His report on El Naranjo was probably accurate, for in 1936 another visitor commented that "in the whole colony there is not one house which fulfills in the slightest the most indispensable requirements of hygiene." The same writer added that, apart from the presence of a school, the situation on San José was also depressing. But whatever the conditions in their colony, the members had, thanks to Cedillo, acquired land of their own. Their gratitude and dependence upon his continuing patronage formed the basis of his power until his death.[14]

Cedillo spent the years 1921 and 1922 largely enjoying the fruits of peace. He began work on rebuilding his home at Palomas and improving the productivity of the property through irrigation. He attended local festivals with their cockfights and dances, and he even courted Juanita Barragán, the cousin of the exiled former governor, whose father, Pablo, had recently returned to the district, one of the few members of the Porfirian oligarchy in the region to do so. Not surprisingly, in view of the bitterness that the Barragán family still felt for Cedillo, the courtship came to nothing, but that it took place at all is an interesting illustration of the marked change in Cedillo's social standing. Beyond such personal matters, Cedillo spent a considerable amount of time tending to his colonies and cementing his power base. He also sought to improve the lamentable education facilities in the district, inviting a young schoolteacher, Valentín Aguilar, to set up a number of schools there. Finally— but with less success—he attempted to reduce alcoholism. (Cedillo himself was never more than a moderate drinker.) Further afield Cedillo established a close relationship with Enrique Henshaw, the CNA representative in the state who was actively encouraging the creation of *ejidos* there.[15]

Several times Cedillo was called upon to demonstrate his loyalty to the administration by helping to suppress revolts in the region. Some of these movements, such as the abortive uprising led by Félix González in February 1922, were connected with General Murguía's attempts to overthrow the national government; others, such as the rebellion led by Manuel Lárraga in the Huasteca later the same year, were the result of power struggles in local politics. By meeting his obligations as a client of the central government in this way, Cedillo cemented his relationship with the new regime, dispelling rumors that he himself might be contemplating a revolt.[16]

Among those who most appreciated Cedillo's loyalty was the state governor, Rafael Nieto. An early supporter of Madero, Nieto became the municipal president of Cerritos in 1911. He subsequently rose through the Constitutionalist ranks to become the under-secretary in the Finance Ministry under Carranza; but having failed to win the governorship of San Luis Potosí in 1919, he joined the president's opponents. It was through the influence of one of them, Plutarco Elías Calles, that Nieto finally became governor in May 1920. Like Calles, Nieto considered that the state should be active in promoting social reform. He established a system of tax relief for those landlords who reduced rents on their properties and he planned an ambitious program of roadbuilding and irrigation. He also put a bill before the state congress designed to give women the vote.[17]

Unfortunately many of Nieto's intended reforms came to nothing; they were either rejected by the state legislature, or, once accepted, never enforced. This was largely due to his lack of an independent power base. As a civilian he had no influence among the military, and neither did he control the local congress or municipal authorities. On certain occasions when he faced conservative opposition in the congress, he organized demonstrations of support from among the urban unemployed; but the loyalties of such elements were fickle, and they could not provide him with a stable and convincing power base. In this situation the consistent support of Cedillo was critical to his ability to govern.[18]

In his relations with the Roman Catholic Church Nieto followed the mild anti-clericalism of the central government. No officials attended the reception for the bishop of San Luis Potosí when he returned from exile in 1922, and the police quickly removed marks of mourning from private houses following the expulsion of the apostolic delegate in January 1923.[19] But as Nieto was aware, religious feeling in the state was strong. Shortly after the bishop's return, for example, a representative of the *Confederación Regional de Obreros Mexicanos* (CROM) was stoned to death in Santa María de la Paz following inflammatory speeches by two Spanish priests. Nieto accused the priests of incitement to murder and they fled the state; but the incident probably reflected the balance of support for the church and for the government-sponsored CROM among the rural population.[20]

In the countryside there was a period of quiet reconstruction under Nieto's administration. The population was exhausted by ten years of violence, and the majority of military chiefs were either dead or, like Cedillo, enjoying the fruits of victory. In some districts the system of production was unchanged; work on *haciendas* and *ranchos* continued as it had during the Porfiriato and wages were at the same level. On Illescas, for example, casual day laborers were given between 0.25 and 0.35 pesos per day, and *peones acasillados* 0.50 pesos, both paid in kind. In other districts a complete transformation in the structure of agricultural production had taken place. *Haciendas* were abandoned and their land was either worked by their former laborers on a casual basis or distributed in the form of colonies or *ejidos*. This usually took place where there had been social tension prior to 1910 and considerable disruption and depopulation during the years of violence. Thus, at the beginning of 1923 there were nine *ejidos* with *posesión definitiva* covering nearly 40,000 hectares, and twenty-five *ejidos* with *posesión provisional* covering 115,000 hectares. But agriculture in the majority of the state lay between these two extremes, and there prevailed an amended form of the pre-revolutionary system of land tenure and production. The *hacienda* remained the basic unit of both, but landlords were conscious of the threat posed by the new agrarian laws. They therefore raised agricultural wages, improved working conditions, and made sharecropping agreements that were more favorable to the sharecroppers than formerly.[21]

Nieto's own views on agrarian reform were in keeping with those of Obregón and his senior ministers. He favored land redistribution as a means of creating a thriving rural middle class of smallholders but opposed wholesale land confiscation or large-scale cooperatives. In July 1921 he passed an agrarian law through the state congress which incorporated these ideas. It also reflected the continuing influence of nineteenth-century liberalism among the state's political leaders, for it was similar to the proposal of 1911 of José Encarnación Ipiña. The law set a maximum limit on the size of a rural property according to its location within the state, which Nieto divided into three zones: the arid north and west (maximum size for any property 4,000 hectares), the more fertile center (maximum size 3,000 hectares), and the humid subtropical Huasteca (maximum size 2,000 hectares). The law also made provision for any excess land to be divided up and sold in individual plots.[22]

This legislation shared the weakness of Carranza's decree of 1915 since it did not oblige the authorities to confiscate and redistribute any land unless they were requested to do so by landless petitioners. ("The owner remains in possession of the lands when there are none who need and solicit them.") Since few *peones acasillados* risked their employers' anger by seeking their land, and independent villagers preferred to use federal legislation to obtain property, no land was distributed under Nieto's law for two years.[23]

Nieto was due to leave office in August 1923, but the question of who should succeed him was overshadowed by the presidential election scheduled for July 1924. It was generally accepted that the next president would be chosen by Obregón. Although he was only *primus inter pares* among the country's military leaders, the virtually dictatorial powers of his office, combined with his own prestige, suggested that he could control the succession. The leading candidates for the post were Antonio Villarreal, the former PLM activist who had been Obregón's first minister of agriculture; Adolfo de la Huerta, the treasury minister, who had won many friends during his brief provisional presidency; General Raúl Madero, who was considered the heir of the revolutionaries of 1910; and General Plutarco Elías Calles, the energetic and ruthless minister of the interior.[24]

In early 1923, Obregón indicated that he favored Calles and thus appeared to guarantee the latter's success. But there was important opposition to his choice in both military and political circles. Several senior army commanders, such as Villarreal and Salvador Alvarado, who had been the virtual dictator of Yucatán from 1915 to 1920, believed that they had a prior claim to the presidency, while others feared that Calles would not indulge them as Obregón had done. The Villista leaders were also hostile to Calles, believing that he was behind the murder of their former chief in July 1923.[25] In their search for a rival candidate, Calles's opponents settled upon De la Huerta, and throughout the summer and autumn of 1923 they urged him to allow his nomination.

Among those who pressed De la Huerta most enthusiastically was Jorge Prieto Laurens, the president of the *Partido Cooperatista Nacional* (PCN). Born into a middle class family in Zacatecas in 1895, Prieto Laurens subsequently attended the National Preparatory School in Mexico City where, in company with other students who later made a mark in national politics such as Luis León, Aarón Sáenz, and Marte Gómez, he became an active Maderista.[26] After holding minor posts under Carranza, he became municipal president of Mexico City under Obregón. The only factor that united the members of his party was their ambition to obtain office; they covered a wide ideological spectrum and had no particular base such as organized labor or the peasantry. In 1923 the PCN formed the majority block in the federal congress and its leaders aspired to convert this position into control of the administration. They realized that the election of Calles would be a blow to their ambitions, since his links were elsewhere—with the CROM, with a minority of army leaders, and with the clientele he had acquired as minister of the interior. A minority of PCN congressmen, led by a friend of Cedillo's from Tamaulipas, Emilio Portes Gil, believed that it was futile to oppose Calles and left the party to join his campaign. But their departure merely hardened the resolve of the majority to press the claims of De la Huerta.[27]

In order to widen his political base Prieto Laurens had earlier decided upon seeking to succeed Nieto as governor of San Luis Potosí. Having been raised there, he claimed to be a "native son" of the state, and he believed that with the support of the PCN his candidacy would be successful. He hoped to receive the backing of local conservatives, but two other candidates also sought their support, Octaviano Cabrera and Samuel de los Santos. Cabrera represented the old Porfirian elite, whose economic interests were still considerable. They retained most of their estates, and outside Catorce, where the mines had been severely damaged during the Revolution, their investments in mining and industry had remained largely untouched. But Cabrera and his associates soon concluded that they had no chance of recapturing the machinery of government and opted instead for collaboration with Prieto Laurens, who among the other candidates appeared most likely to favor their interests. Samuel de los Santos appealed to both the old and new elite but relied for support largely upon his family's influence in the Huasteca and state congress. The Santos clan had been prominent immediately prior to the Porfiriato but had lost influence during the dictatorship. Some members of the family, such as Pedro Antonio de los Santos, were leading local Maderistas, and others later established a powerful *cacicazgo* in the Huasteca under Carranza. During the governorship of Nieto they won control of the state legislature, where they energetically defended their interests.[28]

Neither Samuel de los Santos nor Prieto Laurens had much appeal for local agrarian or labor leaders who supported a third candidate, Aurelio Manrique, Jr. Cedillo and other agrarian leaders had originally urged Antonio Díaz Soto y Gama to stand in their name: his early opposition to Díaz, his association with the Zapatistas—so close in spirit to Cedillo's followers—and subsequent congressional career, all endeared him to agrarian reformers. But he suggested instead Aurelio Manrique, a young and erudite local politician who shared his ideals. Manrique's first involvement in politics had been in 1909, when with other students he founded a Reyista club in San Luis Potosí. He later studied medicine at the National University in Mexico City, but in 1916 he returned to San Luis Potosí to assist Juan Sarabia in his campaign for the governorship. Although Sarabia was defeated, Manrique himself was elected a federal deputy. Two years later he failed to win a seat in the senate, a setback which he ascribed to the machinations of Juan Barragán, who was then governor, but after the overthrow of Carranza he was reelected a federal deputy. When a group of workers' leaders occupied the federal congress in May 1921, Manrique delivered a speech in honor of Emiliano Zapata and planted the red and black Anarchist flag over the speaker's chair. He belonged to the student generation of the late Porfiriato, many of whom achieved political office in the aftermath of the Revolution.[29]

In December 1922 Manrique visited Cedillo in Ciudad del Maíz during the town's annual festival. Cedillo agreed to support Manrique for the governorship in return for promises of further land reform, and in view of this assurance Manrique decided to run. He also had the backing of other groups, including Sarabia's former party, the Reformist Party, and the Labor Party, which was the political front for the CROM. Manrique at once formed a coalition, the Potosí Revolutionary Party, to contest the municipal elections later that month in opposition to the more conservative Liberal Republican Party. Since both sides claimed victory in the elections, the state legislature divided the control of local government between them. During this campaign Manrique encountered the kind of opposition that he would face increasingly in the next few months. At a meeting in Matehuala he invited local workers to petition for land, but some miners present pointed out that their pay was higher than the income of local *ejidatarios*. Manrique's reply was drowned out by hecklers in the pay of some neighboring *hacendados*, and he was forced to abandon the meeting.[30]

The next development in the campaign was the political suicide of the Santistas, which saw the return of Cedillo to the forefront of state politics. In February 1923 Nieto went to Mexico City to consult Calles over the election. It was assumed that the governor could impose his successor, as Juan Barragán had in 1919, and Nieto wisely wished to hear Calles's preference. The Santos faction believed that they enjoyed the support of Obregón, but they feared that Calles, who had a more radical reputation than the president, would favor Manrique. They therefore conspired to use their control of the local legislature to unseat Nieto while he was away and to appoint a provisional governor. At first their plan worked admirably. The local legislature chose Hermilo Carreño to act as interim governor during Nieto's absence, and he immediately purged the administration of the governor's closest collaborators and began impeachment proceedings against him. Nieto returned to San Luis Potosí at once, but Carreño, assisted by federal troops, refused to allow him to resume his duties. Deducing that the Santistas had the support of Obregón, Nieto telegraphed both Calles and Cedillo for assistance. Cedillo hurried to San Luis Potosí, ordered the frightened Carreño to leave office, and reinstated Nieto. Rather than antagonize Cedillo, Obregón chose to sacrifice the Santistas, and the federal garrison made no move to intervene. Gonzalo Santos, the most active member of the Santista faction and mastermind of the attempted coup, fled to Tampico where he invoked the protection of the mayor, Jorge Prieto Lauren's brother Antonio. Shortly afterward the Ministry of the Interior publicly reaffirmed Nieto's legitimacy as governor. Nevertheless, the Santistas continued to cause Nieto problems in the congress until late April when Samuel de los Santos withdrew his candidacy and instructed his supporters to vote for Prieto Laurens.[31]

The election was then a contest between Manrique and Prieto Laurens. Both candidates were protected by armed men from Mexico City—Prieto Laurens by members of his own party, and Manrique by members of the CROM. In consequence, the weeks before the election were stained with violence, and at least eleven people died in clashes between rival supporters in the state capital alone.[32] Shortly before election day the gunmen were reinforced by a number of federal congressmen, including, on Manrique's side, Luis Morones and Celestino Gasca, two of the leading lights of the CROM. The new arrivals used their parliamentary immunity from arrest to full effect, and their presence added to the violence. The ambivalent attitude of the federal authorities, who failed to indicate a preference for either candidate, did nothing to restore calm. But the government was in a dilemma: Calles did not want Prieto Laurens to win control of such a strategically important state as San Luis Potosí, and he also wished to retain the loyalty of Cedillo who backed Manrique; on the other hand, neither he nor Obregón wanted to give the more restless generals the pretext for an uprising by intervening openly in provincial politics. Obregón might also have mistrusted Manrique's radicalism, which was an embarrassment since his regime was then negotiating with the United States for recognition.[33]

If Obregón and Calles hoped that the election would resolve the problem, they were soon disappointed. The voting was a farce, as the American consul observed:

> Governor Nieto tried to identify himself with the election at an early hour of the day, but at the first election booth he was met by a volley of shots which killed the man next to him. After this the governor stayed at home. The chief activity of the election seems to have consisted in sending several automobiles loaded with club bearers and gunmen to each election booth, running the election judges away, and capturing the ballot box. It is claimed that so successful was this method as worked by the opposing parties that long before the hour for closing the polls not a single voting place was open.[34]

In view of the violence the polling booths closed early, and Nieto announced that the results could not be taken seriously. Manrique agreed, but Prieto Laurens, whose followers had "captured" many of the booths, declared that he had won. This provoked Manrique to do likewise, and both factions within the local congress set up an election board that announced that their respective candidates had been elected to the governorship and congress. Manrique, Prieto Laurens, and Nieto then went to Mexico City to put their case before authorities—the first two on their own behalf, Nieto for fresh elections. Cedillo went to Nuevo León to consult Calles and give his version of events and then continued to Mexico City to assist Manrique. Obregón disclaimed any right to intervene, and the question remained unresolved when Nieto left to become ambassador to Sweden on 25 August. Following his departure, the Permanent Commission of the local congress, which reflected the Santista majority among the deputies, stepped in and elected a Prietista, Lorenzo Nieto, as provisional governor with instructions to preside over the transfer of power. Lorenzo Nieto (no relation to Rafael Nieto) at once purged the administration of Manrique's sympathizers and then, in conjunction with the Permanent Commission, announced that Prieto Laurens's supporters had been elected to the state congress.[35]

On the eve of the installation of the new congress, Manrique and thirty-three of his supporters occupied the chamber. Among Manrique's companions were several associates of Cedillo, Epifanio Castillo, Práxedis Olivera, Abel Cano, and Graciano Sánchez. The following day police arrested all the intruders except Manrique, who had parliamentary immunity. The Prietista congress was then installed under the protection of General Luis Gutiérrez, the commander of the local military zone, and at once invited Prieto Laurens to assume the governorship. Unperturbed, Manrique set up a rival congress in his house. A week later, after the murder of one of his "congressmen," he and the others moved to Guadalcázar where they were protected by Cedillo.[36] Obregón then declared the elections null and void, adding that he would shortly appoint a provisional governor. Prieto Laurens obtained an injunction (amparo) against the president's decision and returned to San Luis Potosí where he was duly installed by the congress on 25 September. He at once placed his supporters in all the important positions in the state bureaucracy and began to collect taxes in and around the capital. Obregón countered Prieto Laurens's amparo by referring the matter to the senate, and federal agencies, such as the National Agrarian Commission and the postal and telegraph services, refused to recognize either administration until the senate gave its ruling. Their action soon led to hardship in a number of areas: 300 families were left destitute when a lack of funds caused work to cease on the Mexquitic dam, and local teachers went on strike claiming that their salaries were being diverted into other sectors. Both "governors" continued to be active with words if not with deeds. Manrique issued his first decree at the beginning October. He declared the expropriation of a number of haciendas, the four largest of which, La Parada, Peotillos, Gogorrón, and Cruces, belonged to families that had helped Prieto Laurens during his campaign. In response Prieto Laurens threatened to expropriate land in the Río Verde region belonging to Manrique's supporters, presumably a reference to Cedillo's colonists. Manrique's decree provoked an unfavorable reaction from General Gutiérrez: he sent troops to remove the municipal councils which Manrique had installed in the area under Cedillo's control and ordered Cedillo to cease interference in state politics. Confronted by superior force, Cedillo acquiesced, and since it was expected that the senate would decide in favor of Prieto Laurens, Manrique appeared to have lost his fight. For the moment, at least, it seemed that Obregón was prepared to accept Prieto Laurens as governor, perhaps hoping that by doing so he might wean him away from the opposition to Calles.[37]

However, Prieto Laurens's ambitions in national politics sabotaged his position in San Luis Potosí. On 19 October Adolfo de la Huerta succumbed to the flattery of his friends and offered to be the PCN's presidential candidate. Calles's opponents had the prestigious figurehead whom they needed and began to campaign on De la Huerta's behalf. The leaders of the party maneuvered to gain control of the Permanent Commission of congress, whose task of vetting election results theoretically gave it the power to prevent the imposition of candidates by the executive. The party's strength in both the congress and the senate soon embarrassed Calles, whose active supporters were a minority in both chambers.[38] The election promised to be closely contested, for whereas Calles had the support of the federal authorities, De la Huerta appeared to be more popular. The authorities tried to counter De la Huerta's success by purchasing several newspapers that supported him and by requiring many army officers to declare their loyalty to Calles or resign.[39]

Among his moves to help Calles, Obregón sent Prieto Laurens a message through Governor Zuno of Jalisco offering to recognize him as governor of San Luis Potosí if he abandoned De la Huerta. But Prieto Laurens rejected this bribe, and Obregón thereupon took measures to undermine him. Fearful of the consequences of openly overthrowing any state government, the president moved cautiously. In early November he summoned General Gutiérrez to Mexico City for consultations, ordered the federal garrison in San Luis Potosí to remain in their barracks, and authorized an extraordinary payment of 500 pesos to Cedillo for unspecified purposes.[40] Cedillo and Manrique responded quickly to these gestures of official encouragement. On 10 November they reoccupied Río Verde, and thereafter moved against the other municipalities in the region—Cárdenas, Guadalcázar, Rayón, and Cerritos. Lorenzo Nieto was powerless to prevent the collapse of Prietista local government; he appealed desperately for federal protection and summoned the foreign consuls in San Luis Potosí to ask for their assistance. Although their sympathies lay with Prieto Laurens, the consuls wisely refused to become involved, and in the absence of any federal support Nieto organized a volunteer defense corps of 300 men to try to match Cedillo's *agraristas*.[41]

In Mexico City, Prieto Laurens urged the authorities to send troops against Cedillo, but predictably without success. His difficulties increased on 10 November when the police seized a large consignment of arms and ammunition that he was sending to Nieto's defense force in San Luis Potosí. On 23 November the senate announced their verdict on the election in his favor, but the decision was academic since Manrique and his followers occupied all the major towns to the east of the Saltillo–San Luis Potosí railway line and were threatening Matehuala. They were supported by Cedillo's *agraristas* and financed their activities by collecting taxes in the area they controlled. Only force could have dislodged them, and the federal government refused to provide it. Obregón was doubtlessly pleased to see the erosion of Prieto Laurens's position and took no steps to enforce the senate's decision. When he received a request for help from the municipality of San Luis Potosí, he replied somewhat ambiguously that both parties enjoyed effective authority in the districts they occupied and that federal troops would be used only to keep order. In the opinion of the American consul, Manrique was destined to assume office under Cedillo's protection.[42]

Manrique's triumph came abruptly at the beginning of December when a military revolt erupted in various states of the republic. Ostensibly a political movement in protest against violation of the constitution by the Obregón government, including the sovereignty of the state of San Luis Potosí, it was in fact an attempt to overthrow Obregón and prevent the succession of Calles, following the pattern of the movement of Agua Prieta three years earlier. The nominal leader was De la Huerta; the real leaders were a number of generals who considered their claims to high office to be superior to those of Calles, and who were prepared to revolt rather than see their ambitions thwarted.

For months there had been rumors of plotting among the generals, and Obregón had tried to counter the threat with bribes and changes in the army high command. Nevertheless, the president must have been surprised by the scale of the movement. Over half the army, including the auxiliary forces and a fifth of the 500 generals, rebelled against his administration. There were three centers of revolt, Veracruz, Jalisco, and Oaxaca. On 5 December De la Huerta fled to Veracruz and asked General Guadalupe Sánchez for protection. Sánchez at once withdrew recognition from the federal government in his favor and De la Huerta issued the "Plan of Veracruz" in which he described himself "Supreme Chief of the Revolution."[43] On 7 December General Enrique Estrada, the powerful military commander in Guadalajara, rebelled in the west, and, like Sánchez, recognized De la Huerta as the leader of the revolt. He was soon joined by two of the most prestigious generals in the army, both longtime friends of Obregón, Manuel Diéguez and Salvador Alvarado. In Oaxaca the rebels were led by General Fortunato Maycotte. Obregón had sent him to crush the revolt there with campaign expenses of 200,000 pesos, but the bribe proved insufficient. On 13 December he issued a revolutionary program of his own that recognized the triumvirate of Estrada, Sánchez, and himself as leaders of the revolt.[44]

At this moment of crisis Obregón profited from his administration's program of land redistribution. Faced by a numerically superior army, he ordered the arming of the beneficiaries of the agrarian reform. Reminding the *ejidatarios* that they were indebted for their land to the government and claiming that the rebels would take it back from them, officials loyal to the regime organized them into irregular units. Not all the *ejidatarios* responded positively to the government's appeal. In Durango, for example:

> The farmers around Pedriceña, according to Sr. Fernando Garcinava [the local Spanish vice-consul], who were also given land under the agrarian laws, were approached by the Governor's agents and asked to join the rurales at this city in return for what had been done for them. They all refused and told the agents to take the lands back if they wanted to but they, the farmers, certainly did not expect to fight any more as they were tired of it.[45]

Such a reaction was, however, relatively rare and tens of thousands of *ejidatarios* answered the call. These *agraristas* as they were called either acted as police in districts evacuated by the federal army garrisons or fought in the front line. Some *ejidatarios* who lived in territory occupied by the rebels were mobilized by their leaders to fight as guerrillas. These irregular forces played an important role in the suppression of the revolt, and some observers believed that their support was crucial to the government's success.[46]

One of the most important agrarian leaders to remain loyal to the government was Cedillo. While, on the political front, the De la Huerta revolt marked the triumph of Manrique, on the far more pressing military front it converted Cedillo into a major figure, not just locally but also nationally. On 7 December Obregón dispatched General Luis Gutiérrez to Celaya to check Estrada's advance from Jalisco. Since all important officials including Lorenzo Nieto had fled at the outbreak of the rebellion, Gutiérrez left seventy-five of his men behind to maintain order. On the eighth Cedillo arrived from Ciudad del Maíz to take over the garrison of the city. He was authorized to raise an additional 300 men right away and was placed under the command of General Carlos Vidal, the new head of the local military zone. Manrique arrived with him and assumed office on the evening of the tenth.[47]

Cedillo soon raised the 300 men for the garrison from among his veterans. They entered the state capital in a manner reminiscent of the Zapatistas when they occupied Mexico City in 1914 "to all appearances almost timid at finding themselves in a city of some proportion."[48] Calles arrived on 16 December on a recruiting drive, but he had little success. The inhabitants of the state capital were wearied by the years of intermittent fighting and indifferent to the brutal rivalries of their military leaders, and Calles left the following night with only a handful of volunteers. However, he was back two days later and made his base in the city for the next six weeks. This time he turned his attention to the potentially more fruitful rural sector. On his instructions Cedillo sent his recruiting officers into the districts where land had been redistributed. Their message was similar to that employed by government agents elsewhere in the country. According to Walter Boyle, the American consul:

> The policy of the Government in giving the peons provisional instead of permanent possession of lands, when dividing estates under the Agrarian laws, seems to be justifying itself. According to best reports the soldiers under General Cedillo are visiting outlying districts and informing the provisional holders of land that if they do not enlist the land will be taken away from them and those who are not provisional holders of land are advised to volunteer or be run out of the country.[49]

On the other hand, they were not averse to the use of bribery rather than coercion where it seemed more appropriate. Calles authorized them to grant all sharecroppers who volunteered the release from a year's obligations to their landlords, and in at least one case Cedillo's agents offered land as an incentive for volunteering.[50]

This policy of "stick and carrot" proved successful. By late December Cedillo had raised 1,500 troops, most of them mounted, and his men sought out the few rebels near the capital. Cedillo also requisitioned 3,000 horses which he sent to federal units elsewhere. In the middle of January a consignment of 2,000 rifles and 50,000 cartridges arrived for Cedillo from the United States, and these munitions allowed him to take the offensive. He divided his forces into three regiments of cavalry under Graciano Sánchez, José María Dávila, and Ildefonso Turrubiartes, and one of infantry under Wenceslao Rodríguez. The infantry was drawn from the industrial workers in San Luis Potosí; the cavalry from Cedillo's colonists and local *ejidatarios*. Graciano Sánchez took his contingent, most of whom were *ejidatarios* from around Mexquitic, to fight under Obregón in the Bajío; Dávila first secured the railway line to Saltillo and then moved north to join Calles; and Cedillo led the troops of Turrubiartes and Rodríguez into the east of the state to combat the rebels in the Huasteca. Práxedis Olivera, who had presided over an agrarian convention in San Luis Potosí in January 1923 and who was a close associate of Manrique, raised a further 1,300 men around Cárdenas to police the state in Cedillo's absence.[51]

In the Huasteca campaign Cedillo was supported by a number of local *caudillos*. They included Santana Mendoza and members of the Lárraga and Santos families, as well as Rodolfo Herrera, the assassin of former president Carranza. The leader of the rebels was Marcial Cavazos, who had campaigned against Cedillo in 1917 and 1918 and was popular in the Huasteca Hidalgüense, the part of the Huasteca that extends into the state of Hidalgo. Many local fueds were revived during the campaign, but after three months of bitter fighting Cedillo's forces finally triumphed and Cavazos was killed at the end of April. Although Cedillo thus restored the authority of the state government over the Huasteca, the region continued to resent control from the state capital. In spite of official discouragement, over a thousand people attended Cavazos's funeral, whereas only fifty of Cedillo's soldiers attended the funeral of the officer responsible for his death. Shortly afterward Cedillo returned to San Luis Potosí and disbanded all his forces except a small number of Turrubiartes's soldiers who remained as a nucleus of the garrison. The demobilized troops were, however, allowed to keep their weapons, and a grateful government rewarded many of Cedillo's officers with promotion.[52]

The arrangements made for Cedillo and his men reflected his position as a serving army officer—albeit always in his home district—his wish to retain the force which provided him with his power base, and the government's desire to retain the goodwill of one of its more important supporters in the region. The authorities' treatment of most of the *agraristas* was, however, very different. Having obtained weapons, many *agraristas*, once the revolt was over, began to use them to further their own class interests, e.g., by occupying rural estates by force before the completion of the due process of expropriation. (In view of the many ways, both legal and illegal, in which this process could be and often was delayed, their action is not surprising). This increase in the *agraristas*' power and independence alarmed the authorities for various reasons: it weakened the government's control over the pace of land redistribution, it challenged the monopoly of force enjoyed by the federal army, and it threatened the interests of those members of the regime who had become landowners in their own right. Many military chiefs in particular, either as *hacendados* or through their commercial activities, already had a vested interest in checking widespread land redistribution. Having acquired a stake in the rural economy, they were naturally concerned with protecting it. As the American chargé d'affaires wrote in June 1923:

> Originally the champion of agrarian reform, the Army as reorganized and detached from current politics, has come to play actually a negative role in the operation of this so-called reform. Its customary function has been in late years not to support the undertakings of the friends of agrarianism, but to check the excesses of its extreme enthusiasts. The men of any rank who make up the Army have little legitimately to gain in the redistribution of lands. Moreover, its performance of this police duty of defending the public order against the attempts of overzealous agrarian bands has often brought its officers and men into conflict with men whom they know as "Agraristas." The "Agrarista" has, thus, in some quarters, come to be looked upon by the soldiers as the enemy.[53]

For these reasons the government decided to disarm the *agraristas* as soon as the revolt was over. However, this process often led to violent clashes between recalcitrant *agraristas* and overzealous army officers. The resulting tension between the federal army and the *agraristas* favored the *hacendados*, many of whom actively cooperated with the federal troops. In this way they applied pressure upon local *ejidatarios* and in some cases even had them assassinated.[54] Certain military commanders went beyond disarmament and actively persecuted the *agraristas*. The most notorious of them was General Mange, who, after being responsible for the harassment and murder of *agraristas* in Oaxaca and the Laguna, was sent to Nayarit, where the activities of the *agraristas*, supported by the local governor, were proving embarrassing to the federal government. For six months Mange carried out a clandestine war against the *agraristas* and their political allies and had over two hundred of them murdered. Having thus removed the governor's power base, Mange then forced his resignation. In spite of the activities of Mange and others like him, the disarmament policy was only partially successful. But they had ensured that the *agraristas* were not in a position to press their demands beyond what the government was prepared to concede.[55]

In San Luis Potosí, of course, this campaign to bring the *agraristas* to heel went almost unnoticed. In the months following the De la Huerta revolt Cedillo reinforced his position as an agrarian leader by resettling his war veterans in their colonies and promoting further land redistribution as a reward for war service.[56] While he was thus engaged, Manrique pressed ahead with his plans to convert San Luis Potosí into a model of socialism. The 1917 Constitution gave considerable latitude to state governments in the field of social and economic reform, and Manrique was determined to transform local society. He encouraged labor unrest in the private sector as a justification for government intervention; he favored further agrarian reform, although, of course, land distribution was usually carried out under Cedillo's auspices; and he passed a law prohibiting the sale of alcoholic beverages. Probably only the governor and his closest advisers such as León García, a young former industrial worker, and Graciano Sánchez, a local teacher who had commanded one of Cedillo's columns in the recent revolt, had a clear idea of the political and economic system that they wished to establish; but they were attended by a mass of parasitical camp followers who employed the rhetoric of radical change in pursuit of personal advantage.[57]

Shortly after taking office Manrique appointed León García president of the local Conciliation and Arbitration Board, a body in which the president had a tie-breaking vote between the representatives of capital and labor. García's nomination signalled a period of intense labor agitation in local industry. Manrique's strategy appeared to be to sponsor the creation of unions and then use them either to obtain higher wages for their members or to assist the government in assuming control of local companies. (It was a policy that was being successfully pursued by Emilio Portes Gil, who had recently been elected the governor of neighboring Tamaulipas.) In January the Board forced the Cruz clothing factory to dismiss workers who refused to join a union. In February there was a strike in the city's bakeries which ended only when the owners agreed to employ union labor exclusively and to pay higher compensation in cases of injury. At the same time the American-owned Central Mexican Light and Power Company also conceded the principle of a "closed shop" and higher wages in order to avoid a strike. The following month a brief stoppage of tramway workers forced the company to raise wages and sack non-union labor. Foreign-born managers of local firms feared that if they opposed union demands they might be deported under Article 33 of the constitution, which gave the president discretion in expelling undesirable aliens. By the middle of March Boyle reported that management was rapidly losing control of local industry.[58]

At this point pressure from local businessmen and the central government forced Manrique to change his policies. The focus of their attention was the American Smelting and Refining Company (ASRC), which had recently purchased an unfinished smelter in the state capital for a million dollars. The company intended to complete it and service it from its locally owned mines, an investment expected to create a total of 5,000 jobs. In February ASRC suspended almost all work on the nearly finished smelter because of strikes at its mines in Matehuala and Charcas. Manrique reluctantly withdrew his original backing for the strikes, which soon collapsed. The company was then given assurances of support both by the central government and by Calles during a visit to San Luis Potosí in April and, as a result, renewed work on the smelter. However, in June a strike was called at the ASRC mine in San Pedro. Company officials told Manrique that, since the mine was taking a loss, they were prepared to close it until the smelter could utilize its output two years later. Fearing for their jobs and lacking encouragement from Manrique, the strikers yielded. The governor's change of policy was almost certainly due to pressure from Mexico City. His administration could challenge local industrialists, particularly those as powerful as ASRC, only if it could threaten their interests with compulsory purchase. Only the federal authorities had the necessary funds for this, and it was not their policy. In these circumstances Manrique was forced to give way, and regretfully he turned his reforming zeal to other sectors.[59]

His next initiative was directed at the city's landlords. They were then in a relatively weak position since San Luis Potosí was growing only slowly. Housing was not therefore in great demand, and rents and property taxes were low. Furthermore, most landlords were either Mexicans or Spaniards and consequently lacked the forceful diplomatic support enjoyed, for example, by American mineowners. Altogether Manrique could calculate that an assault upon them carried fewer risks. In December 1924 he permitted the formation of a rentpayer's union and provided it with offices in the government-owned Teatro de la Paz. At the union's instigation the state authorities reduced the lowest rents from 2.50 to 1.80 pesos per month. The landlords claimed that this reduction prevented their maintaining these properties, and a month later the union organized a strike to press for improvements in its members' accommodations. Believing that the state government intended to take over their properties eventually, the landlords proposed that Cedillo should arbitrate in the dispute. The union agreed, but Manrique was incensed by the idea that Cedillo could act as an appeal judge for his decisions. He accused the landlords of acting provocatively and set up an arbitration board consisting of two representatives from each party in the dispute and a chairman, the city's mayor. The committee, on which León García sat on behalf of the rentpayers, reported that the union's leaders were giving the landlords only some of the rent they received from the tenants and were keeping the balance. An embarrassed Manrique therefore instructed the tenants to pay the landlords directly and to use the union solely for negotiations. In consequence, the union eventually ceased to function; but the collapse of a scheme so closely identified with Manrique damaged his prestige and weakened him politically.[60]

One area in which Manrique did have some success was in promoting agrarian reform, and during his two years in office over twelve thousand *ejidatarios* took provisional possession of almost three hundred thousand hectares of land. Some of them were *agraristas* who were being rewarded for their recent war service; other beneficiaries were simply profiting from the governor's sponsorship of the reform. Manrique also organized an agrarian league along similar lines to the much more important one which Adalberto Tejeda had sponsored as governor in neighboring Veracruz. In January 1925 the league held a convention in San Luis Potosí attended by Luis León, the minister of agriculture, and the governors of Morelos, Michoacán, and Aguascalientes. The president of the convention was Manrique's henchman, Graciano Sánchez, and there were 500 delegates from San Luis Potosí. Among those who gave speeches were Cedillo, Enrique Henshaw, by now a federal senator, and an up-and-coming young agrarian leader from Villa de Reyes, Tomás Tapia. Luis León also gave a speech, followed by an exhibition of bullfighting, much to the delight of all those present except Manrique, who disliked the sport intensely.[61]

In spite of his encouragement of land redistribution, however, and the formation of the league, Manrique never succeeded in establishing a firm power base in the countryside, and certainly not one to rival Cedillo's. However well-meaning, the erudite governor was an alien figure as he walked into any village. (His dislike of bullfighting was merely one indication of the cultural gap between himself and his more rustic constituents.) Like his friend Antonio Díaz Soto y Gama, he was an urban-based politician who could pursue his commitment to land reform only through the new agrarian bureaucracy. Furthermore, as a civilian, Manrique was dependent upon the goodwill of the central government and local military authorities in order to enforce his policies. Since the obvious figure to whom he would have to turn for support was Cedillo, who had his own agrarian clientele, Manrique's failure to establish an independent agrarian following is easy to understand. A good illustration of Manrique's weakness was the conflict between the village of Villa de Reyes and the *hacienda* of Gogorrón. The origins of the dispute were common to many cases of agrarian unrest: the juxtaposition of a rich *hacienda* and a landless village. During Carranza's presidency the villagers petitioned for land and received 275 hectares in restitution. After prolonged litigation, during which the villagers' titles to the land were proved to be forged, they received a provisional grant of land in 1921 covering over six thousand hectares, which they immediately occupied in defiance of an injunction obtained by the owners of the estate. During the next few years there was intermittent violence between the villagers and the *hacienda* guards which culminated in April 1924 when the villagers seized and imprisoned a magistrate and officials from San Luis Potosí who were picnicing with the *hacienda* administrator. At the same time they began to syphon off water from the *hacienda*'s irrigation channels which ran across their land, thus causing a shortage on the estate itself. Manrique championed the villagers but was overruled by Obregón, who ordered troops to be sent from San Luis Potosí to free the prisoners. Lacking support from the central government or from Cedillo, who had been in touch with Obregón, Manrique was unable to act effectively on the villagers' behalf, and the dispute remained unresolved when he was overthrown in November 1925.[62]

Manrique's problems with the central government worsened when Calles succeeded Obregón as president in December 1924. Calles had a reputation as a radical and was expected to introduce rapid social change. But he was a reformer, not a revolutionary. He did not intend to restructure the economy but simply to expand it to the benefit of the national bourgeoisie and redistribute some of the wealth it generated to the working classes in the form of higher wages and better conditions. He strengthened the government's links with the CROM but, nevertheless, encouraged the growth of national capitalism. In this he was actively assisted by the leader of the CROM, Luis Morones, whom he appointed industry minister.[63]

In the sphere of agrarian reform Calles's policies were a continuation of those of his predecessor. During his term of office definitive titles were given to almost three million hectares of *ejidos*. The rate of redistribution accelerated slowly during his first three years in office, but showed a marked decline in the final year. This was due largely to a change in the president's views on the agrarian question. Under the influence of the American ambassador Dwight Morrow, and in the face of low levels of agricultural production, he came to favor a reduction in the pace of the reform and greater guarantees for the more productive private sector. Calles also stressed the role of the reform in the development of a rural middle class. He passed the Law of Ejidal Patrimony in December 1925, which overruled the recommendation of the CNA's earlier Circular 51 and instructed that land distributed in *ejidos* should be divided up into individual plots. In a further attempt to assist the *ejidatarios* in becoming more independent, he established two agricultural credit banks for them early the following year: the Banco Nacional de Crédito Agrícola and the Banco de Crédito Ejidal. Unfortunately, as a result of inadequate funding, maladministration, and political interference, neither institution was of real assistance to the majority of *ejidatarios*. Over 80% of the funds of the Banco Nacional de Crédito Agrícola, for example, went to less than one thousand five hundred individuals, usually important politicians, while the Banco de Crédito Ejidal, a government-sponsored cooperative, had branches in only nine states and never possessed a capital of more than 1.4 million pesos, most of which were squandered on poor administration anyway. Both institutions were closed in 1931 when a new effort was made to tackle the problem.[64]

Calles spent the first months of his presidency establishing his personal authority. He filled the higher levels of the bureaucracy with his supporters and also intervened in several states to ensure that they came under the control of men loyal to himself. During his first year in office six governors were forced to resign following difficulties with their state congresses or the local military commander.[65]

As Calles maneuvered to create a power base in the country, Manrique became an increasing nuisance to him. The governor and his associates counted themselves among the spokesmen for revolutionary change within the regime. Perhaps spurred on by an awareness that their failure to establish a socialist system in San Luis Potosí was partly due to central government pressure, they were determined to act as Calles's radical conscience. They made this clear to Calles even before he assumed office, during his visit to San Luis Potosí in November 1924. As part of the official reception committee at the station, Graciano Sánchez, León García, and Manrique himself all delivered highly provocative speeches of welcome. Sánchez and García even went so far as to warn Calles that if he reneged on his revolutionary principles, they would lead an armed revolt to overthrow him. Sánchez repeated this warning in a somewhat more veiled manner a few weeks later during the Agrarian Convention in January. When Cedillo proposed to the assembly that they send telegrams to Obregón and Calles pledging them their support, Sánchez had the telegram to Calles amended to an "offer" of support, accompanied by a proposal that he organize a "Veteran National Guard" to defend the Revolution.[66] Shortly before the convention Manrique had gone on a speaking tour during which he made a number of inflammatory speeches advocating the adoption of more fundamental socialist policies. His journey ended in controversy in Pachuca, the state capital of neighboring Hidalgo, where with the assistance of local *agraristas* he released a number of agrarian and labor activists from the local jail. By this time his activities were becoming too much for Calles, who summoned Cedillo to Mexico City and instructed him to curb Manrique's radicalism.[67]

Calles had turned to Cedillo for two reasons: first because his military power enabled him to carry out the president's wishes, and second because his prior loyalty was to the central government since, as Calles well knew, it was their patronage, not Manrique's, that he needed to help his followers. As W.F. Boyle observed in a report of November 1924:

> The hold of Manrique on the state of San Luis Potosí is greatly overestimated. The real power lies with General Cedillo, but with the support of Federal Command taken from him, he would be but a sorry outlaw holding the same part of the state which he has dominated for years... General Cedillo may be safely counted on as favoring the side having the most power and most likely to reward him by permitting his continued domination of the state, or at least a goodly part of it... he will never align himself with Manrique unless he looks on the Governor as a man of political destiny.[68]

For his part, Cedillo probably welcomed the president's initiative, since as Calles was also doubtlessly aware, his relations with Manrique had recently deteriorated. Originally based upon mutual self-interest, the alliance between Manrique, the intellectual and urbane politician, and Cedillo, the former rancher-turned-guerrilla leader, had soon become strained once Manrique was in office. The governor believed that he had a mandate to introduce his program of reforms, whereas Cedillo believed that his past services to Manrique gave him the right to veto the governor's policies and extract favors from him. There was similar tension between the civilian and military authorities in several states at this time, and almost inevitably it ended in the removal of whoever was less valuable to the central government.[69]

Manrique's efforts to impose his reforms and Cedillo's insistence upon meddling in government inevitably led to friction between them, and Cedillo gradually became the focus for the opposition to Manrique's less popular measures. These included a reduction in state government salaries, in which the governor led by example, and the ban on selling alcoholic drinks. When Calles took office, there were rumors that Manrique would be offered a post in Mexico City and Cedillo would assume the governorship. Shortly afterward Cedillo successfully defied Manrique's ban on the New Year's Day bullfight by offering the promoters his protection. Forced to yield, Manrique went on the speaking tour that had ended in the Pachuca incident. This affair was followed by further cases of petty friction between them. For example, Manrique refused to find jobs for two former supporters of Prieto Laurens whose sister

Cedillo was courting, and in March he had Cedillo's chauffeur arrested for attempted rape. Cedillo insisted upon having the man released for trial in a military court and retaliated by ordering the mayor of Matehuala to deliver some wine that he had confiscated to its rightful owner, a Spanish mine manager.[70]

Any rapprochement between the two men was hindered by the ambitions and machinations of their followers. Enrique Henshaw, for example, one of Cedillo's closest associates, conspired to turn Cedillo against the governor after Manrique had appointed Graciano Sánchez, and not Henshaw, president of the state congress. But it was Sánchez who probably did most to sour relations between Manrique and Cedillo. An intense, energetic, and hot-tempered man, whose political ambitions went beyond the humble stage of San Luis Potosí, he irritated Calles with his radicalism and annoyed Cedillo by seeking to create a personal following among the local *campesinos*. In December 1924 he attempted to impose his candidates in the municipal elections in the Huasteca, a move that Cedillo resisted; but unaffected by this rebuff, he continued to promote his own and Manrique's cause.[71]

As 1925 progressed, Manrique became increasingly isolated, both nationally and within San Luis Potosí. His relations with Calles remained cool, and he caused the president further irritation over the issue of the Mexican Catholic Apostolic Church. This schismatic body, which was founded in February 1925, was the president's own inspiration. It represented one of his first moves in a campaign to reduce the Roman Catholic Church to a position of subservience to the state. Calles expected Manrique to encourage the new organization, especially since the governor was a Protestant, but Manrique knew that the Church was anathema to his electors, and moreover foresaw that such an artificial creation was doomed to failure anyway. True to his principles, he ignored the opportunity to ingratiate himself with Calles and refused to permit the Church to be established in the state. Since the religious question was central to the president's thinking, he probably considered Manrique's action little short of treachery.[72]

Manrique's position was also becoming dangerously exposed within San Luis Potosí. In the agrarian sector he was easily overshadowed by Cedillo, and he even lost some of his support among the urban industrial workers. His labor policies had contributed to a depression in local business which had such an effect upon tax revenue that the municipal authorities in San Luis Potosí cut their employees' salaries by 10% in order to balance their budget. When Manrique tried to encourage investment by refusing to support strikes in the ASRC smelter and the local tramway company, he alienated local workers without convincing the employers of his good faith. Cedillo took advantage of Manrique's discomfiture to intervene in two other labor disputes that broke out shortly afterward, in both cases on the employer's behalf. The governor felt unable to oppose Cedillo's initiatives, which he accepted with barely a word of comment.[73]

Encouraged by Manrique's difficulties, his opponents tried to unseat him. When the governor visited Mexico City at the end of July, the president of the Permanent Commission of congress, Eugenio Jiménez, a well-known Cedillista, tried to have him replaced by a provisional governor. His plan, based upon a dubious interpretation of his legal powers, was resisted by two of the governor's supporters, Hilario Hermosillo and Graciano Sánchez. When Cedillo's chief of staff, Colonel García Rubio, attempted to intercede between Jiménez and Sánchez, the latter sent a telegram to the minister of the interior, Adalberto Tejeda, complaining of Rubio's "interference in the affairs of government." The Manriquista mayor of San Luis Potosí, Juan Martínez, feared that Cedillo might attempt a coup and posted a guard on all government buildings. This precaution was unnecessary, for Cedillo did nothing, and Manrique soon returned. But the governor's relations with Cedillo were irreparably damaged. Manrique suspected, with good reason, that Jiménez would not have moved against him without Cedillo's authority, while Cedillo was angry at Manrique's refusal to refute Sánchez's accusations against Rubio. Each conspired against the other in an atmosphere of mutual suspicion.[74]

Cedillo concentrated his maneuvers against Manrique in the Permanent Commission of the state congress, which he soon came to control through flattery and bribery. In August there were elections for the congress and the Permanent Commission ensured a Cedillista majority in the new legislature. For two months there was legislative paralysis as both Manrique and the congress rejected one another's initiatives. The congressmen complained to Adalberto Tejeda that they could not work under such conditions, but he rejected their protest.[75] However, shortly afterward Tejeda visited San Luis Potosí to interview the parties involved. He and Manrique were close friends—Manrique had assisted in his campaign to become governor of Veracruz in 1920—and Tejeda asked the congress to be more cooperative. Since this appeal had no effect, Tejeda sent Elvira Carrillo Puerto, the sister of the popular governor of Yucatán under Obregón, to mediate in the dispute. She concluded that Manrique was the victim of a congressional conspiracy, but failed in her attempt at mediation. On 9 November Tejeda returned to San Luis Potosí, and the press reported that Cedillo would shortly be transferred. But the final decision lay with Calles, to whom Cedillo's *agraristas* were more important than Manrique's principles and legitimacy; and just as the president had supported action against the governors of Oaxaca and Aguascalientes in the preceding weeks, so he made no effort to prevent Cedillo from overthrowing Manrique.[76]

On the night of 15 November the congress met under the protection of federal troops and voted to remove Manrique from the governorship. In his place they elected a Cedillista deputy, Dr. Abel Cano. Prevented from entering the governor's office by Cedillo's troops, Manrique went to Mexico City to complain to Tejeda. He also appealed to other state authorities to refuse recognition of the congress in San Luis Potosí. Tejeda told him that the federal government could not interfere in the internal affairs of the state—an absurd declaration considering the circumstances. The authorities in the other states were more sympathetic but generally followed Tejeda's line of argument. The only important exception was in the minister's own home territory of Veracruz, where his opponents in the local state congress used the issue to persuade their colleagues to break off relations with the federal government. But the rupture proved harmful and embarrassing to both sides, and in January 1926 relations were restored. Manrique was helpless and retired to Mexico City to await a more favorable climate for his hopes. With him went his closest associates, including Leon García, Graciano Sánchez, and Juan Martínez.[77]

Manrique had sought to create a revolution in San Luis Potosí, without the power base that any revolutionary needs if he is to be even partially successful. His efforts to win support among industrial workers had been frustrated by the central government and Cedillo, and he never gained a significant following in the countryside. His two years in office had been too short a time for him to challenge effectively Cedillo's position there, since when Manrique was overthrown, Cedillo was still regarded by the vast majority of the rural population as the natural agrarian leader of the state. In these circumstances Manrique had contributed to his own downfall by his refusal to compromise his principles. He had continued to press the national government to pursue more radical policies at a time when Calles was moving to the right in economic affairs and had refused to lend his support to the president's anti-clericalism. He had compounded this error within San Luis Potosí by consistently advocating the supremacy of civil over military power. Inevitably this brought him into conflict with Cedillo, who believed that his military power and past services to both Manrique and the national government gave him the right to extract favors from the governor and to interfere in the local administration. Since Manrique lacked a power base comparable to Cedillo's, it was a contest that he could not win without the full backing of Mexico City, and such support was denied to him because of his refusal to accommodate himself to the president's policies. Cedillo, on the other hand, behaved with more astuteness. He increased the already considerable support he enjoyed with the rural population by assisting in further land reform. Realizing "which way the wind was blowing" in Mexico City, he distanced himself from Manrique's more radical ventures such as the rentpayers' union. He also emphasized his loyalty to the central government, thus offering himself as an instrument for Calles's policy of asserting the central government's authority over the provinces. Using his contacts in the state congress and exploiting the weaknesses of local politicians, rather than appealing to their idealism as Manrique did, Cedillo gradually isolated the governor. When the final confrontation came, he proved to Manrique that principles were no substitute for power and engineered his overthrow in a classical coup. As 1926 opened, Cedillo was left the undisputed master of the state.

CHAPTER 5

THE CRISTERO INTERLUDE

GENERAL CEDILLO HELPED TO ORGANIZE THE REDISTRIBUTION OF LAND
AND THAT WAS WHY HE WAS VERY POPULAR.——Manuel Mata, a veteran of
the battle of Tepatitoán.

I AM TAKING STEPS TO CALL TO ARMS ALL THE AGRARIAN COMRADES IN OR-
DER TO FORM REGIONAL BODIES AND PLAY THEM AGAINST THE FANATICS.
——President Plutarco Elias Calles, 1 January 1927

With the overthrow of Manrique, Cedillo was satisfied that he would
henceforth be able to exercise the influence over the state administration that he believed was his prerogative. For the moment, however, he had
more personal matters on his mind; for in December 1925 he married again,
this time to Carmen Wollemberg, the daughter of a German merchant from
Ciudad del Maíz. The Wollembergs had occupied a minor place in the local oligarchy during the last years of the Porfiriato, and with the Barragáns they
were the only such family to resettle in the town when peace returned after
1920. Cedillo had been wooing Carmen ever since his unsuccessful courtship of
Juanita Barragán, but for a long time she resisted his advances. Eventually,
perhaps under pressure from her family, she gave in, but their union was to
prove short-lived. A sophisticated woman by the standards of the district, Carmen found life with her rough-and-ready husband difficult and they soon
parted. In spite of this, Federico Wollemberg, Carmen's brother, became a
close friend of Cedillo and remained one of his most trusted advisers until Cedillo's revolt in 1938.[1]

Manrique's successor as governor, Abel Cano, was born in Coahuila in
1886. As a young man he learned some basic botany and biology and later became a travelling salesman of herbal medicines. He joined the revolutionary
forces against Huerta but returned to civilian life following Huerta's defeat

and exile. In 1923 he stood for the local congress in support of Manrique and took his place there when the latter assumed the governorship. Disillusioned with Manrique's performance, he was one of the members of the state congress who switched allegiance to Cedillo during the summer of 1925 and helped to engineer Manrique's downfall. He was, however, reluctant to replace Manrique as governor. Although he had belonged to the local administration for two years, Cano was best known in the town for his habit of shooting at the ceiling in his favorite restaurant, the Versalles, when reenacting his revolutionary experiences with his former comrades.[2]

Cano immediately took measures to win popularity. He raised government salaries and ensured their prompt payment. He abolished some of the taxes paid by artisans and granted certain outstanding petitions for *ejidos*. In order to finance these measures he ended "prohibition" and imposed a sales tax on alcoholic drinks. Subsequently, he persuaded Calles to divert to his administration some of the fiscal revenue from the oil wells at El Ébano. On the other hand, Cano was ruthless with his opponents. In the weeks following Manrique's departure the police frequently detained his supporters on spurious charges, and early in 1926 they destroyed the printing press on which a Manriquista congressman was producing a news sheet. Such repression, unexceptional by contemporary standards, nevertheless ensured the security of the new regime.[3]

The most immediate problem for Cano was the opposition to the government's religious policy. Relations between the church and the state had been uneasy since independence. In the first half of the nineteenth century the church hierarchy was active in national politics in defense of their sectional interests. Church wealth and influence were used to hamper the reforms of the Liberal Party, and church leaders supported the French intervention in 1862. Although the church was weakened by the Liberals, it remained a powerful institution. During the Porfiriato it reached an accommodation with the government and even regained some of its wealth. However, those who framed the 1917 Constitution were imbued with the Liberals' anticlericalism and approved several articles that contradicted ecclesiastical doctrine. The administrations of Carranza and Obregón were both anticlerical in tone, but they avoided confrontation with the church authorities. Neither passed the relevant *reglamentos* of the controversial clauses of the constitution, and even Obregón's expulsion of the apostolic delegate in 1923 for attending an "illegal" service did not provoke a crisis.[4]

Calles, however, was in no mood for conciliation. He saw the Mexican church as the primary obstacle to the creation of a modern state in which the government would be the exclusive patron of agrarian and labor reform, education, and the social services. He was equally opposed to both conservatives and progressives within the church: the former because their support for large landowners and their hostility to organized labor conflicted with the government's policies; the latter, because they threatened the state's monopoly over reform. He was determined that the church should no longer exert influence on national life.[5] His allies were the freemasons and other anticlericals, and the CROM, whose leaders resented the adoption of certain unions by church progressives. Calles's first move was in February 1925, when, with the CROM, he supported the creation of a schismatic "Mexican Catholic Apostolic Church," independent of Rome. But the new organization failed to win any following, and, soon forgotten, it ceased to exist altogether within a few years. Undaunted by this failure or by the creation by Catholic laymen of the "League for the Defense of Religious Liberty" (LNDLR), Calles resumed the attack the following year. Between February and July 1926 the federal and state governments converted the religious clauses of the constitution into law with varying degrees of harshness. Henceforth, mass could only be celebrated in locations authorized by the government, priests had to register with the authorities and their numbers were restricted, and church schools were closed. In July, in protest at the new laws, the church authorities suspended services, and the LNDLR called for an economic boycott. When this had no effect upon the government, the league turned to violence and in December instigated an armed rebellion. This movement, which lasted until July 1929, came to be called the Cristiada.[6]

Although the spark that ignited the Cristiada was the government's policy toward the church, the rebels' grievances were not exclusively religious. This revolt was a popular reaction against the emergence of a secular state that assumed the right to legislate over every aspect of rural life. Not surprisingly, therefore, it was strongest where the government's agricultural policy was least suitable to local conditions. In the Bajío, for example, largely mestizo *ranchero* communities, in which priests enjoyed considerable influence, fiercely resented the introduction of *ejidos* and the assault upon the church. In contrast, in Oaxaca and Chiapas, where the church still competed with a strong indigenous cultural tradition and the institutions of government had less impact upon most people's daily lives, Calles's religious policies provoked little opposition. There was also less unrest in areas where land reform resulted from a popular movement under local leadership, such as in eastern San Luis Potosí or in districts where *ejidos* had been introduced to meet popular needs without prejudice to local *hacienda* peons.

In those regions where the league's call for a revolt responded to local grievances, the rebellion rapidly assumed serious proportions. By April 1927 the government had lost control of the rural areas of southern Durango, Zacatecas, Jalisco, Guanajuato, Michoacán, Colima, and northern Guerrero. Many federal commanders contributed to the unrest by treating the civilian population with great brutality and by prolonging hostilities for personal profit. In May 1927 General Joaquín Amaro, the minister of war, visited the areas where the fighting was most widespread and directed an offensive. But in the absence of any political initiative he was able only to reduce the unrest while his opponents withdrew to their farms and villages.[7]

In response to the serious threat posed by the Cristiada to his administration, Calles mobilized large numbers of *agraristas,* and for the two and one-half years that the rebellion lasted, they were to bear the brunt of some of the heaviest fighting. By so doing they exposed both the politically divisive nature of the agrarian reform and their own client status. This privileged minority of the rural population, almost all of whom were Roman Catholics, was forced to pay for their land by fighting against rebels motivated by opposition to the government's religious and, to a lesser extent, agrarian policies. Joining the revolt was, by definition, impossible for an *agrarista*, since he would forfeit his land and status. Not surprisingly, the Cristeros regarded them as traitors to the faith, men who had sold their souls for a plot of land; and little quarter was shown in the fighting between the two groups.[8]

In San Luis Potosí, Roman Catholic activists initially reacted to government pressure as their counterparts did elsewhere. Encouraged by their bishop, the popular Monsignor Miguel de la Mora, they formed in 1925 the *Liga Católica Popular Potosina*. The organizers of this local version of the LNDLR belonged to the urban bourgeoisie, some of them, such as Refugio de la Maza, being related to the former Porfirian elite. Many had been too young to participate in the events of 1910–1911, and joining the organization was their first venture into politics. But despite youthful enthusiasm they made little impression on the mass of the population, particularly in the countryside. Their background isolated them from the lower classes, and they never recruited intermediaries to bridge the gap.[9]

When, in February 1926, Calles ordered the state governors to convert the anticlerical clauses of the constitution into law, Abel Cano responded immediately. On 15 February he forced all foreign priests to leave the state, and on 13 March his government passed a *reglamento* covering the relevant articles of the constitution. The number of priests permitted to work in the state was limited to ten for the capital, two each for Matehuala, Río Verde, and Santa María del Río, and one for the remainder of the state. Somewhat surprisingly, Bishop de la Mora obtained an injunction against the decree from a federal judge. Anticlerical elements in the administration thereupon forced the issue. On 18 March the police closed seven churches in the city, claiming that the municipality had not granted permission for their use. De la Mora then ordered the closure of the remaining churches and suspended the holding of mass. A rumor started that his life was being threatened and sympathizers gathered outside his residence. Cedillo unavailingly requested the bishop to renew services and then ordered Colonel García Rubio to disperse the crowd, which he did at the cost of one person dead and several injured. Cedillo's men then patrolled the streets while he sent representatives to negotiate with the bishop. They finally reached an agreement on the twentieth according to which the law remained on the statute book but the authorities promised not to enforce it. Neither party was satisfied with this compromise, but the position of practicing Catholics in San Luis Potosí was relatively privileged even as relations between the church and state in Mexico deteriorated during the summer. The churches remained open for individual worship, and priests continued to hold masses in private houses with only token interference.[10]

Later in the year, activists in the local league made plans for an insurrection in the countryside, but they failed to win popular support for it. Not only did their own social background put them at a disadvantage, but the scale and popularity of the land reform in San Luis Potosí removed many of the grievances exploited by their counterparts in other states. Cedillo's colonies gave him a firm base around the two traditional centers of rural unrest in the state, Río Verde and Ciudad del Maíz, and furthermore, the creation of *ejidos* in San Luis Potosí had not proved as divisive as elsewhere in the Central Plateau. The *rancheros* had been largely unaffected, many *peones acasillados* had illegally received ejidal plots, and most of the confiscated land had belonged to the kind of large landholdings that provoked the hostility of the Cristeros themselves.[11] The *ejidatarios* in San Luis Potosí were not therefore a small minority who had acquired land at the expense of middle class neighbors of landless *hacienda* peons, but a substantial minority whose land had come mostly from the large estates of the old Porfirian elite through the patronage of a relatively popular local *caudillo*.

As a result of these factors, San Luis Potosí remained peaceful in comparison with neighboring states, and there were only three armed movements there in 1927. From January to March a small group under Jesús Posadas operated between Río Verde and Armadillo; in early March eight Cristeros under Ponciano Magallanes were caught by *agraristas* near San Luis Potosí and, with one exception, were executed; and, also in March, General Ignacio Galván died organizing an uprising near Cárdenas. Of these commanders Galván was the most important. He was an experienced guerrilla leader who fought against Díaz in 1910 and 1911 and alongside Cedillo from 1912 to 1920. He broke with Cedillo in 1923 when he supported Prieto Laurens for the state governorship but was pardoned following the De la Huerta revolt and settled in southern Tamaulipas. Persuaded to organize a revolt by the LNDLR, he was betrayed and died in an ambush set for him by Ildefonso Turrubiartes, his former companion-in-arms. Fourteen rebels under a member of the local league—Fidel Muro, the former chauffeur of Miguel de la Mora—attempted to join Galván but were dispersed by a Cedillista patrol. Muro was later captured and escaped execution only when María Azanza Gordoa, a fellow league member whose family was on good terms with Cedillo, interceded with him on Muro's behalf. Muro's captors found a letter on him from Bishop De la Mora urging him not to resort to violence, and they accused the bishop of complicity with the rebels. They did not press the charge—which De la Mora denied— but their suspicions were understandable; for although opposed to any clergyman's participation in the rebellion, the bishop considered the Cristeros' stance to be justified.[12]

The remainder of the year in San Luis Potosí was quiet. Cedillo's *agraristas* contained what little unrest there was in the countryside, and the police were equally vigilant in the towns. Four leading Catholic activists were executed in March, and the others were either arrested or closely watched. (Some of those arrested had unwisely made contact with some supporters of General Arnulfo

Gómez, who was plotting a revolt and whose followers were under surveillance.) On a more conciliatory note Cedillo allowed the churches to remain open and also permitted the discreet practice of religion in private. As for the local league, it proved a paper tiger. Only a few members, such as Fidel Muro, joined the fighting and several opposed the rebellion on principle. Its only contribution to the Cristeros' cause was the irregular supply of money and materials, and neither in the quantities needed.[13]

Although San Luis Potosí itself was undisturbed, Cedillo and his *agraristas* were active in the neighboring states of Guanajuato and Querétaro, where the rebels enjoyed considerable support. The Cristeros were led by General Rodolfo Gallegos, who had years of military experience, first as a Maderista in his home state of Sonora, and later with Obregón. Between 1918 and 1926 he commanded the military district of Guanajuato, where his suppression of banditry earned him great popularity. Relieved of his command by Calles, whose election as president he had opposed in favor of his opponent Angel Flores, Gallegos was recruited by the LNDLR. He rebelled in October 1926 and soon controlled much of Guanajuato. The local military authorities were no match for so formidable an opponent, and in January 1927 General Amaro commissioned Cedillo to move against him. Cedillo raised a force of 2,000 men whom he divided into four mounted columns. He also took a column of infantry from the 76th regiment under Ildefonso Turrubiartes. Cedillo himself moved between San Luis Potosí, Guanajuato, and Mexico City.[14] The campaign soon evolved into a hunt for the elusive Gallegos, but unlike their predecessors, Cedillo's men matched the rebels in mobility and understanding of guerrilla tactics. They gradually gained the initiative, and they located and killed Gallegos on 4 May. His death severely weakened the revolt in the state. None of his subordinates proved able to coordinate the various bands there, and the government regained a loose control over the area.[15]

When Gallegos was killed, Cedillo was in Mexico City arranging his candidacy for the state governorship. He had long been the dominant figure in San Luis Potosí, and following the overthrow of Manrique, he strengthened his position even more. In August 1926 he eliminated a potentially powerful rival by having Leopoldo Lárraga shot in Valles for plotting a rebellion with his brother Manuel. The Lárraga brothers had acquired a formidable reputation as guerrilla leaders in the Revolution, first as Maderistas and then as Carrancistas. Following the fall of Carranza, they retained considerable influence in the Huasteca, despite various attempts by the state authorities to reduce their power. Whether Lárraga was guilty of the charge against him is unclear, but his execution enhanced Cedillo's power. Subsequently, Cedillo had a number of other opponents arrested for supposed complicity in the Cristero revolt and in the abortive uprising of General Gómez in October 1927.[16]

Cedillo's election was a foregone conclusion. His popularity in the countryside, combined with the presence of his *agraristas* at campaign meeting, demoralized and intimidated his opponents, and he was elected unopposed. Shortly afterwards General Obregón visited San Luis Potosí during his presidential campaign. He was accompanied by Aurelio Manrique, who was returning to the state for the first time since his overthrow; but the former governor was careful not to antagonize Cedillo, and his cautious attitude was a tacit acknowledgement of Cedillo's superior standing with the federal government.[17]

In late 1927 there was a resurgence of Cristero activity throughout the country, and by early the following year the British minister calculated that there were over twenty-four thousand rebels under arms:

> The rebel movement, initiated shortly before the Yaqui rebellion of the fall of 1926, grew steadily, although slowly, through that year and the following one—the months of April, May and June of 1927 seeing the peak of the movement. This declined, in turn, up to the Gómez-Serrano armed movement, when sympathetic outbursts flared up especially in the states of Jalisco, Guanajuato and Nayarit. These in turn grew, fed by religious feeling, economic unrest and distrust of the prevailing Government, through the months of October, November and December.
>
> From 8,000 to 10,000 rebels were in arms towards the end of October 1927, this number increasing to 23,400 by the last day of January 1928. In this latter month we find rebel activities scattered throughout the republic—the States of Sinaloa, Nayarit, Jalisco, Colima, Michoacán, Guanajuato, Aguascalientes, Mexico, Zacatecas, Oaxaca, Puebla and Veracruz, possessing the most numerous rebel bands and witnessing the major activity.
>
> Conditions grew slightly worse in February 1928, the end of the month seeing 24,650 rebels in arms, particularly in the States of Sinaloa, Durango, Zacatecas, Guanajuato, Michoacán, Jalisco, Colima and Mexico State. This increase of rebel activities appeared to be due principally to the result of the Secretary of War's policy of concentration of the pacific country element in affected zones, to greater economic pressure, and to the encouragement given by devoted Catholic elements to rebels in certain States, as Jalisco, Michoacán, Guanajuato, Colima, Zacatecas and Aguascalientes.
>
> It might be added, too, that the inefficiency of certain federal chiefs of operations contributed to the rebel successes. Indeed it may be said that the Federal Government barely held its own during these two months of January and February. The one thing lacking among the various rebel bands in certain parts, and especially in the groups of states contiguous to Jalisco, was a leader capable of uniting in greater part these various groups, and directing their energy against important objectives, i.e., the securing of a Pacific port, control over certain areas, as between Guadalajara and Colima, etc.[18]

The federal army was hard pressed and in several states barely maintained control of the major towns. During this period there was unrest even in San Luis Potosí. In February two federal army officers tried to start a rebellion near Zaragoza but were killed by *agraristas,* and shortly afterwards a separate uprising in Armadillo was also crushed. Six people were executed for complicity in this affair, including the unfortunate parish priest of Armadillo who had opposed the movement.[19]

In the summer there was renewed Cristero activity in Guanajuato and Querétaro. The rebels there were obtaining munitions from San Luis Potosí through a member of Cedillo's staff, Captain Tanguma. This officer was eventually caught and shot, along with another soldier and two civilians; but the unrest grew, and in July Cedillo led an expedition to suppress it. Using the same tactics as before, he soon reduced the level of unrest; however, popular antagonism toward the government remained prevalent.[20]

In Cedillo's absence thirty Cristeros under Fiacro Sánchez crossed into San Luis Potosí from Guanajuato. They took Rayón but were then routed by *agraristas* under Ildefonso Turrubiartes. Twelve were captured and Sánchez and four others were shot in company with two local sympathizers. The rest were executed in October, following further unrest in Guanajuato. Among them was Jacinto Loyola, formerly the inspector general of the Cristeros in Guanajuato, Querétaro, and San Luis Potosí. Thereafter, San Luis Potosí was untroubled by Cristero activity. Deprived of their leaders, lacking support in the countryside, and facing increased security measures, the rebels were unable to organize serious resistance there.[21] Elsewhere, however, the insurgents made important advances during the winter of 1928–1929, for they had finally acquired an overall commander to coordinate their operations. In July 1927 the LNDLR recruited a former Porfirian army officer, Enrique Gorostieta, to direct the Cristeros in Jalisco. He assumed command in October, and inspired by his leadership, the rebels there drove the federals onto the defensive. Gorostieta gradually extended his influence, and by late 1928 most of the Cristeros recognized him as their supreme commander, a position which the League formally granted him in December. Under his guidance the Cristeros grew in strength, and by early 1929 stalemate had been reached: the government was unable to suppress the rebellion, but the rebels were equally unable to topple an administration that enjoyed the support of the United States.[22]

The Cristeros, however, believed that the stalemate might soon be broken in their favor, for the murder of the president-elect, General Obregón, by a Catholic fanatic in July 1928 had dealt a serious blow to the regime and had created a climate of political uncertainty. When Calles's term of office expired in December, his minister of the interior, Emilio Portes Gil, became provisional president. At the same time Calles and his associates formed an "official party," the *Partido Revolucionario Nacional* (PNR), and announced a party convention for the following March to select a presidential candidate to succeed Portes Gil. But those who had expected to profit from Obregón's presidency distrusted Calles's intentions, and there were rumors of plotting in the army. Fearing a possible alliance between these dissident generals and the Cristeros, Portes Gil moved to end the Cristiada. He made several conciliatory gestures toward the church hierarchy while at the same time increasing the military effort against the rebels.[23]

The provisional president turned to Cedillo, the most successful commander in the war against the Cristeros, and instructed him to raise 8,000 men to combat Gorostieta. In political terms Portes Gil was demanding a further payment for the land that Cedillo had distributed to his followers. The first installment had been paid during the De la Huerta revolt, and Cedillo's *agraristas*, many of whom held *ejidos* on a provisional basis, probably wondered how many more installments there would be. Nevertheless, they responded to their leader's summons, and within a few weeks the new force, called the *División del Centro,* was ready to move.[24]

Before Cedillo and his men departed, they were directed to meet a new threat. At the beginning of March, while the PNR convention was taking place at Querétaro, the fears of Portes Gil were realized when an army revolt broke out in the north. This movement, subsequently called the Escobar revolt, was led by a group of generals who had been close to Obregón: Escobar, Manzo, Cruz, Topete, and Aguirre. Believing that the PNR would select Aarón Sáenz as the party's presidential candidate, they issued a revolutionary plan in which they accused Calles of imposing him. In fact, their complaint was premature, since the convention eventually chose Pascual Ortiz Rubio, the former governor of Michoacán, and few doubted that the rebel leaders were simply seeking to obtain the spoils of office of which they had been deprived by Obregón's death. The insurgent generals were supported by a number of politicans who shared their disappointment, among them Aurelio Manrique. He had hoped to receive a senior post in Obregón's administration and believed that Calles was implicated in his death.[25]

Since the bulk of the army remained loyal, the rebels had little chance of success, but with the help they might expect from the Cristeros, their defeat promised to be long and costly. They had hoped that Cedillo would join them, but he wisely rejected their overtures and took his men to join General Almazán in Torreón.[26]

After several weeks of hard fighting the revolt collapsed, and by April the majority of rebel leaders were in exile. Their adventurism cost the country nearly forty million pesos and over two thousand lives. The disillusioned Manrique left with them and spent the next few years working as a film extra in Hollywood.[27]

Cedillo arrived in Lagos, Jalisco, in early April. His forces included his most hardened veterans, whose experience of guerrilla warfare made them the most formidable opponents that the Cristeros claimed ever to have faced. Nevertheless, Cedillo's campaign began with a serious reversal. He had divided his forces into three columns and one of them, under General Rodríguez, was almost immediately ambushed at Tepatitlán by Father Reyes Vega, one of the most talented Cristero leaders who was known as "the frocked Pancho Villa." The Cristeros suffered losses of only twenty-five dead—compared with probably three or four times that number among their opponents—but they included Reyes Vega. Lacking his leadership, they failed to follow up their advantage and retired into the hills.[28]

Following this setback, Cedillo amended his tactics and enjoyed greater success. He spread his men across the countryside in columns of 100, with each column maintaining contact with its immediate neighbors. Whenever they encountered any Cristeros, they concentrated in sufficient force to outnumber them, while still keeping in touch with the rest of the division. In this way they combed the Los Altos region and prevented the Cristeros from mounting any large operations there. At the same time, Cedillo also tried to undermine the revolt by more peaceful means. Unlike many other federal commanders, he refused to countenance looting and released any prisoners who promised to remain peaceful. He also promoted land redistribution, but only in accordance with local wishes, and not to the benefit of politicians or army commanders. Cedillo was, of course, aware that, aided by the American ambassador Dwight Morrow, the government was negotiating a settlement with church leaders, and that reconciliation might soon be needed. But he appears not to have profited from the hostilities, and his humane approach toward his opponents reflected his sympathy and respect for them.[29]

Early in June General Gorostieta was killed in a skirmish. Shortly afterward Cedillo returned to San Luis Potosí with 6,000 of his men, leaving Francisco Carrera Torres in command of the others. They were, however, no longer needed, for in mid-June the government reached an agreement with the church hierarchy and hostilities gradually ceased. On 24 June Cedillo disbanded his men in a ceremony in San Luis Potosí attended by both President Portes Gil and General Amaro, the minister of war. Many of them were rewarded with land, so that in 1929 over one hundred thousand hectares of land were distributed in the form of definitive titles to *ejidos* that had previously been held on a provisional basis.[30]

Soon afterward several Cristero leaders from Jalisco sought Cedillo's permission to settle in San Luis Potosí. Although the recent peace agreement had included an amnesty for rebels who surrendered, the desire for revenge was proving irresistible to many government officers, and faced with persecution and possible murder, the Cristeros recalled Cedillo's earlier generous treatment of them. They were not disappointed because he willingly granted them asylum. They were to remain his loyal followers until his eventual overthrow.[31]

The Escobar revolt was the last occasion for which the government mobilized the *agraristas* in large numbers. During the previous decade, however, they had made a major contribution to preserving the existing regimes. Through their programs of land redistribution, Presidents Obregón, Calles, and Portes Gil had partially bridged the gap between the central government and the mass of the rural population, which had been one of the factors in the overthrow of Díaz's regime and in the weakness of Madero's administration. They had established a chain of patronage that led from the presidency and the federal agrarian bureaucracy to the beneficiaries of the land grants, the *ejidatarios*. At first this system was relatively disorganized and dependent upon the relationship between the central government and a number of regional *caudillos,* such as Saturnino Cedillo. Gradually, however, the system became more formal, as the central government strengthened its position in relation to the regions. The government's clients, the *agraristas,* served their patrons in a variety of ways, but their greatest significance was military. They played an important role in protecting the government in 1923 and 1929, possibly a crucial one in the former case, and were also among the fiercest opponents of the Cristeros. They were frequently used by the federal army commanders in the most dangerous engagements where they suffered heavy losses. On the other hand, the government was always careful to keep the *agraristas* under control, and they were never allowed to pursue their interests in defiance of the government's wishes. (Even Cedillo, for example, the *agrarista* leader who enjoyed most freedom of action, was always careful not to contravene overall government policy.) The existence of the *agraristas* made it impossible for the regime's opponents to mobilize the rural population on a mass basis, even to combat the government's religious policy that was highly unpopular among the rural lower classes. In this respect one might argue that in political terms the agrarian reform was a successful example of divide and rule.

Apart from Cedillo's troops, the government deployed other forces of *agraristas* against the Escobar rebels, numbering some 23,000 at the height of the revolt. Both during and after the fighting these other *agrarista* units were treated differently from Cedillo's men, a fact that illustrated Cedillo's importance and relative independence within the regime. Whereas Cedillo's soldiers always operated together under the personal command of Cedillo and his senior officers, such as Carrera Torres and Turrubiartes, the other forces of *agraristas* were usually dispersed among various regiments of the federal army and thus came under the control of regular army officers. The military authorities took advantage of this to discipline or even eliminate the more radical and independent-minded of the *agrarista* leaders. For example, Guadalupe Rodríguez, a former treasurer of the *Liga Nacional Campesina* (LNC)—the first national organization of *ejidatarios* founded in 1926—who had mobilized 200 *agraristas* in his home state of Durango, was shot in May 1929 for "desertion," probably on orders from Calles.[32]

Once hostilities were over, there was again a contrast in the treatment of Cedillo's followers and the other *agraristas*. Cedillo did not want to lose the influence which his *agraristas* gave him and therefore prevailed upon the government to allow them to keep their weapons when they were demobilized. As a result they continued to act as an important army reserve under his personal leadership. Furthermore, he ensured that the land they received was distributed under his auspices, thus fulfilling his obligations to them as their patron. In short, the arrangements he made for them were much the same as in 1924. In contrast, most of the other *agraristas* were disarmed when they were disbanded. Like Cedillo's men, many of them were also given land, but in their case under the patronage of the agrarian bureaucracy, which assumed control over them from the federal army. In this way President Portes Gil strengthened the position of the newly formed, ruling PNR, in whose name the agrarian bureaucracy now functioned, and repeated his achievement in Tamaulipas, where, as governor, he had used land redistribution to create a clientele in the rural sector. At the same time he issued a revision of the Agrarian Code, thus emphasizing the link between the government and its dependents in the countryside.[33]

As one of the main intermediaries between the central government and the *agraristas,* Saturnino Cedillo played an important part in the development of this policy. He was, however, more than just a tool for the authorities in Mexico City; for unlike the other *agrarista* leaders he took advantage of this position to become a major force in national politics. He achieved this status in two ways. First, by gaining control of the state government from Manrique in 1925, he retained the role of power broker between the central government and the rural population which he had acquired in the early 1920s. This gave him a strong geographical, as well as political, base. Second, he used the military campaigns in 1923–1924 and 1926–1929 to build up his *agraristas* into a formidable fighting force, answerable only to himself. While always deploying them within the structure of the federal army, he never relaxed his personal control over the men that he recruited. In the delicate political conditions of the decade, and in view of the important services he rendered, successive presidents and ministers of war tolerated and even encouraged Cedillo's formation of what was virtually a private army, and also sanctioned his use of land redistribution to reward his followers. As time went on, the political risk of disarming his men or incorporating them into regular army units increased, but on the other hand, in view of Cedillo's loyalty to the regime, such measures appeared unnecessary. Certainly Portes Gil, whose administration Cedillo helped to preserve, had no such intentions. Therefore, as 1929 drew to a close, Cedillo's position appeared stronger than ever.

CHAPTER 6

THE CEDILLISTA REGIME

IT IS STILL TRUE, HOWEVER, TO SAY THAT IN SOME OF THE MORE DISTANT STATES THE CENTRAL GOVERNMENT IS MERELY A NAME AND THE INHABITANTS REMAIN AT THE MERCY OF THE INDIVIDUAL GOVERNOR AND AUTHORITIES OF THE STATE.——British Minister Edmund Monson in Mexico City, 1933

GENERAL CEDILLO IS STILL THE POWER THAT CONTROLS POLITICS IN SAN LUIS POTOSÍ, RUMORS TO THE CONTRARY STARTED BY HIS ENEMIES NOTWITHSTANDING.——U.S. Consul George P. Shaw in San Luis Potosí, 1932

From 1929 to 1934 the government of Mexico was dominated by the figure of Plutarco Elías Calles, the former president and the founder of the PNR. Known as the Jefe Máximo (Supreme Leader), a title from which the period has come to be known as the Maximato, Calles controlled the nation's affairs from behind the throne of three successive presidents: Emilio Portes Gil (1928–1930), Pascual Ortiz Rubio (1930–1932), and Abelardo Rodríguez (1932–1934). Although Calles had the rank of general and served as minister of war under both Portes Gil and Ortiz Rubio, his power base was not so much the army as the ruling PNR. With the assistance of lesser machine politicians such as Gonzalo Santos from San Luis Potosí, he manipulated the party in favor of his preferred policies and the continuation of his political hegemony.[1]

While Calles dominated the government in Mexico City, Cedillo reached the high point of his own rule in San Luis Potosí. In the early 1930s his position there appeared unassailable. His regime was, however, different in nature from those of other successful provincial politicians, such as Portes Gil in Tamaulipas, Adalberto Tejeda in Veracruz, or Tomás Garrido Canabal in Tabasco. Tejeda and Garrido Canabal based their power upon the political machines that they organized from the seat of the state government. Having become governors through the influence of patrons in the army or federal government, they used their own powers of patronage to create a personal following. In the urban sector they either reached an accord with local labor leaders, or, if industrial labor was poorly organized, they created unions identified with themselves. In the countryside they formed a clientele through land redistribution and brought their clients together into agrarian leagues.[2]

In contrast, Cedillo's power base was independent of the state bureaucracy, and he acquired it before he assumed political office. Both his position in San Luis Potosí and his value to the central government rested upon his agrarian colonies and the support of the local *ejidatarios*. Together they provided him with a private army, and in return he guaranteed their tenure of land. From this rural and military power base he gradually gained control of the state government: at first through dependents in the congress; then, after overthrowing Manrique, through Abel Cano; and finally, by assuming the governorship himself. Between 1926 and 1929 he installed his clients in all the important posts within the administration: the congress, the bureaucracy, the local representation of the federal government, the municipal authorities and the arbitration boards for labor disputes. From then until his overthrow in 1938, he continued to govern the state in this way.

Cedillo did not, however, take advantage of his dominance to create an organized political movement. Instead of incorporating his rural support into an urban-based party machine, he brought to the state government the atmosphere of the rural municipalities from which he and his companions had originated. The characteristics of his regime were therefore those associated with the rule of a village patriarch: social conservatism, respect for the obligations of kinship, and personal loyalty. From Palomas, where he spent as much time as possible, he distributed largesse and held unofficial court, more like a medieval baron than a modern politician. This help was expressed on an individual basis rather than according to any overall plan. He organized few schemes to irrigate land, build roads, or improve social services; but he always heeded petitioners—finding them jobs, ensuring that lawsuits were speeded up, or making them gifts of money. And, if nothing else, visitors were always given free board while they waited for Cedillo to hear their case.[3]

Palomas was an appropriate setting for the center of such a regime since it accurately reflected the tastes and aspirations not only of Cedillo, the erstwhile *ranchero*, but also of most of his rustic followers. Describing it after a visit there in 1931, the local American consul wrote:

> The house is two stories high, with the first story made of concrete with loopholes on three sides. It has a room for moving pictures which will seat 100 or more people. He [Cedillo] has electric refrigerators, electric lights, a billiard room, a double bowling alley of the latest type. He has drilled three wells for water, and has found some—quantity undetermined. He has a dug well [sic] which furnishes warm hard water. This water is used in his private bath in the basement of his house. It is 16 feet square and 5 feet deep, illuminated with colored

electric lights and bright paintings. It is said to accomodate [sic] large parties. On the ranch the Governor maintains blooded race horses, cattle, swine and fowls.[4]

This environment, in which the trappings of the nouveau riche coexisted uneasily with the coarse rusticity of *ranchero* life, was one in which Cedillo's henchmen and followers felt at ease, one which, given the chance, they would have adopted for themselves. Most of his intimates shared his background. Ildefonso Turrubiartes and Mateo Hernández Netro, who succeeded Cedillo in the governorship, were a former *ranchero* and a *hacienda* peon, respectively, and the original leaders of two of his colonies. Others of a similar ilk were Marcelino Zúñiga, the municipal president of San Luis Potosí in 1929, and Vicente Segura, his successor, both from Ciudad del Maíz, Benigno Sandoval and the brothers José and Epifanio Castillo, all three of whom led troops of Cedillo's *agraristas* in his 1929 campaign. All of these men occupied seats in the state congress—José Castillo for four terms and Zúñiga for three—as well as a number of other posts. Other important figures in Cedillo's "inner group" were Francisco Carrera Torres, the chief of military operations in the state for ten years; Colonel Josué Escobedo, his chief of staff during his campaigns against the Cristeros and secretary of the state government in 1930; Eugenio Jiménez, probably Cedillo's closest political adviser in the early 1930s and the person who usually stood in for him when he was absent during his governorship; Rutilio Alamilla, a state congressman from 1925 to 1931, thereafter a federal senator and finally the secretary of the state government until Cedillo's overthrow; Ignacio Cuellar, the leader of an *agrarista* militia unit in Guadalcázar, who was secretary of the state government under Turrubiartes—a crucial position in view of the fact that Turrubiartes was illiterate—and four times a state congressman; Colonel Ernesto Von Merck, a German soldier of fortune who arrived in San Luis Potosí in the 1920s, was befriended by Cedillo, and became the chief of police in the state capital; Luis Lárraga, another militia commander, who was a state congressman for nine years and one of Cedillo's bodyguards; Efrén González, Cedillo's brother-in-law and another of his bodyguards; Hipólito Cedillo, his nephew, who was municipal president of San Luis Potosí in 1934; and José Arvide, his personal secretary.[5]

Perhaps Cedillo's regime was best exemplified in the person of Ildefonso Turrubiartes, whose friendship with Cedillo dated from before 1910, when he was a *ranchero* near Cerritos. Turrubiartes fought with Cedillo from 1912 to 1920 and was rewarded with the command of the largest of the agrarian colonies, "Alvaro Obregón." He later acquired a small property near the colony from the former *hacienda* of Lagunillas. A resourceful guerrilla leader, Turrubiartes served with Cedillo during the De la Huerta revolt and the Cristero rebellion. The occupation of the governorship by this illiterate farmer was both proof and symbol of Cedillo's power, for Cedillo imposed him against the wishes of President Ortiz Rubio. (The president's own choice for the post was Lamberto Hernández, also an associate of Cedillo, who was a senator and the head of the Federal Government Central Department.) Turrubiartes's election represented the victory of the countryside over the town, and of the rural militia who had borne the brunt of the fighting during the Revolution over the urban middle classes who had stayed at home. Within the rest of Mexico few men like Turrubiartes held important posts by 1930. Most of his counterparts had either been liquidated during the regime's consolidation from 1916 to 1929, or had been absorbed into the bourgeoisie. In San Luis Potosí, however, under the aegis of Cedillo, they controlled the administration, assisted by opportunistic civilians bent upon self-enrichment.[6]

Away from the two main centers of power of San Luis Potosí and Palomas, Cedillo controlled the state through a network of *caciques*—local political bosses. The most important of them—until he began to distance himself from Cedillo about eighteen months before Cedillo's overthrow—was Gonzalo Santos. After his family's precipitate action in 1923, Santos had preserved the clan's position in the Huasteca by aligning himself with Cedillo. When Cedillo was ordered to combat the Cristeros in Guanajuato in 1928, Santos raised a troop of cavalry from among the Huasteca Indians, leading them personally during the campaign. While accepting Cedillo's hegemony over the state, Santos was ruthless in protecting his personal domain from any local rival, as he showed on more than one occasion. He was, however, a shrewd politician, and one of the first to recognize the potential of the PNR as a power base. Elected to the federal congress, he was appointed to the Permanent Commission of that body in 1929. He worked closely with Cedillo and also, during the first years of the PNR, with Calles.[7] Other more parochial, but nevertheless important, figures were Pedro Izaguirre in Tamasopo, Severo Aguilar in Salinas, Tomás Tapia in Villa de Reyes, J. Pilar García in Mexquitic, Alberto Araujo in Charcas, Benigno Sandoval in Matehuala, Gabriel Barrientos in Vanegas, Santana Mendoza in Rayón, Rafael Anaya in Cárdenas, and Magdaleno García in Villa Hidalgo. Their power bases varied; most of them commanded the local militia of *agraristas* that Cedillo founded when he disbanded his forces in 1929. Some, such as Araujo, also controlled the municipal administration; Izaguirre ran a sugar producers' cooperative in Tamasopo, while Tapia's strength lay in the *ejidatarios* whom he had organized around Villa de Reyes. Like Gonzalo Santos, they were ruthless in defending their position when they deemed it necessary, but this was not frequently the case until Cedillo's whole regime came under pressure in 1936–37.[8]

Although Cedillo exercised the same influence over the state economy as he did over its political life, he did not acquire wealth on the same scale as most of the other leading figures within the regime. He lacked the entrepreneurial instincts and talents of men like General Abelardo Rodríguez, who had become a peso millionaire through the gambling saloons he established when governor of Baja California, or General Andreu Almazán, whose business interests were worth five and one-half million dollars in 1940. Cedillo's most important business concern was probably his control over the production and marketing of *ixtle*, conducted through *La Compañía Nacional Ixtlera* and the *Banco Ixtlero*, which he shared with, among others, Francisco Carrera Torres and two local *hacendados*, Eduardo Meade and Ignacio Curiel. Together these two enterprises had a virtual monopoly on marketing the state's *ixtle* output. He also owned the local bus company, and his sister, Higinia, shared the franchise for the municipal slaughterhouse in San Luis Potosí with Rutilio Alamilla.[9] Otherwise, Cedillo's money-making interests were largely parasitical: taking a percentage from the profits of local business or dipping into the state treasury. Sometimes his demands upon the state had a serious impact upon local government finances, particularly when the depression affected the revenue from mining. When, for example, Cedillo went to Europe in June 1930, he not only extracted enforced contributions toward his expenses from local politicians and members of the state bureaucracy, but he also collected the taxes for the balance of the year from all the principal businesses in San Luis Potosí. The effect of this action was temporarily to leave the local authorities in some financial embarrassment. In 1932 the American consul reported that Cedillo was receiving 200 pesos per day from the state governor and 100 pesos per day from the municipal president of San Luis Potosí, his brother-in-law, Efrén González. When Cedillo became minister of agriculture under Cárdenas in 1935, he treated the funds of the Ministry in a similarly cavalier fashion. Although it was common at this time for Mexican ministers to find jobs and sinecures for their friends and followers—for example Tomás Garrido Canabal, Cedillo's predecessor in the post, "employed," under the Ministry's auspices, members of the student organization popularly known as the Red Shirts, which he sponsored in his home state of Tabasco—Cedillo's enemies claimed that his activities in this respect cost the treasury more than a million pesos over two years. He also made occasional gifts from official funds to his clients or camp followers. Finally Cedillo also used the Ministry's money to acquire weapons for his militia, although equally damaging malpractices were far from uncommon elsewhere in the government during this period.[10]

Such a personal and parasitical style of government caused economic stagnation in San Luis Potosí. Local businessmen initially welcomed the rise of Cedillo, pleased by the change in official attitudes toward labor unrest and to government interference in industry and commerce. However, they were soon disappointed, for Cedillo's regime gave them little assistance such as tax concessions or government investment in the infrastructure of the local economy. As a result neither mining nor industry prospered as much as before 1910, and San Luis Potosí languished in comparison with other northern cities. With the onset of the Great Depression this situation worsened. Oil production at El Ébano dropped sharply, and, with the collapse in metal prices, mining and smelting—the most important sector of the state's economy in terms of the value of production—were also badly affected, several of the more important mines being forced to close or operate at a much lower rate of output. This naturally had an important spin-off effect upon a number of local businesses and also reduced government revenues.[11]

The government's inability to manage its finances satisfactorily in the strained circumstances of the depression led to the only public challenge to Cedillo's regime in San Luis Potosí during the Maximato. Unable to meet all its commitments—including its subsidies to Cedillo—on a reduced income, the administration began to hold back salaries, and from April 1931 onward the 168 teachers in the capital were not paid. At the end of August, 106 of them went on strike and circulated a petition to Cedillo outlining their grievances. The authorities reacted quickly to the strike: they appointed a new director of education, closed the printing press that had been used for the petition, and replaced the teachers with strike breakers, mainly nurses and minor bureaucrats. Undaunted, the teachers appealed for help to their union, the *Confederación Nacional de Organizaciones Magisteriales* (CNOM), which publicized their plight in the national press. They also received support from local unions and parents' associations, which formed a "defense committee" to assist them. Efforts by the government to obtain money for the teachers proved unavailing, and on 22 November some of them began a protest march to Mexico City, accompanied by members of the defense committee. The teachers involved were immediately arrested on the orders of Turrubiartes, but that night twenty-one of them were removed from the penitentiary by Ernesto Von Merck, the chief of police, and local officials. The six women teachers were sent to detention in Guadalcázar, while the men were taken to Palomas and put to work repairing roads and tending Cedillo's estate.[12]

In Mexico City the kidnapping caused a sensation. The CNOM requested the intervention of President Ortiz Rubio, and friends of the teachers met with Manuel Téllez, the interior minister, to seek his help. In San Luis Potosí, some of the other teachers began a hunger strike, and several hundred workers and students demonstrated outside the governor's office. Turrubiartes was embarrassed by the kidnapping—which had been carried out on Cedillo's instructions—and at the instigation of Carrera Torres, who was transmitting orders from Calles, he had the detained teachers released. Shortly afterward he resolved the problem by obtaining the federal government's agreement to cover the debts of his administration.[13]

The teachers' strike exposed the financial mismanagement and political ineptitude of Cedillo's regime and in so doing tarnished its image. It also underlined the rift between Cedillo and organized labor. Cedillo never understood the problems of industrial laborers, whose environment was so distinct from his own. For their part, local industrial workers, whom Manrique had favored, resented Cedillo's preference for rural interests and his tendency to support employers in disputes. At first lukewarm toward Cedillo's regime, they later opposed it actively. Cedillo also neglected the local miners, except those living in rural communities who were eligible for *ejidos*. But the position of nonagricultural labor in San Luis Potosí was vulnerable. First, industrial and mining workers together numbered only 25,186 in 1930, compared with the 130,800 persons employed in agriculture (including the 32,732 *ejidatarios*). More importantly, however, they lacked the support of a powerful national labor organization that they would have needed to confront Cedillo. The once mighty

CROM had gone into decline after President Portes Gil, who had earlier clashed with the organization when he was governor of Tamaulipas, had broken with it shortly after taking office. (Portes Gil had taken advantage of the fact that many senior generals had suspected Luis Morones, the leader of the CROM, of involvement in the assassination of Obregón.) Without government patronage the CROM disintegrated, as many of its member groups sought to reach an independent accommodation with the authorities. This fragmenting of the labor movement had seriously prejudiced the position of workers in states such as San Luis Potosí, where they didn't enjoy local government favor. Finally, industrial workers and, even more, miners were the major victims of the hardship and unemployment caused by the depression, which further reduced their ability to defend their interests.[14]

In the countryside in San Luis Potosí, the Maximato was a period of stabilization and retrenchment, marked by a reduction in the pace of land redistribution. Perhaps somewhat surprising at first sight, there are several reasons why Cedillo failed to give greater impetus to agrarian reform in these years. In the first place, relative to the national government's ambivalent and self-interested encouragement of land reform, much had already been achieved in the state. By May 1930, apart from the eleven agrarian colonies that Cedillo had established by then, and including both provisional and definitive *ejidal* grants, 811,800 hectares of land had been distributed to 32,732 *ejidatarios* among the 130,800 persons employed in agriculture. This was the third largest area of land distributed in any state (behind Chihuahua and Yucatán) and in both percentage and absolute terms easily the highest total of *ejidatarios* among those working in agriculture in any of the eleven states in the north of the country. (It was followed by Zacatecas with 16,307 *ejidatarios* out of 108,522 and Chihuahua with 11,082 out of 102,413.) Although 81,200 persons, or 62.1% of those making their living out of agriculture, were still landless, this figure was nevertheless below the national average. From the perspective of a peasant in most of the republic, San Luis Potosí did not seem a bad locality. In the second place, until the new Agrarian Code was issued in April 1934, the majority of the rural population, the *peones acasillados*, were ineligible to petition for *ejidos*. Although Cedillo had never paid too much attention to legal niceties, this fact inevitably acted as an inhibition upon wholesale land redistribution.[15]

Apart from these considerations, Cedillo was not an agrarian ideologue like Aurelio Manrique or Antonio Díaz Soto y Gama. He did not favor wholesale confiscation of land, the bureaucratization of land tenure, or the establishment of collectives. Rather he saw the reform as a means by which the rural population could be provided with land for its own use, whether in colony, *ejido,* or *hacienda.* His initial support for land redistribution in the Ciudad del Maíz region had been designed to reward his followers and establish a power base. When Nieto and Manrique subsequently promoted further land redistribution, he generally supported them, both for reasons of social justice and in order to extend his rural clientele. He opposed their efforts only when they conflicted with the interests of his colonists or orders from Mexico City, or were inappropriate to local circumstances (e.g., where an *ejidal* grant would have deprived the *peones acasillados* on the *hacienda* in question of their means of sustenance).[16]

Following the resettlement of his veterans after the Escobar revolt, Cedillo took a more cautious approach to further land redistribution, which thereafter declined.[17] He had already ceased to be the *bête noir* of the local *hacendados* and now assumed the role of mediator in petitions for land. As a local *hacendado* later recalled, "[In 1932] we were in the middle of the Cedillista dictatorship. He was lord and master of the state, and nothing was resolved unless 'the chief' had given a direct order to that effect. It was necessary for one to be constantly going to Palomas where he lived."[18] This situation fitted in with Cedillo's position as supreme arbiter of the affairs of San Luis Potosí and his desire to offer the kind of guarantees to the private sector that might encourage investment and increase production. On the other hand, there was also less pressure for land redistribution. This was partly due to the fact that the more urgent demands for it had been met and that wages and the conditions for renters and sharecroppers had generally improved.[19] But it was also because, for some potential *ejidatarios*, the possible cost of obtaining land was too high. The price of an *ejidal* plot anywhere in Mexico was client status, usually to an ambitious governor or agrarian politician. In San Luis Potosí this status took the form of obedience to Cedillo's political or military needs. For many this had been, and continued to be, an acceptable price to pay. But for others it was not. When, for example, in 1929, a CNA official asked the inhabitants of Milpitas, near Río Verde, why they didn't want land, they replied that it was due to "the certainty they felt that with the land they would also acquire the obligation to serve the government arms in hand, and that they were not disposed to be soldiers."[20] Three years later the same official was told by the members of the Anteojos *ejido* that they didn't want an addition to their existing landholding since "they were aware that in the recent recruiting of auxiliary forces which the state commissioners carried out, the commissioners made it clear that any individual who might want land would necessarily have to serve as a soldier."[21]

In declining to lend his support to increased land redistribution during the Maximato, Cedillo was undoubtedly influenced by the knowledge that his attitude fitted in with the overall policy of the regime. For under Ortiz Rubio the agrarian reform program virtually ceased. There were two main causes for this. The first was that with the end of the Cristero revolt and the diminishing threat of a military uprising, the government no longer relied as heavily upon the *agraristas*. The second reason was economic. The men who dominated the regime in 1930, Calles and his inner circle of confidants, had always regarded agrarian reform as an instrument of pacification and a means of furthering the development of a rural middle class. With the land and credit provided by the government, the *ejidatarios* were expected to accumulate capital and then extend their interests on their own account. They were, in effect, to merge into the private sector. In practice, however, most *ejidatarios* were given land without the means to become commercial farmers. They remained an exploited minority within the rural population, since the failure of the government agricultural credit banks meant that they had to resort to private money lenders, whose exorbitant terms of business crippled them. Similarly they often depended upon intermediaries to market their goods and were thus at a disadvantage in comparison with large private producers enjoying direct access to the market. Above all they were subject to abuse from politicians and agrarian bureaucrats, many of whom used their privileged position to exploit the *ejidal* sector for personal profit. In view of these factors many grew only what they needed for their own consumption and failed to produce a market surplus.[22]

On the other hand, even though the *ejidos* remained a backward pocket in the rural economy, their existence impeded the recovery of the private sector from the ravages of the years 1910 to 1920. A period of uninterrupted peace and large injections of capital had been needed after 1920 to restore productivity, but neither was forthcoming. Since conditions remained unsettled in many areas, some *hacendados* never returned to their properties. Others who had remained during the decade of violence or returned soon afterward lost some of their most productive land in *ejidal* grants to nearby communities. But the most damaging effect of the agrarian laws was the creation of an atmosphere that deterred investment. Landowners were often reluctant to carry out improvements in their properties, fearing that this might increase the possibility of expropriation. This was less true of plantation owners whose properties were protected under the law, but even they were reluctant to invest in some states, such as Yucatán or Veracruz. The general rule among *hacendados* was to seek short-term profits while allowing their estates to run down.[23]

Faced with this situation, the authorities had two choices: they could either improve the agrarian bureaucracy, increase land redistribution, provide the *ejidos* with adequate capital, and make them the basic unit of agricultural production; or, as the influental American ambassador Dwight Morrow advocated to Calles, they could halt land redistribution and create a feeling of confidence among landowners which would stimulate investment in agriculture. For reasons of self-interest and in accordance with their ideological preference for private rather than state farming, they chose the latter course. Ortiz Rubio purged the agrarian bureaucracy of radicals and tried to raise the proportion of compensation for expropriated land which was paid in currency rather than in government bonds. (The bonds, which had previously been almost the only form of compensation, were quoted at 10% of their face value in private dealings.) He also instructed state governors to set a time limit on further petitions for land.[24]

Among the majority of state governors who complied with Ortiz Rubio's request—at least on paper—was Cedillo. In view of his firm power base in the countryside, he saw no political risks in accepting the president's mandate, and for the reasons already mentioned he was authorizing a decreasing number of provisional *ejidal* grants. On the other hand, even after he informed the congress in September 1930 that "the first phase of the agrarian problem, in other words the granting of land, has ended in this state," he did not halt land redistribution altogether. Ever a pragmatist, he considered that some petitions should still be met, primarily in order to maintain his position as the final arbiter in the state in such matters.[25]

Cedillo's relations with Mexico City continued to be based upon mutual expediency. For as long as the central government allowed him a free hand in San Luis Potosí, he was willing to remain basically loyal. On the other side, while there was little love lost between Ortiz Rubio and Cedillo, the president did not want to provoke him into revolt. From the point of view of Calles, Cedillo was a useful instrument to assist him in keeping a check on the president, in case he showed any tendency toward excessive independence.

In the 1929 elections Cedillo used his control over the state to ensure an almost unanimous vote for Ortiz Rubio. Thereafter, however, his relations with the president deteriorated. Contrary to expectation, Ortiz Rubio did not offer Cedillo a cabinet post. Then, on his inauguration day, the president was the victim of an assassination attempt by Daniel Flores, a young man from Charcas in San Luis Potosí. In spite of being cruelly tortured, Flores refused to say why he had acted against Ortiz Rubio. It was rumored that Calles had inspired the attempt in order to maintain his dominance in national politics; and the fact that Cedillo was counted among his most loyal supporters, coupled with Flores's origins, was used to support this theory. For his part Ortiz Rubio linked the assassination attempt to his plans to purge the national congress of certain well-known Callistas, including Gonzalo Santos, whom he considered hopelessly corrupt. The affair was never resolved and cast a cloud over both the president's first months in office and his relations with Cedillo. Flores, who probably acted upon his own initiative, died in prison in 1932, having destroyed his family by his action.[26]

Some months later, in the summer of 1930, Cedillo took a leave of absence and went on a tour of Europe. It was widely rumored that the president wanted him out of the way, perhaps because he still believed that Cedillo was plotting against him. In any event he made a 30,000-peso contribution to Cedillo's expenses. General Joaquín Amaro, the war minister, also contributed 10,000 pesos to the trip. This was probably largely a gesture of goodwill designed to win Cedillo's support for his presidential ambitions, but Amaro was also involved in carrying out a radical reorganization of the army and might have considered that Cedillo's absence would make the task easier. Cedillo spent most of his time in Europe in Spain, where he looked up some traders who had once lived in Cerritos and had helped him when he was being hunted by the Carrancistas fifteen years before. He also visited a number of other countries and later informed his friends that he had been particularly impressed by the achievements of Kemal Ataturk and Benito Mussolini, although he hoped that the latter would make his regime more democratic in due course. Cedillo soon became homesick for Palomas, however, and returned to San Luis Potosí where he completed his term as governor.[27]

In the summer of 1931 there were a series of complex political maneuvers in

Mexico City as Ortiz Rubio, aided by Amaro, sought to weaken Calles's influence over his government. In retaliation Calles used his supporters in the congress, led by Gonzalo Santos, to force Ortiz Rubio to make some cabinet changes. As a result Cedillo became minister of agriculture and joined Amaro, Lázaro Cárdenas, and Andreu Almazán as the fourth general in the new cabinet. Calles then inspired rumors of a fresh cabinet crisis, and, at his instigation, Almazán and Cedillo approached Cárdenas in October and persuaded him that they and Amaro should all resign. They then put the proposal to Amaro, who grudgingly accepted. Calles had thus achieved his aim of removing Amaro and weakening Ortiz Rubio. Cedillo, always loathe to be away from Palomas for very long, but slightly piqued at not being given a post in the reformed cabinet, returned home.[28]

For the next two years Cedillo remained in San Luis Potosí. His dominance there continued to be absolute. In June 1932, for example, he ensured the unopposed election of the PNR candidates throughout the state, all of whom he had previously approved. That same year he had the name of Ciudad del Maíz changed to Magdaleno Cedillo, in honor of his dead brother.[29] A more significant indication of his power, however, was his reaction to the government's policy of "socialist education." This doctrine, first debated in 1932 by Narciso Bassols, Ortiz Rubio's education minister, and adopted by the PNR as official party policy at its second national convention in December 1933, was finally incorporated into an amendment to Article 3 of the constitution in December 1934. The policy was never clearly defined—Article 3 stated that its objective was to create in children's minds "a rational and exact concept of the universe"—but was basically an attempt to establish the supremacy of secular over religious education. It was, however, open to a variety of interpretations: according to Ignacio García Téllez, the minister of education under Lázaro Cárdenas, its objective was to "inculcate the youth of the country with a revolutionary spirit, with a view to their fighting against the capitalistic regime and to establishing a dictatorship of the proletariat."[30] Left-wing teachers often used it as authority to launch attacks upon the church or to give instruction in the basic tenets of Marxism. Not surprisingly the policy evoked a fierce reaction from Catholic activists and led to frequent incidents of violence between teachers and religious extremists. Cedillo, who ever since the Cristero war had permitted an unusual degree of religious toleration in San Luis Potosí in comparison to the rest of the country, considered the new policy provocative and a gratuitous cause of offense to the local population. He therefore discouraged its implementation in the state, prohibited the introduction there of the new textbooks based upon the doctrine, and allowed private schools to flourish. By 1934, rich Catholic families from other parts of Mexico had begun to send their children to be educated in San Luis Potosí. The central government, aware of the unpopularity of socialist education in many quarters, permitted Cedillo to have his way.[31]

In September 1932 Ortiz Rubio resigned, the victim of Calles's determination to remain in control of national politics. His successor was General Abelardo Rodríguez, the millionaire governor of Baja California, a Sonoran who had risen to power with Obregón and Calles.[32] When Rodríguez assumed office, Mexico was suffering from the effects of the depression. The prices of agricultural and mineral exports, on which the country's economy remained heavily dependent, had fallen sharply, causing serious problems for producers. There were signs of popular discontent in both the cities and the countryside, where wage laborers agitated for access to land, and *ejidatarios*, under the new landlord class of agrarian bureaucrats, agitated for the freedom to grow subsistence crops.[33] In these circumstances many younger members of the PNR lost faith in the capitalist orthodoxy practiced by Calles and his associates under the influence of the former American ambassador Dwight Morrow and called for more radical solutions to the country's problems.[34]

Rodríguez, an astute politician, deemed it prudent to appease these younger radical elements. In July 1933 he restored the right to petition for land and with it those state agrarian commissions that had been abolished.[35] In September he established a minimum wage and in December reorganized the agrarian bureaucracy. The CNA was abolished and replaced by the Agrarian Department, the *Departamento de Asuntos Agrarios y Colonización* (DAAC), which concerned itself with all aspects of the reform. That same month the PNR published a Six-Year Plan, a detailed program for the administration of the country during the next presidential term (1934–1940). This also reflected the views of the radicals and was in itself an indication of this new approach to government. Finally, in April 1934, a new and more comprehensive agrarian code was published, the most important feature of which was that for the first time *peones acasillados* were given the right to petition for land, although renters and sharecroppers were still excluded. Rodríguez did not, however, intend these moves to herald a fundamental departure from previous government policy. Having restored the right to petition for *ejidos*, he did not, for example, give a stimulus to land redistribution. He was acting to preempt dissent and maintain party unity during the period up to the 1934 presidential elections.[36]

Nevertheless, the PNR's radical "Young Turks" took heart from his reforms, and, led by Manrique's former collaborator, Graciano Sánchez, they turned their attention to the selection of the party's candidate for the elections. Seeking to end Calles's domination of the PNR, they resisted the widely expected choice of one of his intimates—probably Manuel Pérez Treviño—for the office. They formed a tactical alliance with other, more influential figures who shared their aims, either for personal reasons, or because they feared that Calles's virtual dictatorship threatened the stability of the regime. The latter group included Andreu Almazán, Lázaro Cárdenas, Portes Gil, Cedillo, and President Rodríguez himself. Together they sought a candidate who was acceptable to Calles but prepared to respect the pressure for reform.[37]

The three most likely choices were Adalberto Tejeda, Lázaro Cárdenas, and Cedillo. Of the three, Cárdenas was the strongest candidate: Tejeda was regarded by many as too radical, and Cedillo, whom the anticlericals considered too conciliatory toward the church, was reluctant to accept nomination.[38] Before putting his name forward, Cárdenas wanted a guarantee of military support if he should clash with Calles. He received this assurance from Cedillo, who had advocated Cárdenas's candidacy as early as May 1932. Cedillo then discussed the question with Calles, who, while obviously preferring Pérez Treviño, agreed to accept Cárdenas if he proved to be the party's choice. On 1 May Cárdenas's supporters, led by Portes Gil and Cedillo, launched his candidacy at an agrarian congress in San Luis Potosí. His official nomination remained in doubt until Calles's two sons also endorsed Cárdenas. Erroneously assuming that they spoke for their father, numerous politicians and generals hastened to join the Cárdenas bandwagon. Shortly thereafter, Pérez Treviño admitted defeat and withdrew from the race.[39]

Cárdenas's victory was then guaranteed, but he nevertheless went on an unprecedented campaign tour covering over 27,500 kilometers. During this journey he began to hint that once in office he might pursue more radical policies than those favored by Calles, a fact displeasing to the Jefe Máximo:

> There have been rumors of late that General Calles and the inner ring of politicians who control the country are beginning to have serious doubts as to whether General Cárdenas is going to prove to be as accommodating and amenable as was at first supposed. To judge from his recent speeches General Cárdenas has got a little out of control and shows signs of moving more and more to the left.[40]

However, in spite of his concern, Calles still believed that he would be able to manipulate Cárdenas as he had his predecessors. With his blessing the PNR machine and the government bureaucracy ensured Cárdenas's election by an overwhelming margin.[41]

As for Cedillo, he appeared to be at the height of his power. His control of his home state was unchallenged, and although his relations with the central government were not always harmonious, he nevertheless remained a pillar of the regime. Moreover, his close identification with the election of Cárdenas appeared to have strengthened his position even further. Beneath the surface, however, the underlying currents of Mexican politics were beginning to flow against him, and there were just a few indications that all might not be well. The basis of Cedillo's power as a regional *caudillo* and his value to the government lay in his agrarian colonies and his ability to mobilize large numbers of *agraristas*. In this respect he had been of great service to the regime in the unstable climate of the 1920s. But the end of the Cristero rebellion and the suppression of the Escobar revolt, combined with the foundation of the PNR, were to herald a new period in the country's political life: one in which the institutions of government were to be further strengthened and centralized. The age of the machine politician and the agrarian bureaucrat was dawning, personified by men such as Gonzalo Santos and Graciano Sánchez. In this context Cedillo's highly personalized and informal rule in San Luis Potosí—exemplified by his arbitrary handling of the teachers' strike—was beginning to look incongruous. If he were to retain his dominant position in the state during the next presidential term, he would need to adapt both his regime and his own political style to this development of more institutionalized government in the country as a whole. Nothing he had said or done during the last years of the Maximato indicated that he recognized this. Nor, to date, had he demonstrated that he possessed the qualities that he would need if he were to thrive in the emerging era of machine politics. As 1935 opened, Cedillo's political future was less assured than he or most of his close associates probably appreciated.

CHAPTER 7

CEDILLO AND CÁRDENAS

IF GENERAL CEDILLO CONTINUES TO SHOW OPPOSITION TO THE GOVERN-
MENT, I WILL PUT HIM INTO A MINISTRY. I WOULD PREFER TO KEEP THE
COUNTRY PERFECTLY AT PEACE, SO AS TO CARRY FORWARD THE ECONOMIC
PLAN IN FAVOR OF THE WORKERS, RATHER THAN HAVE TO CARRY OUT A MIL-
ITARY CAMPAIGN.——Lázaro Cárdenas in his diary, 15 March 1935

During his six years as president (1934–1940), Lázaro Cárdenas paid more attention to agrarian and labor reform than did any of his predecessors. His activity in these fields formed part of his overall policy of strengthening the role of the central bureaucracy and of promoting social justice. To a certain extent his dedication to reform was also motivated by the economic and political problems that he confronted when he assumed office. Although it is difficult to assess the impact of the depression upon the Mexican economy, it undoubtedly had a detrimental effect upon some sectors. Metal production fell sharply after 1929 as a consequence of falling demand on world markets, and at least for a short time some of the country's manufacturing industries were affected by a similar decline in the home market. Moreover, oil exports virtually ceased in 1931 when it became cheaper for the oil companies to import oil into Mexico than to continue production.[1] In agriculture there was a sharp drop in the volume and prices of exports, particularly of cash crops such as sugar, cotton, tobacco, coffee, and sisal. In contrast, subsistence agriculture—which meant much of the *ejidal* sector—was, of course, largely untouched by such external factors. There was also the social problem caused by the repatriation of Mexican workers from the United States, who numbered over 240,000 during the two years 1931 and 1932. In these circumstances there was pressure in some quarters to increase land redistribution in order to alleviate the difficulties of those workers most affected by the crisis.[2] On the political front a credibility gap had opened between the government's past promises and current achievements. In the PNR, Calles had forged a powerful instrument for executing policy. But the regime commanded the loyalty of only the privileged minority who benefitted from its powers of patronage. As the Cristero war had revealed, the government remained in power because it could suppress opposition, rather than because of its popularity. The growing isolation of the country's leaders was illustrated by the rise of the young radicals in the PNR who had campaigned to put Cárdenas into office. In association with some of their leaders, such as Graciano Sánchez, Cárdenas was to pursue policies designed to raise living standards, particularly in the rural sector, and thus to increase the government's popularity and power base.[3]

Cárdenas's first cabinet was a careful balance of radicals and conservatives. The former, who were newly appointed to cabinet rank by Cárdenas, were Gabino Vázquez (head of the Agrarian Department), Ignacio García Téllez (Education), Francisco Múgica (National Economy), and Silvano Barba González (Labor). The latter were closely associated with Calles, and included Rodolfo Calles (Communications), Juan de Dios Bojórquez (Interior), Tomás Garrido Canabal (Agriculture), and Aarón Sáenz (head of the Department of the Federal District). The structure of the cabinet suggested that Cárdenas intended to continue the cautious renewal of land reform and the guarded support for organized labor instigated and shown by Rodríguez.[4] In retrospect, however, the new president's choice of a cabinet appears to have been the first in a series of calculated moves designed to strengthen his position within the regime. Cárdenas was determined to assert his personal authority over the government but was aware that he could not challenge Calles openly. In order to allay any suspicions which Calles may have harbored about him, he introduced a number of well-known "Callistas" into the cabinet. But he appointed his own men as minister of labor and head of the Agrarian Department, which covered the two spheres of government in which he expected to be most active and where he intended to mobilize a personal following. He also forged a close alliance with a radical young labor leader, Vicente Lombardo Toledano, the head of the *Confederación General de Obreros y Campesinos de México* (CGOCM). This organization had resulted from a schism within the CROM in December 1933 and, under Lombardo Toledano, was rapidly supplanting it as the main labor federation.[5]

Cárdenas did not waste time in developing his strategy. Within a few weeks the new administration began to redistribute large tracts of land. The president also permitted a wave of strikes, the most important of which were in foreign concerns such as the Huasteca Oil Company (U.S.), the Mexican Tramway Company (Canadian), and the San Rafael Paper Company (French and Spanish).[6] Conservatives in the government were worried and looked to Calles for leadership. Calles was in the United States for medical treatment, but in early February he sent Abelardo Rodríguez to advise Cárdenas to restrain the "left wing" of the cabinet. Their activities, so Rodríguez told Cárdenas, were an embarrassment to the American government. Cárdenas delayed giving a reply and in the meantime sought a guarantee of support in any future conflict with Calles from General Andreu Almazán in Nuevo León and Saturnino Cedillo in San Luis Potosí. Neither man was well disposed toward Cárdenas's more radical supporters or the policies that they espoused; and in Cedillo's case Cárdenas had felt obliged to warn him the previous month that his expressions of discontent with the administration were acting as an encouragement to the country's "reactionary elements."[7] On the other hand, he knew that both wished to see the influence of Calles reduced, and their command of virtually independent forces would make them key figures in any confrontation with the Jefe Máximo. The two generals agreed to help Cárdenas against Calles, but only on condition that he kept the more radical labor leaders under control. In view of their response, Cárdenas summoned Rodríguez and promised to comply with Calles's request.[8]

Calles remained in the United States until March and then spent two months recuperating in the north of Mexico. His long absence from the capital proved fatal to his political position; for during this period Cárdenas strengthened his links with organized labor, peasant leaders, and younger elements in the bureaucracy and armed forces. He also cultivated those leading politicians who had clashed with Calles in the past, such as Ortiz Rubio and Portes Gil. The leaders of the Callista establishment were thus undermined and outflanked; little by little they were drawn into taking an open stand on the president's policies. This was most observable in the congress, which divided into two blocks: a minority group, the "left wing" based upon the nine deputies from the president's home state of Michoacán, and firmly committed to him; and the remaining majority, who considered Calles as their natural leader.[9]

In April and May there was renewed labor unrest discreetly encouraged by Cárdenas. There was even a strike in the Mexican Telephone and Telegraph Company, in which Calles had shares.[10] Calles decided to act and made a widely publicized attack upon Cárdenas's policies, particularly in industrial relations. Many politicians and senior officials believed that Cárdenas was about to be forced out of office as Ortiz Rubio had been and assured Calles of their loyalty. Contrary to these expectations, however, Cárdenas responded to the threat with great skill and energy. He used his contacts with labor leaders to organize mass demonstrations in his favor, forced the removal of the Callista president of the PNR, General Matías Ramos, and obtained the resignation of the cabinet. He also replaced certain Callista generals with younger men loyal to himself. Portes Gil became the new president of the PNR and required all leading officials to pledge their wholehearted support to Cárdenas. Like Portes Gil, Cedillo also sided with Cárdenas. He accepted the president's invitation to become minister of agriculture in place of Garrido Canabal, who apparently refused to disown Calles and sought to remain neutral. The remainder of the new cabinet was wholly Cardenista in composition; Barba González, for example, whose performance as minister of labor had been specifically criticized by Calles, was promoted to the key post of minister of the interior. When it became clear that, far from being forced to resign, Cárdenas had been strengthened by the crisis, many Callista politicians switched their allegiance, and a month later the former "majority" block in the congress announced its dissolution. As for Calles himself, he retired to Sonora in a tacit admission of defeat.[11]

Cedillo's decision to support Cárdenas in his confrontation with Calles was probably critical to the president's success.[12] It almost seemed—for a few weeks at least—as if Cedillo himself had become the arbiter of the nation's political destinies in place of the fallen Calles. Certainly the country's Roman Catholics hoped that this might be the case, and several thousand of them greeted him when he arrived in Mexico City to take up his new post, in "a spontaneous demonstration of enthusiasm for the uncrowned king of the only state where the Roman Catholics have nothing to complain of." Nor were the Roman Catholics' hopes that Cedillo's presence in the cabinet would help them wholly unjustified. A month later, apparently at his instigation, Cárdenas repealed his earlier decree of the previous February banning the transmission of religious material by post.[13] Appearances could easily deceive, however, and Cedillo's position was not as strong as it seemed. Unlike in the past, his services on this occasion were not to bring the reward of continuing to enjoy a free hand in San Luis Potosí. For having wrested control of the ruling party machine from its creator, Calles, Cárdenas was to extend its powers even further, at the expense of, among others, his benefactor Cedillo.

The president's first move in this process was to eradicate the remaining pockets of Callista influence. In the weeks following his victory, in a purge reminiscent of Calles's own in 1925, he replaced all unrepentant Callistas in the higher levels of the bureaucracy, and following a shooting incident in the congress on 11 September, that body expelled the eighteen most prominent Callista deputies. The president also moved against those state governors and provincial *caudillos* most identified with Calles: the governors of both Tabasco and Tamaulipas were forced to resign, and an anti-Callista governor was chosen to succeed Saturnino Osornio in Querétaro.[14]

The tactics employed by Cárdenas in removing one of the governors, Rafael Villarreal in Tamaulipas, and in demolishing the *cacicazgos* of Garrido Canabal in Tabasco and Saturnino Osornio in Querétaro, presaged those he was to use against Cedillo three years later. With the help of Calles, Villarreal had defeated Portes Gil in the 1932 gubernatorial elections. Protected by his patron, who had important sugar interests in the state at El Mante, Villarreal conducted a ruthless campaign against the agrarian organizations established by Portes Gil while he was governor in the 1920s. When Portes Gil became president of the PNR, he used his agrarian contacts to organize a series of demonstrations against Villarreal. Lacking any support from Mexico City, the governor's position soon became untenable, and he took an indefinite leave of absence. The political strongman of Querétaro, Saturnino Osornio, whom Cedillo had assisted to come to power, was the victim of a press campaign in June and July which recounted his various crimes, including involvement in the murder of a political opponent. Once he lost his immunity from prosecution bestowed by the governorship, Osornio was charged with murder;

and although he was never tried, his political career was finished. A year later the last vestiges of his regime were removed when the Agrarian Department sent a commission to Querétaro "to resolve the agrarian problem there." The estates of the former governor and of his associates were confiscated for use as *ejidos,* and the local Agrarian League was purged of his supporters.[15] In Tabasco the regime of Garrido Canabal was overthrown by violence. A group of young Tabascan exiles returned home from Mexico City to organize an opposition party in the state elections. They had the blessing of two cabinet ministers, General Francisco Múgica and Luis Rodríguez, but no overt official support. Following a murderous clash between the exiles and some of Garrido's followers in Villahermosa, there were demonstrations against his regime in Mexico City. Within days the congress withdrew recognition from the state government, and the governor, a Garrido nominee, resigned. Garrido Canabal himself accepted Cárdenas's offer of diplomatic exile and went to Costa Rica on an agrarian mission.[16]

In December Calles returned to Mexico City to defend himself against attacks in the press. His return provided the president with an excuse for further purges in the administration. The senate expelled five of its members for conspiracy against the government and then voted to withdraw recognition from the governors of Sonora, Sinaloa, Durango, and Guanajuato, thus forcing their resignation. Following these moves, the president retired several leading generals, including the military commanders of the Federal District and Veracruz, and also the once-powerful General Joaquín Amaro, whose attendance at the airport to meet Calles cost him his job as director of military education. The absence in military circles of any protest at these changes underlined the extent to which the army had lost its interventionist role in politics and had become subordinated to the ruling party, an increasing number of whose leaders were civilians.[17] Four months later, in April 1936, Cárdenas completed his triumph by sending Calles and three of his most faithful lieutenants, Luis León, Melchor Ortega, and Luis Morones, into exile in the United States.[18]

The departure of Calles symbolized Cárdenas's political supremacy. Within eighteen months of taking office he had restored the authority of the presidency after six years of rule by the Jefe Máximo, achieved control over the government and PNR bureaucracies, and appeared to have the loyalty of the once-turbulent army leadership. He also enjoyed the support of organized labor. In February 1936, with the president's backing, Lombardo Toledano had converted the CGOCM into a new and more powerful confederation of unions, the *Confederación de Trabajadores de México* (CTM). With the exception of some of the smaller unions and the textile workers in the Orizaba area, the CTM soon gained control of organized labor, leaving older federations such as the once powerful CROM relatively impotent.[19]

Cárdenas emphasized his determination to retain his overriding authority when, in August 1936, he forced the resignation of Portes Gil as president of the PNR. For some months Portes Gil, who with Cedillo represented the more conservative element in the government, had been locked in a power struggle with General Múgica, the radical minister of communications, among whose supporters was Lombardo Toledano. During this time Portes Gil used his position to build up a personal following in the party machine. Concerned that the wily Portes Gil might eventually construct an independent power base within the government bureaucracy, Cárdenas moved to check him. In August the "left wing" of the senate vetoed the election of five "Portes Gilista" senators, and Portes Gil felt obliged to offer Cárdenas his resignation. Cárdenas promptly accepted it, but then emphasized his control over the situation by also obtaining the resignation of Portes Gil's three leading opponents in the senate and by ordering the dissolution of the "left wing" groups both there and in the chamber of deputies.[20]

The removal of Portes Gil demonstrated that Cárdenas would not tolerate any challenge to his hegemony within the central bureaucracy. Outside the federal government, only two of the provincial warlords who had dominated the country's politics during the previous decade still retained a significant power base of their own: Saturnino Cedillo in San Luis Potosí and General Andreu Almazán in Nuevo León. The remainder had either been eliminated in the military revolts of those years or had lost their independent military following during the course of General Joaquín Amaro's army reforms. Cedillo's position, of course, rested upon his *agraristas*. Almazán's power derived from his position as chief of the military region of Nuevo León, a post which he had occupied for several years. During this time he had amassed considerable wealth, and by providing his forces with up-to-date equipment and the most modern barracks in Mexico, he had converted them into a formidable force loyal to himself. As the British minister commented following a visit to Monterrey early in 1936:

> The maintenance of order depends far less upon the Governor and local police than on the enigmatic general Almazán and his virtually private army which he maintains in magnificent cantonments on the outskirts of the town. These cantonments, which I also visited, were constructed by the army with material practically all of which was supplied gratis by the various brick and cement works under pain of incurring the General's displeasure. The buildings are well designed and well laid out and the comfort of all ranks thoroughly catered for by a cooperative store, swimming pools, football, polo, basketball and other grounds. The General is thus assured of a contented and loyal force, of a brigade or more which will accept his orders and deal with any situation that may arise in accordance with his ideas, whether they should or should not happen to coincide with those of the federal government.[21]

Amaro's downfall indicated that neither Almazán nor Cedillo alone could hope to challenge Cárdenas; but their military power and conservatism made them a potential focus of opposition to the more radical elements within the administration. It was in Cárdenas's interests to reduce their independence and bring them under presidential control before the elections of 1940. Almazán, however, protected his position with skill. He publicly proclaimed his loyalty to the president but declined to serve in the cabinet and avoided any open involvement in national politics. Instead, he remained with his troops in Monterrey, where his close association with the most prosperous city in the country made it difficult for his enemies to attack him.[22]

Cedillo, however, behaved less astutely, for although he still maintained an independent power base in San Luis Potosí, he allowed himself to be brought into the limelight of the cabinet. He had accepted a post there in order to help the president in his struggle with Calles, but he lacked the skills necessary to survive in high public office. He found himself wooed by landowners and industrialists—a strange turn of fate for a man once feared and hated by such men—but was also correspondingly the target for harsh criticism in the left-wing press, such as *El Machete,* the organ of the Communist party. He became embroiled in bureaucratic in-fighting, but usually without much success. General Múgica, for example, the radical minister of communications and one of Cedillo's leading opponents, as he had been of Portes Gil, wrested from him control of the construction of the San Luis Potosí–Antiguo Morelos highway. This was Cedillo's pet project, which he had been promoting not only for the benefit it would bring to the economy of San Luis Potosí, but also because, when completed, it would facilitate access to his agrarian colonies. Finally, Cedillo must have soon realized that he lacked the confidence of the president and that Cárdenas was keeping him in the cabinet, not for his advice, but in order to prevent him from becoming a rallying point for opposition to the president's policies outside the government. While not criticizing Cedillo in public, the president would sometimes deliberately distance himself from Cedillo by his actions, as when he failed to attend the inauguration of Mateo Hernández Netro as governor of San Luis Potosí in September 1935.[23]

The major policy differences between Cedillo and the president were over religion, education, and agriculture. An agnostic in his own religious views, Cedillo had never shared the anticlericalism of Calles and Tejeda, which he believed was an unnecessary cause of antagonism for the mass of the population. He fought in the Cristero war for political, not doctrinal, reasons, and welcomed those of his former opponents who later chose to settle in San Luis Potosí. When Calles unleashed a further wave of religious persecution in 1934 and Cárdenas initially gave rabid anticlericals such as Garrido Canabal a free hand, Cedillo made San Luis Potosí a haven for Roman Catholics. In 1935 almost a quarter of the priests in the whole country were domiciled there, and nowhere else did they dare to appear in public wearing the markings of their office.[24] As we have seen, Cedillo was also opposed to socialist education and continued to prevent its introduction in San Luis Potosí, in spite of the president's enthusiastic support for the policy. Commenting on the religious and educational tolerance in San Luis Potosí at this time, an American visitor to the state wrote:

> I understand that no Protestant work has been interfered with and that there are private schools which are practically Catholic. There are nearly as many private schools in the state as public, and as a matter of fact the parents seem to show a preference for the private schools. On visiting some of the priests in San Luis Po-

tosí I was interested to observe that, regardless of federal laws, they were permitted to wear clerical collars in the streets. They expressed faith in General Cedillo.[25]

Cedillo's defense of the church could not have endeared him to Cárdenas, and his rejection of socialist education must have been an irritant. But they were not important enough issues to cause an open rupture between the two men. The first six months of Cárdenas's presidency were marked by frequent attacks upon the church, both verbal and physical. The most notorious incident was in December 1934 when there was a shooting affray between a group of Garrido Canabal's youthful supporters, the infamous Red Shirts, and some Catholics in the Mexico City suburb of Coyoacán. Gradually, however, the president curbed the activities of the anticlericals in his administration, and in a speech in March 1936 he promised that his government would not repeat the error of earlier administrations in giving overall priority to religious policy. "Anti-religious campaigns," he explained, "do not fall within the competence of the government."[26] There continued to be friction, particularly over the activities of rural teachers, but officially inspired persecution of the church ceased.

However, the most important disagreement between the two men was over agricultural policy. During his campaign tour in 1934 Cárdenas had been made acutely aware of the minimal impact that the agrarian reform had had upon the living standards of the rural population. He concluded that any improvement could be made only if there was a dramatic increase in land redistribution. As he noted in his diary for 1 January that year:

> It is the responsibility of the present generation to distribute land to all the villages which lack it and provide the credit necessary for its cultivation. The Revolution requires both the ejidos and the dissolution of the great estates so that production can be increased and with it the purchasing power of the rural masses to the benefit of the economy as a whole.[27]

Unlike the Sonorans, Cárdenas considered the *ejido* as quite distinct from the private smallholding and intended to make it just as important a unit of agricultural production as the other. He might even have planned to make it more important; in a speech to the nation from Torreón in November 1936 he suggested that the *ejido* should be the main supplier of the nation's food.[28] During his presidential term he presided over the redistribution of 17,906,429 hectares of land, almost all in the form of *ejidos*, to 811,115 recipients. By 1940 *ejidos* accounted for one-half of the country's total farmland and well over one-half of the arable land under cultivation.[29]

In support of his program of land redistribution Cárdenas increased the size and scope of the agrarian bureaucracy. The DAAC became, under Cárdenas, one of the most important departments of the government. For the majority of the rural population DAAC employees were their only contact with the civilian authorities of the central government. More comprehensive agricultural credit banks were also established to provide the beneficiaries of the land reform with access to the credit that they had previously had to seek from money lenders, middle-men, or wealthy neighbors. Cárdenas also considered that, where appropriate, *ejidatarios* should be encouraged to work their land on a co-operative basis; and he supported the creation of a number of extensive collective *ejidos,* of which the largest were those in the Laguna region.[30]

Unfortunately, the detrimental effect of the agrarian reform upon production, which had been noticeable in the 1920s, was even more marked under Cárdenas. Landlords declined to invest, and when they feared imminent expropriation, they decapitalized their estates by selling machinery and stock. In spite of the reformed agrarian credit banks the *ejidatarios* lacked adequate working capital. They tended to fall back upon subsistence crops, such as maize and beans, rather than risk the production of commercial crops whose profits could more easily pass into the hands of their creditors, whether private or bureaucratic.[31] Summing up the first effects of the stimulus that Cárdenas gave to land redistribution, the British minister reported:

> Whereas he used to have his regular wage, small though it may have been, his house and a piece of ground to cultivate for his own use, the peasant whose demand for a smallholding has been satisfied is now thrown on his own resources. Hampered by lack of capital for the purchase of seeds, farm implements, etc., he becomes disillusioned, and many have abandoned their holding to seek work elsewhere.
>
> Whatever justification there may be for the slogan that "the land is for the tiller of the soil," the general effect of the policy appears to be that no one, with the possible exception of some local political bosses, has benefited. Not only are the landlords impoverished, but the working of the system is uneconomic, both for the smallholders and the community in general. There is a tendency to cultivate only the simple food crops such as beans and maize on which the cultivator and his family depend and for which there is always a market should there be any surplus, to the detriment of money crops like wheat, cotton, sugar and henequén. The net result appears to be that production has gone down, with the consequent increase in prices for the town dweller. Furthermore, crops such as henequén, sugar cane etc., can only be economically grown on large estates, and are definitely unsuitable for cultivation on smallholdings.[32]

The government intended that the much-vaunted collective *ejidos* would solve these problems but, initially at least, they proved a disappointment. The system was imposed from above with little regard for the traditions or wishes of the recipients of the land, who often distrusted the idea and desired a plot of their own. And even where the collective appeared suitable for local conditions, e.g. on estates producing commercial crops on a large scale, they often failed in practice. The *ejidatarios* depended for credit and marketing facilities upon the enlarged agrarian bureaucracy, which soon assumed a role similar in some ways to that of the former landlords. Unfortunately, many of the officials in that bureaucracy behaved with an arrogance and despotism associated with the worst of their *hacendado* predecessors. Working in collaboration with local politicians, they milked the profits from the *ejidos,* leaving the *ejidatarios* as badly off as before. In February 1937 Senator David Ayala of Guanajuato, who headed a study group on the *ejidos,* issued a report highly critical of the system. In a remarkably frank analysis of the agrarian reform for a PNR politician, Ayala claimed that 80% of the land distributed as *ejidos* was less productive than formerly, leading to rises in the prices of agricultural goods. He also accused the DAAC's regional superintendents of exploiting the *ejidatarios* in their district in various ways, either alone or in league with the leaders of *ejidal* communities. Concluding gloomily that "those campesinos who have freed themselves from the hacendado have simply fallen into the hands of the agrarian leader, someone with no virtues or scruples," he recommended the establishment of an Ejidal Department to root out the abuses that he had highlighted.[33] Ayala's criticisms were borne out in the most famous of the cooperative *ejidos,* those of the Laguna region. The government had set them up in 1936 and intended them to be a showplace for the system; yet within two years the project was much discredited by financial scandals involving some of the most important officials connected with it. Such malpractices, of which there were other examples elsewhere, tended to demoralize the *ejidatarios.*[34]

The short-term social cost of the agrarian reform under Cárdenas was high, which is hardly surprising in view of the vast readjustment in land tenure involved. As Ian Jacobs has recently shown in his analysis of the agrarian reform in northern Guerrero, not only *hacendados* but also *rancheros* suffered from the creation of *ejidos* in their locality. So too, on occasions, did renters and sharecroppers, while some rural workers still regarded the *ejidatarios* as thieves and government stooges, men who refused to work to acquire land but preferred to sell their political independence for it. *Hacienda* laborers who opposed the division of their employers' estates were forced to accept *ejidos* under the threat of the land being given to outsiders. Even Cárdenas, in a typically honest speech in Guadalajara in July 1935, admitted that the reform was causing serious divisions at all levels of rural society.[35]

Nevertheless, Cárdenas pressed ahead with his program of land redistribution in spite of these problems. He did so largely for three reasons: first, whatever the resistance to the reform in predominantly *ranchero* states such as Guerrero, Guanajuato, and Jalisco—where it was considerable—in other areas, such as the coastal states of Veracruz and Sinaloa, there was widespread pressure for some kind of land redistribution. In the interests of social justice, Cárdenas was determined to respond to such demands. Second, an extension of the government-controlled *ejidal* sector fitted in with the president's policy of centralizing political power. As a British diplomat observed in May 1937:

> The division of agricultural land into smallholdings, the owners of which are entirely dependent for the capital with which to work them on the state controlled Banks of Ejidal and Agricultural Credit, is clearly calculated in effect if not in intention, to provide the state with the means of exercising political pressure greater even than the old system of caciques.[36]

Third, Cárdenas sincerely believed that the creation of a large *ejidal* sector would be economically beneficial, in that it would lead to an increase in agricultural production and would be more responsive to governmental economic policy than would the private sector. In all respects he was to be justified during the years that followed his presidency, for his program of massive land redistribution reduced a large sector of the rural population to the status of government clients and thus allowed his successors to ensure the provision of cheap agricultural inputs to assist industrialization.[37]

Cedillo, for his part, was hostile to such a bureaucratization of agriculture, which, of course, also threatened his power base in San Luis Potosí. He opposed the introduction of collective *ejidos*—which he considered alien to the nature of the Mexican *campesino*—and defended the system of individual *ejidal* plots. He believed that the family farm, whether a small property or an *ejidal* plot, should form the basis of land tenure. He also considered that farmers should be allowed to grow the crops they wanted—unlike members of cooperative *ejidos* who had to follow the dictates of the agrarian bureaucracy. As he once said to his secretary, "a plot of land which isn't your own; machinery which you all share and spare parts which you can only obtain by paying a bribe; paying dues to a more voracious master than his forebears—the agrarian bureaucrat; all of this is worse than the system before the Revolution."[38]

Cedillo's views were shared by many in the rural population, particularly the owners of small properties who feared the growth of the *ejidal* sector. Aware of this fact, Cárdenas often stressed the inviolability of small property in his public statements. He also took Cedillo's advice and passed legislation protecting from expropriation all but the largest farms which were devoted exclusively to cattle raising or sheep breeding. But as Cárdenas himself was aware, these gestures were largely ineffective, and in practice the DAAC did little to protect smallholders from the demands of potential *ejidatarios* for their land.[39]

A good illustration of how Cedillo's perception of land reform differed from that of Cárdenas was their respective treatment of the Colorado River Land Company. Toward the end of the Porfiriato the company acquired 277,144 hectares of land in Baja California for producing cotton. Over 100,000 hectares of land were subsequently irrigated; 100,000 were *temporal,* i.e., dependent upon rainfall for water, and 80,000 were unsuitable for cultivation. The company sublet the land to farmers, many of them Japanese and Chinese, on condition that they grew cotton. The scheme apparently benefited both parties; for even *El Machete,* which was vehemently opposed to the company's operations, admitted that the tenant farmers were well off. In April 1936 the company reached an agreement with Cedillo's Ministry of Agriculture to partition 16,700 hectares of its property into ten agricultural colonies. According to the contract, the colonists were to be allowed twenty years to purchase their plots of land. Shortly afterward, however, a petition was placed before the Agrarian Department to grant as *ejidos* 42,000 hectares of the company's estates, including the majority of the land earmarked for the colonies. The petitioners followed up their request by occupying the area that they wanted. *El Machete* claimed that the squatters were local *campesinos* although the paper admitted that "from a revolutionary point of view the seizure of the land left much to be desired." According to the company, however,

> applications for ejidos have been faked in a manner which is only too familiar, claims have been put in by colonists, urban dwellers in Mexicali, vagabonds and others not natives of the district, and the *poblados* claiming land in many cases consist but of a single hut.[40]

Whatever the origin of the would-be *ejidatarios*—and it seems probable that the company's claims were not without foundation—they were soon successful. For after several months of sporadic violence, Cárdenas decreed in March 1937 that the land in dispute should be distributed in the form of *ejidos,* thus overruling Cedillo's earlier agreement.[41]

In spite of his differences with the president and the increasingly vociferous attacks upon him in the press, Cedillo still enjoyed a reputation as an important agrarian leader, and this enabled him to acquire a powerful base in the largest agrarian confederation, the *Confederación Campesina Mexicana* (CCM). The CCM was founded during a meeting of a splinter group of the *Liga Nacional Campesina* (LNC), the so-called LNC "Úrsulo Galván" faction, which was held in San Luis Potosí in May 1933 under the patronage of Saturnino Cedillo, Emilio Portes Gil, and Marte Gómez, a former minister of agriculture. The executive committee was formed by delegates from San Luis Potosí, Chihuahua, Michoacán, Nuevo León, Oaxaca, Guerrero, México, and Tamaulipas. The delegate from San Luis Potosí was Tomás Tapia, the radical young politician from Villa de Reyes; while the delegate from Tamaulipas was Graciano Sánchez, who overcame his antipathy toward Cedillo for the sake of his commitment to organizing the peasantry.[42]

The CCM grew rapidly although it was heavily dependent upon the patronage of Cedillo and Portes Gil. Cedillo's influence was shown during the CCM's third annual congress in Mexico City in December 1934, which was attended by 200 delegates from nineteen states. A delegation from the conference held a meeting with Cárdenas and asked him to create a new department charged with organizing the various agrarian leagues in the country into one federation to be headed by Cedillo and to be directly dependent upon the president. But Cárdenas wanted to form a national peasant league without direct reference to any existing federation such as the CCM. He intended to bind the organized peasantry to the central bureaucracy that he was extending and streamlining. In July 1935 he instructed the executive committee of the PNR to organize peasant leagues in all the states into a new organization, the *Confederación Nacional Campesina* (CNC). In September the PNR subcommittee charged with the task organized a congress in Mexico City to discuss the project. Among those who were invited to attend was Cedillo, who was "greeted with a thunderous applause by the delegates and numerous spectators."[43] The conference confirmed that the new federation would be organized by the government and would operate in an "open spirit of class struggle." By using the party apparatus in this way, Cárdenas reserved patronage over the movement for himself and prevented any ambitious politician from using it as a power base in pursuit of the presidency. For the next two years the organizing committee went to work to carry out his instructions.[44]

Cárdenas's decision to organize the peasantry within the PNR was consistent with his policy of political centralization and a crucial step in his creation of a corporate state. However, the new organization represented a threat to Cedillo's political power base, and his reception at the CNC congress in September 1935 was deceptively flattering. For, once the central government established direct lines of communication to the beneficiaries of the land reform through a national peasant league, there would be no need for regional *caudillos* such as Cedillo who acted as intermediaries between local *agrarista* groups and the federal authorities. A new system of bureaucratic and military patronage under the control of party functionaries would replace the cruder kind of political and military patronage that still survived in San Luis Potosí. Regional *caudillos* who wished to retain their influence would henceforth have to operate from within a centralized bureaucracy, a role that was alien to Cedillo's character or inclinations.

There were, however, more immediate threats to Cedillo's position than those posed by the establishment of the CNC. During 1936 and 1937 Cedillo's opponents, both inside and outside the government, became increasingly outspoken and provocative, and it was clear from the way that Cárdenas tolerated their activities that he was using them to erode Cedillo's power. Cedillo realized what was happening; he could have surrendered his control over San Luis Potosí to the central government and followed either Garrido Canabal into diplomatic exile or Portes Gil into private life. Instead, he succumbed to the flattery of friends and associates who fuelled his ambitions in order to further their own careers. They persuaded him that he could, and should, play a role in the presidential election of 1940. This combination of pressure from without and ambition from within eventually proved fatal to him.

Cedillo's first problems came from industrial labor, whose champion, Aurelio Manrique, he had overthrown ten years previously. As we have seen, industrial workers were still a relatively insignificant minority of the labor force in San Luis Potosí, and Cedillo controlled them through the *Federación Regional de Obreros y Campesinos* (FROC). This was a tame labor federation that included almost all the local unions. It claimed a membership of approximately 14,500, one-half of whom were in the state capital. In 1937 the FROC was run by Manuel Anaya, one of Cedillo's most trusted collaborators; he was assisted by the leaders of the member unions, some of whom saw the organization as a channel for their own advancement in local politics, while others saw it as the only practical way to help the men that they represented. The FROC enjoyed good relations with the local employers' organization, the *Centro Patronal de San Luis Potosí*, which had a membership of almost two hundred.[45] The leaders of the two organizations, working closely with the local Arbitration and Conciliation Board, usually prevented unrest in local industries. Only workers in nationally based industries, such as the railways or the American Smelting and Refining Company (ASRC), could express their demands outside the Cedillista labor machine. Toward the middle of Cárdenas's presidency, however, the industrial workers in San Luis Potosí received the attentions of Lombardo Toledano, who wished to incorporate them into the *Confederación de Trabajadores Mexicanos* (CTM). Toledano's plans threatened Cedillo's hegemony and contributed to the movement to overthrow him.

The first political embarrassment that Cedillo suffered over labor relations was not, however, the result of CTM activity. It came from a rare failure on the part of the Arbitration and Conciliation Board to resolve a dispute in a local textile factory, the Atlas, whose workers were not affiliated with the CTM . In November 1934 the workers asked for a wage raise. (They were paid between fifty and eighty cents per day, which was approximately the same as an agricultural laborer and low by industrial standards.)[46]

Local arbitration officials felt inhibited in dealing with the dispute because Jerónimo Elizondo, the factory owner, was a friend of Cedillo, and they failed to resolve it. The case then went before the head of the Labor Department, Juan de Dios Bojórquez, who ruled that the company should raise its wages to the minimum for the jute fiber industry. (These rates had been fixed in a national agreement in 1927, which Elizondo had never implemented.) It soon became clear, however, that Elizondo had no intention of complying with the decision. In August 1935, therefore, the workers called in an inspector from the Labor Department to prepare evidence for a judicial enquiry. At the same time seventeen small workers' groups in the city formed a united body, the *Frente Único de Trabajadores de San Luis Potosí*, and offered the Atlas workers their support. In response, the senior staff at the factory impeded the inspector's work, and Elizondo hired a former army captain to discipline his labor force.[47]

In late 1935 the workers went on strike and the following January declared their intention of staging a hunger march to Mexico City. In a gesture of solidarity the *Frente Único de Trabajadores* called for a general strike in the city to begin on 20 January. Cárdenas thereupon offered to arbitrate in the dispute himself, and the general strike was called off. Two months later the president gave his judgment. He ordered Elizondo to implement Bojórquez's ruling and to give the workers the balance of what they ought to have received from the time of the decision in November 1934, but he added that Elizondo should pay the workers only 30% of their wages, for the period of the recent strike. This proved too much for Elizondo's resources—as Cárdenas might have guessed it would—and in November 1936 the government took over the factory on the grounds that he had failed to meet his obligations. Eventually, in January 1938, the factory was reconstituted as a workers' cooperative. Although Cedillo was not directly involved in the affair, he was criticized in the press for his purported sympathy toward Elizondo.[48]

Other labor unrest in San Luis Potosí in 1936 was related to the activities of national labor federations. In late August the workers in the ASRC plant in San Luis Potosí went on strike for higher wages, and the company suspended work both there and at its three other operations in the state at Matehuala, Barranco, and San Pedro. Since ASRC paid approximately one million pesos per month in wages, local merchants soon suffered from a drop in demand. The state arbitration machinery was unable to bring much pressure to bear on the strikers, who belonged to the nationally based *Sindicato de Mineros, Metalúrgicos y Similares,* and the company was equally unsuccessful in breaking the strike with "blackleg" labor. A settlement was not reached until December, after lengthy negotiations between the company and union representatives in Mexico City.[49]

The leaders of the CTM took advantage of the strike to accuse Cedillo of hostility to organized labor and of being an ally of "international fascism." They were supported in their attacks on him by General Múgica, the left-wing minister of communications, who wanted to force Cedillo's resignation from the cabinet.[50] In response, Cedillo issued a lengthy *apología* to the press. Having disclaimed any connection with the far right, he defended his record in labor affairs:

> When I was governor of San Luis Potosí and military commander there for four years, I never broke up a strike or defended strike breakers; for my actions were designed to balance the two factors of production and always to seek maximum advantage for the workers. There was never a strike in my time as governor since agreement was always reached in a way which did not harm the workers' interests.[51]

This mendacious and somewhat illogical statement was given scant coverage in the official PNR daily newspaper, *El Nacional*—an indication, as the British minister observed, of Cedillo's weakness and isolation in government circles.[52] In San Luis Potosí, in contrast, it was received with ritual congratulation from the state legislature and local judiciary, whose members chose to forget his reaction to the teachers' strike there four years earlier. The following month, in a gesture clearly designed to emphasize Cedillo's strength in his home territory, the government of the state awarded him the title of *hijo predilecto* (favored son). A medal was struck to commemorate the occasion and a banquet was held in his honor, attended by several hundred members of the local civilian and military establishment.[53] Seemingly the battle lines were being drawn for a confrontation which both sides involved considered inevitable.

The next challenge to Cedillo's authority, as if in response to this ceremony, was on the political front and came during the campaign for the elections to the federal congress in 1937. In previous years the national committee of the PNR had never disputed Cedillo's exercise of patronage in the selection of party candidates; it was a mutually accepted factor in the structure of patron-client relationships which linked the federal government to the population of San Luis Potosí. In 1937, however, the government and the national committee of the party broke this unwritten understanding to a small, but significant, extent. The CTM actively supported candidates who were challenging the local PNR machine as independents; and the national committee of the PNR refused to ratify two of the candidates selected by the party's state committee. The opposition candidates were united only in their hostility to Cedillo. They included both members of the PNR who had quarreled with the local state machine and a number of independents. Initially they were supported by the local labor organizations affiliated with the CTM; later, when the PNR national committee took an interest in the election, some of this support fell away. The most prominent of these candidates was the indomitable Manrique, who returned to state politics after an absence of eleven years. Together with several others, he formed a *Partido Renovador Potosino* (the Party for the Renovation of San Luis Potosí) and began to campaign vigorously. *El Universal's* correspondent compared him to Rodolfo Brito Foucher, the leader of the Tabascan students whose participation in the elections there two years earlier had led to the fall of Garrido Canabal's regime.[54] Manrique might well have seen himself in such a role; certainly, as in Brito Foucher's case, his campaign provoked a violent reaction from the local authorities. Several of his early meetings were disrupted by Cedillo's supporters, and in March another opposition candidate, Rafael Armendáriz, died in suspicious circumstances near Peotillos. According to the authorities, he was killed in a car accident, but according to his friends, he was murdered by Cedillista gunmen.[55]

Toward the end of the campaign Manrique held a rally in San Luis Potosí, during which he listed what he considered to be the most glaring instances of corruption in the state government:

1. Local government employees were paid in bonds which rapidly became devalued;

2. The state ixtle commission, which was controlled by Cedillo's friend General Francisco Carrera Torres, the commander of the local military zone, purchased fibers at below their market value and sold them at a large profit in New York to Carrera Torres's benefit;

3. Cedillo's sister had the franchise for the municipal slaughter house;

4. The Mexquitic dam, near San Luis Potosí, which had cost the government 600,000 pesos to build, was subsequently sold to an "agrarian cooperative" controlled by Carrera Torres for 70,000 pesos. Carrera Torres paid for the dam in government bonds which were worth only 10% of their face value, so that it only cost him 7,000 pesos. Furthermore, he had diverted the waters of the dam, which were intended for the city, to irrigate his hacienda of El Peñasco.[56]

The insignificance of these misdeeds in comparison with the corruption in several other states did not diminish the force of Manrique's arguments. His speech, delivered in Cedillo's own capital, proved too much for the latter's supporters. Led by four recent or current members of the state congress, Alberto Araujo, Juan Infante, Vicente Segura, and Marcelino Zúñiga, a group of them assaulted Manrique and shaved off his luxuriant beard.[57] Cedillo's enemies made full use of this incident for propaganda purposes, and the national press, which closely followed Manrique's campaign, gave it wide coverage.

León García, Manrique's former collaborator in his days as governor, and now a senior CCM official working on the organization of the CNC, addressed a protest meeting in Mexico City. On the other hand, representatives of the state employees in San Luis Potosí issued a statement denying that they were paid in government bonds. Cárdenas ordered an investigation into the affair but the results were never published.[58]

The assault upon Manrique was not the last act of violence prior to the elections, but his own campaign lost much of its vigor thereafter. Opposition candidates continued to be molested by Cedillo's followers, and the only printer of opposition propaganda was found dead shortly afterwards—a suicide victim according to the local authorities—but no one expected the candidates of the *Partido Renovador Potosino* to be elected. Manrique probably best described how he—and the federal government—saw his role in the election when he once publicly stated that he had "express orders from the President to systematically attack General Cedillo," a claim which Cárdenas never denied.[59] By the middle of the campaign Manrique's quixotic gestures had been overshadowed by the controversy over the selection of the PNR's own candidates.

In early May the state PNR committee submitted to the national committee a list of its candidates for the elections. Previously the national committee had ratified such lists without demur, but this time it rejected two of the nominees: Antonio Díaz Soto y Gama, the former associate of Emiliano Zapata in Morelos and sponsor of Manrique for the governorship of San Luis Potosí in 1923, and Santiago Rincón Gallardo, a local machine politician. In the case of Díaz Soto y Gama the committee claimed that his ideas conflicted with the principles of the PNR, but added that since he enjoyed the confidence of the authorities in the district which he hoped to represent, they would not put up an official party candidate.[60] In Rincón Gallardo's case they selected Arellano Belloc, his rival in the local party primary, as the PNR candidate, even though the local committee claimed that Belloc had been overwhelmingly defeated. They added insult to injury by informing the local committee that Belloc would be elected "with or without votes," an honest if hardly tactful statement. Since Belloc was a well-known opponent of Cedillo, the national committee's insistence upon his election had obvious political implications, for it emphasized the growing rift between Cedillo and the central government. Recognizing this, Cedillo sent a telegram to Cárdenas protesting the decision and warning the president that by supporting Belloc's imposition he was "gaining a new friend but losing other trūe friends." But neither Cedillo's gesture nor the subsequent protests of the local PNR committee had any effect, and Belloc was duly elected in July with the other PNR candidates, who were all Cedillistas.[61]

These elections made it clear that Cárdenas wished to dismantle Cedillo's regime. First, neither the federal government nor the PNR national committee gave Cedillo the collaboration that he might have expected. Second, the way the elections were covered in the national press supported this idea. Violence and malpractice were commonplace in Mexican politics during this period. Almost all state elections were accompanied by murder and denunciations of fraud, and reporting of such events tended to be routine and low key. This was not, however, the case with the election campaign and its aftermath in San Luis Potosí. Even conservative newspapers, such as *El Universal* or *Excélsior*, gave long and detailed coverage of the electoral disorders there and of the less savory aspects of Cedillo's rule, which they illustrated. No editor of a major newspaper would have dared to do this without the approval, or more probably the encouragement, of those close to the president. The implications for Cedillo's standing in the government and for his rule in San Luis Potosí were clear.[62]

It was, therefore, no surprise when a month later Cedillo resigned as minister of agriculture. His tenure in the post had never been happy, partly because of his disagreements with the president over policy, and partly because it had exposed him to criticism from his political opponents. However, it was not an ideological issue over which he resigned, but a more personal one—Cedillo's appointment of an incompetent director of the Agricultural School at Chapingo, near Mexico City. On 20 July, after a period of unrest, the students at the school went on strike in support of three demands: the establishment of a directive council for the school, comprising both students and teachers; improvements in the school's facilities; and the removal of the director, Ing. Conrado Rodríguez. Of these demands the third was the most important. The strikers claimed that Rodríguez was a drunkard who chose his staff without regard to their suitability. On 21 July, 200 students held a protest meeting outside the Ministry in Mexico City. They declared their support for Cedillo, whom they described as "an outstanding member of the cabinet," but pressed for their demands to be met. Cedillo was in a difficult position, and he appointed a commission headed by the under-secretary of agriculture, Dr. José Parres, to look into the affair. Since Parres was a professional civil servant who enjoyed the confidence of Cárdenas, this move defused the tension. On the twenty-sixth, the commission reported that the students' demands for technical improvements would be met and the director replaced, but that the students would not be given a share in administering the school since "they should devote themselves to study and not political activism." When the new director was appointed, however, the students refused to accept him. Cedillo thereupon decided to take disciplinary action against them and telegraphed Cárdenas to seek his support. The president's response was short and to the point. From Yucatán, where he was presiding over a land redistribution program, he sent Cedillo a telegram accepting his resignation. Cedillo was angered and astonished. He had not offered to resign and felt insulted by what he considered his summary dismissal. It was a bitter end to fourteen uncomfortable months in the cabinet.[63]

Cedillo's departure from the Ministry of Agriculture was a victory for his opponents within the administration, notably Francisco Múgica and Lombardo Toledano. According to Cedillo's friends, both of them were involved in the Chapingo strike, working behind the scenes in its later stages. But the most important aspect of Cedillo's "resignation" was that it marked a decisive rupture in his relations with Cárdenas. By accepting it, Cárdenas had indicated publicly his lack of confidence in the man who had helped him to reach and remain in the presidency. As Cedillo retired to lick his wounds in Palomas, he must have wondered how long his regime in San Luis Potosí could survive the president's increasingly obvious determination to destroy it.

C H A P T E R   8

THE OVERTHROW OF CEDILLO

No se levantó—lo levantaron. (He didn't rebel—they forced him to rebel.)——Juan Ochoa Vázquez

Following his resignation, Cedillo retired to his bailiwick at Palomas and began to search for allies to protect his endangered position. At the same time both opponents and supporters of the government came to regard him as the natural leader of the conservative opposition. Friends and advisers pressed him to participate in the presidential election of 1940. Assuming that neither he nor any of his nominees would win the blessing of the PNR hierarchy, they urged him either to stand as an independent or to support the candidate of his choice. Those who gave him this advice were motivated more by their own ambition than by concern for Cedillo's political future, since they were suggesting that he challenge the right of the central government to control the presidential succession, but Cedillo succumbed to their persuasion. He planned to retain what he could of his power within San Luis Potosí and run for office in the election. If, as he expected, he was defeated by government manipulation of the polls, he intended to rebel. If the situation prior to 1940 appeared to favor a revolt, he was prepared to move before then. During the autumn of 1937 he started to build up political support for his campaign while also making preparations for a possible uprising.[1]

In seeking to form an opposition alliance Cedillo was encouraged by the knowledge that the administration was not as popular as government propaganda suggested. As the British minister reported in January 1938:

A large body of public opinion heartily dislikes the present trend of events; indeed the army, the middle classes, the more conservative and religious peasantry are all equally opposed to it. But thanks to the lack of a strong personality round whom they can rally, to their inertia, and to the shrewd way in which the Government has tied their hands, they lack any means of making their views felt.[2]

Those most disenchanted with the president's policies were the small and medium industrialists, the middle classes, particularly those on fixed incomes, a large number of older army leaders, the remaining *hacendados*, and those other members of the rural community who were displeased with the way in which Cárdenas carried out agrarian reform. The industrialists feared that with the support of the CTM Cárdenas intended to expropriate their companies and convert them into state industries or workers' cooperatives. They organized a nationwide network of employers' associations, the *Confederación Patronal de la República Mexicana* (CPRM), which was formally constituted in 1936. The middle classes also feared the growth of a workers' state, and those on fixed incomes suffered from the sharp inflation of the years 1936 and 1937. The more religious among them were also angered by government persecution of the church. Many senior army officers were jealous of the power of the CTM, and concerned that Cárdenas might eventually replace the army with workers' and peasants' militias. Their fears were fuelled by the CTM itself and the Communist party, which both pressed for the creation of such militias and whose propaganda gave the impression that they exercised more influence than was in fact the case. Those officers most disposed toward political intervention in order to protect what they considered the army's rights—by no means all of them generals—were encouraged by the recent uprising of General Franco in Spain, which by 1937 appeared likely to succeed. (The very fact that such men saw Franco as someone they might imitate reveals how conservative the officer corps in general had become by this time.)[3]

In the rural sector the *hacendados* were not alone in their hostility to the president's commitment to widespread land redistribution. Their views were shared by many smallholders, and even by certain other members of the *hacienda* community: the administrators and foremen who stood to lose their privileged position, those *peones acasillados* who preferred the security of lowly station to the risks and responsibilities of life as *ejidatarios*, and the tenants and sharecroppers for whom their landlords had been a major source of credit and who found the government's agricultural credit banks an inadequate substitute. In Guanajuato the opponents of the agrarian reform had turned to violence—on a large scale, according to a British landowner there:

> Señor Carlos Furber, a British landowner resident in Irapuato, gave me some extremely interesting information in regard to the general situation in the state of Guanajuato. It is widely known that in the mountainous region in the northeast of the State, there are a number of insurgents at large, whose principal enemies are the communal smallholders. Mr. Furber placed their number at 3,000 and told me that they are so well organized that they even produce a newsheet called *Hechos de Armas* (Feats of Arms) in which they record their exploits. He did not think that they had originally been incited to rebel by the property-owners, but that they consisted of men thrown out of work by agrarian reform who had no other employment open to them. Thus, if his own ranch were expropriated the land would be sufficient only to support 60 men out of the 90 at present employed on it. These sixty communal smallholders would only grow maize or

corn, and casual labour previously employed, for instance, on the melon crop as well as the residue of thirty would quite likely take to the hills.[4]

The situation in Jalisco seems to have been similar, and conditions in Durango and Zacatecas were little better. The agrarian discontent was aggravated by continuing friction between church and state and by the government's insistent support for the introduction of Socialist Education, which together caused a resurgence of the Cristero movement. In late 1935, when the renewed revolt was at its height, Cristero rebels were active in fifteen states, and their protest did not die down completely for several years.[5]

The disillusionment with the government felt by the above groups, both rural and urban, did not, however, lead to the growth of important opposition parties. The strength of the regime, and the ease with which it manipulated all elections, created a sense of helplessness among its opponents and deterred all but the most committed from any action. In looking for formal political support Cedillo could count upon only a number of small right-wing organizations and pressure groups which fed upon the middle class fears of the CTM and the Communist party. The members of these groups shared a belief that by increasing the role of the central bureaucracy Cárdenas was laying the basis for a totalitarian state modeled upon that of the Soviet Union. They included both conservative social democrats, Roman Catholic extremists, and fascists and were largely drawn from disgruntled former officials, the remnants of the old Porfirian elite, and the professional classes. Their financial backing came mainly from industrialists, merchants and small businessmen, and a few politicians such as Cedillo who had a personal interest in supporting them. The three largest organizations were Mexican Revolutionary Action (*Acción Revolucionaria Mexicana*—ARM), an overtly fascist organization founded in 1934 by Nicolás Rodríguez, a former Villista general, and modeled upon Mussolini's Black Shirts; the National Union of Revolutionary Veterans (*Unión Nacional de Veteranos de las Revolución*—UNVR), established in 1935, whose strength was in the army; and the Confederation of the Middle Class (*Confederación de la Clase Media*—CCM), formed in 1936.[6] In addition, there were a few smaller organizations, such as the Social Democrat Party and the Confederation of Independent Parties, and numerous diminutive splinter groups. Among the latter were National Civic Action, the Civic Action Party of the Middle Class, the Spanish Anti-Communist and Anti-Jewish Association, the Anti-Reelectionist Party, Mexican Nationalist Youth, the National Committee in Defense of the Race, and the Party of National Action.[7]

The most coherent expression of the grievances and aspirations of the supporters of these groups was probably the founding manifesto of the Confederation of the Middle Class (CCM), whose main points were as follows:

a) The aim of the Confederation of the Middle Class is the improvement of the moral and economic conditions of the workers of that class, and of all other workers in Mexico.

b) Communism—or Scientific Socialism—is an unrealizable utopia and a divisive force among the Mexican people.

c) The working conditions of civil servants are intolerable. They can be dismissed at any time, and are forced to make "voluntary donations" and ascribe to certain social and political views.

d) Private sector office workers are in a similar position since the legal machinery intended to protect them functions so slowly.

e) Cottage industries no longer complement larger industries or supplement family incomes. Instead they are exploited by a small number of middle-men to the detriment of both larger industrialists and the working class.

f) The army still lives like a nomadic tribe and the middle ranking officers are underpaid.

The Confederation of the Middle Class therefore recommends:

a) the organization of middle sector pressure groups;

b) the creation of "white collar" unions;

c) that Article 123 of the Constitution be fully implemented;

d) an end to the use of the unions for political purposes;

e) that capital be protected from unjustified attack, and that the legitimate demands of labor be met;

f) respect for both the gains already made under the agrarian laws and for small property; the creation of agricultural colonies for those villages lacking land; and the immunity from further loss of properties already affected by the agrarian laws;

g) respect for seniority within the army and a salary increase for middle ranking officers financed by eliminating wasteful expenditure;

h) the promulgation of a Civil Service Law requiring that civil servants be sentenced by a court of law before they can be dismissed;

i) the organization of consumers' cooperatives among cottage industrialists in order to reduce the costs of their raw materials, and also of credit unions among them, so that they do not fall into the hands of money lenders, and of mutual insurance schemes.[8]

Although the largest of these organizations had branches in several state capitals, often in association with the local office of the CPRP, they were numerically and financially weak. The most important was the ARM, which at its height in 1935 had several hundred members and drew up to 5,000 sympathizers to its parades. But the following year, Nicolás Rodríguez, its leader, was sent into exile after being involved in political violence, and his organization was officially banned. Thereafter, the numbers of its active supporters dwindled rapidly, and by the time Cedillo resigned as minister of agriculture they probably numbered well under two hundred.[9] The CCM and UNVR were in a similar position, probably counting upon only a few hundred paid-up members each. But in the absence of any alternative Cedillo believed that these and other right-wing groups offered a nucleus for a potential opposition coalition to the PNR in the 1940 elections, and he cultivated their leaders from 1936 onward. Among those with whom Cedillo made contact was his erstwhile opponent Jorge Prieto Laurens, who had returned from exile some few years before and was president of one of the less extreme right-wing groups, the Constitutionalist Democratic Party. For Prieto Laurens and his associates Cedillo offered the only possible channel to power, although they could not have been optimistic about their chances of achieving their goal.[10]

Because of Cedillo's connections with these organizations, the left-wing press associated him with international fascism. For example, according to the British newspaper, *The Daily Worker*:

> That General Saturnino Cedillo is actively supporting reactionary elements who are plotting to establish a Fascist dictatorship in Mexico is revealed by the publication of photostat copies of two sensational documents in *El Machete*. . . . The documents show that Cedillo handed over 1,000 pesos to the National Union of Veterans of the Revolution, an organisation which works together with the Gold-shirt Gangsters, which in turn is [*sic*] connected with the Calles groups, who are closely related to certain American financial interests.[11]

This is a misinterpretation of the facts.

First, the National Union of Revolutionary Veterans lacked a coherent ideology and could not be described as fascist. Cárdenas himself considered the organization relatively harmless. In mid-August 1937 Lombardo Toledano denounced the existence of a "fascist plot" in Mexico and accused the CCM and UNVR of involvement in it. Following his speech, the police raided their offices and closed them down. Cárdenas, however, who was in Yucatán, telegraphed the authorities in Mexico City, ordering them to allow both organizations to go unmolested.

Second, although Cedillo certainly saw representatives from the embassies of the two leading fascist powers, Italy and Germany, on occasions, such contacts appear to have been of little significance. For example, a meeting that he held with the Italian ambassador and a member of the German legation in February 1937, in order to discuss the possibility of purchasing airplanes for the National Aviation School which Cedillo sponsored in San Luis Potosí, proved to be unproductive. When Cedillo next purchased more aircraft, he acquired them in the United States. Nor has any evidence yet emerged that the Italian or German legations came to his assistance in the winter of 1937–1938 when he badly needed funds to prepare for a possible revolt.[12]

Third, Cedillo himself was politically unsophisticated to say the least. His support for the right-wing groups mentioned did not derive from any particular sympathy toward fascism, which he did not understand, but from his search for allies to defend him against attacks from left-wing elements within the administration. As the British novelist Graham Greene observed, in his perceptive account of an afternoon that he spent with Cedillo at Palomas during a visit he made to Mexico early in 1938:

> Of course one doesn't trust the word of a general or politician, but there was something genuine in the bull-frog rage, the hopeless bewilderment of the man when I asked him about the German officers. He spluttered, he turned eyes of desperate inquiry on the old teacher. . . what would his enemies say next? He was caught in a maze of friends and enemies with similar faces. That is how I see him—the young Indian trooper with the round innocent face turned middle-aged, the bitterness of political years souring the innocence. People who were his

friends milked him, and he had to milk the state, and then there was a drought and the water system was antiquated and the Governor had no money to deal with it—and the trade unionists complained to the President, the President who wouldn't have been in Chapultepec now without his help, without the support of the troops which had enabled him to deport Calles. He had to get money from the state—for his friends, for his farm—and from capitalists. And capitalists wanted "things" in return, things like the suppression of labor agitation, and so politics crept in. I think he was inclined to hate the man who came bothering him with questions about Fascism and Communism. He swelled and sweated and said "Democracy." He had been happier at sunset, jolting over the stony fields in an old car, showing off his crops and his canal.[13]

Finally, although Cedillo allowed the ARM to print much of its propaganda in San Luis Potosí during the early days of the movement and enjoyed good relations with a number of Gold Shirt officers, some of whom he helped with jobs or money when he was still minister of agriculture, Nicolás Rodríguez refused to offer him his support or collaboration. According to a government agent, when Cedillo wrote to Rodríguez in the late summer of 1937 seeking a promise of help should he decide to revolt, Rodríguez replied "in a haughty manner, saying that he was an honorable and completely nationalist Mexican, who would have no truck with a Cedillo; that he had suffered greatly during the Revolution in Madero's day and was no traitor to his country, and that he would not therefore support Cedillo who should look to others to satisfy his desires."[14] Nor, indeed, as the British consul general in Mexico observed, was a fascist government a serious possibility in the country. The circumstances that produced fascist movements in Germany and Italy did not exist there. The PNR was unassailable; and unless the party itself assumed a fascist form— which was unthinkable under Cárdenas—there was no likelihood that a fascist administration would evolve.[15]

During the autumn of 1937 Cedillo also contacted certain other senior generals who were either under similar pressure as himself or equally opposed to Cárdenas's policies. He wished to know if they would be prepared to join him in a revolt. The most prominent of those whom he approached were Generals Yocupicio, Almazán, Magaña, Ríos Zertuche, and Bañuelos. As a colonel, Yocupicio had joined the Escobar revolt in 1929 but was later pardoned and reincorporated into the army. His election as governor of Sonora in 1937 over the "official" PNR candidate was due to his close links with the Yaquis. He shared Cedillo's instinctive conservatism, and since assuming office, he had been criticized by Lombardo Toledano for suppressing organized labor in the state. General Almazán knew that his dominance in Monterrey could not have been any more pleasing to Cárdenas than Cedillo's in San Luis Potosí, and that eventually he was likely to come under similar pressure from the central government. General Magaña, a former Zapatista and the governor of Michoacán, shared Cedillo's views on agrarian reform and his opposition to collective *ejidos*. General Ríos Zertuche was a leading member of the UNVR. He had, however, lost much of his power shortly before when Cárdenas moved him from command of the military zone in Zacatecas to head the cavalry department in the Defense Ministry. General Bañuelos, the governor of Zacatecas, had been assisted by Cedillo in imposing his nominees in the municipal councils on the Zacatecas–San Luis Potosí border, and also disliked what he considered to be the Communist leanings of the administration and the over-riding influence of organized labor.[16]

Yocupicio in particular should have been susceptible to Cedillo's approach. For some months he had been secretly arming the Yaquis, but in October 1937 Cárdenas undercut his power base by personally redistributing land to the inhabitants of the Yaqui valley. To Cedillo's annoyance, however, Yocupicio informed his emissary that in spite of Lombardo Toledano's provocation he remained loyal to the president. The others were equally unenthusiastic about a revolt: none rejected the possibility, but all believed that they should await the next presidential election campaign.[17]

The government was aware of Cedillo's activities and moved to weaken his position in San Luis Potosí. In early September 1937 the Defense Ministry purchased the eleven planes and equipment of the National Aviation School which it then transferred to near Mexico City. Cedillo had founded the school in 1928 and regarded it as virtually his own property. He subsequently acquired five new airplanes which he paid for with forced loans from the municipalities in the state and with the money that he received from the government in compensation for the school's removal, but his overall position had been weakened.[18] At the same time the defense minister, General Manuel Ávila Camacho, made some changes in the composition of the federal army forces in San Luis Potosí. The state was garrisoned by the 36th regiment led by General Francisco Carrera Torres, whose officers had been vetted by Cedillo. While leaving Carrera Torres in charge, Ávila Camacho transferred some of the other officers to distant parts of the country. At the same time he dispatched the 38th regiment to San Luis Potosí; the regiment's loyalty was unquestioned, and it thereafter acted as a fifth column in the state. Cedillo maintained a public silence about these changes, which he was unable to prevent, but he complained bitterly about them to his friends. He knew that the loyal troops in the state would prevent him from imitating the rebellious generals of the previous decade by raising a whole region in revolt. In the event of an uprising he would be forced on the defensive, and would have to rely upon guerrilla warfare until he received assistance from outside the state.[19]

While the government took measures to weaken Cedillo's military power base, his political opponents sought to discredit his reputation as an agrarian reformer. On 20 September the executive committee of the *Confederación Campesina Mexicana* (CCM), which included two of Manrique's former henchmen, Graciano Sánchez, the secretary general of the organization, and León García, published an attack upon Cedillo in *El Universal*. The writers stated that for tactical reasons the CCM had collaborated in the past with "exclusively political elements and opportunists, men who used the disorientation of the rural masses to give themselves the fictitious appearance of being their leaders." They cited Cedillo as an example, claiming that he had always intended to use the agrarian movement as a base from which to overthrow the government and to establish a fascist dictatorship. They said that his ambitions had led the CCM to break with him in December 1936 when its fourth congress rejected a proposal that he be declared a "hero of national agrarianism." They then refuted Cedillista accusations that Sánchez and García had a "counterrevolutionary" past and claims that both had received subsidies from Cedillo during previous administrations. They concluded by attacking Cedillo's record in San Luis Potosí, accusing him of having suppressed strikes and having protected the local *hacendados*. Overall the manifesto fell rather flat—for the most part because Sánchez and García were using the agrarian movement for personal political ends and because the more specific charges made against Cedillo were lightweight. Two weeks later the local agrarian league in San Luis Potosí published a reply that sought to answer the charges against Cedillo and to substantiate those against Sánchez and García. On the whole the second document was more persuasive, but neither party emerged unscathed from the exchange.[20]

The CCM leaders' claim that Cedillo protected the local *hacendados* was a willful misinterpretation of the facts. He was concerned with helping the rural population but did not regard further land redistribution as necessarily the best solution to their problems. He encouraged the creation of new *ejidos* where he believed that this would raise the living standards of the *campesinos* involved; but he opposed land redistribution where he considered that it would replace a large-scale agricultural unit with unproductive subsistence plots. Such pragmatism was ill-received by both his opponents and the more doctrinaire members of the administration. In a speech in early October Arellano Belloc repeated the charges made by Sánchez and García, citing as evidence Cedillo's friendship with Hermenegildo Gutiérrez, the owner of the *hacienda* of Illescas, which had lost relatively little of its original vast size of 245,786 hectares. Belloc claimed that Cedillo protected the estate from further expropriation and ignored the murder by the *hacienda*'s "white guards" of villagers who had petitioned for *ejidos* there. Gutiérrez published a spirited reply to Belloc in the national press. Dismissing Belloc's charges of murder, he went on to state that fourteen *ejidal* grants covering almost 60,000 hectares had been made from the property to all but one of the nuclei of population within its boundaries, that earlier in the year the government had expropriated the *hacienda*'s irrigation works which were worth 100,000 pesos, and that he was in the process of selling off the *hacienda*'s herds of horses to the Banco de Crédito Ejidal. He also pointed out that since Illescas was in the arid and sparsely populated western region of San Luis Potosí, it was therefore suitable only for cattle raising and not for the crop or plantation farming which was customary on *ejidos*. Cedillo's enemies, however, were unimpressed by Gutiérrez's exposition of his case and continued to raise the subject in their public utterances.[21]

In this atmosphere of semiofficially inspired suspicion about Cedillo's credentials as an agrarian leader, Cárdenas struck at the heart of his power base: the rural population of San Luis Potosí. For two years the DAAC had been encouraging landless laborers in the state to petition for *ejidos*, thus seeking to win their allegiance and to challenge Cedillo's monopoly of patronage over land redistribution there. In October 1936, in response to this pressure, Cedillo had even granted provisional possession of an *ejido* covering 6,582 hectares on Palomas itself. Although the grant made little difference to the *ejidatarios'* life style—they remained dependent for their welfare upon Cedillo's patronage— the gesture reaffirmed his credentials as an agrarian leader.[22] Cedillo's opponents were not, however, going to be appeased by such symbolic concessions. The following year the DAAC entered into a negotiation with the government of San Luis Potosí designed to lead to a radical restructuring of land tenure in the state. Agreement on a program was soon reached, and in October the head of the DAAC, Gabino Vázquez, traveled to San Luis Potosí with a team of agronomists to carry it out. Vázquez was certainly no friend of the *hacendados*; a former peon on a Spanish *hacienda* in Cárdenas's own state of Michoacán, he was, according to one observer, "imbued with a cold hatred of all landowning classes."[23] Upon his arrival Vázquez stated that he intended to speed up the solution of the 484 petitions which he claimed were outstanding, and to encourage the landless who were eligible for *ejidos* to exercise their rights. He also stated that with the cooperation of the local military authorities and schoolteachers he hoped to supplement the land redistribution with other social reforms such as the provision of better medical facilities.[24]

In strictly agrarian terms such a high-level commission was not as necessary as the press suggested. In comparison with most other states a relatively high percentage of the farmland in San Luis Potosí had already been affected by the land reform. Vázquez himself admitted that by 30 November 1934, 985,000 hectares of land had been distributed to 43,998 *ejidatarios*, and between then and 16 September 1937 a further 381,000 hectares had been distributed to 15,191 *ejidatarios*. As a result about one-half of the agricultural work force in the state had *ejidal* land.[25] Moreover, at least some of the landless had refused to receive *ejidos*. There were, therefore, more pressing cases for such a commission than San Luis Potosí. Just as the press exaggerated the need for the commission's visit, so it exaggerated its achievements. When Vázquez and his men left at the end of November, they reportedly had distributed over another half million hectares benefiting 10,000 persons. This was clearly an overstatement, since in many cases the commission merely confirmed *ejidatarios* in their rights to land that they already possessed on a provisional basis.[26] As a result, less than 400,000 hectares physically changed hands. Furthermore, not all those who were granted land were satisfied with what they received. Some, such as the *ejidatarios* of La Labor in Ciudad del Maíz, wanted land elsewhere.[27] A few, such as many of the *ejidatarios* of Bledos, in Villa de Reyes, did not want land at all, fearing the political or economic consequences of becoming *ejidatarios*.[28]

The national press studiously ignored the most important aspect of the visit—its effect upon the balance of power within the state. Before the intervention of the commission, the beneficiaries of the land reform owed their allegiance primarily to Cedillo, who was their patron, and only indirectly to the federal authorities. He had stimulated land redistribution in the 1920s and had been personally involved in establishing certain *ejidos*. The majority of *ejidatarios* regarded him as their protector; and they would have followed him in the rebellions of 1923, 1927, and 1929, whichever side he had chosen. The visit of Vázquez disturbed these loyalties. The recipients of the new *ejidos* were indebted for their land to the Agrarian Department and depended upon it for the future provision of credit. Even those who had received only additions to their *ejidal* plots were under an obligation to that department and might prove loyal to their new and more powerful benefactors in a time of crisis. After the land distribution of the autumn of 1937 Cedillo could not be sure of how much active support he would receive from the state's *ejidatarios* in a rebellion against the government.

There remained, of course, his colonies, but even here the commission sought to interfere. In line with a decree of 2 November, the commission granted individual titles to the eighteen colonies which by then Cedillo had either founded or sponsored. (See Table 8.) In theory the colonists were thereafter dependents of the DAAC, but in practice, neither Cárdenas nor Vázquez expected their change of status to have any impact upon them. Unlike in the case of the *ejidatarios*, the gesture of granting them titles to their land was symbolic, even if it was also a pointer to the future.[29]

While the commission was in San Luis Potosí, the growing pressure upon Cedillo provoked a violent reaction from the more hot-headed of his supporters. Incidents of repression or even murder in the state had become more frequent during the past year as the mounting hostility to Cedillo's regime from Mexico City—epitomized by the elections the previous summer—had encouraged Cedillo's opponents to express their dissent more openly and forcibly. His enemies had formed the "Popular Committee of Revolutionary Action" (*Comité Popular de Acción Revolucionaria*), headed by a renegade Cedillista chief, Herminio Salas, to coordinate their activities. Associated with the committee were other well known adversaries of Cedillo, such as Arellano Belloc and Juan V. Torres, a magistrate in the state capital who had once been imprisoned seven times by Cedillo within a few days, only to be released on each occasion by a federal judge.[30]

On 3 October Belloc, Torres, and a number of other opponents of Cedillo went to Valles purportedly to prepare for an agrarian congress scheduled to be held in the town. In fact, they also wanted to attend an election meeting organized by the Road Workers' Union (*Frente Único de Trabajadores de Caminos*), an affiliate of the CTM, which was putting forward its own candidates in the forthcoming municipal elections there in rivalry to the "official" Cedillista nominees. The gathering soon became an act of protest against Cedillo and his regime. In particular, speakers criticized the local mayor, Tomás Oliva, whom Cedillo had put into office two months earlier following the murder of the pre-

TABLE 8: A LIST OF THE AGRARIAN-MILITARY COLONIES FOUNDED BY
OR FOUNDED WITH AID FROM SATURNINO CEDILLO
(AS OF 2 NOVEMBER 1937)

Colony	Municipality and State	Area (in Hectares)
El Llano or Magdaleno Cedillo[a]	Magdaleno Cedillo, S.L.P.[b]	4,405
Ollita de las Vacas	Magdaleno Cedillo, S.L.P.[b]	5,564
Lagunillas	Magdaleno Cedillo, S.L.P.[b]	7,561
Álvaro Obregón y Palmas	Magdaleno Cedillo, S.L.P.[b]	45,891
Guajolote y Morita or Libertad	Magdaleno Cedillo, S.L.P.[b]	17,980
Agua Nueva del Norte	Magdaleno Cedillo, S.L.P.[b]	7,153
El Salto	Magdaleno Cedillo, S.L.P.[b]	27,000
El Naranjo	Cárdenas, S.L.P.	2,021
San José	Guadalcázar, S.L.P.	3,782
La Gavia	Villa Juárez, S.L.P.	5,144
Ojo de Agua de Solano or Cleofas Cedillo[b]	Ciudad Fernández, S.L.P.	3,984
San Isidro Cerros Blancos	Mier y Noriega, Nuevo León	14,894
Madrugadores	Doctor Arroyo, Nuevo León	1,696
Cruces	Tula, Tamaulipas	10,683
La Peña	Miquihuana, Tamaulipas	18,948
Santa María de Guadalupe	Ocampo, Tamaulipas	5,816
San Pedro de los Hernández or Los Saldaña[a]	Jaumave, Tamaulipas	8,663
Meca del Norte y Meca del Sur	Jaumave, Tamaulipas	16,810

[a]Formerly known as Ciudad del Maíz.
[b]Where a colony had two names, one referred to the traditional name for the site of the colony, and the other was the title given to the colony when it was founded. In practice, however, no distinction was made between the use of the two names; and both appear in legal documents such as the one quoted here.

Source: *Diario Oficial,* 2 November 1937.

vious incumbent. Eventually Oliva appeared with some of Cedillo's hench-men, including Marcelino Zúñiga, the president of the PNR state committee, Luis Lárraga, a member of the state congress, and Vicente Segura, a former member of the same body. After an exchange of insults shooting broke out, and in the ensuing gunfight four people were killed, including Torres, and seven others were wounded. Federal troops intervened and arrested a number of those involved in the affray, one of whom was Lárraga.[31]

The incident provoked an immediate wave of protests from Cedillo's ene-mies, who accused him of being indirectly responsible for Torres's death. On the other hand, local officials claimed that Belloc provoked the violence in or-der to persuade the federal authorities to withdraw recognition from the state administration and to appoint him governor instead. Both parties were par-tially correct: whether or not they acted upon his orders, Cedillo's followers showed that they would not relinquish power peacefully; whereas Belloc, whatever his personal ambitions, was equally intent upon Cedillo's overthrow. Responsibility for the shooting was never established and Torres's murderers were not put on trial.[32]

The determination of Cedillo's most committed supporters not to tolerate opposition was underlined a week later by the murder of Tomás Tapia, the substitute president of the state PNR committee and a deputy in the state congress. Tapia, who was also on the executive committee of the *Confederación Campesina Mexicana* (CCM), had formerly been a protegé and loyal associate of Cedillo, but he broke with him when the CCM came under the control of Cedillo's adversaries. His reasons for abandoning Cedillo were personal ambition and a determination to survive Cedillo's regime with his political reputation unscathed. He realized that Cedillo was a declining force in agrarian affairs and that his own future would be more secure with influential bureaucrats such as León García and Graciano Sánchez. According to the American consul in San Luis Potosí, Sánchez had actually advised him to break with Cedillo while he still could, since "Cedillo could only last a short time longer." In switching allegiance to the Sánchez faction of the CCM, Tapia also adopted their collectivist views, something which brought him into further disagreement with Cedillo, who still believed that the *ejidatarios* should be given individual plots. During August and September 1937 he promoted these ideas among the landless population of rural San Luis Potosí, urging them to petition for land prior to the visit by Vázquez's commission.[33]

Tapia's distancing of himself from Cedillo did not develop into marked personal animosity between the two men—any more than it did in the case of Gonzalo Santos, for example. This was not, however, true of all of Cedillo's followers, some of whom regarded Tapia as a traitor to his benefactor and a dangerous example to others who might be wavering in their support for his regime. Two of Cedillo's inner circle, the brothers Arturo and José María Leija, who were smarting from Tapia's recent denunciation of them as "oppressors of the rural poor," eventually decided to make him pay for his disloyalty. On their orders two of their retainers waylaid Tapia in San Luis Potosí on 7 October and murdered him. Again there was an immediate outcry in the national press, and Gonzalo Santos, eager to demonstrate his independence of Cedillo's inner group, called upon Cárdenas to order an investigation into the murder. Several members of the state congress also subscribed to Santos's request, either from friendship with Tapia or in order to protect themselves from any repercussions of the affair. Cedillo himself was saddened by Tapia's death and angry at the Leija brothers' blunder. Tapia's funeral in Villa de Reyes was attended by the governor, Hernández Netro, and most of the state deputies. Tapia had recently organized the redistribution of 7,500 hectares of land in the district, and over a thousand *campesinos* were also present. Their shouts of "Death to the murderers Leija" were a further embarrassment to Cedillo, although they did not publicly associate his own name with the crime. Tapia's murderers were imprisoned, but the Leija brothers escaped and went into hiding—to all appearances under Cedillo's protection.[34]

Following these incidents, a high-level delegation from the CTM met Cárdenas to protest about the situation in San Luis Potosí. The president's response to their criticism was noncommittal, a reaction that encouraged the CTM to step up its campaign against Cedillo's regime. In the autumn of 1937 there was a serious drought in the state. The water supply in the town was inadequate and unhygienic, and rationing was soon imposed. Shortly afterward there were cases of typhus in the poorer quarters of the city. The CTM announced that it planned to call a strike against the authorities' failure to provide water from other sources. Mention was made again of Cedillo's co-ownership with Carrera Torres of the main local dam.[35] The state government sent to the United States for pumping equipment and also appealed for help to the federal government. Cárdenas ordered drilling equipment to be sent from Durango and Mexico City for the construction of new wells. None of these measures alleviated the immediate problem, and on 29 November the CTM began their threatened strike in the state. The following day Cárdenas offered 300,000 pesos of federal aid toward improving the city's water supply. By waiting until the strike had begun before making his second offer, the president caused the state authorities to suffer considerable embarrassment, and their discomfiture increased when the CTM organized a demonstration in the main square of San Luis Potosí on 1 December. Officially it was called to express gratitude for the federal aid to Dr. Siurob, the director of the Public Health Department, who was in the city on the president's behalf. But the meeting was a humiliating spectacle for the state government, and when one of the speakers severely criticized the local authorities a shot was fired at the crowd. Fortunately no one was seriously hurt, and the presence of Dr. Siurob prevented further violence.[36]

Unfortunately, the authorities could not install the necessary equipment immediately and the water shortage continued. This permitted Cedillo's opponents to maintain their press campaign against him. The leaders of the local CTM affiliated unions asked the senate to withdraw recognition from the state government. But before this pressure could bring any results, enough rain fell to fill the local dams. The CTM also mounted a challenge to Cedillo in the municipal elections in late December. Although they failed to weaken his grip upon local government, they further discredited the state authorities by obliging them to impose certain unpopular officials by force.[37]

The authorities in San Luis Potosí were not the only ones coming under attack. At the same time the Permanent Commission of the federal congress publicly criticized the governors of Guerrero, Tlaxcala, and Zacatecas, and sent a representative to Guanajuato to investigate accusations that the governor was in sympathy with the Cristero rebels there. But the commission's activities were simply routine steps in Cárdenas's campaign to establish the authority of the central government over the provinces.[38] The pressure upon San Luis Potosí was more specific. It was designed to undermine Cedillo's regime and recalled the campaigns against fallen *caudillos* such as Garrido Canabal. The governor of San Luis Potosí, Mateo Hernández Netro, recognized this fact and published an emotional *apología* in *El Universal*. He launched a fierce attack against his own and Cedillo's opponents in the CTM and defended his record in office.[39]

This pressure from the central government acted as a spur rather than a deterrent to Cedillo's plotting. As he unwittingly told a government spy, he was convinced that he was being forced to revolt and was preparing accordingly.[40] His agents purchased additional munitions in the United States which they then smuggled into Mexico and stockpiled in San Luis Potosí and neighboring states. Others among his supporters produced antigovernment propaganda with which they intended to create the climate for a revolt. In both Monterrey and San Luis Potosí, for example, the local *Centro Patronal* distributed a pamphlet entitled "Cedillo is not a Traitor to the Revolution," which defended Cedillo and called for an uprising against the government.[41]

Cedillo also redoubled his efforts to obtain the support of disgruntled politicians and generals. The majority of those whom he approached advised him not to contemplate a revolt before the elections of 1940, but, as Cedillo knew, his position in San Luis Potosí was unlikely to remain intact until then. None of his more powerful sympathizers, such as General Andreu Almazán, was prepared to risk participating in a premature rebellion. The only military commanders who agreed to join him unconditionally were men of the second rank such as Generals Sintora, Córdova, Barbosa, and Carmona in Nuevo León, Arango in Veracruz, Rubio and Carranza in Querétaro, and Frías in Guanajuato.[42] He knew that he could also count upon the groups of Cristeros in neighboring Guanajuato, whom he was probably supplying with arms. But although they were a "large and well-organized force," their activities were confined to the northeast of the state, and they were easily kept in check by the army.[43]

Nor could Cedillo depend upon any opposition party's supporting an armed movement. However enthusiastic Cedillo's allies of the extreme right might have been as propagandists, they were unlikely to join in a revolt. They usually belonged to the same middle-class urban sectors from which the League for the Defense of Religious Liberty had drawn its following ten years earlier and like many of the members of the league they were more inclined to a war of words than of bullets. In the final analysis they had too much to lose materially to take up the rigorous life of rural guerrillas.

The only group that was willing to engage in a military revolt was the fascist ARM, but Nicolás Rodríguez continued to reject Cedillo's overtures and maintained his closest links with his fellow exile, ex-president Calles. In any case the ARM lacked significant support, as was shown in January 1938 when Rodríguez attempted to organize an insurrection in Tamaulipas. A group of his supporters smuggled three lorries across the U.S. border and attacked Matamoros. The authorities were forewarned that such an action was likely, and both the town garrison and the local *agraristas* were alerted. As a result the Gold Shirts were easily repulsed; sixteen of them were killed and twenty-five captured. The whole affair was a fiasco and must have acted as a somber warning to Cedillo that the chances of a successful rebellion were slight.[44]

One of Cedillo's most pressing problems as he contemplated revolt in the spring of 1938 was a shortage of funds. His needs were considerable: he was constantly asked for money in return for political allegiance; he was building up his private arsenal; and he was helping to finance the various right-wing organizations with which he was involved. Access to the state treasury was inadequate to meet his needs, for although the state authorities cooperated as much as they could, they simply lacked the money. For the period from January to May 1938 the state's fiscal department budgeted the sum of 5,475 pesos for "unforeseen and extraordinary expenses"—the term which often covered payments to Cedillo—whereas they were called upon to spend 48,241 pesos under that heading. Since they had to find the additional sum by cutting back on other expenditures, there was a limit to what they could do for him.[45] In March 1937 Cedillo obtained a loan of 150,000 pesos from a representative of the Monterrey Chamber of Commerce. This was soon exhausted, and toward the end of the year he looked elsewhere. Through an intermediary, Alfonso Loyola, whose cousin was a legal adviser to the Huasteca Petroleum Company, Cedillo sought a loan from the foreign-owned oil companies in Mexico. These companies were then locked in a pay dispute with their workers, who were supported by the CTM. Although the companies would undoubtedly have liked to see Cárdenas replaced by someone more sympathetic to their cause, they were aware that the U.S. government would not support them in any plot to overthrow him. They must also have known that Cedillo was under close surveillance by the Mexican government, and that if they spent money on him their relations with the regime would worsen even more. As a result of these factors the negotiations came to nothing, and neither then nor apparently later did Cedillo obtain funds from this source.[46]

Following this disappointment, Cedillo sent agents to the United States to try to negotiate two huge loans, one of a million and one-half pesos, and the other of two million. The first was purportedly for establishing cotton production on Palomas, and Cedillo offered the property as security. Cedillo's representative could not interest anyone in such an unlikely scheme, particularly since Palomas was at most worth 100,000 pesos. The second was based upon a decree by the state congress authorizing the floating of such a loan to finance irrigation projects within San Luis Potosí. It was to be repaid over ten years with 15% of the state's annual revenues. The Chase National Bank showed a slight interest in this project, which, in theory at least, appeared plausible, but insisted that it be approved by the Mexican National Congress. Knowing that such approval would not be granted, Cedillo's agents gave up their efforts. To complete their misfortune, one of them, an American freelance pilot called Lloyd Clevenger, was arrested and imprisoned for violation of the neutrality laws. In September 1937 he had flown to Mexico two of the planes that Cedillo had purchased in the United States without the permission of the relevant American authorities.[47]

While Cedillo strove to construct a defensive alliance and the government maneuvered to undermine his position, developments in San Luis Potosí were overtaken by events of greater national consequence. In December Cárdenas reaffirmed his control over the governing bureaucracy by announcing that the PNR was to be restructured. The party's name was changed to *Partido de la Revolución Mexicana* (PRM), and it was to be divided into four sections: the army, organized labor, the peasantry, and middle sector groups. In taking this step Cárdenas was moving toward the creation of a corporate state, but restructuring the ruling party assisted him to bring the government more closely under his personal control. Then shortly before the organization of the PRM was completed, the president made the most dramatic move of his six years in office. On 18 March 1938 he announced the expropriation of the foreign-owned oil companies operating in Mexico. This decision, which followed months of legal proceedings and tense negotiations between the government and the companies, was extremely popular in all but certain business circles. It provoked a wave of nationalism, and there were spontaneous expressions of support for the president throughout the country. In a skillfully managed campaign the government identified itself with the national interest. Normally vociferous critics of the administration fell silent, either believing that the country should present a united front in the face of foreign hostility, or deeming the moment inappropriate to speak out. In such circumstances the government could brand anyone who rebelled as a traitor and the tool of foreign interests.[48]

This change in the political atmosphere was recognized by General Magaña, who had previously contemplated supporting Cedillo if he rebelled. He and General Bañuelos, the governor of Zacatecas and another potential ally of Cedillo, obtained an interview with Cárdenas. They assured the president of their loyalty and offered to visit Cedillo in order to dissuade him from any rebellious action. Cárdenas had presumably seen references to Magaña and Bañuelos in the reports of Cedillo's plotting and welcomed their initiative. The two governors travelled to Palomas and interviewed Cedillo. They emphasized to him the political consequences of the oil expropriation, explained that they would not participate in any armed movement, and urged him to abandon his preparations for a revolt.[49] This was a serious blow to Cedillo, who realized the futility of any revolt confined to San Luis Potosí. He therefore agreed not to commit himself until the elections of 1940 but insisted that he would defend himself if attacked. At the beginning of April another of Cedillo's potential allies, General Yocupicio, publicly reaffirmed his loyalty to Cárdenas, thus hinting to Cedillo that he would not join any armed movement. In spite of these indications to the contrary, Cedillo still hoped to count upon General Magaña and other disgruntled generals in an emergency.[50]

Cárdenas also appreciated the political advantage that the oil expropriation gave him, and decided to use the opportunity to eliminate Cedillo as a force in national politics. Within a week of the expropriation he transferred the local military commander in San Luis Potosí, Cedillo's friend Francisco Carrera Torres, to become head of the military zone in Oaxaca, almost as far from San Luis Potosí as he could have sent him. He replaced Carrera Torres with General Genovevo Rivas Guillén, a career officer whose loyalty to Cárdenas was unquestioned but who was also on good terms with Cedillo. Guillén brought with him additional troops, so that Cedillo began to look like a man under siege in a war zone.[51]

Cárdenas then turned his attention to Cedillo himself. Shortly after Cedillo's resignation as minister of agriculture, he had offered him an ambassadorship, but Cedillo had refused this traditional path to political exile and oblivion, preferring to remain in San Luis Potosí. The offer that Cárdenas now made to Cedillo did not permit him the option of refusal. On 31 March he ordered him to assume immediate command of the military zone of Michoacán with his headquarters in Morelia. Such a move was consistent with the bloodless way in which Cárdenas had dealt with other political opponents such as Calles or Garrido Canabal. Although Cedillo was a stranger to the local population of Michoacán, the governor of the state was his close friend and erstwhile fellow conspirator Gildardo Magaña. By ordering Cedillo to Morelia, Cárdenas offered him an honorable exit from political life, and not, as certain of Cedillo's advisers told him, a trap from which he would not escape alive.[52]

Cedillo was not prepared to leave San Luis Potosí and face political extinction, but he knew that refusal to obey the order was tantamount to rebellion. He therefore tried to delay any decision by claiming that he was unfit to travel. The minister of defense, General Manuel Ávila Camacho, knew that Cedillo was perfectly capable of travelling, but on Cárdenas's instructions he gave him six weeks leave with orders to present himself in Morelia by 16 May. In the meantime Cedillo's adjutant, Colonel Josué Escobedo, was ordered to assume command in Morelia on his behalf.[53]

During this period Cedillo vacillated between four possible courses of action: acceptance of the order to go to Michoacán; resignation from the army and remaining at Palomas in the faint hope that he would be left in peace; striving to reach an agreement with Cárdenas which would leave his position in San Luis Potosí undisturbed; and, finally, rebellion. Believing that his life would be threatened if he went to Mexico City, he negotiated with Cárdenas through his representatives there. Whether an obstinate and rebellious Cedillo could ever have come to terms with a government apparently determined to dismantle his regime is doubtful; but he made the task more difficult by dealing with Cárdenas through intermediaries. Cedillo was surrounded by men whose political survival depended upon his regime, some of whom were prepared to push him into revolt in order to protect their privileges. Cárdenas counted among his closest advisers left-wing ideologues such as Múgica and Lombardo Toledano who considered Cedillo to be the natural leader for a fascist *putsch* against the government. Between them was a group of dubious middlemen, dedicated to furthering their careers and in many cases indifferent to the eventual fate of their original patron.

It was commonly believed that Cedillo could call upon between 10,000 and 15,000 *agraristas,* most of them mounted.[54] But he lacked the resources to mobilize even one-half that number before the government could take countermeasures; furthermore, many of his former soldiers had received land during the visit by Gabino Vázquez a few months earlier, and it was uncertain whether they would place their *ejidal* plots at risk by rebelling against their benefactor. Altogether, therefore, Cedillo could expect to put about 5,000 men into the field under the command of his former officers. Assisted by the planes that he had recently purchased, such a force could certainly embarrass the government, particularly if it was supported by sympathizers elsewhere in the country.

Throughout April, while Cedillo hesitated over his next move, the tension in San Luis Potosí increased. Some of Cedillo's friends advised him to leave for Michoacán. They included the state governor, Mateo Hernández Netro, who believed that in this way a conflict with the central government could be avoided. Others close to Cedillo who shared Netro's view were Miguel Aranda Díaz, Arturo Leija, Enrique Alatorre, and Colonel Josué Escobedo, all of whom considered that an uprising would lack popular support and informed Cedillo accordingly. On the other hand, several of his oldest friends, including Marcelino Zúñiga and Vicente Segura, assured Cedillo that a rebellion would be successful. Cedillo veered toward the latter view, still convinced that if he actually launched a rebellion, other dissident generals such as Magaña and Yocupicio would feel obliged to join him. It was a grave misjudgment, and the preparations for an uprising continued unabated.[55]

On 18 April Rubén Sánchez Gascón, Cedillo's chief publicity adviser, arrived in Río Verde to supervise the printing of two revolutionary documents: the first, a decree by the state government withdrawing recognition from the federal administration, and the second, a personal manifesto from Cedillo explaining the reasons for his revolt. Sánchez Gascón ordered 4,000 copies of each. At Palomas a workshop for making bombs was established, and emergency airfields were marked out nearby for the use of Cedillo's planes. In addition, Cedillo informed some of his former commanders that they might shortly be called upon again and instructed them to make the appropriate preparations. Most were not given any further explanation, and several assumed that another campaign was being planned against the Cristeros.[56]

Cedillo knew that he could not delay a revolt indefinitely, and despairing of reaching agreement with Cárdenas, he set 5 May as the date for his uprising. However, encouraging reports from his agents in Mexico City shortly before the appointed day led him to alter his plans. He decided to retire from the army, a move that would give him more time to negotiate with Cárdenas and would allow him to remain at Palomas. He hoped that if he promised to keep the peace, he could persuade the president to replace Rivas Guillén with a general of his choice, such as Turrubiartes. But in case Cárdenas refused this offer, he set a new date for the uprising, 15 May. He telegraphed the defense minister, General Ávila Camacho, on 8 May seeking permission to retire from the army for reasons of ill health. To allay any suspicions aroused by this request, he added that he wanted no further involvement in politics and intended to devote himself to farming. At the same time he sent Eugenio Jiménez, probably his closest political adviser and one of the senators for San Luis Potosí, to Mexico City with a letter for the president reiterating the contents of the telegram.[57]

On 5 May Enrique Alatorre, one of Cedillo's most trusted associates, visited General Magaña in Morelia and advised him that a revolt was imminent. Magaña repeated his warning of a month earlier: that the oil expropriation had changed the political picture, that a rebellion at that moment was doomed to fail, and that neither he nor any other of Cedillo's more important fellow conspirators would join an uprising. He added, however, that he was prepared to act as a mediator between Cedillo and Cárdenas. Alatorre therefore proposed that Cedillo should be offered the command of the military zone in San Luis Potosí, explaining that like Andreu Almazán in Nuevo León, he would thus remain in his home territory, but under government control. Magaña agreed to suggest this compromise to Cárdenas, and Alatorre travelled to Palomas to obtain Cedillo's approval for it.[58] Cedillo reacted favorably to Alatorre's idea and gave him the following memorandum for Magaña to read before speaking to the president. This document accurately reflects Cedillo's tendency to see his differences with Cárdenas in personal rather than political terms and also his somewhat confused state of mind at this critical moment:

Palomas, S. L. P., 9 May 1938
Memorandum for General Magaña

1. I have repeatedly told you that I have no intention of acting precipitately. I have been preparing to defend myself from any aggression. An intense effort is being made to destroy my group; so far those involved have only managed to disorient a small number of my friends.

2. I authorize you to arrange with the President for me to be given command of the military zone in San Luis Potosí, so that I can be operated upon for my hernia. If the Government agrees to this move, it need have no reason to fear any danger; I will personally guarantee [the President] both peace and support for his Administration. If the authorities do not trust me with the command of the military zone in San Luis Potosí, I would like them to appoint General Turrubiartes, who is at present a Brigade General, to assume command there; he will be able to ensure peace and quiet without the need for one extra man to be sent to help him.

3. Please repeat to the President, who is a very humane man, that I am preparing to defend myself in view of the threats which have been made against my life and in view of the constant boasting of his friends who claim that they are going to destroy me. If the President really wants to do me justice, it is not a lot to ask him to allow me command of this zone in return for my word of honour that I will answer for its tranquillity and that for my part there will not be the least intention of denying his government my support. The honour of the government will lose nothing by this since my illness prevents me going to Michoacán.

As you will understand my honor and dignity as a man require me to protect my group, which is not, strictly speaking, Cedillista, it is simply that I am the link which holds them together. This group gave the President its whole-hearted support when he was a candidate, and could very easily become Cardenista again if it were treated with justice. We are not seeking privileges, simply justice, but if, instead of paying heed to us, the President continues to listen to mean and petty-minded elements and wishes to destroy me, then he should know that many heads will roll and that he will have a fight on his hands, and let him make no mistake about it, the fight will be long and the consequences uncertain; for I do not sell my dignity and honour for all the gold in the world; I prefer to die on my feet, like a man, rather than allow my group to be destroyed without just cause, or even less rather than to die on my knees as some people intend.

Saturnino Cedillo[59]

Magaña was concerned about the defiant tone of the memorandum, but he nevertheless took it to Mexico City on the tenth. His presence there at the same time as Jiménez left Cárdenas confused and suspicious; for both claimed to represent Cedillo but made contradictory proposals.[60] In the meantime Cedillo's subordinates prepared for an uprising on 15 May, and ordered the commanders of his *agraristas* to concentrate their forces at Palomas and other strategic points by that date. At the same time, in a bizarre incident Marcelino Zúñiga organized the theft of some colonial paintings from the town hall in San Luis Potosí. He intended to sell the pictures, which were valued at 150,000 pesos, to help to finance the revolt. The scheme backfired when the federal police investigating the crime learned who was responsible, recovered the pictures, and found with them a number of compromising documents concerning Cedillo's plotting. This affair, farcical though it was in some ways, nevertheless provided Cárdenas with further evidence of the seriousness of the situation.[61]

On 14 May, Arnulfo Hernández, a federal congressman for San Luis Potosí, sent Cedillo a telegram from Mexico City informing him, incorrectly, that Cárdenas was prepared to grant his request for retirement and to appoint Turrubiartes the military commander in San Luis Potosí.[62] This implausible report persuaded Cedillo to postpone the revolt yet again. Over fifteen hundred *agraristas* had assembled at Palomas on the fourteenth, ready to move the following day. Cedillo thanked them, explained that they were not needed after all, and instructed them to return home. He sent similar messages to his commanders in other parts of the state. He retained only a token force as a personal guard and some key individuals such as telegraphists and pilots. Several groups apparently did not receive the counter-orders, and they remained under arms awaiting instruction. Two of them took the initiative and attacked the federal garrisons in Tamazunchale and Valles. Hearing of this, General Rivas Guillén sent a message to Cedillo advising him to go to Mexico City and offering to act as a hostage for his safety. Even in these circumstances Cedillo refused to risk abandoning San Luis Potosí. He still believed that his representatives in Mexico City could reach an agreement with the president by which he could remain in San Luis Potosí and retain control of affairs there. He therefore stayed at Palomas and informed the press that he was peacefully attending to his estate.[63]

At this point Cárdenas decided to intervene personally and force Cedillo to either submit to central government authority or openly revolt. Although a natural enough reaction in view of the conflicting information that he was receiving from San Luis Potosí, the president's desire to bring matters to a head was not, however, due solely to Cedillo's seditious activities. He had recently received reports of plotting by a number of generals who had not previously been associated with the more prominent dissenters from his government's policies, such as Magaña or Cedillo himself. Among the names mentioned in this connection were those of Ramón Iturbe, the brothers Emilio and Miguel Acosta, and Máximo Ávila Camacho, the governor of Puebla and brother of the defense minister. Such men were concerned at the possible economic consequences of what they considered to be the government's extremist labor policies. In addition, they feared that the army's position might be threatened by the rapid growth of the CTM and what they saw as the increasing militancy of its leaders. Although their discontent had not reached the point where they were definitely planning a revolt, they had nevertheless prepared a manifesto purporting to come from "the Organizing Committee of the National Anti-Fascist and Anti-Communist Association." Several of these dissident generals, such as Iturbe, were on the army reserve list, but they were believed to have the sympathy or even support of the more important regional army commanders and a number of younger officers, particularly those whose thinking had been influenced by the authoritarian doctrines of General Amaro when he was director of the Military College. Since they were also in touch with the oil companies, the potential threat that they posed was not to be taken lightly. In these circumstances Cárdenas was naturally anxious to deal with Cedillo as quickly as possible. He might also have calculated that if he provoked Cedillo into a precipitate and abortive uprising, it would be a lesson to other possible rebels. He would remind them of his presidential power and demonstrate that, in spite of the oil expropriation, they could not expect to receive the support of Washington.[64]

On the night of 17 May, Cárdenas took a train to San Luis Potosí accompanied by his ministers of the interior and education, Ignacio García Téllez and Gonzalo Vázquez Vela, and a bodyguard of secret police. He was followed a few hours later by General Manuel Ávila Camacho, the minister of defense, Luis Rodríguez, the president of the newly formed *Partido de la Revolución Mexicana* (PRM), and finally Cedillo's long standing antagonist, Graciano Sánchez, who was director of the Department of Indian Affairs. Cedillo heard of the president's journey, but in keeping with his disposition to see their political differences in terms of a personal quarrel, he believed that Cárdenas wished to resolve their dispute in a face-to-face meeting. He therefore instructed his followers to allow the presidential train to proceed unhindered and ordered the governor, Mateo Hernández Netro, and other officials to receive Cárdenas with all due honors.[65]

Cárdenas went at once to the government palace and delivered a speech to the assembled crowd. He detailed his government's priorities in the fields of social and economic reform, referred to the difficulties it faced, including the external pressure resulting from the oil expropriation, and then stated that at such a time of national crisis there was talk in San Luis Potosí of a possible revolt. He ascribed such seditious rumors to the rebellious attitude of Cedillo, and he concluded by calling on him to give the government all the arms and munitions that he had acquired, and to retire into private life. Cedillo heard the speech on the radio at Palomas while he was having a bath. Rather than go to San Luis Potosí and make his peace with Cárdenas, which in the mood of the moment could have been dangerous, he gave orders that his appointed commanders should be told to begin the revolt. About 1,500 of his followers answered his call and, like their leader, took to the hills.[66]

The rebels were opposed by 10,000 federal troops in the state capital and several thousand elsewhere in the state under the overall command of the minister of defense, General Ávila Camacho. Cárdenas, however, was reluctant to use the force at his disposal. He was adamant that bloodshed should be minimized and the rebels be given every opportunity to surrender voluntarily. Initially, therefore, Camacho's only offensive gesture was to dispatch a column of soldiers to Palomas under José Beltrán, one of Cedillo's former officers. Beltrán found the property deserted but nevertheless sacked it. Camacho also reinforced the garrisons of all the towns in the eastern region of the state. Otherwise, he concentrated upon psychological warfare and a peaceful solution to the problem. Aircraft dropped leaflets containing extracts of Cárdenas's speech and stating that rebellion against an administration dedicated to help the rural poor was absurd. A number of local teachers had long been carrying out propaganda work for the government and undermining support for Cedillo; their efforts were now augmented by teams of officials from the Ministry of Education and the Department of Agriculture who visited remote villages under the protection of federal soldiers. Finally, censorship made it difficult for the isolated and uncoordinated groups of rebels to receive reports of Cedillo's movements.[67]

These tactics proved successful. Confused by the propaganda and censorship, the rebels soon began to surrender, many of them before they were involved in any action. On 26 May Cedillo issued instructions to his followers to lay low until the political situation favored a renewal of the revolt. (He presumably wanted to save his forces from fruitless loss of life or forcible disarmament, so that he could still call upon them at a later date.) Thereafter, the majority of his men still under arms either went home or surrendered to the nearest federal unit. Those who surrendered were deprived of their weapons and then encouraged to return to their villages.[68] Some of Cedillo's closest associates died before he issued his orders to disband, and others chose to fight on regardless. The first such victim of the revolt was Melitón Luna, the private secretary of the state governor, Mateo Hernández Netro, who died in a skirmish at Estación Manuel on 20 May. Hipólito Cedillo, Saturnino's nephew and a member of the state congress, was killed on 23 May. Marcelino Zúñiga, whose men blew up a troop train on 3 June, killing the driver and fireman, was killed soon afterward with his son and nephew. Pedro Izaguirre surrendered with 201 men that he had raised in his home district of Tamasopo on 27 May, only to be murdered a few weeks later in a fight between his own men and a rival faction of the sugar cooperative there. Aureliano Anaya, Ramón Verástegui, Ignacio Castillo, and their men surrendered to General Figueroa on the twenty-eighth. Bruno Jasso and sixteen of his men gave themselves up on the twenty-ninth. Federico Wollemberg, Cedillo's brother-in-law, who had acted as one of his intermediaries in the abortive negotiations with the oil companies, was captured on 10 June with Manuel Collado and Florencio Turrubiartes. Alberto Araujo, the municipal president of San Luis Potosí during the last months of Cedillo's rule, accepted the offer of an amnesty from Cárdenas when the president was in Araujo's home town of Charcas in late June, although he was arrested for robbery with violence soon afterward on the orders of a magistrate in Salinas. Other chiefs who surrendered with their followers at about the same time were Vicente Segura, Félix Cura, the Leija brothers, one of whose bands numbered about one hundred fifty men, Arnulfo Hernández, Genaro Morales, Antonio Jaramillo, the head of the agrarian colony of Ollita de las Vacas, and Feliciano Najera, with forty-three men from Palomas. Adelaido Barrón, who was leading a group of rebels near Ciudad del Maíz, was killed on 8 August and his men were dispersed. By early September probably less than one hundred fifty rebels remained under arms, and when J. Guadalupe García was killed in an ambush and his band broken up at the end of the following month, the federal army declared the revolt to be officially over. Nevertheless, individual followers of Cedillo remained at large, and many did not surrender for several months after that.[69]

Not all of Cedillo's associates joined him in rebellion. Colonel Josué Escobedo, his aide-de-camp for over ten years, immediately reaffirmed his loyalty to the central government. Senator Eugenio Jiménez, one of Cedillo's main representatives in his recent negotiations with Cárdenas, issued a statement pledging his support to the president; Rutilio Alamilla, various times the secretary of the state government during Cedillo's regime and a man who had enriched himself in Cedillo's shadow from urban real estate, also publicly disowned his former patron. Gonzalo Santos, always quick to advance his career, went even further—he at once flew to San Luis Potosí and offered to join the hunt for Cedillo. The bitterest blow of all was the attitude of Ildefonso Turrubiartes. Either for his own safety, or perhaps for Cedillo's, the old guerrilla fighter assisted the federal army in their search for him.[70]

Any hopes which Cedillo's supporters had of retaining control of the government while their leader went into hiding were soon shattered. On 21 May Cárdenas was given an official lunch in San Luis Potosí by the state authorities. During the meal two of Cedillo's airplanes flew over the city. One of the pilots dropped four bombs, apparently aimed at where the lunch was being held or at the government palace where Cárdenas was staying, and the other, a number of leaflets. They then retired to their base near Ciudad del Maíz. The bombs missed their mark and fell harmlessly nearby. The leaflets were copies of Cedillo's manifesto and of the decree—signed by the governor, Hernández Netro, and three state congressmen—by which the state authorities withdrew recognition of the national government. The air raid took everyone by surprise, especially Hernández Netro, whose hopes of salvaging his regime had been sabotaged by the release of the decree. Although Cárdenas assured him that he regarded Cedillo alone as being responsible for the incident, the governor decided that his position was untenable. He resigned from his post that night and went into hiding, leaving his administration in the hands of the president of the state supreme court.[71]

Following Hernández Netro's resignation, the senate complied with a request from Cárdenas to declare that "the powers of the state administration had disappeared," and thus left the national congress to choose a provisional governor. There were three candidates for the post: General Rivas Guillén, the local military commander, Reynaldo Pérez Gallardo, a former associate of Cedillo who had turned against him some time before, and Arellano Belloc. At Cárdenas's instigation the congress chose Rivas Guillén. This was a conciliatory move on the president's part since he was by far the most popular choice of the three among Cedillo's friends.[72]

The new state authorities at once began a purge of the municipal administrations in which Cedillista *caciquismo* had been most marked. Cárdenas himself presided over elections in the most important municipalities such as Charcas and Matehuala. He also visited several others, such as Ciudad del Maíz and Ciudad Mante in neighboring Tamaulipas. By traveling around the state—albeit with a strong military escort—the president emphasized the failure of Cedillo's revolt and conveyed an impression of normalcy. By autumn the Cedillista regime had been dismantled, and only minor officials and a few popular local councilors remained in office.[73]

In keeping with Cárdenas's customary treatment of his opponents, there was little persecution of members of the previous administration. A few were arrested, although most were soon released; and a number of deaths during the revolt might have been acts of personal revenge. But the prevailing mood was of reconciliation rather than retribution. Those of Cedillo's closest associates who survived the rebellion lost their privileges, but at least they remained alive. The majority of them retired to the countryside, where many had property in one form or another. Several, such as Hernández Netro and Vicente Segura, settled in the agrarian colonies, where their authority, like that of their absent leader, was still respected.[74]

Outside San Luis Potosí Cedillo received almost no support at all. General Yocupicio in Sonora dispelled any government fears that he might join the revolt by publicly reaffirming his loyalty to Cárdenas on 22 May, and the other state governors, including Magaña and Bañuelos, issued a joint statement along similar lines the following day. Not unexpectedly, perhaps, Andreu Almazán also remained loyal to the administration and abandoned Cedillo to his fate. Refugio Huerta raised a guerrilla band in support of Cedillo near Guadalajara but surrendered on 13 June. On the same day the police in Chipilo,

Puebla shot and killed Cedillo's local representative, General Enrique Espejel Chavarría, when he resisted arrest. In Oaxaca three local military chiefs, Generals Cuéllar, Brena, and Avendaño, abandoned their attempts to raise support for Cedillo through lack of funds and went into hiding. In Tamaulipas and Nuevo León there were insignificant clashes between members of Cedillo's colonies and federal soldiers. Elsewhere, there was no reaction to the revolt at all, and censorship of the press and radio—for the minority of the population with access to them—made the movement appear even less significant than it was.[75]

Cedillo survived the downfall of his regime by six months. On 19 May he fled from Palomas to a cave at Milpaís near El Custodio where he had stores and radio equipment prepared. Four days later federal army units approached, and he moved on to San Juan del Meco, accompanied by thirty or forty loyal followers. There, on the night of the twenty-sixth, he held a council of war. Having concluded that resistance was futile, he decided to take refuge in the mountains that he knew so well. He arranged to be kept informed about the movements of the federal army and to be supplied with food and ammunition, and then he ordered most of those present to return home. He kept with him about fifteen of his most devoted companions, men without family ties who could endure the hardships of a guerrilla existence.[76]

Thereafter, Cedillo moved around the east of the state, his freedom depending upon his intimate knowledge of the terrain and upon the support of the local population. Sometime in late June or early July he issued a second manifesto. In it he roundly condemned the state governments of Zacatecas, Michoacán, and Sonora for not coming to his assistance, claiming that they and the local administration of San Luis Potosí had earlier made an agreement to support one another if the central government withdrew recognition from any of them. He also denied again any connection with international fascism, rejected accusations of being in the pay of the foreign-owned oil companies, and made a further attack upon Cárdenas's agrarian policies. The manifesto was shorter and more emotional than his previous one—he referred to Cárdenas, for example, as "His Serene Highness." It also reflected his sense of betrayal by those generals that he expected to help him—Magaña, Yocupicio, and Bañuelos—even though such expectations had been wholly unrealistic. (The mutual defense pact which it mentioned had been at most a loose and informal understanding between Cedillo and the other generals concerned; and as we have seen, Magaña and Bañuelos had specifically warned him after the oil expropriation that they would not join him in a revolt.) But above all, the manifesto was a statement of self-justification and defiance, and as far as the government was concerned, it offered no hope that Cedillo could be persuaded to surrender.[77]

Shortly after Cedillo issued this document, an intrepid journalist from the right-wing periodical *Hoy* sought an interview with him through mutual friends. In conditions of great secrecy the journalist was eventually taken to a rendezvous in the hills near Ciudad del Maíz. Of necessity Cedillo's meeting with the man was short, but it revealed that his spirit was undaunted by the failure of his rebellion. In what was to be his last public statement, he stoutly defended the legality of his action. He referred the journalist to the decree of the recently deposed state government in which it had withdrawn recognition from Cárdenas and had appointed Cedillo "Chief of the Constitutionalist Army of Mexico." He also reaffirmed his opposition to the introduction of collective *ejidos* and again denied any connection with the oil companies. On a more personal note, Cedillo added that he was in better health than for many years. This was confirmed by a photograph which the journalist took; having previously been badly overweight and out of condition, he now looked slimmer and more active. In parting, Cedillo expressed his confidence that he could evade capture indefinitely:

> I know this region as no one knows it. In these hills and valleys I spent my life as a revolutionary. Before any federal soldiers approach I have been given detailed information concerning their movements which allows me either to flee or prepare an attack upon them.[78]

The obvious improvement in Cedillo's health was an unhappy omen for the government, for it indeed suggested that he would be able to persist in his revolt for far longer than anyone would have imagined, seeing him two months earlier. In fact, he intended to remain at large until the presidential elections of 1940, when he expected his fortunes to improve. He believed that if the elections were fair, the "official" candidate would be defeated, in which case he himself could hope for an amnesty from the new administration. On the other hand, if the government chose to impose its candidate through electoral chicanery, he assumed that General Andreu Almazán and other right-wing elements would join him in revolt. Cárdenas appreciated the reasons for Cedillo's continuing defiance. He too anticipated a possible uprising in 1940 and was eager to obtain Cedillo's surrender before the election campaign began. Through intermediaries he made him several offers of safe conduct into exile, but Cedillo, believing that time was on his side, rejected these overtures.[79]

Eventually, however, treachery succeeded where other methods had failed. At the beginning of January 1939 Cedillo saw his beloved Palomas for the last time. On the night of 10 January he and his companions camped near La Ventana. Their presence there was betrayed to the federal army by two of the men involved in supplying them with food, Blas Ruíz, a former secretary of the state Agrarian League, and Magdaleno García, the former *cacique* of Guadalcázar. The following morning the Cedillistas were surprised by a federal patrol under Captain Castrejón. In the resulting skirmish three of Cedillo's companions were killed, including his son Elodio. Cedillo himself was only wounded but was then given a *coup de grâce,* some say by Blas Ruíz himself. His body was taken back to Ciudad del Maíz and thence transported to Palomas for burial. With his death he had paid the price for refusing to surrender to a man whom he helped to the presidency but whom he now considered his enemy. He had not, however, lost either the respect or affection of the vast majority of the local *campesinos*. In spite of everything—his mismanagement of the state's affairs, the oppression of many local *caciques* who had acted in his name, the corruption of his friends, and the governments's efforts to blacken his reputation—he still retained their loyalty. In a last gesture of esteem for their former patron, thousands of them braved official displeasure to attend his funeral.[80]

CONCLUSION

The decade of violence that followed the overthrow of the dictator Porfirio Díaz in 1910–1911 was in essence a struggle for political power. The failure of Díaz to rejuvenate his aging administration provoked a crisis within the regime that ended in an armed revolt led by a member of the ruling elite, Francisco Madero. This uprising heralded a prolonged period of civil unrest which eventually evolved into a multifactional fight for control of the central government. Within this political conflict there ran a strong current of agrarian revolt, whose roots lay in the development of large-scale commercial agriculture during the late Porfiriato. This rural unrest, which proved prolonged and bloody, gave the Revolution its character, so that many historians consider it the first important peasant revolution of the twentieth century. As events proved, however, the agrarian issue was of secondary importance to the question of renovating the Porfirian state. The eventual winners in the power struggle from 1910 to 1920 were not the Zapatistas or their allies, with their parochial world view and agrarian-oriented aims, but a group of restless and hard-headed young men from the northwestern state of Sonora, whose experience of agrarian unrest was confined to the frontier wars against the obstinate Yaqui and Mayo Indians. Led by the most talented general to emerge from the civil wars, Álvaro Obregón, the Sonorans set out to modernize the country along classical capitalist lines, while at the same time realizing personal ambitions that had been frustrated in the stifling atmosphere of the late Porfiriato.

The country's new rulers appreciated the fact that in order to pacify the country they had to make a response to the aspirations of the Zapatistas and their counterparts elsewhere, even if they considered them to be outdated and incompatible with their own vision of the country's long-term future. Therefore they promoted the agrarian reform introduced by the previous administration of Venustiano Carranza. Their view of the scope of this reform was relatively limited; it was intended to assist in the pacification of the more troubled parts of the country but not to challenge the dominance of private estates in Mexican agriculture. Within this process some of the rural *caudillos* who had survived the Revolution, such as Saturnino Cedillo in San Luis Potosí and Genovevo de la O in Morelos, played an important role, acting as brokers between the authorities in Mexico City and the local population. But in most of the country the agrarian reform came under the control of urban-based, provincial politicians who saw it as a platform for their ambitions, and in this way it was rapidly absorbed into the expanding central bureaucracy. Those who received land under the reform became clients of the bureaucracy, and their status was underlined when the government used them to combat the various rebellions of the 1920s. Moves by the rural dispossessed to seize and occupy land outside the framework of the agrarian bureaucracy were usually suppressed by the federal army.

Lázaro Cárdenas built upon the foundations laid by the Sonorans, and his administration witnessed the consolidation of the modern Mexican state. In many ways a continuation of the Porfirian system, with a strong president and a highly centralized bureaucracy, the postrevolutionary regime as it came to fruition under Cárdenas was, however, less rigid and better able to absorb the demands of the middle and lower classes. In the rural sector Cárdenas made the agrarian reform the focal point of his agricultural policy. He extended land redistribution in an unprecedented manner, so that by 1940, *ejidatarios* accounted for almost one-half of those employed in agriculture, and in line with his general policy of political centralization he increased the size and scope of the agrarian bureaucracy. As a result the government eventually came to exercise patronage over a large proportion of the rural population, and the relationship between the agrarian bureaucracy and its clients under Cárdenas was similar in many ways to that between the *hacendados* of the Porfiriato and their laborers. The many *campesinos* who had fought in the Revolution and who subsequently obtained land under the agrarian reform found that their new master, the postrevolutionary state, was, in practice, barely less burdensome than their former one, the old Porfirian oligarchy.

Against this background the career of Saturnino Cedillo provides a useful illustration of the part played by agrarian revolt and reform in the history of Mexico between the late Porfiriato and the 1940 presidential elections—the wide spread within the country of the phenomenon known as Zapatismo; the use of land redistribution to achieve pacification after 1920; the employment of the beneficiaries of such land, the *agraristas*, against the rural opponents of the Callista state, the Cristeros; and the incompatibility of the rural *caudillos* who emerged from the Revolution with the new, postrevolutionary, bureaucratic state created by Obregón and Calles, and consolidated by Cárdenas.

In a strict sense, Zapatismo should be used only to describe the rural unrest in Morelos between 1910 and 1920, where Emiliano Zapata led the resistance of the local villagers to the expansionism of the state's sugar plantation owners. But conflicts between commercially minded *hacendados* and their poorer neighbors were not confined to Morelos, and contemporaries soon employed the terms "Zapatismo" and "Zapatista" to describe similar struggles and their protagonists in other states, such as Veracruz, Puebla, Sinaloa, and San Luis Potosí. The objectives of the rebels were reactionary: opposition to the future for rural society envisaged by the dynamic agricultural entrepreneurs of the late Porfiriato, in which all available resources were to be geared to maximum production along classical capitalist lines. The *hacendados* saw the recalcitrant villagers as a barrier to progress; the latter were fighting for a return to an imagined past in which *hacendados* had happily coexisted with smallholders and independent landowning communities. Between these two extreme positions lay the growing numbers of *rancheros* who were, in part, the product of the increasing commercial opportunities of the late Porfiriato. Eager to develop their properties, but often fearful of the government-backed aggression of the *hacendados*, the *rancheros* frequently provided the leadership for the rural revolts.

Around Ciudad del Maíz in San Luis Potosí, the equivalent of the powerful landowning families of Morelos were the Espinosa y Cuevas, Ipiña, Arguinzóniz, and Martínez families, who were equally commercially minded and who exercised the same control over local government. Stimulated by the same rapid growth in the market for their products in the late Porfiriato, they also increased their demands upon the local resources of land, labor, and water and in so doing provoked similar friction with their neighbors. In Morelos this social tension led to serious unrest even before the fall of Díaz; around Ciudad del Maíz violence erupted when the leaders of the local oligarchy attempted to reassert their position after the triumph of Madero.

The leaders of the rural revolt in Ciudad del Maíz, and the counterparts of Emiliano Zapata in Morelos, were the Cedillo brothers. As the sons of a *ranchero* they shared Zapata's rural, petit-bourgeois origins; and their relative wealth and education gave them prestige in a community where most members were sharecroppers or day laborers. Furthermore, their involvement in petty trade took them beyond the confines of the local *haciendas*—the world of the *peón acasillado*—and gave them a number of contacts in neighboring municipalities. But they still identified closely with their community, primarily through kinship and a shared distrust of the local oligarchy, and there was no doubt where their sympathies would lie in any conflict between the *hacendados* and other members of the rural population. When, therefore, the renewed commercial drive of the local oligarchy in the tense conditions of 1912 provoked a violent reaction from their workers and poorer neighbors, the Cedillos were the natural leaders for the popular revolt that followed.

The Cedillos' objective, like that of the Zapatistas, was not the destruction of the *hacienda* system but its containment, combined with active support for the growth of the rural middle class. Lacking a clear ideology, the Cedillos shared the Zapatista vision of an agrarian sector in which every man could acquire a plot of land, even if he chose to work as a laborer or sharecropper on a *hacienda*. Their program appealed to two groups in particular: dispossessed smallholders and disgruntled *peones acasillados*. The former had lost land, grazing, or water rights, etc., to those *hacendados* who had extended their own operations both inside and outside their *hacienda* boundaries, sometimes by chicanery or force. The latter had some grievance against their landlords, such as inherited debts, a refusal to grant them a plot of land to work for themselves, or demands on their families to provide unpaid domestic service.

Like the Zapatistas the Cedillos and their followers fought a succession of governments in Mexico City between 1910 and 1920. The reasons for their prolonged resistance to central authority were not exclusively related to their demands for land reform. From their early successes against the Huerta government in late 1913 until the death of Magdaleno Cedillo in November 1917, they established a loose authority over much of eastern San Luis Potosí which they were reluctant to yield; and once committed to a guerrilla war against the Carranza government, they must have deemed it more dangerous to surrender than to continue fighting. In the case of Saturnino Cedillo this strategy was justified. Due to a combination of circumstances—his skill as a guerrilla leader, the ineptitude and unpopularity of the Constitutionalist army in a region where it was in essence an army of internal occupation, and his considerable good fortune—he remained alive until the revolt of Agua Prieta in 1920. By joining the movement in its early stages he regained respectability for himself and his men and ingratiated himself with the new regime. He did not again rebel against the government in Mexico City until his last gesture of defiance in 1938.

The settlement that Cedillo made with the Obregón administration established a chain of patronage between the central government and Cedillo's followers. The key to this arrangement was Cedillo's establishment of military-agrarian colonies. The central government authorized his confiscation of the land that he needed for the colonies; and Cedillo confirmed his prestige and popularity in the region by providing both his soldiers, and later other members of the rural poor, with access to land. In return, the beneficiaries were obliged to obey his orders, particularly with regard to military service, and he was expected to meet any demands that the central government made of him. On a personal level he was rewarded with command of the local garrison in Ciudad del Maíz and was able to develop his property at Palomas.

This arrangement was in the mold of similar agreements reached between military leaders and the central government after the wars of the nineteenth century and should be seen in the context of the Obregón administration's efforts to pacify the country. This policy of national reconciliation was only partially successful. The federal army which emerged from the Revolution was a coalition of private forces, often regionally based, whose first loyalty was to their commander. Many of these warlords were unwilling to abandon their privileged existence and retained their power within the loose structure of the army. But wherever possible—and this was the case with Francisco Villa in Chihuahua and Saturnino Cedillo in San Luis Potosí—the federal government arranged for the demobilization of troops, often through resettlement on the land, leaving their leaders with a small personal bodyguard. In such instances the bulk of the demobilized troops came to form a strategic reserve at the disposition of their former commanders and, more theoretically, of the central government.

The majority of semi-independent army commanders disappeared from the scene during the decade 1920–1930 in three futile military rebellions. The first of these, the De la Huerta revolt in 1923–1924, was the most serious, and came close to toppling the government of Obregón. It also proved the most destructive to the warlords, witnessing the death or banishment of such prominent figures as Salvador Alvarado, Guadalupe Sánchez, Manuel Diéguez, Enrique Estrada, and Fortunato Maycotte. The second, the movement led by Generals Gómez and Serrano in 1926, never got off the ground, but it led to a further pruning of the top ranks of the military; and the third, led by General Escobar in 1929, virtually completed the process. Paradoxically, it was during this period of the decline of the revolutionary warlords that Saturnino Cedillo grew to his full stature as a regional military *caudillo*. Having remained loyal to the government in 1923, he was rewarded with its confidence thereafter; and, lacking ambitions in national politics, he was given a free hand in San Luis Potosí. He thus extended his influence over the whole state and increased his clientele by encouraging land redistribution under the agrarian laws and exercising a general political patronage. The basis of his power remained military—his control over his revolutionary veterans and his ability to mobilize the local *ejidatarios*. But he soon dominated the civilian administration also, replacing Manrique with a puppet governor in late 1925 and assuming the governorship himself two years later.

Cedillo's military power increased further during the Cristero revolt when a harassed administration called upon him to raise 8,000 irregular troops to fight the rebels. By the time of the Escobar uprising in 1929 he was considered one of the government's most valuable pillars of support. But Cedillo's command remained very much his own, and his soldiers continued to respond to the government only through his orders. This situation contrasted with the trend in the remainder of the federal army, which, as a consequence of the military revolts and the reforms of Calles's ruthless minister of defense, General Amaro, was largely depersonalized. In 1930 the only figure of comparable power to Cedillo was General Andreu Almazán, who controlled the important army command of Nuevo León as if it were one of his many business interests. General Amaro also exercised great influence over the federal army, but he lacked Cedillo's regional base and was too involved in the political scene in Mexico City to build up an independent command as Almazán had.

Cedillo's position was strongest during the Maximato of Calles (1929–1934). He had established himself as one of the foremost supporters of the regime, and since he lacked ambitions in national politics, it suited a succession of governments to allow him freedom of action in San Luis Potosí. Cedillo constructed a regime there more familiar to students of the previous century in Mexico than the present one. The formal structure of government was the same as in other states, but power was exercised in a very personal manner. Municipal government was in the hands of Cedillo's nominees, the congress was composed of his closest collaborators, his followers held all the important posts in the state bureaucracy and local representation of the federal government, and the head of the federal garrison, Francisco Carrera Torres, was his friend and erstwhile companion-in-arms. Cedillo did not use his power to build a sophisticated, urban-based political machine but imposed the values of a rural municipality upon the whole state. He controlled San Luis Potosí not from the state capital but from his ranch at Palomas, where he held court, dispensing favors and receiving a stream of petitioners. Cedillo's regime survived for only two reasons. The first was his popularity among many of the local *campesinos*—probably the majority—as a patron of agrarian reform. The core of this support lay in his agrarian colonies, which provided him with an impressive political power base, but he also enjoyed a widespread following in the other districts where he had sponsored or approved land redistribution. The second mainstay of his regime was the network of lesser *caciques* who owed allegiance to him and kept his opponents in check. Some of these figures, such as Gonzalo Santos, belonged to families whose influence pre-dated Cedillo's political ascendence and who had deemed it prudent to ally themselves with him. The majority, however, were men of Cedillo's own background who had achieved power in their locality through their association with him. Most of these *caciques* were prominent among the officers of his *agrarista* militias.

Cedillo's military campaigns during the 1920s made an important contribution to the gradual restoration of central government authority and the growth of institutional rule, but, ironically, these very developments reduced his value to the regime. Cedillo's support for Cárdenas during his conflict with Calles was crucial to the president's triumph, but his importance declined once the latter was the undisputed master of the country. Cedillo's power was undiminished in his home state, but this in itself gradually became a cause for offense in Mexico City.

At a time when Cárdenas was striving to assert the pre-eminence of the central government, Cedillo's semi-independent administration of San Luis Potosí represented the principle of regional autonomy; and Cedillo used this excuse for ignoring several government policies of which he disapproved, such as socialist education and the tight control—some said persecution—of the church. His highly personal rule challenged the exercise of presidential patronage through the central bureaucracy, a fact which must have been particularly irritating to Cárdenas with regard to agrarian reform, another issue over which the two men differed. Cedillo's patronage of land redistribution in San Luis Potosí gave him a base from which to reaffirm his support for the individual *ejidal* plot and to resist the introduction of the collective *ejidos* which the president favored.

It was therefore in Cárdenas's interest to dismantle Cedillo's regime, and when the latter allowed himself to become the figurehead for the right-wing and neofascist opposition to the president, conflict between them was almost inevitable. As Cárdenas was aware, the opposition to his policies was far more widespread, even in the countryside, than official propaganda or the government-controlled press suggested. Unrest in the military, the disenchant-ment of the urban middle classes with many of the government's measures, and the disruption in rural society caused by the agrarian reform offered a po-tential power base to any opposition leader. (In the election campaign of 1940 they provided the opposition candidate, General Andreu Almazán, with such a following that he would have probably won the presidency if the government had not resorted to electoral fraud.) Cárdenas therefore feared that if left alone, Cedillo might lead or assist a successful challenge to the "official" can-didate in the 1940 elections and was determined to destroy his power base be-fore that date. Cedillo, for his part, was not prepared to surrender his position in San Luis Potosí even if he had to revolt in order to defend it.

During the winter of 1937–1938 Cedillo was out-maneuvered; his regime was weakened by government pressure, both political and military, and his power base was eroded by the land redistribution forced upon him by the Agrarian Department. The expropriation of the oil companies, which he cannot have anticipated, was the final blow to his chances of political survival, for it al-lowed the president to brand Cedillo's opposition to his policies and attempts to preserve his regime as treachery at a time of national crisis. When Cedillo was finally forced into an uprising, it was in far less favorable circumstances than he might have hoped when he resigned as minister of agriculture some nine months earlier. His movement was easily crushed, and he survived only for as long as he did because of his popularity among the local *campesinos*.

There are no monuments to Saturnino Cedillo in the city of San Luis Potosí to indicate to the casual visitor that he once ruled the state. Nor are there any streets that bear his name there, although both "Calle Carlos Díez Gutiérrez" and "Calle Espinosa y Cuevas" are to be found as a reminder of the Porfi-riato. And as for the brief denomination of Ciudad del Maíz as Ciudad Magdaleno Cedillo, it has long since passed into oblivion. Yet Saturnino Ce-dillo is not forgotten in his home state, at least among the older members of the population. He is still referred to in conversation more often than one would expect after so long, particularly in official circles or at meetings of agrarians. The victors in the Revolution, of course, can afford to be indulgent, and local politicians—the heirs of Graciano Sánchez or Gonzalo Santos—tend to speak of him with tolerance or condescension, as of a mildly aberrant ancestor. The losers, Cedillo's old foes, the Porfirian oligarchs, are long since dead; but their older descendents still tend to see him as the embodiment of the destructive force that they identify with the Revolution. "The Cedillos were like a plague," one of them once told me, "a plague upon the whole state."

Saturnino's friends, naturally enough, remember him differently. Every 11 January, on the anniversary of his death, a group of aging men gather at Palo-mas to hold a lunch in his honor. Their numbers are dwindling rapidly with the years; they are the grizzled veterans of Cedillo's campaigns, both military and political. They drink to his health, exchange news, and recall old times.

The food on the table is *ranchero* fare: chicken with mole, rice and tortillas, swilled down with copious quantities of beer. In 1979 one of Cedillo's former aides invited me to attend this gathering. I sat between a former member of the state congress and one of Cedillo's telegraphists, a man who was with him when he died. Together they talked of their experiences and gave their views on the Mexico of today. At one point in the conversation one of them turned to me and said, "We loved the General, you know. Everything we have, everything we are, we owe to him. That is why we still come here, in spite of everything." Personal loyalty toward their leader and pride in their association with him, the rewards of patronage and the penalties of clientship—in those few sentences he summarized Cedillo's regime.

APPENDICES

Hacienda	Municipality	Size (in hectares)[a]	Owner[a]
La Parada	Ahualulco	17,736	Petrolina Ipiña de Gutiérrez
Santa Teresa	Ahualulco	46,000	José Encarnación Ipiña
Pozo del Carmen	Armadillo	11,600	José Encarnación Ipiña
Guascamá	Carbonera	10,279	José Encarnación Ipiña
Ojo de León	Carbonera	10,768	F. Vázquez
Cárdenas	Cárdenas	39,325	M. Barajas Viuda de Díez Gutiérrez
Poblazón	Catorce	12,756	José Encarnación Ipiña
Potrero	Catorce	10,935	Gregorio de la Maza
Solís	Catorce	60,021	Luis Hernández Ceballos (in 1926)
El Sotol	Cedral	33,356	R. Barrenechea (in 1926)
San Pablo	Cedral	43,890	P. Irrizarri (in 1928)
Agua del Toro y Tanque de Angeles	Cerritos	21,199	Juan Hernández Ceballos
Labor de Nietos	Cerritos	14,472 (in 1937)	E. Chamberlain (in 1938)
Charcas	Charcas	25,185	Pilar Toranzo Viuda de Hernández Soberón (in 1926)
Laguna Seca	Charcas	96,035	Ricardo Muriedas (in 1928)
Cañada Grande	Ciudad Fernández	8,793	R. Manrique de Lara
Diego Ruíz	Ciudad Fernández	11,835	R. González de Vadillo
Ojo de Agua	Ciudad Fernández	20,308	Carlos Fernández Galán (in 1928)
Concepción[b]	Ciudad del Maíz	15,256 (in 1935)	Cunningham Investment Co. (in 1935)
El Custodio	Ciudad del Maíz	31,420	Juan Hernández Ceballos (in 1925)
Lagunillas	Ciudad del Maíz	8,669	Joaquín Arguinzóniz
La Leoneña	Ciudad del Maíz	20,000 (in 1934)	E. Moctezuma Viuda de León (in 1937)
Llano del Perro	Ciudad del Maíz	13,380	Mariano Arguinzóniz
Minas Viejas	Ciudad del Maíz	13,492	David E. Thompson
Montebello	Ciudad del Maíz	37,593	Zeferino Martínez
Papagallos	Ciudad del Maíz	28,000	Adela Toranzo Viuda de Cuevas (in 1926)

Puerta de Santa Gertrudis	Ciudad del Maíz	6,892	Joaquín Arguinzóniz
Buenavista	Guadalcázar	13,283	Manuel Gómez (in 1923)
La Hincada	Guadalcázar	29,835	Serapio de la Garza (in 1924)
Norias del Refugio	Guadalcázar	32,163	Rafael Hernández Ceballos (in 1928)
Pozo de Acuña	Guadalcázar	12,360	William O. Jenkins (in 1922)
Presa de Guadalupe	Guadalcázar	103,915	Eduardo Meade
Santo Domingo	Guadalcázar	34,403	Pilar Toranzo Viuda de Hernández Soberón (in 1926)
San Rafael	Lagunillas	12,889	Rosa y Mariana Escandón
Maravillas	Matehuala	11,962 (in 1915)	Refugio Bouvi Viuda de De la Maza (in 1929)
Pastoriza	Matehuala	42,411	Leopoldo de la Maza (in 1925)
San José de las Trojes	Matehuala	7,885	Refugio S. Viuda de Barrenechea (in 1928)
El Peñasco	Mexquitic	17,551	Espinosa y Cuevas brothers
San Francisco	Mexquitic	26,208	Valentín Soberón y Castro
San Antonio de Rul	Moctezuma	24,831	Salvador Dosamantes Rul (in 1929)
Tambaca	Palma[c]	60,000	Compañía Fraccionadora de Grandes Propiedades
El Carro	Ramos	63,201	The Nation
Punteros	Ramos	75,491	José Escandón (in 1922)
Estancita	Rayón	41,620	José Encarnación Ipiña
La Boquilla	Rayón	43,604	Heirs of Casimiro García Verástegui (in 1926)
Amoladeras	Río Verde	38,610	Fernando González (in 1929)
Angostura	Río Verde	178,050	Espinosa y Cuevas brothers
Canoas	Río Verde	8,060	R. Martínez (in 1929)
Cañada Grande	Río Verde	8,738	Heirs of R. Manrique de Lara (in 1929)
Cieneguilla	Río Verde	21,075	Teresa Verástegui Viuda de P. de Hoyo (in 1921)
Jabalí	Río Verde	45,280	Pablo Escandón
San Diego	Río Verde	5,365	José Encarnación Ipiña
San José de Tepanco	Río Verde	24,382	María de la Luz, María Socorro Garfías, and Pedro Gómez
Bocas	San Luis Potosí	35,112	Genaro, Antonio, and Jesús Y. García
Valle Umbroso	San Luis Potosí	17,556	José Domínguez (in 1926)
Santa Catarina	San Nicolás Tolentino	15,368	Arturo Martí
Calabazas	Santa Catarina	14,317	Antonio Arguinzóniz
El Salvador	Santa Catarina	17,041	Genaro de la Torre
El Trigo	Santa Catarina	70,224	Manuel González and partners

Cruces	Santo Domingo	186,945	Guadalupe Soberón Viuda de Hernández (in 1922)
Illescas[d]	Santo Domingo	245,786	Hermenegildo Gutiérrez
Guanamé	Santo Domingo	251,051	Mariano Hernández Ceballos (in 1922)
Sierra Hermosa[e]	Santo Domingo	463,734	Francisco and Federico Moncada (in 1924)
El Limón[f]	Valles	112,266	José Rodríguez Cabo
Rascón[g]	Valles	465,075	Compañía Manufacturera y Desarrolladera de Rascón
San Antonio	Valles	13,492	D. J. Spillane
El Salado	Vanegas	105,337	Mariano Arguinzóniz
Santa Rita[e]	Vanegas	58,670	Luis Barcena Blanco (in 1937)
San José de Vanegas	Vanegas	130,671	Leopoldo de la Maza (in 1926)
La Coronada	Venado	6,939	Juan Hernández Ceballos (in 1924)
San Francisco de Obregón y anexo San Mateo	Venado	14,727	Heirs of Celso Llano (in 1925)
Peotillos	Villa de Arista	196,627	Pilar Toranzo Viuda de Hernández Soberón; J. Valle y Cavia Viuda de Muriel; I. Muriel (in 1929)
Santiago	Villa de Arriaga	10,000	A. and F. Garfías (in 1926)
Vallejo	Villa de Guadalupe	47,391	Rafael Hernández Ceballos (in 1924)
La Boca	Villa de la Paz	8,188	Carmen Barrenechea Viuda de Sánchez Lozano (in 1926)
La Presita	Villa de la Paz	9,308	O. Nuncio Viuda de Ibarguengoytia
La Pila[h]	Villa de Pozos	15,946 (in 1934)	Francisco Sánchez Barrenechea (in 1934)
Bledos	Villa de Reyes	25,717	José Encarnación Ipiña
Carranco	Villa de Reyes	9,733	T. Elorduy Viuda de Meade (in 1934)
Gogorrón	Villa de Reyes	36,015	Felipe Muriedas
Jesús María	Villa de Reyes	20,941	F. Vázquez Barrenechea (in 1938)
La Sauceda	Zaragoza	18,738	Pedro Barrenechea (in 1907)
San Isidro	Zaragoza	4,991	José Encarnación Ipiña
Carbonera[i]		51,270	Leopoldo de la Maza (in 1928)

Note: *Viuda* means "widow."

[a]In 1910 unless otherwise stated.

[b]The source for this data is DAAC 23/20218. La Concepción, Papagallos, and La Mula originally formed part of the *hacienda* of Rascón, comprising 70,200 hectares José Rascón, an owner of the

estate in the late nineteenth century, made them into separate properties. Since Papagallos measured 28,000 hectares (DAAC 23/11442) and La Mula, 5,272 hectares (DAAC 23/1415), La Concepción must have then contained 36,928 hectares.

^cNow a part of Tamasopo municipality.

^dThere is some confusion over the original size of this vast property. Enrique Henshawe, the local CNA delegate, in a letter of 9 September 1922, gave it as 184,945 hectares, which was also mentioned in a separate report by another CNA official, Ignacio Nuñez. But CNA delegate Carlos Macías in his earlier report to the CNA (20 March 1918) gave the size as 140 *sitios de ganado mayor* (245,700 hectares); and this is the area referred to in the presidential decree of 27 March 1918 awarding *ejidos* from the *hacienda* to the village of Santo Domingo. (The various papers are in DAAC 23/4198.)

^eMore than half of these properties were outside the state.

^fOnly 60,000 hectares of this *hacienda* were in San Luis Potosí (DAAC 23/4227).

^gIt is uncertain exactly how much of this property was in San Luis Potosí; but according to a plan in the Archivo Cartográfico in Mexico City, which gives the size of the *hacienda* in 1890 as 491,428 hectares, over half of it was in the state.

^hVilla de Pozos is now in the municipality of San Luis Potosí. Jan Bazant, in *Cinco Haciendas Mexicanas* ([México 1975], p. 135), gives the size of La Pila at the beginning of the century as 31,000 hectares.

ⁱThe *Diario oficial* (4 January 1928) makes no reference to the municipal location of this *hacienda*.

Sources: Archive of Octaviano Cabrera Ipiña (AOC); Archive of the Secretaría de la Reforma Agraria (DAAC); *Périodico Oficial de San Luis Potosí, 1920-1938; Diario oficial, 1920-1939*; Archive of the Secretaría de Defensa Nacional (SDN).

APPENDIX 2: THE PRICES OF SEVERAL LEADING PRODUCTS ON THE HACIENDAS OF MONTEBELLO (1889–1911) AND BLEDOS (1884–1911)

Price per *Arroba*[a]
(in Pesos)

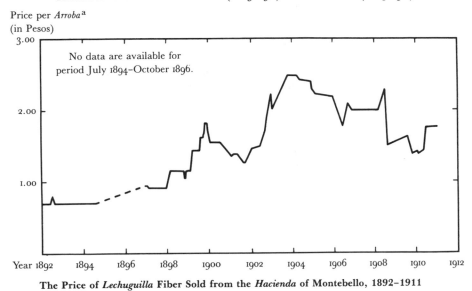

No data are available for period July 1894–October 1896.

The Price of *Lechuguilla* Fiber Sold from the *Hacienda* of Montebello, 1892–1911

[a]1 *arroba* = 25 pounds, or 11.506 kilograms.

Source: *Libro diario* of the *hacienda,* Archive of Octaviano Cabrera Ipiña.

Price per *Arroba*[a]
(in Pesos)

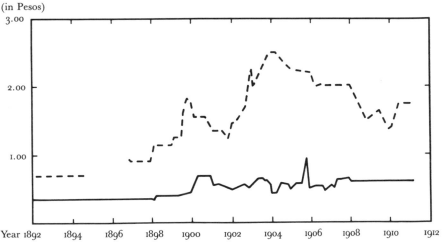

Montebello *Palma* Sales and Wages, 1892–1911

– – – – Price paid to the fiber cutters on Montebello for each *arroba* of fiber they produced, 1892–1911.

———— Price of *palma* fiber sold from Montebello, 1892–1911.

Source: *Libro diario* of the *hacienda,* Archive of Octaviano Cabrera Ipiña.

Price per *Fanega*[a]
(in Pesos)

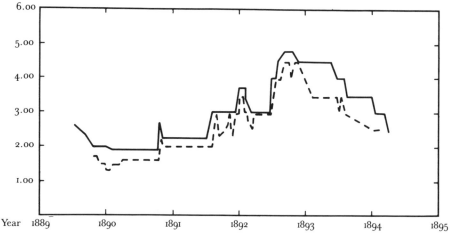

Maize Rations and Deposits on Montebello *Hacienda,* 1889–1895

———— Value of the maize ration of the *peones acasillados* on Montebello *hacienda,* 1889–1895.
- - - - Value of the maize deposited in the *hacienda* store, Montebello, 1889–1895.
[a]1 *fanega* = 0.908 hectoliters.

Price per *Hectoliter*
(in Pesos)

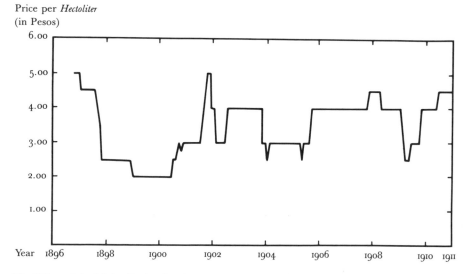

The Value of the Maize Ration for *Peones Acasillados* on Montebello *Hacienda,* 1896–1911

Source: *Libro diario* of the *hacienda,* Archive of Octaviano Cabrera Ipiña.

Price per *Fanega*[a]
(in Pesos)

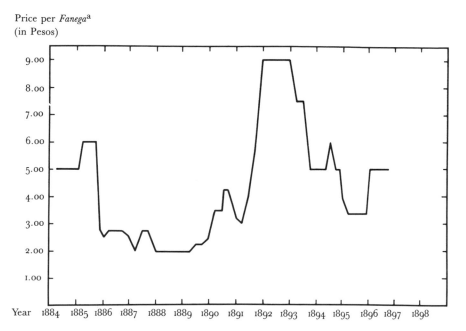

Year

The Value of a *Fanega* of Black Beans *(Frijoles)* Deposited in the *Hacienda* Store, Bledos, 1884–1897

[a] 1 *fanega* = 0.908 hectoliters.
Source: *Libro diario* of the *hacienda,* Archive of Octaviano Cabrera Ipiña.

Price per Hectoliter
(in Pesos)

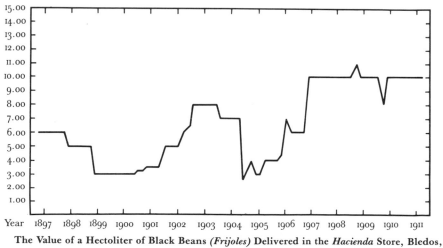

Year

The Value of a Hectoliter of Black Beans *(Frijoles)* Delivered in the *Hacienda* Store, Bledos, 1897–1911

Source: *Libro diario* of the *hacienda,* Archive of Octaviano Cabrera Ipiña.

APPENDIX 3: THE PROFITS OF THE *HACIENDAS* OF MONTEBELLO (1889-1910)
AND BLEDOS (1883-1935)

The Profits of the *Hacienda* of Montebello, 1889-1890 to 1909-1910

Year	Profits[a]	Year	Profits[a]
1889-1890	561	1900-1901	11,811
1890-1891	7,081	1901-1902	11,937
1891-1892	3,968	1902-1903	28,046
1892-1893	397	1903-1904	32,626
1893-1894	5,892	1904-1905	29,331
1894-1895	2,292	1905-1906	21,135
1895-1896	1,197	1906-1907	17,858
1896-1897[b]	-2,976	1907-1908[b]	-4,832
1897-1898	2,240	1908-1909[b]	-1,996
1898-1899	4,602	1909-1910	8,940
1899-1900[c]	13,937		

The Profits of the *Hacienda* of Bledos, 1883-1935[d]

Year	Profits[a]	Year	Profits[a]
1883-1884	24,663	1905-1906	66,625
1884-1885	3,538	1906-1907	41,617
1885-1886	19,855	1907-1908	57,141
1886-1887	25,194	1908-1909	35,191
1887-1888	20,806	1909-1910	56,676
1888-1889	21,277	1913-1914	37,089
1889-1890	30,759	1914-1915	65,937
1890-1891	28,212	1915-1916	210,161
1891-1892	35,823	1916-1917	72,898
1892-1893[b]	-1,906	1917-1918	10,899
1893-1894	28,381	1918-1919	17,063
1894-1895	8,392	1919-1920	58,514
1895-1896	35,758	1920-1921	35,867
1896-1897	29,187	1921-1922[b]	-23,478
1897-1898	60,069	1922-1923	31,314
1898-1899	35,184	1923-1924	19,503
1899-1900[c]	17,405	1924-1925	30,351
1900-1901	19,520	1929-1930	-30,031
1901-1902	17,818	1930-1931[b]	-868
1902-1903	63,846	1931-1932	8,760
1903-1904	47,924	1933-1934	8,689
1904-1905	53,700	1934-1935	2,177

[a]In pesos to the nearest peso.
[b]Years of loss.
[c]Refers to the fourteen-month period between 1 March 1899 and 30 April 1900.
[d]No evidence is available for Bledos *hacienda* for the years 1910-1911, 1911-1912, 1912-1913, 1925-1926, 1926-1927, 1927-1928, 1928-1929, and 1932-1933.

Source: *Libro diario* of the *hacienda,* Archive of Octaviano Cabrera Ipiña.

APPENDIX 4: THE MARKET PRICE OF SELECTED BASIC FOODSTUFFS IN
SAN LUIS POTOSÍ, 1931–1940

Price per Kilogram
(in Pesos)

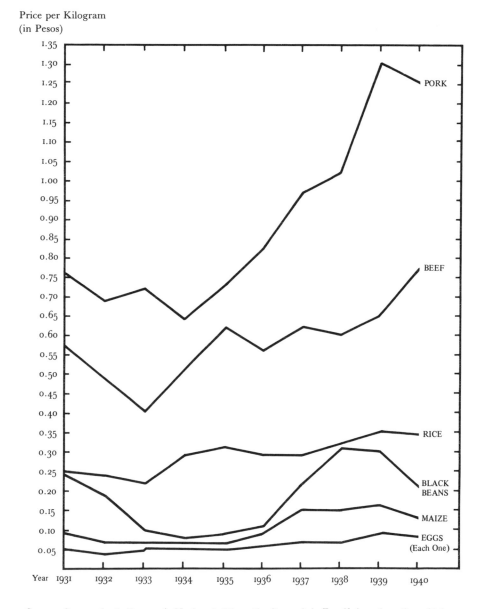

Source: Secretaría de Economía Nacional, Dirección General de Estadística, *Anuario estadístico,
1940*, p. 705.

APPENDIX 5: THE OFFICIAL RATE OF EXCHANGE BETWEEN THE MEXICAN PESO AND THE U.S. DOLLAR, 1900–1940

Pesos per Dollar

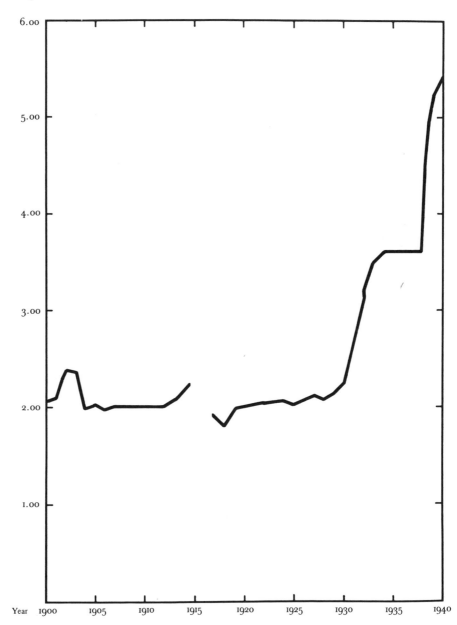

Source: Nacional Financiera S. A., *Statistics on the Mexican Economy* (Mexico, 1966), p. 171.

APPENDIX 6: MEXICAN AGRICULTURAL PRODUCTION: SELECTED CROPS, 1900–1907 AND 1925–1940 (IN THOUSANDS OF METRIC TONS)

Year	Cotton	Rice	Sugar Cane	Beans	*Henequén*	Corn	Wheat	Coffee
1900	22	21	1267	167	79	2100	274	21
1901	22	18	1311	180	96	2378	252	27
1902	23	20	1618	157	84	2330	268	27
1903	24	22	1570	169	108	2257	281	26
1904	29	26	1714	159	101	2060	246	26
1905	31	25	1565	150	100	2167	280	27
1906	29	28	1562	154	101	2339	295	21
1907	34	33	1907	159	111	2128	293	29
Annual Average	26.75	24.1	1564.25	161.9	97.5	2219.9	273.6	25.5[a]
1925	43	86	2873	188	137	1968	251	34
1926	78	91	3158	199	117	2135	281	40
1927	39	83	2997	190	133	2059	324	41
1928	60	83	2947	176	139	2173	300	42
1929	53	67	3029	95	129	1469	308	42
1930	38	75	3293	83	96	1377	312	39
1931	46	72	3694	136	84	2139	442	38
1932	22	72	3405	132	123	1973	263	33
Annual Average	47.4	78.6	3174.5	149.9	119.75	1911.6	310.1	38.6
1933	56	67	2778	186	96	1924	330	44
1934	48	69	2774	124	72	1723	298	37
1935	68	71	3573	121	81	1656	292	42
1936	86	86	4341	107	115	1597	370	49
1937	74	75	4056	104	101	1635	288	60
1938	66	80	4132	105	80	1693	325	57
1939	68	76	4556	148	86	1977	402	55
1940	65	108	4973	97	96	1640	363	52
Annual Average	66.3	79	3897.9	124	90.9	1730.6	333.5	49.5

[a]Eyler N. Simpson gives somewhat higher figures for agricultural production during the Porfiriato, with an average annual production for the years 1901–1907 as follows: cotton: 54; rice: 25; sugar cane: 2015; beans: 182; *henequén*: 90; corn: 2653; wheat: 295; and coffee: 33 (*The Ejido: Mexico's Way Out* [Chapel Hill, N.C., 1937], p. 672).

Source: *Estadísticas económicas,* pp. 65–78; Secretaría de Economía Nacional, Dirección General de Estadística, *Anuario estadístico,* 1938, pp. 182–83; *Compendio estadístico* 1941, p. 625.

APPENDIX 7: TRANSLATIONS OF CEDILLO'S MANIFESTOS TO THE NATION
IN 1938

Manifesto to the Nation, 16 May 1938——When I ceased to collaborate with the Cárdenas Government in the Cabinet, I had the firm intention of dedicating myself to my agricultural interests; but from the time I retired until the present, the Cárdenas Government has continued to take great strides down the path which is leading to the country to ruin and desolation of every kind, both socially and economically. Before the unanimous clamor of the country, which requires my cooperation to prevent the total ruin of our Fatherland, I have therefore decided to accept the appointment with which the XXXV Legislature of my State has honored me, that of Commander-in-Chief of the Constitutional Army, so that peace and order may once again rule, and so that the Constitution, which has been foully trampled upon in its most elemental principles, may again be respected. Private property has been violated, the rights of free men have been violated; freedom of conscience has been prohibited; there is no law other than the caprice of the farcical leaders who surround Cárdenas, whom, in my character as Commander-in-Chief of the Constitutional Army, I accuse before the Nation and the civilized world of trying to change our democratic regime, in order to establish one based upon the Soviet.

FACTS: In Yucatán, with the foreknowledge and approval of Cárdenas, the National Anthem was suppressed in our schools and replaced by "The International"; some Ministers have also taken to singing this chorus at official celebrations. Teachers have been sent to state schools throughout the country with the task of bringing up the children with Marxist doctrines, and in numerous government establishments instead of there being pictures of the heroes of our Independence, you find Russian leaders such as Lenin, Stalin, and others.

I ACCUSE Cárdenas of being anti-agrarian, because he has allowed a great stigma to be attached to the individual *ejidal* plot and the small rural property, yet both the man who sows his *ejidal* plot and the one who sows his smallholding are agrarians. Cárdenas, without weighing the consequences of his actions and with no more knowledge than his theory, is communizing the *ejido*; that is to say, he is disguising communism with the word collectivism. He is converting the engineers of the Bank into overseers; and as can be shown with concrete examples, they are proving more greedy than the *latifundistas* of former times. His achievement with all this is that agricultural production is going down and down, the *ejido* has become nobody's land, the *campesino* doesn't know where his plot is, and he cannot say with pride that he has his own title to land that he can pass on as an inheritance to his relatives when he dies.

We who have struggled in the past, leading a hazardous existence for many years, dreaming just as Zapata dreamed, of a plot of free land for a free *campesino*, cannot allow the defilement of an ideal which is noble, which is sacred, and which truly gives freedom to our peasantry. Once the rule of law has been reestablished and the fatal clique which is plunging the country into misery has disappeared from public life, the Law of Family Patrimony will be vigorously applied, so that there won't even be an attempt to return to the latifundia of former times. For that is the risk which will be run if Cárdenas presses on with his maniacal folly of converting agrarianism into communism. This is what he has done in the Laguna, where to date there is only misery, and where a small group of employees of the Bank that the disastrous Peralta directs are the only ones who have profited from that business by charging the *ejidatarios* dearly for their implements and seeds, with the foreknowledge and approval of Cárdenas. But these employees will continue robbing for only a few days more, since, whatever they may want, they have already drained the Nation dry.

I accuse Cárdenas of being anti-worker, because in a criminal fashion he is supporting, assisting, and giving preference to the CTM, with the power bestowed upon him in his character as Senior Official in the country. He disregards all workers who are not in that Confederation, with the fatal consequences of which the country is already aware, such as the criminal murders of workers by workers carried out in the factories of Puebla and Veracruz. Moreover, as a result of his administration, many workers are without bread, because with capital's present difficulties, factories have been closing down daily, a long list of them. And with the recent rise in the value of the dollar, raw materials have gone up in price, with the result that the workers of the Federal District will shortly be working a three-day week; and many small workshops have been forced to close their doors, leading to hunger among our laborers.

I ACCUSE Cárdenas of humiliating the Army and of relaxing its discipline by subordinating it to unscrupulous leaders such as Luis Rodríguez and Lombardo Toledano, his intention being that the swords of the Generals, Commanders, and Officers may subsequently serve to support and sustain the miserable and bastard ambitions of these scoundrels.

I ACCUSE Cárdenas of being a traitor to the Fatherland because, while knowing that we are a weak and impoverished country, he is provoking stronger countries, and in the end Mexico will suffer outrages and abuses because it is always the strong who impose humiliating conditions upon the weak. Cárdenas has admitted, first through Lombardo Toledano, then recently himself at the so-called Congress of the CTM that Mexico does not have any oil tankers and is not in any position to develop its oil industry. And yet even though he knows this, he is provoking the total ruin of the aforementioned industry, something which will cause misery and hunger to the oil workers themselves.

During his political campaign Cárdenas promised not to disarm the *campesinos*, but he has broken this commitment as well by disarming the *campesinos* in various places within the country. The most recent example of such disarmament has been the State of San Luis, where he has also sent a large number of federal soldiers.

After the preceding review of what the whole country has witnessed, and no one can claim that it is not true, I solemnly declare that with zeal and faith I place myself at the head of this legalist movement, putting aside any petty personal ambition and with the sole desire to establish in Mexico a truly democratic regime. I also totally reject the accusation of being a fascist which is made against me by the unprincipled politicians who surround Cárdenas. The Mexican people hate dictatorships and will resist the communist dictatorship which Cárdenas is seeking to impose at all cost.

In this grave hour, in which the country needs the cooperation of honorable men, I hope for the sincere and frank cooperation of the precursors of the Revolution. Many of these men, in return for their sacrifices, are at present being humiliated; and attempts are being made to replace them with others whose credentials as revolutionaries are farcical. I invite these precursors to strike a decisive blow at such ludicrous time-servers and to give to the true revolutionaries the position they deserve. The present legalist movement has nothing to do with personality cults or private ambitions. It has no "isms" attached to it but simply seeks to obtain the cooperation of every good Mexican. And let the generals, commanders, and officers of our glorious National Army be aware that inescapable duty calls them to place their swords at the service of a democratic government. For it has been clearly proven that Cárdenas doesn't represent Institutional Government, since he has villainously trampled upon the Constitution which he promised to respect and see respected. The only persons whose positions are secure are the politicians who burn incense and go down on their knees before him, for Cárdenas has cast aside the old participants in the revolutionary struggle and has overlooked the precursors of the Revolution. Instead he has given preference in the "famous" PRM to someone like Luis Rodríguez, whom our dignified and honorable soldiers now have the bestial obligation of supporting, and has passed over General Juan José Ríos, even though the representatives of our Army and the workers grouped together in the CROM and CGT asked for him to be appointed.

Neither the Nation's prisons nor its finances will be enough to stop a truly popular movement. Ninety percent of the Mexican Nation is against Cárdenas, and all the means at his disposal will be insufficient to silence the voices of a people clamoring for mercy before an avaricious clique, which is dragging the Fatherland to disaster with gigantic steps.

SOLDIERS OF THE REPUBLIC: Do not stain your swords by making them accomplices of the betrayal of the Revolution and our institutions. Do not support a man like Cárdenas who, in the interests of his own political ambitions gives preference within a party to a sycophant like Luis Rodríguez rather than to a glorious soldier of our Army.

He who addresses you has faith in justice; and since he is deeply convinced that if necessary the country will call for the sacrifice of his life, he willingly offers it. He does not mind losing it because his sole desire is that Mexico should be a great country, free and respected.

PEOPLE OF MEXICO, duty calls you to be wholeheartedly on the side of the Government of San Luis Potosí, which has boldly thrown down the glove before the tyrant who has converted the country into a personal fief for himself, his family, and his group of friends.

San Luis Potosí, S.L.P., 16 May 1938
The Commander-in-Chief of the Mexican Constitutional Army
Divisional General, Saturnino Cedillo

A copy of the original manifesto appears in M. Fernández Boyoli and E. Marrón de Angelis, *Lo que no se sabe de la rebelión Cedillista* (México, 1938), 320–24.

Manifesto to the Nation of the Commander-in-Chief of the Mexican Constitutional Army——In view of the treachery of the Governments of the States of Sonora, Michoacán, and Zacatecas, which had a Pact of Honor with the Government of San Luis Potosí, so that if General Lázaro Cárdenas, the Dictator modelled upon Stalin, should carry out his threat to declare the Powers of any of the before-mentioned States dissolved, they would support it in order to defend its sovereignty; and as Cárdenas has carried out his threat, declaring the Powers of the state of San Luis Potosí dissolved, the Government of San Luis Potosí has bravely reasserted its Sovereignty and designated the signatory of this document to be the Commander-in-Chief of the Constitutional Army which the Decree of 16 May 1938 created. And since the before-mentioned Governments have failed to keep their word, the Legislature of the Local Congress has ceased to operate on account of a lack of guarantees, with some Deputies in flight and others dead, and the legitimate Governor is now committed to the struggle waiting for the legalist cause to triumph and for the overthrow of His Serene Highness Lázaro Cárdenas, who with his errors is compromising the Country just as Santana compromised it in 1847.

For the above reasons I have been forced to divide my Army into guerrilla units, until they can be given the necessary organization to undertake serious operations. And I declare solemnly that as I am defending the Constitution and Sovereignty of my State, my flag is wholly Legalist, and there is nothing nor anyone that can make me change my viewpoint, since the struggle will continue until the legalist cause is crowned with success. And in view of the calumnies with which people are trying to stain my name, with both Cárdenas himself and his voracious leaders saying that I am defending the interests of the oil Companies, I must again roundly declare that I know none of the executives of the oil Companies and that neither do I have any links with Fascism, since I am struggling and will struggle to the last against the COMMUNIST character which Cárdenas is trying to impose on all the *ejidal* grants of the country, disguising them as collectives, leading the *Ejido* in this way to its ruin and, in consequence, to the disrepute of agrarianism in the Republic. For as a long-time fighter for the agrarian cause I will not allow it to be stained by the vultures who have recently adopted it. I have absolute faith, since I know the *campesino* of my country, that the agrarianism which Zapata invoked will not fail and that production will increase when every man farms his own plot by himself, with his own title to it and knowing that should he die, his family will continue working it. The collectivist system of Cárdenas is fine in theory, but in practice it has been a failure. Cárdenas, to date, has been able to count only upon the force which Power and the Nation's Treasury can give, but the immense majority of the country hates him for the sectarian system which he has established, overwhelming the radicals with sinecures and wealth, while the Country sinks daily deeper into horrendous misery. While the Country's sources of wealth are daily being exhausted, it is being deceived in all the official state organs, which proclaim that the authorities are carrying out a transformation with new methods, which in fact are good only in the theories of individuals who have no knowledge of Mexican realities.

May the Country and the whole world know that I ASKED FOR MY RETIREMENT FROM THE ARMY in order not to serve a Government that is corrupting THE TRUE MEXICAN REVOLUTION and bringing ruin and misery to all homes, and I serenely await the judgment of History without paying any attention to the cheap and cowardly insults which Cárdenas and all the sycophants who adore him have cast upon my name.

CONSTITUTION, JUSTICE AND LAW

Headquarters in the Municipality of Ciudad del Maíz, S.L.P.

S. Cedillo

A copy of this manifesto can be found in AGN, Ramo presidentes, Cárdenas, legajo 559.1/53-57.

AGN, ramo presidentes, Cárdenas, 559.1/53-57.

GLOSSARY

Administrador. A manager; usually used here to refer to a *hacienda* manager.

Agrarista. A supporter or beneficiary of the postrevolutionary agrarian reform. Usually used here to refer to those recipients of land under the reform who were mobilized as irregular soldiers during the 1920s.

Agricultor. General word for farmer.

Amparo. A court injunction.

Arrendatario. A tenant farmer.

Arroba. A measure of weight of approximately 25 pounds.

Baldío. See *Tierras baldías.*

Cacique. A local political boss; sometimes used to mean *caudillo.*

Caciquismo. Rule by political bosses.

Campesino. Literally, a person from the fields. Used here, as in Mexico, to describe a member of the rural lower classes, e.g., poorer *rancheros,* sharecroppers, wage laborers, and *ejidatarios.*

Caudillo. An important political boss, often used to describe influential politicians with a regional power base. A *caudillo*'s position usually rested upon a combination of force, patronage, and a close personal relationship with his followers.

Caudillismo. Government by one or more *caudillos.*

Científicos. The small group of businessmen/politicians who were influential in government during the latter years of the Porfiriato.

Condueñazgo. A property held jointly by several heads of families.

Congregación. A rural settlement, normally smaller than a *pueblo.*

Cristero. A participant in the Cristiada.

Cristiada. The religious revolt against the government in Mexico from 1926–1929.

Donación. A grant. Used here to refer to a grant of land under the agrarian reform laws to which the petitioners had either a claim unprovable by law or no claim at all.

Ejidatario. A member of an agrarian community possessing *ejidos.* A recipient of land under the agrarian reform.

Ejido. Originally the term for the "common land" of a village; later used to describe a grant of land made by the government under the post-1910 agrarian reform.

Estancita. A small farm; fraction of a *hacienda.*

Ganadero. A cattle rancher.

Hacendado. The owner of an *hacienda*.

Hacienda. A large rural estate worked by paid laborers.

Jefe Máximo. Supreme Chief. The title given to Plutarco Elías Calles by his supporters during the years 1928–1934 when he was at the height of his power.

Jefe político. A district commissioner during the Porfiriato.

Lista de raya. The payroll in a mine, factory, or *hacienda*.

Maximato. The period (1928–1934) during which the government of Mexico was dominated by Plutarco Elías Calles, known popularly as the Jefe Máximo.

Mestizo. A person of mixed Indian and Spanish descent.

Partido. (1) During the Porfiriato, an electoral division of a state covering several municipalities. (2) A political party, as in Partido Liberal Mexicano.

Peón. A landless agricultural laborer, especially *hacienda* laborers.

Peones acasillados. Landless wage laborers domiciled on the estate where they worked.

Pequeña propiedad. A small private property.

Pequeño propietario. The owner of a small private farm.

Poblado. A small village.

Posesión definitiva. The definitive possession of something. Used here to refer to the final legal tenure of land granted as *ejidos*.

Posesión provisional. The provisional possession of something. Used here to refer to the provisional legal tenure of land granted as *ejidos*.

Porfiriato: The period from 1876 to 1910 when Mexico was ruled directly or indirectly by Porfirio Díaz.

Presidente municipal. The senior elected official in a municipality; town mayor.

Pueblo. A village.

Rancho. A smallholding, either a private or a rented property, which could be worked with family labor and occasional seasonal help.

Ranchero. The owner or tenant of a *rancho,* who could be either a *pequeño propietario* or *arrendatario*.

Reglamento. The legislative act necessary to convert articles of the constitution into law.

Restitución. Restoration of anything to its rightful owner. Under the agrarian reform, a grant of land which the petitioners claimed to have been stolen from their community in the past.

Rurales. The police force founded by President Porfirio Díaz for controlling the countryside.

Sinarquismo. A right-wing political movement that acquired a significant following in certain rural areas of Mexico during the 1940s.

Sinarquista. A supporter of sinarquismo.

Temporal. See *Tierra temporal*.

Tienda de raya. A store attached to a factory, mine, or *hacienda* for the use of its employees.

Tierras baldías. Public land; land to which no legal title exists.

Tierras demasiadas. Unclaimed land; the area between property boundaries to which no one has a legal title.

Tierra temporal. Arable land dependent only upon rainfall for water.

Since Mexican politics in the early twentieth century was highly personalized, I have also followed the common practice of naming the political movements of the time after their leaders, e.g., Maderismo, Reyismo, and Zapatismo (to describe the movements led by Madero, Reyes, and Zapata), and of referring to their adherents in the same way, e.g., Huertistas, Carrancistas, and Cedillistas (to denote the followers of Huerta, Carranza, and Cedillo).

NOTES

A List of the Abbreviations Used in the Notes

SD   The Archive of the U.S. State Department in the Library of Congress, Washington, D.C.; Record Group 59, 812.001/ series, documents relating to the internal affairs of Mexico, 1910–1929; and 812.00/San Luis Potosí, reports from the U.S. consuls in San Luis Potosí, 1930–1938.

AGN   Archivo General de la Nación, Mexico City. Followed by the section *(ramo)*, file *(legajo)*, and document number.

FO   The British Foreign Office Archive in the Public Record Office, London. Followed by the series and file number and the document reference in brackets.

DAAC   The Archive of the Departamento de Asuntos Agrarios y Colonización, now held in the Secretaría de la Reforma Agraria in Mexico City. Followed by the file reference.

SDN   The Archive of the Secretaría de Defensa Nacional, Mexico City. Followed by the file reference.

AOC   The Archive of Señor Octaviano Cabrera Ipiña, San Luis Potosí, Mexico.

"Arvide"   The unpublished manuscript biography of Saturnino Cedillo by his former secretary, Colonel José Arvide. (Made available to me by the author in San Luis Potosí.)

HAHR   Hispanic American Historical Review.

Note to Preface

1. For the works by these and other authors mentioned in this preface, see the bibliography at the end of the volume.

Notes to Chapter 1

1. For the early history of San Luis Potosí, see Primo Feliciano Velázquez, *Historia de San Luis Potosí* (México, 1946), vols. 1 to 3; and H. G. Ward, *Mexico* (London, 1829), 2:225–58. According to official statistics in the 1878 *Boletín de la Sociedad de Geografía y Estadística de la República* (4:58), the population of the state during the nineteenth century was as follows:

Year	Population	Year	Population
1794	168,002	1849	367,320
1829	297,590	1869	476,500

These figures are, of course, very approximate because of the difficulty of collecting reliable data at that time. Ward, for example, gives a figure of 250,000 (*Mexico*, p. 226); and Mayer Brantz, an American visitor writing twenty years later, said that the population numbered "over 300,000" (*Mexico: Aztec, Spanish, and Republican* [Hartford, Conn., 1853], 325). For the political unrest in the state in the years between 1869 and 1876, see Laurens B. Perry, *Juárez and Díaz: Machine Politics in Mexico* (DeKalb, Ill., 1978), 141-44, 282-83.

2. Ambassador Henry Lane Wilson to the Secretary of State, 31 October 1910, SD 812.00/355; Lázaro Gutiérrez de Lara and Edgcumb Pinchón, *The Mexican People, Their Struggle for Freedom* (New York, 1914), p. 318; J. W. Kitchens, "Some Considerations on the *rurales* of Porfirian Mexico," *Journal of Inter-American Studies* 9, no. 3 (July 1967): 441-55; Paul J. Vanderwood, "Mexico's *rurales:* Image of a Society in Transition," *HAHR* 61, no. 1 (February 1981): 52-83; and Paul J. Vanderwood, *Disorder and Progress: Bandits, Police, and Mexican Development* (Lincoln, Neb., 1981), 63-138.

3. F. Macías Valadez, *Apuntes geográficos y estadísticos sobre el estado de San Luis Potosí* (San Luis Potosí, 1878), 25-129; Secretaría de Fomento, Colonización e Industria, Dirección General de Estadística, *Tercer censo de población de los Estados Unidos Mexicanos 1910* (México 1918), 451; Philip Wayne Powell, *Capitán Mestizo: Miguel Caldera y la frontera norteña. La pacificación de los chichimecas* (México, 1980).

4. Macías Valadez, *Apuntes*, pp. 25-129. Macías Valadez provides figures for the value of real estate on the basis of tax returns for 1873 and 1874. The population of the Huasteca may have been slightly greater since many of its inhabitants lived in remote settlements. For the distinction between a *rancho* and an *hacienda* see George M. McBride, *The Land Systems of Mexico* (New York, 1923), 82. See also n. 45, this chapter.

5. Octaviano Cabrera Ipiña, "San Luis Potosí: Monografía de un estado" (San Luis Potosí, n.d.), 38, 46, and 112.

6. Emiliano Bustos, *Estadística de la República Mexicana. Resumen y análisis de los informes rendidos a la Secretaría de Hacienda* (México, 1880), 1:189, 199.

7. For a full discussion of the consequences of the railway construction for the Mexican economy, see John H. Coatsworth, *Growth against Development: The Economic Impact of Railroads in Porfirian Mexico* (DeKalb, Ill., 1981). See also Francisco R. Calderón, "Los Ferrocarriles," in *Historia moderna de Mexico, El Porfiriato. La vida economica*, ed. Daniel Cosío Villegas, 1:488-684; Andrés Molina Enríquez, *Los grandes problemas nacionales* (México, 1909), 232.

8. John Coatsworth, "Railroads, Landholding, and Agrarian Protest in the Early Porfiriato," *HAHR* 54, no. 1 (February 1974): 48-71; El Colegio de México, Seminario de Historia Moderna de México, *Estadísticas económicas del Porfiriato. Fuerza de trabajo y actividad económica por sectores* (México, n.d.), 29 (hereafter cited as *Estadísticas económicas*); Secretaría de Fomento, *Boletín semestral de la Dirección General de Estadística*, no. 9 (México, 1892), 24; Fernando Rosenzweig Hernández, "El desarrollo económico de México," *El Trimestre Económico*, 32 (3), no. 127 (July-September 1965): 419-21; Secretaría de Economía, Dirección General de Estadística, *Estadísticas sociales del Porfiriato 1877-1910* (México, 1956), 10-11. On the unrest around Tamazunchale, see p. 19.

9. Velázquez, *Historia* 4:72-73, 91-100; James D. Cockroft, *Intellectual Precursors of the Mexican Revolution* (Austin, Tex., 1968), 14; Perry, *Juárez and Díaz*, pp. 264, 282-83; W. E. Carson, *Mexico: The Wonderland of the South* (New York, 1909), 406. Commenting upon the city of San Luis Potosí, Carson wrote, "Twenty years ago this old town, which was founded in 1566, was but little known to the outside world; but since the advent of the railways it has become a thriving commercial place."

10. Cockroft, *Intellectual Precursors*, p. 21; *The Mexican Year Book, 1909/10* (London,

1910), p. 609; *1911*, p. 78; *1912*, pp. 155, 163; and *1914*, p. 134; David M. Pletcher, *Rails, Mines and Progress: Seven American Promoters in Mexico, 1867–1911* (New York, 1955), 233–38; Guadalupe Nava Oteo, "La Minería," in *Historia moderna de México, El Porfiriato. La vida económica,* ed. Cosío Villegas, 1:224–83; Ipiña to Kilton, 4 October 1906, AOC; *El Agricultor Mexicano* 19, no. 1 (January 1905).

11. Compare the comment of the editor of the San Luis Potosí daily, *El Estandarte:* "The modern hacendado is the 'soldier of work.' The public wealth is in his hands, and his fortune lies in his technical knowledge and sense. He needs the learning of a geologist, meteorologist, economist, chemist, mechanic, administrator, and worker. He ought to know about business, the state of the country, politics, finance and national trade. He should give the earth its appropriate cultivation, labor, water, air, light, shade, salt, manure; he should make war on the obstacles and plagues of agriculture. . . . he ought to prefer machinery to labor and modern to antiquated machinery" (11 January 1910).

12. Octaviano Cabrera Ipiña, *Archivo histórico de una hacienda* (Bledos, San Luis Potosí, 1958), 97; Jesús Silva Herzog, *Una vida en la vida de México* (México, 1972), 18–19; Secretaría de Fomento, Colonización e Industria, *Anuario estadístico de la República Mexicana, 1906,* p. 166; Nereo Rodríguez Barragán, interview with author, 16 July 1974; of Alejandro Espinosa Pitman, interview with author, 16 August 1974; Consul Wilbert Bonney to the Secretary of State, 16 October 1912, San Luis Potosí, SD 812.00/5310.

13. Secretaría de Fomento, Colonización e Industria, *Anuario estadístico, 1898,* pp. 644–49; *Anuario estadístico, 1903,* p. 572; *1904,* pp. 372, 414; *1905,* pp. 418–32; and *1906,* pp. 502–27. The figures for Montebello are taken from the hacienda's *Libro diario* for the years 1892 and 1902, in AOC. For *henequén* production in Yucatán in this period, see Siegfried Askinasy, *El problema agrario de Yucatán* (México, 1936), 100–101.

14. From the following *Anuarios estadísticos: 1898,* pp. 528–688; *1903,* pp. 516–60; *1904,* pp. 364–77, 406–49; *1905,* pp. 368–81; and *1906,* pp. 406–71.

15. Cockroft, *Intellectual Precursors,* p. 24; Velázquez, *Historia,* 4:155–62; Gabriel A. Menéndez, *Doheny el cruel* (México, 1958), 285.

16. Secretaría de Fomento, Colonización e Industria, Dirección General de Estadística, *Primer censo de población de los Estados Unidos Mexicanos 1895,* p. 9; *Tercer censo de población de los Estados Unidos Mexicanos,* p. 21.

17. See the *Anuarios estadísticos* for *1898* (pp. 469–71); *1903,* pp. 387–99; *1904,* pp. 261–74; *1905,* pp. 265–78; and *1906,* p. 279; McBride, *The Land Systems of Mexico,* pp. 73–77; José L. Cossío, *Monopolio y fraccionamiento de la propiedad rústica* (México, 1914), 6; Jesús Silva Herzog, *El agrarismo Mexicano y la reforma agraria. Exposición y crítica* (México, 1959), 82–86, 112–15.

18. Moisés González Navarro, *La vida social,* in *Historia moderna de México,* ed. Cosío Villegas, p. 196; John Womack, Jr., *Zapata and the Mexican Revolution* (London, 1972), 80–92; Friedrich Katz, "Pancho Villa, Peasant Movements and Agrarian Reform in Northern Mexico," in *Caudillo and Peasant in the Mexican Revolution,* ed. D. A. Brading (Cambridge, 1980), 59–75; Coatsworth, "Railroads, Landholding, and Agrarian Protest in the Early Porfiriato," p. 63; Vanderwood, *Disorder and Progress,* pp. 90–91; Héctor Aguilar Camín, *La frontera nómada: Sonora y la Revolución Mexicana* (México, 1977), 47–48. For resistance to the survey companies see the correspondence of José Encarnación Ipiña for March 1889, AOC, and Gutiérrez de Lara and Pinchón, *The Mexican People,* p. 316.

19. Secretaría de Fomento, Colonización e Industria, *Anuario estadístico de los Estados Unidos Mexicanos, 1898,* p. 469; *1903,* pp. 387–99; *1905,* pp. 265–78; *1906,* pp. 283–98. The

Colonia Díez Gutiérrez was founded in 1881–1882 on land the government gave to 410 Italian immigrants to the east of Ciudad del Maíz. Many of the Italians soon left, and the colony never became prosperous. In 1908 it contained 139 foreign colonists and 454 Mexicans; their total holdings together amounted to just under 3,000 hectares (Moisés González Navarro, *La colonización en México, 1877–1910* [México, 1960], 46–50).

20. Secretaría de Fomento, Colonización e Industria, Dirección General de Estadística, *División Territorial del Estado de San Luis Potosí*, Appendix, p. 1. According to *Estadísticas económicas* (p. 27), 430,109 persons lived in the 2,299 communities of fewer than 2,500 inhabitants in San Luis Potosí in 1900.

21. *Mexican Year Book, 1909/10*, p. 507; Cockroft, *Intellectual Precursors*, pp. 25–27; *El Estandarte*, 23 July 1910; Rafael Nieto, *Exposición de los motivos que el ejecutivo del estado tuvo para pedir al H. Congreso la expedición de la ley agraria* (San Luis Potosí, 1921), 2–5.

22. Matilde Cabrera Ipiña de Corci, *Cuatro grandes dinastías Mexicanas en los descendientes de los hermanos Fernández de Lima y Barragán* (San Luis Potosí, 1956), 46; Cockroft, *Intellectual Precursors*, p. 26.

23. Nereo Rodríguez Barragán, *El Canónigo Mauricio Zavala, apóstol del agrarismo en el Valle del Maíz* (San Luis Potosí, 1972), 9, 16, and 26–33; Leticia Reina, *Las rebeliones campesinas en México (1819–1906)* (México, 1980), 271–77; Coatsworth, *Growth against Development*, pp. 165–66.

24. Reina, *Las rebeliones campesinas*, pp. 278–87. After his capture Cortina was sent to San Luis Potosí for trial, but his ultimate fate is unknown. Zavala subsequently returned to Mexico, although not to San Luis Potosí, and became a canon of Mérida Cathedral. While in Yucatán he published a number of works on education, theology, and the Mayan language, which he considered superior to Spanish. He died in 1914 at the age of eighty-two (Rodríguez Barragán, *El Canónigo Mauricio Zavala*, pp. 12, 13, 23).

25. Rafael Montejano y Aguiñaga, *El Valle de Maíz S.L.P.* [San Luis Potosí, 1967], 341–42. In 1905 the *hacienda* of Minas Viejas belonged to the American ambassador, David Thompson (*El Estandarte*, 29 April 1909).

26. Details of these cases may be found in DAAC 23/8905, 23/4263, and 23/4208.

27. The documents relating to this case are in DAAC 23/4202. They include a copy of the accusation of slander brought before the judge of Villa de Carbonera by the legal secretary of the Compañía Deslindadora de Terrenos Baldíos, concerning remarks alleged to have been made by Antonio Espinosa y Cervantes.

28. The documents relating to this case are in DAAC 23/4284. For the events of 1898 to 1902 see also Wistano L. Orozco, *Los negocios sobre terrenos baldíos. Resoluciones judiciales y estudios del Licenciado Wistano Luis Orozco en el caso especial de Agustín R. de Ortiz contra los Moctezumas* (San Luis Potosí, 1902). For Orozco's own life, see Elena Sánchez Orozco's prologue to Wistano Luis Orozco, *Los ejidos de los pueblos* (México, 1975), 31–42. Orozco subsequently married Teresa Sánchez, a girl from Ciudad del Maíz.

29. Ingeniero R. Bufano to the Comisión Nacional Agraria, 7 October 1929, DAAC 23/4284; *El Estandarte*, 3 January 1911, pp. 3, 5, 7, 9; 18 May 1911; and 9 and 29 June 1911.

30. *Estadísticas económicas*, pp. 27–30; Secretaría de Economía Nacional, Dirección General de Estadística, *Estadísticas sociales del Porfiriato* (México, 1956), 41.

31. For an instance of the division of an *hacienda* between heirs to the property, see the case of La Parada, divided between José Encarnación Ipiña and his sister Petronila, in Jan Bazant, *Cinco haciendas Mexicanas. Tres siglos de vida rural en San Luis Potosí (1600–1910)* (México, 1975), 135–39. Frans J. Schryer, in his study of a *ranchero* community in neighboring Hidalgo, also notes a "growing differentiation of wealth among

landowning farmers" at the end of the Porfiriato (*The Rancheros of Pisaflores. The History of a Peasant Bourgeoisie in Twentieth Century Mexico* [Toronto, 1980], 34-35).

32. For prices see Appendix 2. The sources for wages during this decade are *Anuario estadístico, 1903*, pp. 498-99, 508, 514-15, and 524; Montejano y Aguiñaga, *El Valle de Maíz S.L.P.*, p. 345; Silva Herzog, *Una vida en la vida de México*, pp. 16-17, where he refers to the existence of a food ration on Angostura; Bazant, *Cinco haciendas Mexicanas*, pp. 175, 223; *El Estandarte*, 27 October 1909; and Consul Wilbert Bonney to the Secretary of State, 4 December 1912, where he describes conditions on Cerro Prieto (SD 812.00/5665). For conditions on José Encarnación Ipiña's *haciendas*, see the account books for the properties in AOC. Unfortunately, however, all but two of the *listas de raya* for the properties are missing; it is therefore impossible to make a general assessment of the size of the individual food ration or the level of wages.

33. José Encarnación Ipiña, as quoted in Cabrera Ipiña, *Archivo histórico de una hacienda*, p. 123; *Estadísticas económicas*, pp. 27, 28, and 46; McBride, *The Land Systems of Mexico*, p. 32; *El Agricultor Mexicano* 19, no. 1 (January 1905).

34. In a letter to Anastasio Obregón in July 1888, José Encarnación Ipiña wrote, "I want my sons to have a thorough knowledge of how to organize the division and colonization of estates . . . since for those who wish to be rich in Mexico, this will have to be their principal business" (quoted in Cabrera Ipiña, *Archivo histórico de una hacienda*, p. 106). Ipiña was a firm advocate of the division of large estates into smallholdings and frequently turned to this theme in his correspondence.

35. Francisco Bulnes, *Toda la verdad acerca de la Revolución Mexicana. La responsabilidad criminal del Presidente Wilson en el disastre Mexicano* (México, 1960), 136. For the profits of Montebello see Appendix 3. The administrator's comment is in the *hacienda*'s *Libro diario* for the year 1908/09, AOC. The Espinosa y Cuevas brothers mortgaged Angostura to José Encarnación Ipiña for 300,000 pesos (Nereo Rodríguez Barragán, interview with author, 16 July 1974; and Octaviano Cabrera Ipiña, interview with author, 28 July 1974). For an example of the prejudicial effect of the 1907 credit squeeze upon landowners in Coahuila, see William K. Meyers, "Politics, Vested Rights, and Economic Growth in Porfirian Mexico: The Company Tlahualilo in the Comarca Lagunera 1885-1911," *HAHR* 57, no. 3 (August 1977): 425-54, 438.

36. *El Estandarte*, 27 October 1909.

37. *El Estandarte*, 17 February and 6 April 1909. The problems of Rascón were not typical of other American-owned *haciendas* in the state, of which there were several. During the Maderista revolt in 1911, for example, the administrator of Rascón was the only manager of an American-owned estate in San Luis Potosí who felt it necessary to request an armed guard from the authorities. Consul Wilbert Bonney to the Secretary of State, 14 May 1911, SD 812.00/1847. I believe that Cockroft (*Intellectual Precursors*, pp. 52-54) exaggerates the extent of lower-class unrest in rural San Luis Potosí in the two decades prior to the Maderista revolt in 1910. In view of the decline in lower-class living standards there were remarkably few instances of protest or incipient revolt.

38. *Estadísticas económicas*, pp. 47-48, 106-9; *The Mexican Year Book, 1909/10*, p. 609; and *1911*, p. 78; Fernando Rosenzweig Hernández, "La industria," in Cosío Villegas, ed., *Historia moderna de México, El Porfiriato. La vida económica*, 1:404.

39. *El Estandarte*, 24 April 1908; John Kenneth Turner, *Barbarous Mexico* (New York, 1911), 208; Molina Enríquez, *Los grandes problemas nacionales*, p. 232; Jesús Silva Herzog, *Breve historia de la Revolución Mexicana* (México, 1960), 1:43; Rodney D. Anderson, *Outcasts in Their Own Land: Mexican Industrial Workers, 1906-1911* (DeKalb, Ill., 1976), 214-15.

40. Cockroft, *Intellectual Precursors,* pp. 92-163; Silva Herzog, *Breve historia de la Revolución Mexicana,* 1:76-107. For a full discussion of the relationship between the PLM and Mexican industrial workers, see Anderson, *Outcasts in Their Own Land,* pp. 268-70, 289-90, and 313-19, who concludes that "what evidence there is about the PLM's relationship to Mexican workers suggests that the PLM was a marginal factor in their existence, a vaguely known, sympathetic, but distant force, not central to what they did or thought about their problems" (p. 316).

41. Wilson to the Secretary of State, 31 October 1910, SD 812.00/355.

42. *El Estandarte,* 25 August 1909; Bulnes, *Toda la verdad,* p. 113; Félix F. Palavicini, *Mi vida revolucionaria* (México, 1937), 16; Consul Richard Stadden in Manzanillo to the Secretary of State, 19 March 1911, SD 812.00/1085; Wilson to the Secretary of State, 31 October 1910, SD 812.00/355. For a good illustration of this point, see Ian Jacobs's illuminating description of the background to the revolution in the state of Guerrero, *Ranchero Revolt: The Mexican Revolution in Guerrero* (Austin, Tex., 1982), pp.17-28.

43. Consul Albert Brickwood to the Secretary of State, Tapachula, 19 March 1911, SD 812.00/1412; Consul W. W. Graham to Thomas Hohler, the British chargé d'affaires in Mexico City, Durango, 27 April 1911, FO 371/1147 (17946). See also Consul Norman Rowe to the American Consul-General in Mexico City, Guanajuato, 3 April 1911; former Consul Edward Thompson, Progreso, 19 March 1911; and an unsigned U.S. naval intelligence report, 14 March 1911, Veracruz, SD 812.00/1300, 1260, and 1162; Henry Baerlein, *Mexico, The Land of Unrest* (London, 1914), 21-38 and 238; Turner, *Barbarous Mexico,* pp. 148-49; Hohler to Sir Edward Grey, the British foreign secretary, 1 February 1911, FO 371/1146 (5446); Jacobs, *Ranchero Revolt,* pp. 20-22 and 25; Charles Macomb Flandrau, *Viva Mexico* (London, 1982), 70-71.

44. *El Estandarte,* 3 January 1911; 3, 5, 7, 18 May and 9 and 29 June 1911; Ingeniero R. Bufano to the Comisión Nacional Agraria, 7 October 1929, DAAC 23/4284; Nereo Rodríguez Barragán, *Biografías Potosinas* (San Luis Potosí, 1976), 128-30; Bulnes, *Toda la verdad,* p. 114.

45. "The rancheros...can be distinguished from the large *hacienda* owners in a number of ways. Unlike the *hacendados,* who were absentee landlords, the *rancheros* resided on their small estates or in small rural communities. They also managed their own farms or were actively engaged in local commerce or the small-scale processing of agricultural products grown on such small estates. Like the large absentee landowners, the majority of *rancheros* employed seasonal wage laborers or peons as well as renting out part of their land. Unlike the *hacendados,* however, they shared the dress, deportment, and speech of their economic subordinates. These small landowners or rich peasants can be characterized as a peasant bourgeoisie. This term is used to emphasize both their 'peasant' or rustic style of life, which gave them low status in the eyes of the metropolitan elite, and their actual economic position as employers and entrepreneurs" (Schryer, *The Rancheros of Pisaflores,* p. 7).

46. "Arvide," pp. 1, 2.

47. "Arvide," pp. 3-8; Isaac Grimaldo, *Vida del Divisionario Saturnino Cedillo* (San Luis Potosí, 1935), 12; Lic. José Perogordo y Lasso, interview with author, 7 August 1974. Perogordo y Lasso was the district judge in Ciudad del Maíz in 1912 and a friend of Amado Cedillo.

48. Gildardo Magaña and Carlos Pérez Guerrero, *Emiliano Zapata y el agrarismo en México* (México, 1951), 2:169; Luís Noyola Barragán, *Como murieron los Generales Magdaleno y Saturnino Cedillo* (San Luis Potosí, 1964), 7 and 8; Sra. María Zuñiga, interview with author, 10 April 1974. Sra. Zuñiga was a close friend of Saturnino Cedillo during

the years 1910 to 1920. For the income of the fiber-cutters on Montebello, one of the *haciendas* in the district, see Appendix 2.

49. "Arvide," p. 9.

50. Montejano y Aguiñaga, *El Valle de Maíz*, p. 345; Magaña and Pérez, *Emiliano Zapata y el agrarismo en México*, 2:170; Antonio Diaz Soto y Gama, "Los hermanos Cedillo, destacados agraristas," *El Heraldo de San Luis Potosí*, 2 July 1952; Juan Muñiz Silva, "Saturnino Cedillo," *El Sol de San Luis Potosí*, 3 January 1954.

NOTES TO CHAPTER 2

1. "The President of the Republic is really an autocrat ruling and governing through republican forms" (Henry Lane Wilson to the Secretary of State, 31 October 1910, SD 812.00/355.

2. Rodney D. Anderson, *Outcasts in Their Own Land: Mexican Industrial Workers, 1906-1911* (DeKalb, Ill., 1976), 208-11; Francisco Bulnes, *Toda la verdad acerca de la Revolución Mexicana. La responsibilidad criminal del Presidente Wilson en el disastre Mexicano* (México, 1960), 101-36.

3. For Madero and his book see Stanley R. Ross, *Francisco Madero, Apostle of Mexican Democracy* (New York, 1955).

4. *El Estandarte*, 6 March 1909, 20 December 1910, 3 January and 8 April 1911; Charles C. Cumberland, *Mexican Revolution: Genesis under Madero* (Austin, Tex., 1974), 55-69; Anderson, *Outcasts in Their Own Land*, pp. 250-67.

5. Bulnes, *Toda la verdad*, p. 114; *El Estandarte*, March to September 1909 and 3 November 1909; Anderson, *Outcasts in Their Own Land*, p. 247; Consul G. B. McGoogan to the Secretary of State, 19 March 1911, Progreso, SD 812.00/1084.

6. Cumberland, *Mexican Revolution: Genesis under Madero*, pp. 70-85; Madero's views on economic questions may be summarized by a remark he addressed to a crowd at an election rally in Orizaba: "You do not want bread; you only want freedom because it will serve you to win bread" (as quoted by Ross, *Francisco Madero*, p. 103).

7. Cumberland, *Mexican Revolution*, p. 98.

8. Cumberland, *Mexican Revolution*, pp. 99-105; *El Estandarte*, 20 November 1910 and 7 July 1911; Luis F. Bustamante, *Quién es el Coronel Juan Barragán?* (San Luis Potosí, 1917), 14. According to Anderson, the historian of the industrial working class of Porfirian Mexico, "on the eve of the great Mexican Revolution of 1910, industrial workers around the nation were largely pro-Madero" (*Outcasts in Their Own Land*, p. 254).

9. *El Estandarte*, 5, 6, 12, 16, 23, 26, and 28 June 1910; Cumberland, *Mexican Revolution*, p. 114; Nereo Rodríguez Barragán, *Biografías Potosinas. Introducción bibliográfica y notas de Rafael Montejano y Aguiñaga* (San Luis Potosí, 1976), 95-103.

10. *El Estandarte*, 23 June 1910.

11. James D. Cockroft, "El maestro de primaria en la Revolución Mexicana," *Historia Mexicana* 16 (April-June 1967): 573-75; Alberto Alcocer Andolón, "El General y Profesor Alberto Carrera Torres," *Archivos de Historia Potosina* no. 1 (July-September 1969): 32-48. Under the electoral system then in force, the population of the state was divided into groups of approximately five hundred persons, who chose a representative to vote on their behalf. Saturnino, the most literate of Amado's sons, was the choice of the community of Palomas. The only reference I have found to Saturnino's visit to Madero is in "Arvide," p. 10. Unfortunately, "Arvide" provides no details of their en-

counter; but as far as I am aware, there is no reason to doubt his assertion that the two men met.

12. Primo Feliciano Velázquez, *Historia de San Luis Potosí* (México, 1946), 4:218; Jesús Silva Herzog, *Breve historia de la Revolución Mexicana* (México, 1960), 1:125; Madero and Barrenechea were fellow directors of the Santa María de la Paz Mining Company at Matehuala. *The Mexican Year Book, 1909/10* (London, 1910), 516.

13. Velázquez, *Historia*, 4:218; Octaviano Cabrera Ipiña, *San Luis Potosí: Monografía de un estado* (San Luis Potosí., n. d.), 147; *El Estandarte*, 7 to 12 August 1910. The revolt in Tancanhuitz seems to have been the culmination of a series of incidents of municipal unrest caused by the tyranny of local officials, rather than, as Cockroft has asserted, a part of a "revolutionary movement of workers and peasants, abetted by the Precursor Movement, championed by the P.L.M., and directed against the Mexican bourgeoisie and foreign businessmen" (James D. Cockroft, *Intellectual Precursors of the Mexican Revolution* [Austin, Texas, 1968], 156).

14. *El Estandarte*, 20, 22, 24, 25, and 26 November 1910.

15. Vice-Consul Percy G. Holms in Guadalajara to British chargé d'affaires Thomas Hohler in Mexico City, 17 April 1911, FO 371/1147 (16692); Cumberland, *Mexican Revolution*, pp. 124-25.

16. Ambassador Wilson to the Secretary of State, 26 November 1910, SD 812.00/484; Ross, *Francisco Madero*, p. 127.

17. "In Chihuahua the rebellion is rather against the unpopular state authorities than against the federal government. This state has been under the control of the Terrazas family for fifty years and all public positions have been filled by members of that family or persons acceptable to them" (Wilson to the Secretary of State, 29 December 1910, SD 812.00/622). William H. Beezley, *Insurgent Governor: Abraham González and the Mexican Revolution in Chihuahua* (Lincoln, Neb., 1973), 13-54; Michael C. Meyer, *Mexican Rebel: Pascual Orozco and the Mexican Revolution, 1910-1915* (Lincoln, Neb., 1967), 10-15.

18. "The leaders of the (revolutionary) party are mainly people of some local consideration who have suffered some injustice or loss at the hands of the administration, and who, being unable to obtain redress, have decided to follow the example set them by Madero last year, and strike out for a new government in the hope of better things. Their local influence enables them to start out with a band over which they are able to exercise a greater or less degree of discipline" (Hohler to the British Foreign Secretary, Sir Edward Grey, 30 May 1911, FO 371/1148 [23276]). See also Patrick O'Hea, *Reminiscences of the Mexican Revolution* (México, 1966), 16, 161, and 174; Pastor Rouaix, *Diccionario geográfico, histórico y biográfico del Estado de Durango* (México, 1960), 37, 38, 102, 118, 369, and 473; John Womack, Jr., *Zapata and the Mexican Revolution* (London, 1972), 113, 121; *El Estandarte*, 1, 4, 6, and 31 January, 7 February, 11 March, 7 and 9 May, and 20 August 1911; Hohler to Grey, 17 May 1911, FO 371/1147 (20780); Ian Jacobs, *Ranchero Revolt: The Mexican Revolution in Guerrero* (Austin, Tex., 1982), xiii, 79.

19. Vice-Consul W. W. Graham to Hohler, 27 April 1911, Durango, FO 371/1147 (17946); Rouaix, *Diccionario*, p. 102.

20. This account of the pattern and nature of the unrest is drawn largely from the American consular reports for the period from November 1910 to May 1911, SD 812.00/390-1888; the British consular and embassy reporting for the same period, FO 371/1146-1148; and *El Estandarte*, January to June 1911, which contains surprisingly full and frank coverage of the rebellion. The revolt in Yucatán was summarized for the Secretary of State by G. B. McGoogan, the American consul in Progreso, on 19 March 1911:

The revolutionary spirit is due to several causes. The peons on the large plantations are really chattels of the owner. Many peons are born, live and die on the same plantations. It is an unwritten law of the henequén planters that they will not employ a laborer from another plantation. These peons are paid very little, and some are treated very badly, and whipped and punished in various ways. They become like enraged animals subdued by their keeper and have taken advantage of the present situation to revolt and have destroyed some property and assasinated [sic] two of the planters, but having no leader or organization are gradually quietening down. Another class are rebellious on account of the administration of the local judges and jefe politícos (mayors of cities) who are claimed to be tyrannical and unfair. Several of these local officials have been assassinated. . . . A large majority of intelligent Mexicans are opposed to the present government because they feel Díaz and Corral were not elected, but retain their power by violating the Mexican constitution, intimidation and tyranny.

They say that the friends of Díaz in Mexico are able to obtain concessions and franchises from the government which enrich the few at the expense of the many.

This is the middle class, the skilled mechanic, merchants and professional men, but they cut but little figure in the present situation, as they are not inclined to risk their lives or fortunes in a revolution.

This report is in SD 812.00/1084.

21. Bonney to the Secretary of State, 18 March 1911, in SD 812.00/1071; *El Estandarte,* 2 and 22 February 1911. According to the newspaper, there were 800 prisoners in the penitentiary by early February.

22. "Only in capital letters can be described the Maderista effervescence in the east of the state. . . . Two factors exist why the inhabitants of this distant region are Maderistas body and soul. The first is the discontent which exists with the government for having disposed of land which the local people consider their own; when these lands were denounced as vacant, the government accepted the denunciation. The second is that the *jefes políticos* and Municipal Presidents are chosen from the most despotic *caciques"* (*El Estandarte,* 3 January 1911). In spite of the tone of this report, incidents of violence were still very few in January; sympathy for Madero only expressed itself in widespread direct action much later.

23. *El Estandarte,* 3 January, 21 and 24 February, and 24 March 1911; Bonney to the Secretary of State, 18 March 1911, SD 812.00/1071. In Bonney's opinion the local government's defenses were so relaxed that a force of five hundred rebels could have captured the state capital. He added, however, that rebel activity was confined to raids on property in remote localities and concluded that "there is scarcely likely to be any independent movement begun in this district unless some new incitement arise."

24. *El Estandarte,* 4, 8, and 12 April 1911.

25. Paul J. Vanderwood, "Response to Revolt: The Counter-Guerrilla Strategy of Porfirio Díaz," *HAHR* 56, no. 4 (November 1976): 551-79; Hohler to Grey, 1 February 1911, FO 371/1146 (5446); Wilson to the Secretary of State, 29 March 1911, SD 812.00/1210; Ross, *Francisco Madero,* pp. 135-75.

26. *El Estandarte,* 23 March, 18 April, and 12 May 1911; Bonney to the Secretary of State, 4 and 14 May 1911, SD 812.00/1774 and 1770.

27. *El Estandarte,* 1-20 May 1911. "It has become a physical impossibility for the authorities to protect the various country properties which have asked for guards . . . . to the east of this capital the situation is confused. Small bodies of men under arms, from twenty to fifty each, move from point to point committing depredations upon planta-

tions and attempting to raise recruits, with some success" (Bonney to Secretary of State, 14 May 1911, SD 812.00/1847).

28. *El Estandarte,* 9 and 19 May 1911; Bonney to the Secretary of State, 4 and 14 May 1911, SD 812.00/1774 and 1847. The grievances of the inhabitants of the district of Santa María de Acapulco are detailed in their 27 February 1922 petition for an *ejido,* DAAC 23/4263. See also chap. 1, p. 16–17.

29. *El Estandarte,* 14 and 24 May 1911.

30. *El Estandarte,* 20 May to 3 June 1911; Ross, *Francisco Madero,* pp. 135-75; Alcocer Andolón, "El General y Profesor Alberto Carrera Torres," pp. 32-33; Cockroft, "El maestro de primaria en la Revolución Mexicana," p. 575; Romana Falcón, "¿Los orígenes populares de la revolución de 1910?—El caso de San Luis Potosí," *Historia Mexicana* 29 (July 1979-June 1980): 212; "Arvide," p. 23. Three of the six members of Pedro Antonio de los Santos's staff in the Huasteca—his brothers Samuel and Miguel, and another close relative, Fulgencio M. Santos—were also members of his family. Of the three new *jefes políticos* they appointed in the region, two—Santos Pérez in Valles and Rafael I. Santos in Tancanhuitz—belonged to their family (*El Estandarte,* 1 June 1911).

31. Wilson to the Secretary of State, 11 July, 4 August, and 30 November 1911, SD 812.00/2219, 2257, and 2601; Consul Luther Ellsworth to the Secretary of State, 24 July 1911, Ciudad Porfirio Díaz, and Consul William O. Jenkins to the Secretary of State, 13 July 1911, Puebla, SD 812.00/2239 and 2222; Meyer, *Mexican Rebel,* pp. 39-40; Womack, *Zapata and the Mexican Revolution,* pp. 105-78.

32. *El Estandarte,* June to August 1911; see especially 15, 21, and 22 June 1911.

33. Bonney to the Secretary of State, 4 May 1911, SD 812.00/1774. For the incidents of agitation in the countryside see *El Estandarte,* 22 June, 20 August, 20 September, and 5 October 1911.

34. Joaquín Meade, *Semblanza de José Encarnación Ipiña* (San Luis Potosí, 1956), 24-31; Velázquez, *Historia,* 4:225.

35. *El Estandarte,* 20 and 29 August; 6, 15, and 22 September 1911; Bonney to the Secretary of State, 30 September and 16 December 1911, SD 812.00/2401 and 2659; American chargé d'affaires Fred Morris Dearing to the Secretary of State, 5 August 1911, Mexico City, and Ambassador Wilson to the Secretary of State, 30 November 1911, SD 812.00/2268 and 2601; Cumberland, *Mexican Revolution,* p. 168.

36. Madero once summarized his agrarian policy as follows: "I have always advocated the creation of small property but that does not mean that any landowner is going to be deprived . . . . it is one thing to create small property through constant effort, and another to divide up large estates which I have never considered nor offered" (*El Imparcial,* 28 June 1912). See also Luis Cabrera, *Obras completas* (México, 1975) 1:137-65; William H. Beezley, "Madero: The 'Unknown' President and His Political Failure to Organize Rural Mexico," in *Essays on the Mexican Revolution: Revisionist Views of the Leaders,* ed. George Wolfskill and Douglas W. Richmond (Austin, Tex., 1979), 19; Jesús Silva Herzog, *El agrarismo Mexicano y la reforma agraria. Exposición y crítica* (México, 1959), 199-206; Ross, *Francisco Madero,* pp. 240-46.

37. Alberto J. Pani, *En camino hacia la democracia* (México, 1918), 17-18 and 31-32; Ramón Eduardo Ruiz, *Labor and the Ambivalent Revolutionaries: Mexico, 1911-1923* (Baltimore, 1976), 29-36; Marjorie Ruth Clark, *Organized Labor in Mexico* (Chapel Hill, N.C., 1934), 19-23.

38. Consul Marion Letcher to the Secretary of State, 4 and 20 March 1912 and 17 October 1913, Chihuahua, SD 812.00/3192, 3424 and 9484; Meyer, *Mexican Rebel,* pp. 45-58 and 62-83; Beezley, *Insurgent Governor,* pp.55-88.

39. On the unrest outside Chihuahua see the reports of the American consular representatives to the Secretary of State: Gaston Schmutz from Aguascalientes (7 March 1912), Wilbert Bonney from San Luis Potosí (12 March 1912), Lewis Haskell from Salina Cruz (30 April 1912); William Alger from Mazatlán (1 May 1912), John Glenn from Guanajuato (25 May and 17 September 1912), Alphonse Lespinasse from Frontera (2 July 1912), Clarence Miller from Tampico (16 May 1912), and Theodore Hamm from Durango (14 August 1912), SD 812.00/3231, 3303, 3851, 3910, 4126, 5084, 4378, 4055, and 4674. For the Zapatistas see Womack, *Zapata and the Mexican Revolution*, pp. 187–220, 543.

40. Wilson to the Secretary of State, 12 March 1913, SD 812.00/6840; Ross, *Francisco Madero*, p. 278; Cumberland, *Mexican Revolution*, pp. 227–43; Friedrich Katz, *The Secret War in Mexico: Europe, The United States and the Mexican Revolution* (Chicago, 1981), 87–115; Michael C. Meyer, *Huerta—A Political Portrait* (Lincoln, Neb., 1972), 71–82.

41. *El Estandarte*, 6 and 7 June, 7 July, and 15 August 1911; Bonney to the Secretary of State, 19 December 1911, 30 March and 13 August 1912, and 14 January 1913, SD 812.00/2664, 3497, 4461, and 5908.

42. Bonney to the Secretary of State, 16 and 19 December 1911, 13 February, 12 and 30 March, and 30 April 1912, SD 812.00/2659, 2664, 2837, 3303, 3497, and 3814.

43. Bonney to the Secretary of State, 28 May, 5 and 21 June, and 13 August 1912, SD 812.00/4119, 4193, 4319, and 4661.

44. M. Teresa Barragán, *Figuras de la actualidad* (San Luis Potosí, 1930), 16.

45. Bazant, *Cinco haciendas Mexicanas*, p. 223; Bonney to the Secretary of State, 26 September, 16 October, 2 and 18 November 1912, SD 812.00/5140, 5310, 5446, and 5575.

46. Bonney to the Secretary of State, 2 November 1912, SD 812.00/5446.

47. Bonney to the Secretary of State, 16 October, 2 and 18 November, and 4 December 1912, SD 812.00/5310, 5446, 5575, and 5665.

48. Bonney to the Secretary of State, 26 September 1912, SD 812.00/5140. In November Bonney reiterated to the Secretary of State the agrarian and economic origins of the unrest (18 November 1912, SD 812.00/5575):

> The gulf between the classes is impassable. Those employers who have treated agricultural labor with most severity have been the worst sufferers in the raids in this State; there has been an obvious effort on the part of the raiders to discriminate against harsh administrators. There has never been personal contact between workman and owner, and this now prevents them uniting, although it happens that both are opposing themselves to the existing government. It is continually doubtful whether the middle class is sufficiently strong or numerous to stand alone, and this condition results in the existing insecurity and impossibility of predicting the future. There is also doubt as to whether the middle classes are united or loyal to their own leaders. It seems certain that antagonism between the classes is the strongest motive in the present situation and it seems probable that the land owning class have lost control.
>
> It is only in the towns and cities that there is a middle class. In agriculture there are practically only the rich employers and the laborers. It is therefore a question as to which of these two shall control the plantations. There is no middle class there to effect a compromise. To the laborers there appears only the alternative of continuing the feudal system or killing the administrator and taking possession of the property . . . . There is then, here, a district scarcely able to support its people, in which wealth has been created for a few hundred people by exploiting native labor; a middle class somewhat more numerous, and a vast illiterate lower class who have become discontented. All have been accustomed to one-man power. A class struggle

has begun in a guerrilla manner. There is little open conflict. The peon raids property when it appears safe to do so. The middle class instigate the arrest of wealthy land owners. The land owners secretly plot against the middle class officials. Editors are in constant danger of arrest. All classes attempt to use the courts for personal or class ends. At times the soldiers scarcely know which class they are supporting.

49. The Moctezumas to the Comisión Nacional Agraria, 4 January 1921, DAAC 23/4284.

50. The Moctezumas to the Comisión Nacional Agraria, 4 January 1921, DAAC 23/4284. Manuel Garza Aldape, the Minister of Development under President Victoriano Huerta, subsequently canceled the survey's findings.

51. Gildardo Magaña and Carlos Pérez Guerrero, *Emiliano Zapata y el agrarismo en México* (México, 1951), 2:169-71; "Arvide," p. 26.

52. Magaña and Pérez, *Emiliano Zapata y el agrarismo en México* 2:171-72; Meyer, *Mexican Rebel*, p. 64.

53. "Arvide," p. 34.

54. Luis Noyola Barragán, *Como murieron los Generales Magdaleno y Saturnino Cedillo* (San Luis Potosí, 1964), 10 and 11; Juan Barragán Rodríguez, *Historia del Ejercito y de la Revolución Constitucionalista* (México, 1946), 1:164; "Arvide," pp. 34-35; Bonney to the Secretary of State, 18 November 1911, SD 812.00/5575.

55. Bonney to the Secretary of State, 13 February 1913, SD 812.00/6365; "Arvide," p. 41. Rafael Montejano y Aguiñaga, in *El Valle del Maíz S.L.P.* (San Luis Potosí, 1967, p. 347), claims that the Cedillos took 800,000 pesos from the train robbery.

56. Bonney to the Secretary of State, 4 December 1912, 14 January, 13 February (twice), and 18 February 1913, SD 812.00/5665, 5908, 6365, 6368, and 6417.

NOTES TO CHAPTER 3

1. The best account of Huerta's government is to be found in Michael C. Meyer, *Huerta: A Political Portrait* (Lincoln, Neb., 1972).

2. Charles C. Cumberland, *Mexican Revolution: The Constitutionalist Years* (Austin, Tex., 1972), 12-22, 71-74; Douglas W. Richmond, "Carranza: The Authoritarian Populist as Nationalist President," in *Essays on the Mexican Revolution: Revisionist Views of the Leaders*, ed. George Wolfskill and Douglas W. Richmond (Austin, Tex., 1979), 50; Consul Philip Holland to the Secretary of State, 19 and 21 February 1913, Saltillo, SD 812.00/6272 and 6472. "The tone of the Sonoran rebellion was that of a nation closing its ranks and abolishing internal contradictions in order to confront another nation attacking it" (Héctor Aguilar Camín, "The Relevant Tradition: Sonoran Leaders in the Revolution," in *Caudillo and Peasant in the Mexican Revolution*, ed. D. A. Brading [Cambridge, 1980], 109). Aguilar Camín provides an excellent account of the Sonoran revolt in *La frontera nómada. Sonora y la Revolución Mexicana* (México, 1977), 265-359.

3. "The real danger lies in the attitude of the old Maderista revolutionaries who have subsequently been employed as rurales and irregulars in policing the outlying districts. . . . It is evident that disaffection is spreading among their ranks" (Consul Theodore Hamm to the Secretary of State, 5 March 1913, SD 812.00/6789, Hamm to the

Secretary of State, 13 March 1913, and Ambassador Wilson to the Secretary of State, 15 May 1913, SD 812.00/6977 and 7652; John Womack, Jr., *Zapata and the Mexican Revolution* (London, 1972), 229; Cumberland, *Mexican Revolution*, p. 27; Ian Jacobs, *Ranchero Revolt: The Mexican Revolution in Guerrero* (Austin, Tex., 1982), 96.

4. Michael C. Meyer, *Mexican Rebel: Pascual Orozco and the Mexican Revolution, 1910–1915* (Lincoln, Neb., 1967), 98; Hamm to the Secretary of State, 24 and 28 February and 13 March 1913, SD 812.00/6733, 6734, 6977; Patrick O'Hea, *Reminiscences of the Mexican Revolution* (London, 1981), 59. According to Meyer, apart from the revolts led by Carranza, Villa, and the Sonorans, there were smaller uprisings against Huerta in the spring of 1913 in thirteen other states (*Huerta*, p. 90).

5. Canada to the Secretary of State, 4 September 1913, SD 812.00/8851.

6. Cumberland, *Mexican Revolution*, p. 73; Alexander Dye (former U.S. consul in Nogales) to the Secretary of State, 15 March 1913, SD 812.00/6806; Womack, *Zapata and the Mexican Revolution*, p. 273; Linda B. Hall, *Álvaro Obregón: Power and Revolution in Mexico, 1911–1920* (College Station, Tex., 1981), 10–58; Vicente Blasco Ibañez, *El militarismo Mejicano* (Valencia, 1920), 107; Francisco Naranjo, "Los millionarios de la Revolución," *El Diario de Yucatán*, 4 August 1948.

7. Bonney to the Secretary of State, 25 February and 7 March 1913, in SD 812.00/6510 and 6537. According to John Silliman, the U.S. Consul in Saltillo, Carranza had "counted certainly" upon Cepeda's support in his rejection of Huerta. Cepeda was subsequently escorted north to bargain with Carranza on Huerta's behalf, but his mission was a failure and he was returned to jail (Silliman to the Secretary of State, 19 April 1913, SD 812.00/7397). See also Meyer, *Huerta*, p. 92.

8. Bonney to the Secretary of State, 28 March 1913, SD 812.00/7041; Carlos Purata Gómez, "Integrantes del poder legislativo de San Luis Potosí del constituyente de 1824 a la fecha," *Boletín de la Escuela de Jurisprudencia de la Universidad Autónoma de San Luis Potosí*, no. 5 (August 1965): 1–27.

9. Pastor Rouaix, *Diccionario Geográfico, Histórico y Biográfico del Estado de Durango* (México, 1960), 37; *El Imparcial*, 28 July 1914; Bonney to the Secretary of State, 4 March and 29 April 1913, and Hamm to the Secretary of State, 13 March 1913, SD 812.00/6736, 7428, and 6977. The American administrator of Agua Buena hacienda near Tamasopo decided to cease operations on the property in June because of rebel depredations, saying "it is a common remark among our men here that as soon as we close and there is no more work, that there is nothing for them to do but join the rebels" (quoted by U.S. Consul Clarence Miller to the Secretary of State, 25 May 1913, Tampico, SD 812.00/7690).

10. "In the eastern part of this district several bands of rebels under the Cedillo brothers grew rapidly after the new government was proclaimed, February 18 1913, and they now claim more than eight hundred men in all. Some of them recognize President Huerta but refuse to recognize Governor Cepeda. They are terrorizing the country between Río Verde, Cerritos, Cárdenas and Ciudad del Maíz. Upon entering Cárdenas on February 27th they carried a red flag and claimed to be partisans of Pascual Orozco and Vázquez Gómez. They have control of the short railway between Río Verde and San Bartolo. They are socialistic in their political ideas and the whole force of the Cedillo brothers grew from a simple band of robbers into a political unit in two weeks and the Federal Government is now treating with them" (Bonney to the Secretary of State, 4 March 1913, SD 812.00/6736. "Arvide," pp. 44–48; Victoria Lerner, "Los fundamentos socioeconómicos del cacicazgo en el México postrevolucionario—El caso de Sa-

turnino Cedillo," *Historia Mexicana* 29 (July 1979–June 1980): 403. Bonney to the Secretary of State, 15 April 1913, SD 812.00/7145, refers to the Cedillos' first operations against the new regime.

11. James D. Cockroft, "El maestro de primaria en la Revolución Mexicana," *Historia Mexicana* 16 (April–June 1967): 577–79.

12. Bonney to the Secretary of State, 29 April and 8 May 1913, SD 812.00/7428 and 7675.

13. Primo Feliciano Velázquez, *Historia de San Luis Potosí* (México, 1946), 4:250. Bonney to the Secretary of State, 8 and 28 May 1913, SD 812.00/7675 and 7790.

14. Bonney to the Secretary of State, 18 December 1913, SD 812.00/10466.

15. Bonney to the Secretary of State, 9 September 1913, SD 812.00/8911.

16. "Arvide," pp. 58–59; Bonney to the Secretary of State, 18 December 1913, SD 812.00/10466.

17. Bonney to the Secretary of State, 18 December 1913, SD 812.00/10466.

18. "The anti-American feeling is coherent, organized, expressive, because it is lodged in the writing classes. The anti-Spanish feeling is silent, incoherent and expressed in acts of personal violence, because it is harbored by the illiterate working class" (Bonney to the Secretary of State, 28 May 1913, SD 812.00/7790). The popular resentment of the Spaniards was embodied by Francisco Villa, who took a number of discriminatory measures against the local Spanish population when he occupied Chihuahua City in February 1914. When Marion Letcher, the American consul there, interceded with Villa on the Spaniards' behalf, Villa told him that "his people had been robbed from time immemorial by the Spaniards, that their liberties had been taken away from them and that then [*sic*] had been kept in the darkest ignorance in order that they might be better exploited; that Spanish priests and nuns, the whole organization of the Catholic Church, in fact, had used their offices to the same end: and that now that the power to do so had come into his hands, he was going to drive them out of Mexico to the last soul" (Consul Letcher to the Secretary of State, 21 February 1914, Chihuahua, SD 812.00/11043). The Chinese community, which was active in commerce in the north of the country, was the other major foreign victim of reprisals by the revolutionaries (Alan Knight, "Peasant and Caudillo in Revolutionary Mexico, 1910–1917," in *Caudillo and Peasant*, ed. Brading, p. 52; and Henry Baerlein, preface to *Mexico, The Land of Unrest* [London, 1914], xiii).

19. Rafael Montejano y Aguiñaga, *El Valle de Maíz S.L.P.* (San Luis Potosí, 1967), 353; *El Imparcial*, 18 May 1914; Consul Silliman to the Secretary of State, 6 September 1913, Saltillo, SD 812.00/8884.

20. Velázquez, *Historia*, 4:253. See also Eugenio Martínez Nuñez, *La Revolución en el estado de San Luis Potosí* (México, 1964), 41.

21. Bonney to the Secretary of State, 18 December 1913, SD 812.00/10466.

22. Friedrich Katz, *The Secret War in Mexico: Europe, The United States, and the Mexican Revolution* (Chicago, 1981), 145. Katz provides an excellent analysis of the origins and development of Villa's movement in this work. Villa's personal background was extremely varied: he had been an *hacienda* peon, a miner, tenant farmer, peddler, and bandit (see pp. 38, 137). For Calixto Contreras see O'Hea, *Reminiscences*, pp. 49–52 and 75–76. For the fighting in the winter of 1913-1914, see Álvaro Obregón, *Ocho mil kilómetros en campaña; relación de las acciones de armas efectuadas en más de veinte estados de la República durante un periodo de cuatro años* (México, 1959), 82–122; and Juan Barragán Rodríguez, *Historia del Ejercito y de la Revolución Constitucionalista* (México, 1946), 1:148-66. Consul

Theodore Hamm to the Secretary of State, 15 October and 16 December 1913, Durango, SD 812.00/9658 and 10406, describes Villa's capture of Torreón and Ciudad Chihuahua.

23. Hall, *Álvaro Obregón*, pp. 50–54; Barragán Rodríguez, *Historia del Ejercito*, 1:522–64; Martín Luis Guzmán, *Memorias de Pancho Villa* (México, 1951), 461–62; *El Imparcial*, May–July 1914; Cumberland, *Mexican Revolution*, p. 217; Douglas W. Richmond, "Venustiano Carranza," in *Essays*, ed. Wolfskill and Richmond, p. 76; Meyer, *Huerta*, pp. 198–203; Zachary Cobb (U.S. customs collector) to the Secretary of State, 4 June 1914, El Paso; and Leon Canova (President Wilson's special envoy to Carranza) to the Secretary of State, 8 July 1914, Saltillo. (The Cobb and Canova documents are in SD 812.00/12160 and 12474.) A full account of the political and military developments in Mexico during the period March to July 1914 may be found in the reporting of the various U.S. consuls and special agents in the country in SD 812.00/11130 to 12780.

24. Bonney to the Secretary of State, 19 March and 22 August 1914, SD 812.00/11212 and 13074.

25. *El Imparcial*, 18 June and 19 July 1914; "Arvide," pp. 61–64; Martínez Nuñez, *La Revolución en San Luis Potosí*, p. 43; Vice-Consul Thomas Dickenson, 2 August 1914, San Luis Potosí, in SD 812.00/12770; Meyer, *Huerta*, pp. 207–8.

26. Vice-Consul Dickenson to the Secretary of State, 2 August 1914, San Luis Potosí, and Cobb to the Secretary of State, 2 November 1914, SD 812.00/12770 and 13657; Velázquez, *Historia*, 4:257–60; John M. Hart, *Anarchism and the Mexican Working Classes, 1860–1931* (Austin, Tex. 1978), 127. A copy of Gutiérrez's labor law is to be found in Patronato de la Historia de Sonora, *Fuentes para la historia de la Revolución Mexicana* (México, 1954), 1:188.

27. "Arvide," p. 69; Jesús Silva Herzog, *Una vida en la vida de México* (México, 1972), 37; Velázquez, *Historia*, 4:260; Bonney to the Secretary of State, 19 August 1914, SD 812.00/13002. José María Espinosa y Cuevas, the other co-owner of Angostura, died in Mexico City in 1928. When news of his death reached San Luis Potosí, local business houses closed their doors in mourning for a few hours. (Nereo Rodríguez Barragán, *Biografías Potosinas* [San Luis Potosí, 1976], 129).

28. "Arvide," p. 69.

29. "On the whole, conditions, although unsatisfactory to many, at present tend to the betterment and reformation of the unhappy country" (Vice-Consul Dickenson to the Secretary of State, 2 August 1914, San Luis Potosí, SD 812.00/12770). One of the administration's more popular measures was to abolish the military courts which had functioned under Huerta (Bonney to the Secretary of State, 19 August 1914, SD 812.00/13002).

30. Robert E. Quirk, *The Mexican Revolution, 1914–1915: The Convention of Aguascalientes* (Bloomington, Ind., 1960), 75–136.

31. Rouaix, *Diccionario*, pp. 37–39, 102, 118, and 473 (s.v. "Argumedo," "Arrieta," "Contreras," "Chao," and "Urbina")); Canova to the Secretary of State, 21 October and 6, 11, and 12 November 1914, SD 812.00/13633, 13788, 13741, and 13923; Luis F. Bustamante, *Perfiles y bocetos revolucionarios* (San Luis Potosí, 1917); Dye (former U.S. consul in Nogales) to the Secretary of State, 15 March 1913, SD 812.00/6806. For two excellent analyses of the reasons the two sides aligned as they did, see Katz, *The Secret War*, pp. 123–55 and 257–97; and Knight, "Peasant and Caudillo in Revolutionary Mexico, 1910–1917," in *Caudillo and Peasant*, ed. Brading, pp. 17–58.

32. *El Monitor*, January to April 1915; American consuls and special agents in Mexico

to the Secretary of State, January–October 1915, SD 812.00/14173 to 16794; Katz, *The Secret War*, p. 268; Hall, *Álvaro Obregón*, p. 93.

33. Martínez Nuñez, *La Revolución en San Luis Potosí*, p. 57, "Arvide," pp. 70–79; Cockroft, "El maestro de primaria en la Revolución Mexicana," p. 580.

34. A copy of Carranza's decree may be found in an attachment to a letter from American chargé d'affaires George Summerlin to the Secretary of State, 6 July 1923, México, SD 812.52/1105.

35. Womack, *Zapata and the Mexican Revolution*, pp. 359–60; Eyler N. Simpson, *The Ejido: Mexico's Way Out* (Chapel Hill, N.C., 1937), 54–61.

36. Quirk, *The Mexican Revolution, 1914–1915*, pp. 174–75; Bonney to the Secretary of State, 8 March 1915, SD 812.00/14627; José Vasconcelos, *Obras completas* (México, 1957), 1:948–55.

37. "Arvide," pp. 79–97; Alberto Alcocer Andolón, "El General y Professor Alberto Carrera Torres," *Archivos de Historia Potosina*, 1, no. 1 (July–September 1969): 41; Bustamante, *Perfiles y bocetos revolucionarios*, s.v. "Manuel Lárraga" and "Samuel de los Santos"; Bonney to the Secretary of State, 8 April and 26 July 1915, SD 812.00/14869 and 15728.

38. Elena Sánchez Orozco, "Prologue" to Wistano Luis Orozco, *Los ejidos de los pueblos* (México, 1975), 39.

39. Ibid., pp. 36–39; Womack, *Zapata and the Mexican Revolution*, pp. 271–72.

40. Bonney to the Secretary of State, 8 April, 25 June, and 26 July 1915, SD 812.00/14869, 15374, and 15728.

41. Consul William Davis to the Secretary of State, 9 November 1915, Guadalajara, SD 812.00/16835. See also the reports of the American consular representative, C. A. Williams, 3 December 1915, Torreón, SD 812.00/16965; and Bonney, 3 November 1915, San Luis Potosí, SD 812.00/16764; and Rouaix, *Diccionario*, p. 37, s.v. "Argumedo."

42. On Alvarado and Múgica, see reports to the Secretary of State by American consuls Gaylord Marsh in Progreso and William Canada in Veracruz, 21 and 29 February 1916 and 2 October 1916, SD 812.00/17332, 17410, and 19522; and also G.M. Joseph, *Revolution from Without: Yucatán, Mexico and the United States, 1880–1924* (Cambridge, 1982), 93–149. On depredations by Constitutionalist commanders elsewhere, see the reports from American consuls Homer Coen in Durango (30 April 1916), Gaston Schmutz in Aguascalientes (16 March 1916), William Davis in Guadalajara (4 December 1915 and 24 April 1916), William Alger in Mazatlán (4 November 1915), Claude Dawson in Tampico (24 July 1916), William Canada in Veracruz (22 January and 27 May 1915), and Zachary Cobb in El Paso (23 February 1916), SD 812.00/18157, 17605, 17258, 18168, 16796, 18832, 14322, 15352, and 17342. These abuses continued into 1917 and 1918, largely unchecked. Consul Frederick Simpich, for example, wrote on 11 January 1918 from Guaymas to the Secretary of State: "Officers may, and do, violate the personal and property rights of civilians with utter impunity" (SD 812.00/21690). Consul Dawson reported to the Secretary of State from Tampico on 19 June 1918 that "absolute quiet and public order reign throughout the region, foreigners are unmolested, the native inhabitants are comparatively prosperous and contented. The arrival of government troops is always followed by a reversal of these conditions—the countryside is terrorized, troops are allowed to loot, steal and plunder" (SD 812.00/22098). Charles Furber, a British landowner in Guanajuato, similarly ascribed the continuing unrest there in 1918 to the rapacious activities of the Constitutionalist soldiers (British chargé d'affaires H.A. Cunard Cummins to Arthur Balfour, the British Foreign Secretary, 23 April 1918, México, FO 371/2429 [87167]).

43. *El Demócrata,* 4-6, 11, 14, 16, 17, 22, and 30 December 1915, and 3-6, 8, 18, 19, and 29 January 1916; Vice-Consul Thomas Bevan to the Secretary of State, 27 September 1915, Tampico; and Bonney to the Secretary of State, 3 and 24 November 1915, SD 812.00/16414, 16764, and 16892.

44. In a letter of May 1915, Mariano Jara, the administrator of Bledos, reported to his employer, Roberto Ipiña: "We are not too badly off here in Bledos, since we have enough in store to feed our people, a miracle at times like these. I am sending maize to the other haciendas from San Luis Potosí, since they have been left with nothing at all . . . . The price of maize has gone up alarmingly. I bought a freightcar load at 130.00 pesos the hectoliter, (rather more than the 4.00 we paid before the revolution. . .) and I had to bribe the police not to steal it from me. But cost what it may, I will continue buying more so that none of the people on any of your haciendas lacks sustenance" (quoted in Octaviano Cabrera Ipiña, *Archivo histórico de una hacienda* [Bledos, San Luis Potosí, 1958], 137–38). For Stackpole, see Bonney to the Secretary of State, 30 August 1915, SD 812.00/16135.

45. Bonney to the Secretary of State, 7 and 29 March 1916, SD 812.00/17477 and 17730. The Cedillos used classical guerrilla tactics: "All of the Cedillos' forces are familiar with the territory in which they are operating, and as soon as they are attacked by a superior force they scatter into small bands and hide in the mountain retreats, and do not congregate until the pursuers have given up the chase" (Vice-Consul Bevan to the Secretary of State, Tampico, 11 November 1915, SD 812.00/16813).

46. Bonney to the Secretary of State, 24 November 1915 and 7 March 1916, SD 812.00/ 16892 and 17477. See also Velázquez, *Historia,* 4:277; Douglas W. Richmond, "Factional Political Strife in Coahuila, 1910–1920," *HAHR* 60, no. 1 (February 1980): 65. For the effect of the inflation upon the profits of the *hacienda* of Bledos, see Appendix 3. In May Bonney commented, "Trains are coming and going daily from the frontier and Mexican communications are fairly good. There are no extortions or forced loans, no street fighting, no confiscation of houses and furniture, no arrests of civilians for party reasons, no monopoly of railways by soldiers. This is in marked contrast with conditions ten months ago" (Bonney to the Secretary of State, 8 May 1916, in SD 812.00/ 18148).

47. Blocker to the Secretary of State, 11 October 1916, SD 812.00/19544. For Dávila's attitude toward agrarian reform, see Velázquez, *Historia,* 4:277; Katz, *The Secret War,* p. 291; and Bonney to the Secretary of State, 24 November 1915, SD 812.00/16892.

48. Cumberland, *Mexican Revolution,* p. 350. For a full discussion of the debates over these articles, see E. V. Niemeyer, *Revolution at Querétaro: The Mexican Constitutional Convention, 1916–1917* (Austin, Tex., 1974), 60–100.

49. Marjorie Ruth Clark, *Organized Labor in Mexico* (Chapel Hill, N.C., 1934), 47; Comisión Nacional para la Celebración del Sesquicentenario de la Proclamación de la Independencia Nacional y del Cincuentenario de la Revolución Mexicana, *Diario de los debates del Congreso Constituyente 1916–1917* (México, 1960), 2:1181–1222; Pastor Rouaix, *Génesis de los artículos 27 y 123 de la Constitución Política de 1917* (México, 1959), 103–41.

50. Niemeyer, *Revolution at Querétaro,* pp. 134–65; Jesús Silva Herzog, *El agrarismo Mexicano y la reforma agraria. Exposición y crítica* (México, 1959), 250–60.

51. Parker to the Secretary of State, 10 January 1917, SD 812.00/20433.

52. Katz, *The Secret War,* pp. 287–93; Womack, *Zapata and the Mexican Revolution,* pp. 355–92; U.S. Consul Coen to the Secretary of State, 3 May 1916, Durango, SD 812.00/ 18141; Silva Herzog, *El agrarismo Mexicano,* p. 248; James W. Wilkie, *The Mexican Revolution: Federal Expenditure and Social Change since 1910* (Berkeley, Calif., 1970), 188.

53. James D. Cockroft, *Intellectual Precursors of the Mexican Revolution* (Austin, Tex., 1967), 76–80, 226–28; Luis F. Bustamante, *¿Quién es el Coronel Juan Barragán?* (San Luis Potosí, 1917); Juan Muñiz Silva, "Saturnino Cedillo," *El Sol de San Luis Potosí*, 14, 21, and 28 February 1954; Cobb to the Secretary of State, 16 April 1917, El Paso, SD 812.00/20834. Cobb's report is based on information from an American merchant in Matehuala, who refers to Barragán's unpopularity as a candidate. For the elections in Tamaulipas and Coahuila, see the unsigned report of 23 April 1918, "Conditions in Mexico," prepared by the U.S. Office of Naval Intelligence, U.S. Navy Department, Washington, D.C., in SD 812.00/21949; and Consul Blocker to the Secretary of State, 10 January 1918, Piedras Negras, SD 812.00/21652. See also Cumberland, *Mexican Revolution*, pp. 366–70.

54. Consul Dawson to the Secretary of State, 7 March 1917, Tampico, SD 812.00/20662. Carrera Torres's injury in 1911 had led to an amputation and the fitting of an artificial leg, an operation paid for by Madero himself. (Cockroft, "El maestro de primaria en la Revolución Mexicana," pp. 575, 581). A year later, in an irony typical of the period, Caballero himself was being hunted as a rebel in the same region. (Cumberland, *Mexican Revolution*, pp. 369–70.) For a copy of the document in which the Cedillos declared their adherence to Carrera Torres's decree, see *Unica*, 6, no. 60 (January 1969): 48–53. "Arvide," p. 98, describes the defection of Enrique Salas.

55. Dawson to the Secretary of State, 13 October and 7 December 1917, SD 812.00/21381 and 21557; Memorandum of the Huasteca Petroleum Company, 5 November 1917, SD 812.00/21457; Katz, *The Secret War*, pp. 463–65.

56. Montejano y Aguiñaga, *El Valle de Maíz S.L.P.*, pp. 359–60; Luis Noyola Barragán, *Como murieron los Generales Magdaleno y Saturnino Cedillo* (San Luis Potosí, 1964), 18–22; *Excélsior*, 6 November 1917, which reported that upon hearing of Magdaleno's death "the local hacendados have congratulated General Manuel M. Diéguez, the *jefe de operaciones*, for having released them from the threat hanging over them"; Juan Muñiz Silva, "Saturnino Cedillo," 17 January 1954.

57. "It has been stated that the Cedillo brothers had as many as three thousand or three thousand five hundred men a year ago. As they have completely overrun the district until quite lately and are bandits pure and simple few persons have ventured into their territory, hence the information concerning them is very vague. From the extent of territory covered by their operations, and the nature of the depredations committed it is quite evident they are exceedingly numerous, and their influence in the country is accentuated by the friendly attitude of the civil population" (Consul Dawson to the Secretary of State, 7 December 1917, Tampico, SD 812.00/21557). "Arvide," pp. 98–101; Muñiz Silva, "Saturnino Cedillo," 14 February 1954; British Vice-Consul Dr. Harry E. Nolan in San Luis Potosí to Edward Thurston, British chargé d'affaires, 20 August 1917, Mexico, FO 371/2963 (305). For the attack upon Tamasopo see the report of Consul General Philip Hanna to the Secretary of State, 20 September 1918, San Antonio, SD 812.00/22272. Beginning in the second half of 1915, the national press frequently reported successful engagements against the forces of the Cedillos and Carrera Torres, with predictions of their imminent capture. Such reports merely served to emphasize the strength and resilience of the rebels. See, for example, *El Demócrata*, 8, 13, 17, and 30 September and 6, 11, 16, and 17 December 1915, and 3, 7, and 10 February 1916; also see *Excélsior*, 6 and 7 November and 5 December 1917, and 7 and 19 August 1918.

58. Ernest Gruening, *Mexico and Its Heritage* (New York, 1928), 319. According to Carleton Beals, another contemporary American observer, "the army is built up in a pyramidal fashion on the basis of shifting personal allegiance" (*Mexico: An Interpretation*

[New York, 1923], 179). The Spanish novelist Vicente Blasco Ibañez provides an amusing and unflattering account of the Constitutionalist army in *El militarismo Mejicano* (Valencia, 1920).

59. Consul E. M. Lawton to the Secretary of State, 15 January 1918, Nogales, SD 812.00/21668; Consul H. S. Bursley to the Secretary of State, 21 July and 8 August 1928, Guaymas, SD 812.00/Sonora, etc.; Hall; *Álvaro Obregón*, pp. 200–202.

60. Patrick O'Hea, the acting U.S. consul in Gómez Palacio, wrote about General Luis Gutiérrez that "his reputation is not savoury in regard to the many commercial transactions of decidedly doubtful character that he conducted for his own benefits, availing himself of the advantage of his military position. This, of course, is universal" (O'Hea to the Secretary of State, 14 December 1917, SD 812.00/21595). Information about the other generals can be found in reports from Consul Simpich in Guaymas (11 January and 23 February 1918); Cobb in El Paso (4 June 1917); J. A. Wright of the War Trade Board in El Paso (26 June and 2 July 1918); Consul Canada in Veracruz (11 September 1916); Consul General Hanna from San Antonio, Tex. (23 May 1918), and Consul Blocker in Piedras Negras (13 December 1917 and 19 June 1918), SD 812.00/21690, 21778, 20981, 22089, 22130, 19256, 22015, 21570, and 22073. See also Edwin Lieuwen, *Mexican Militarism: The Political Rise and Fall of the Revolutionary Army, 1910–1940* (Albuquerque, N.M., 1968), 39.

61. A letter from an unnamed "prominent English businessman" to Consul General Philip Hanna, December 1917. Quoted by Hanna to the Secretary of State, 24 December 1917, San Antonio, Tex., SD 812.00/21636.

62. See the report by an unnamed American employee at the ASRC smelter in Matehuala to Consul-General Hanna in San Antonio, Texas, written in the spring of 1918 and quoted by Hanna in a letter to the Secretary of State, 6 May 1918, SD 812.00/21974.

63. Hanna to the Secretary of State, ibid.

64. See, for example, Ramón Eduardo Ruíz, *Labor and the Ambivalent Revolutionaries: Mexico, 1911–1923* (Baltimore, 1976), 51–70.

65. Ibid., pp. 51–70; Clark, *Organized Labor*, p. 58; Consul-General Hanna to the Secretary of State, 6 May 1918, San Antonio, Tex., SD 812.00/21974; Barry Carr, *El movimiento obrero y la política en México 1910–1929* (México, 1976), 1:70–102, 121–34.

66. Velázquez, *Historia*, 4:308; *El Universal*, 19 May 1919; Vice-Consul Knox Alexander to the Secretary of State, 21 October 1920, San Luis Potosí, SD 812.00/24743. Knox Alexander commented that "it is generally understood that Nieto received the majority of the votes for governor in the last state elections, held over a year ago; but Ing. Severino Martínez took charge of the office at that time with the support of the late President Carranza."

67. *El Universal*, 12 April 1919; Katz, *The Secret War*, p. 324; Hall, *Álvaro Obregón*, p. 184. According to Lloyd Burlingham, the American consul in Salina Cruz, "There is an astonishing lack of adhesion to the government in power in this district. . . . If the rebels had a sufficient supply of arms and ammunition, the present pretense of control by the Carrancista government could not last a day in the states of Oaxaca and Chiapas" (Burlingham to the Secretary of State, 11 April 1919, SD 812.00/22641). See also reports from American consuls Thomas Bowman in Frontera (10 April 1919), Dawson in Tampico (16 April 1919), Charles Arthur in Oaxaca (1 May 1919), and Paul Foster in Veracruz (12 May 1919), SD 812.00/22643, 22649, 22712, and 22738. For Esteban Cantú, see George Carothers to the Secretary of State, 25 March 1917, El Paso, SD 812.00/20732; Carothers had been a U.S. consul in Torreón. Alberto Pineda's matronymic was Ogarrio but he was always referred to as Pineda O.

68. Hall, *Álvaro Obregón,* pp. 233-44.

69. Roberto Guzmán Esparza, *Memorias de don Adolfo de la Huerta, según su propio dictado: transcripción y comentarios del Licenciado Roberto Guzmán Esparza* (México, 1957), 153-67; *El Universal,* 1 February and 20 May 1920; Womack, *Zapata and the Mexican Revolution,* pp. 494-96; Gruening, *Mexico and Its Heritage,* p. 357; Clark, *Organized Labor,* p. 72; Peter V. N. Henderson, *Felíx Díaz, The Porfirians and the Mexican Revolution* (Lincoln, Neb., 1981), 144; Hall, *Álvaro Obregón,* pp. 245-48; British chargé d'affaires H. A. Cunard Cummins to the Marquess Curzon of Kedleston, the Foreign Secretary, 13 April, 26 July, and 4 December 1920, Mexico, FO 371/4492 (A2812/65/26) /4496 (A5896/65/26) and /4497 (A9079/65/26).

70. Katz, *The Secret War,* pp. 143-44.

71. Rouaix (*Diccionario,* p. 102) claims that Contreras died in 1918; but Homer Coen, the American consul in Durango, reported Contreras's death in August 1916 (Coen to the Secretary of State, 30 August 1916, SD 812.00/19042).

NOTES TO CHAPTER 4

1. Ernest Gruening, *Mexico and Its Heritage* (New York, 1928), 319. Gruening's valuable book is an indispensable source for the politics of the period.

2. Linda B. Hall, "Álvaro Obregón and the Politics of Mexican Land Reform, 1920-1924," *HAAR* 60, no. 2 (May 1980): 215.

3. Narciso Bassols Batalla, *El Pensamiento Político de Álvaro Obregón* (México, 1967), 136. See also Gruening, *Mexico and Its Heritage,* p. 147, and Eyler N. Simpson, *The Ejido: Mexico's Way Out* (Chapel Hill, N.C., 1937), 87. For Obregón's own business interests see Consul H. S. Bursley to the Secretary of State, Guaymas, 21 July 1928, SD 812.00/ Sonora etc.

4. H. A. Cunard Cummins to the Marquess Curzon of Kedleston, the Foreign Secretary, 30 July 1921, FO 371/5586 (A6143/337/26).

5. Hall, "Álvaro Obregón and the Politics of Mexican Land Reform, 1920-1924," pp. 219-23; Simpson, *The Ejido,* pp. 87-88.

6. Manuel Fabela, *Cinco siglos de legislación agraria en México* (México, 1941), 347-91; Simpson, *The Ejido,* pp. 318 and 721. A copy of the CNA's "Circular 51" may be found in the attachments to a letter from George Summerlin, U.S. chargé d'affaires, to the Secretary of State, 6 July 1923, SD 812.52/1105.

7. For Adalberto Tejeda see Heather Fowler Salamini, *Agrarian Radicalism in Veracruz, 1920-1938* (Lincoln, Neb., 1978), 25-140; for Emilio Portes Gil see his own book, *Raigambre de la Revolución en Tamaulipas* (México, 1972), 173-99. For José Zuno see Vice-Consul Percy Holms in Guadalajara to Esmond Ovey, the British Minister in Mexico City, 17 February 1927, FO 371/12001 (A1574/52/26).

8. Robert Haberman, "Bandit Colonies," *Survey Graphic* V, no. 2 (May 1924): 148.

9. The report of Juan Correa Martínez of the Army Paymaster's Department on the demobilization arrangements for Cedillo's troops, n.d., SDN XI/III/I-244, vol. 1. For Cedillo's rank see his correspondence with the Ministry of War for March 1921 in SDN XI/III/I-244, vol. 1. The equipment Cedillo's men received from the ministry included a tractor, 25 ploughs, 800 machetes, 800 axes, 800 picks, 800 shovels, 800 hoes, and 800 hectoliters of maize (Cedillo to the Ministry of War, 21 June 1920, SDN XI/III/ I-244, vol. 1).

10. For the superior social standing of colonists over *ejidatarios* see the letter from Ing. M. Gómez Félix of the Agrarian Department to the department's delegate in San Luis Potosí, 25 January 1934, DAAC 23/4477.

11. *El Universal*, 20 January 1922; Haberman, "Bandit Colonies," p. 196; Director of Waters, Lands, and Colonization of the National Agrarian Commission (CNA) to José Arteaga, 29 August 1930, DAAC 23/4477.

12. Quoted in a memorandum by the Sub-Director of the Department of Justice, Records and Library, the Ministry of War and Marine, 30 August 1922, SDN XI/III/I–244, vol. 1.

13. Cedillo to the Ministry of War, 5 October 1921; and Obregón to the Ministry of War, 12 September 1921, SDN XI/III/I–244, vol. 1. The *ejidatarios* of El Labor finally obtained their land after Cedillo's overthrow; see Memorandum by Ing. S. Tueffer, Agrarian Department, 8 February 1940, DAAC 9296/Colonies.

14. R. Ayluardo to the Technical Director of the CNA, 28 April 1931, Ing. J. M. Rebentum to the CNA, 11 February 1931, and Juan Argumedo to the CNA, 10 May 1936, all in DAAC 9296/Colonies; Ing. Rafael Bufano to the CNA, 8 October 1929, and Ing. José de Jesús Martínez, *informe* of 20 January 1927, both in DAAC 23/4284; *Ejidal* Committee of Victoria to the Mixed Agrarian Commission, 19 January 1942, DAAC 23/9137.

15. "Arvide," pp. 106–24. I have found no record of the fate of Cedillo's first wife, who was presumably dead by this time.

16. *Excélsior*, 25 November 1922; Consul Walter F. Boyle to the Secretary of State, 25 February and 9 October 1922, San Luis Potosí, SD 812.00/25416 and 25976; Chief of Military Operations to Cedillo, 10 October 1922, San Luis Potosí, and Cedillo to the War Ministry, 10 October 1922, SDN XI/III/I–244, vol. 1.

17. *El Estandarte*, 14 June 1911; Boyle to the Secretary of State, 13 and 16 May 1921, SD 812.00/25599 and 24799; *El Universal*, 10, 18, 19, 24, and 31 January 1922; Jorge Prieto Laurens, *Cincuenta Años de Política Mexicana* (México, 1968), 141.

18. Compare the remark of Consul Boyle in 1924: "For the last few years it has been clearly demonstrated that the only political element that can control the state is the element which can count on the Agrarian support of General Cedillo" (Boyle to the Secretary of State, 1 August 1924, SD 812.00/27336); on Nieto's government generally, see Boyle to the Secretary of State, 13 May 1922, SD 812.00/25599.

19. Boyle to the Secretary of State, 10 July 1922 and 20 January 1923, SD 812.00/25780 and 26174.

20. Gruening, *Mexico and Its Heritage*, p. 222.

21. Information on wages and sharecropping may be found in *Diario Oficial*, 4 July 1925, and in the petitions for land by the *ejidal* committees of Sta. María Acapulco, Tampate, Villa de la Paz, Villa Carbonera, Tamuín, and Guaxcamá, DAAC 23/4263, 4208, 4231, 4202, 4227, and 4311. For the land redistribution see *Resumen de posesiones provisionales y definitivas desde la promulgación de la ley de 6 de enero de 1915 a la fecha*, AGN, Ramo Obregón/Calles 106/6 818–E–38.

22. Rafael Nieto, *Exposición de los motivos que el Ejecutivo del Estado tuvo para pedir at H. Congreso la expedición de la ley agraria* (San Luis Potosí, 1921).

23. The Hon. Claude Stanhope, General Manager of Salinas of Mexico Ltd., to the board of the company in London, 29 August 1923, FO 371/8472 (A6344/2904/26).

24. Cummins to Curzon, 27 July and 22 October 1923, FO 371/8466 (A4998/187/26 and A6661/187/26).

25. Summerlin to the Secretary of State, 5 June 1923, SD 812.00/26384; Cummins to

Curzon, 16 August 1923, FO 371/8466 (A5546/187/26). For Alvarado's administration of Yucatán, see G. M. Joseph, *Revolution from Without: Yucatán, Mexico and the United States, 1880–1924* (Cambridge, 1982), 93–149.

26. Prieto Laurens, *Cincuenta años,* pp. 9, 18, and 19.

27. Emilio Portes Gil, *Autobiografía de la Revolución Mexicana* (México, 1964), 362–63; Summerlin to the Secretary of State, 28 September 1923, SD 812.00/26467. Portes Gil had recently come to know Cedillo when the latter sought his assistance in founding an agrarian colony for the former followers of the Carrera Torres brothers in southern Tamaulipas ("Arvide," p. 119).

28. Boyle to the Secretary of State, 18 December 1922, SD 812.00/26153; Prieto Laurens, *Cincuenta años,* p. 141.

29. Others included Alberto Pani, the treasury minister under Obregón and Calles; Emilio Portes Gil, then a congressman and later president; Marte Gómez, the minister of agriculture in 1929; José Vasconcelos, the minister of education from 1921 to 1924; Félix Palavicini, an influential editor and member of the Constituent Assembly in 1917; and, of course, Prieto Laurens himself. For Manrique's background see *El Estandarte,* 19 June 1909; *Excélsior,* 16 and 29 July 1918; Juan Muñiz Silva, "Saturnino Cedillo," *El Sol de San Luis Potosí,* 14 March 1954; John W. F. Dulles, *Yesterday in Mexico: A Chronicle of the Revolution, 1919–1936* (Austin, Tex., 1967), 129.

30. "Arvide," p. 113; Muñiz Silva, "Saturnino Cedillo," 14 March 1954; Boyle to the Secretary of State, 18 December 1922, SD 812.00/26153.

31. "Arvide," pp. 111–12; *El Universal,* 3 March 1923; *Excélsior,* 19 April 1923; Boyle to the Secretary of State, 26 February and 30 April 1923, SD 812.00/26226 and 26338. See also Prieto Laurens, *Cincuenta años,* pp. 186-87.

32. Boyle to the Secretary of State, 10 July 1923, SD 812.00/26410.

33. Boyle to the Secretary of State, 2 June and 10, 13, and 21 July 1923, SD 812.00/26378, 26410, 26413, and 26415. Alfonso Gama to the Secretary of War, 26 June 1923, SDN XI/III/I-244, vol. 4.

34. Boyle to the Secretary of State, 7 August 1923, SD 812.00/26423.

35. Boyle to the Secretary of State, 13 and 22 August 1923 and 5 September 1923, SD 812.00/26427, 26437, and 26452.

36. Juan Muñiz Silva, "Saturnino Cedillo," 21 and 28 March 1954; Consul David J. D. Myers to the Secretary of State, San Luis Potosí, 18, 26, and 29 September 1923, SD 812.00/26459, 26462, and 26465.

37. Consul Myers to the Secretary of State, 6, 15, and 22 October 1923, San Luis Potosí, SD 812.00/26470, 26478, and 26479.

38. Summerlin to the Secretary of State, 19 October and 23 November 1923, SD 812.00/26483 and 26526; Cummins to Curzon, 22 October 1923, FO 371/8467 (A6661/187/26).

39. Summerlin to the Secretary of State, 16 November and 7 December 1923, in SD 812.00/26513 and 26612. For the popularity of De la Huerta in the provinces see the reports from American consuls William Chapman (Mazatlán, 8 December 1923), A. R. Willson (Matamoros, 15 December 1923), Lee Blohm (Aguascalientes, 13 December 1923), William Jenkins (Puebla, 8 December 1923), John Dye (Ciudad Juárez, 6 December 1923), and Harry Walsh (Nuevo Laredo, 26 November 1923), SD 812.00/26620, 26643, 26644, 26661, 26568, and 26523. In Guaymas, however, the hometown of De la Huerta, Calles was more popular (Consul B. T. Yost to the Secretary of State, 20 December 1923, SD 812.00/26645; Héctor Aguilar Camín, *La frontera nómada* [México, 1977], 85).

40. Summerlin to the Secretary of State, 16 November 1923, SD 812.00/26514; Prieto Laurens, *Cincuenta años,* p. 146; the Paymaster General to the Minister of War, 8 November 1923, SDN XI/III/I-244, vol. 3.

41. The Municipal President of Río Verde to General Gutiérrez, 18 October 1923, SDN XI/III/I-244, vol. 3; Consul Myers to the Secretary of State, 22 and 30 October 1923, San Luis Potosí, and Consul Boyle to the Secretary of State, 11 and 13 November 1923, San Luis Potosí, SD 812.00/26479, 26492, 26499, and 26504; *El Universal,* 4 December 1923.

42. Boyle to the Secretary of State, 26 November and 12 December 1923; and Summerlin to the Secretary of State, 16 and 24 November 1923, SD 812.00/26528, 26630, 26514, and 26527.

43. Luis Monroy Durán, *El último caudillo* (México, 1924), 111; Cummins to Curzon, 16 November and 12 December 1923 and 25 January 1924, FO 371/8467 (A7399/187/26) and (A7647/187/26) and 371/9560 (A1091/12/26).

44. Gruening, *Mexico and Its Heritage,* pp. 320-22; Monroy Durán, *El último caudillo,* pp. 95-112.

45. Myers to the Secretary of State, 13 December 1923, Durango, SD 812.00/26636. Myers reported a similar response from the *ejidatarios* in Tapones, where the governor claimed he had an army reserve of two thousand men, though only thirty came forward to fight.

46. Jesús Silva Herzog, *El agrarismo mexicano y la reforma agraria. Exposición y análisis* (México, 1959), 310; Fowler Salamini, *Agrarian Radicalism,* pp. 41-45. A full account of the De La Huerta revolt and the role of the agraristas in helping to suppress it may be found in FO 371/9557 to 9561.

47. *El Universal,* 7-14 December 1923; the Chief of General Staff to the Infantry Department, 12 December 1923, SDN XI/III/I-244, vol. 1; Boyle to the Secretary of State, 8 and 12 December 1923, SD 812.00/26549 and 26630.

48. Boyle to the Secretary of State, 12 December 1923, SD 812.00/26630; John Womack, Jr., *Zapata and the Mexican Revolution* (London, 1972), 302.

49. Boyle to the Secretary of State, 5 January 1924, SD 812.00/26758.

50. The President of Rascón *Ejidal* Committee to the President of the State Agrarian Commission, 14 April 1924, DAAC 23/4315; Boyle to the Secretary of State, 12 January 1924, SD 812.00/26792.

51. "Arvide," pp. 142-45; *El Universal,* 19 January 1924; Consul Boyle to the Secretary of State, 5 and 12 January 1924, SD 812.00/26758 and 26792.

52. "Arvide," pp. 145-52; General Amaro to the General Staff Department, 7 August 1925, SDN XI/III/I-244, vol. 1; *The Times,* 23 April 1924, p. 13; Boyle to the Secretary of State, 3 May 1924, SD 812.00/27234.

53. Summerlin to the Secretary of State, 21 June 1923, SD 812.00/26398. For land seizures by *agrarista* groups in the wake of the De la Huerta revolt see Cummins to James Ramsay MacDonald, Foreign Secretary, 3 May 1924, FO 371/9562 (A3164/12/26); for complaints about the anti-agrarian attitude of certain military commanders see the claim of the president of the Comisión Local Agraria in Michoacán to Obregón (21 November 1921) that the military commanders in the state were "systematically obstructing the breaking up of latifundios and the granting of ejidos," AGN, Ob/Calles pq. 106.6, 818-E-28; Antonio Díaz Soto y Gama to Obregón, 27 October 1921, AGN Ob/Calles, pq. 106.6, 818-E-28; the *ejidal* committee of Tlahuac, Xochimilco, to Obregón, 26 February 1923, AGN pq. 11/1-leg. 4, Exp. 818-T-93; and the Sindicato de Obreros y Campesinos de la Región Lagunera to Obregón, 4 May 1924, AGN pq. 106.6. 818-E-

51. See also Hans-Werner Tobler, "Las paradojas del ejercito revolucionario: su papel social en la reforma agraria Mexicana 1920–1935," *Historia Mexicana* 21 (July–September 1971): 38–79.

54. Minister of Agriculture Luis León quoted in *El Universal,* 7 February 1926; Paul Friedrich, *Agrarian Revolt in a Mexican Village* (Chicago, 1977), 130.

55. Consul William Blocker to the Secretary of State, 17 February 1927, Mazatlán, SD 812.00/28257; *El Machete,* 19 March 1925; Senator Huitron to Obregón, 19 April 1924, Coahuila, AGN pq. 106.6. 818–E–51.

56. "Arvide," p. 154; Boyle to the Secretary of State, 1 August 1924, SD 812.00/ 27336.

57. "No-one calls him (Manrique) dishonest or insincere, only fanatical and bent on socializing the state . . . in contrast to himself Governor Manrique's followers are perhaps the most ignorant, selfish and dishonest horde that has ever come to power" (Boyle to the Secretary of State, 1 August 1924, SD 812.00/27336). See also Gruening, *Mexico and Its Heritage,* p. 471.

58. Portes Gil, *Raigambre,* pp. 141–46; Boyle to the Secretary of State, 7, 15, and 29 February and 11 March 1924, SD 812.00/27002, 27017, 27080, and 27126.

59. Boyle to the Secretary of State, 11 March, 22 and 28 April, 15 June and 1 August 1924, SD 812.00/27126, 27225, 27230, 27302, and 27336. In January 1925 a Canadian banker familiar with Mexico found that the government's attitude to the private sector was inducing "a decided feeling of hopefulness in all business circles" (British Ambassador Sir Esme Howard to Sir Austen Chamberlain, the British Foreign Secretary, 4 February 1925, Washington, FO 371/10627 [A812/216/26]).

60. *El Universal,* 29 January 1924; Boyle to the Secretary of State, 31 December 1924, 20 and 31 January, and 14 and 31 March 1925, SD 812.00/27486, 27497, 27499, 27510, and 27517.

61. According to official figures, 292,286 hectares were given in provisional possession to 12,802 *ejidatarios* in the years 1924 and 1925 in San Luis Potosí (Secretaría de Agricultura y Fomento, Comisión Nacional Agraria, *Estadística 1915–1927* [México, 1928], 76). For the agrarian congress see Boyle to the Secretary of State, 20 January 1925, SD 812.00/27497; and "Arvide," p. 162.

62. *El Universal,* 30 April and 5 and 7 May 1924. The documents dealing with the case of Villa de Reyes are in DAAC 23/4201 (724.3).

63. For the Calles presidency see Jean Meyer, *Historia de la Revolución Mexicana. Periodo 1924–1928. Estado y sociedad con Calles* (México, 1977). The close relations between Calles and the CROM are described in Ovey to Chamberlain, 5 April 1926, FO 371/ 11146 (A2279/48/26).

64. Simpson, *The Ejido,* pp. 377–90; Report of the Congress of Agricultural Communities of Guanajuato, *El Universal,* 10 June 1930; *Segunda Convención de la Liga de Comunidades Agrarias del Estado 1927* (n.p., 1927), 117–221; Ovey to Chamberlain, 13 April 1926, 10 December 1927, and 16 May 1929, FO 371/11144 (A2429/14/26), /12768 (A63/32/26), and /13496 (A3745/220/26).

65. "Several governors have been dismissed and various others are said to be scheduled for early removal. There seems to be no doubt that the dismissals have been the exclusive work of the President" (Consul Drew Linard to the Secretary of State, Piedras Negras, 2 December 1925, SD 812.00/27661). The governors who resigned were those from Oaxaca, Aguascalientes, Zacatecas, Coahuila, Nuevo León, and, as we shall see, San Luis Potosí. See also Gruening, *Mexico and Its Heritage,* pp. 399–403, 413–17, and 468–73.

66. *Rojo y Negro*, 11 November 1924; Boyle to the Secretary of State, 12 November 1924 and 20 January 1925, SD 812.00/27449 and 27497. Commenting on the first incident, Boyle wrote, "The spectacle of speakers telling the President-elect that they would resort to arms to overthrow him if he proved a traitor to their cause, and the President-elect replying that he had no intention of being a traitor, was certainly edifying."

67. Boyle to the Secretary of State, 20 January 1925, SD 812.00/27497.

68. Boyle to the Secretary of State, 12 November 1924, SD 812.00/27449. Compare Boyle's prophetic observation two months later: "The whole Manrique following would crumble to pieces if General Calles were to send one batallion of troops of the line into the state and use any one of the score or so legal methods by which Mexican officials understand how to get rid of officials not to their liking, to dispose of Manrique as governor" (Boyle to the Secretary of State, 20 January 1925, SD 812.00/27497).

69. David Kelley, the British chargé d'affaires in Mexico City, to Chamberlain, 26 April 1927, in FO 371/12001 (A3079/52/26). Cedillo had successfully defied Manrique's authority as early as January 1924, but his subsequent involvement in the De la Huerta revolt and its aftermath led to a lull in their rivalry; see Boyle to the Secretary of State, 12 and 28 January 1924, SD 812.00/26792 and 26926.

70. Muñiz Silva, "Saturnino Cedillo," 25 April and 9 May 1954; Boyle to the Secretary of State, 31 December 1924 and 20 January and 14 March 1925, SD 812.00/27486, 27497, and 27510.

71. Muñiz Silva, "Saturnino Cedillo," 2 May 1954; Boyle to the Secretary of State, 31 January 1925, and U.S. Consul-in-Charge Don S. Haven to the Secretary of State, 1 May 1925, San Luis Potosí, SD 812.00/27499 and 27531.

72. Jean Meyer, *La Cristiada* (México, 1974), 2:154; Muñiz Silva, "Saturnino Cedillo," 25 April 1954.

73. Boyle to the Secretary of State, 21 March 1925, and Haven to the Secretary of State, 21 May 1925, San Luis Potosí, SD 812.00/27514 and 27542.

74. Muñiz Silva, "Saturnino Cedillo," 9 and 23 May 1954.

75. Boyle to the Secretary of State, 26 August 1925, SD 812.00/27595; *Excélsior*, 5 November 1925; Muñiz Silva, "Saturnino Cedillo," 16 and 23 May 1954; Gruening, *Mexico and Its Heritage*, p. 471.

76. Ambassador James Sheffield to the Secretary of State, 17 November 1925, in SD 812.00/27655; Muñiz Silva, "Saturnino Cedillo," 30 May 1954; *Excélsior*, 12 November 1925. For Elvira Carrillo Puerto, see Joseph, *Revolution from Without*, pp. 217-18.

77. Muñiz Silva, "Saturnino Cedillo," 6 June 1954; U.S. Consul-in-charge in Mexico City, Reed Paige Clark, to the Secretary of State, 12 November and 7 December 1925, SD 812.00/27660 and 27670; Consul General Alexander Weddell to the Secretary of State, 11 January 1926, SD 812.00/27694; *Excélsior*, 10-29 November 1925.

NOTES TO CHAPTER 5

1. "Arvide," p. 177.

2. Juan Muñiz Silva, "Saturnino Cedillo," *El Sol de San Luis Potosí*, 13 June 1954; "Arvide," pp. 159-60.

3. Muñiz Silva, "Saturnino Cedillo," 13 June 1954.

4. Memorandum by Ernest Lagarde, the French chargé d'affaires in Mexico City,

to Aristide Briand, the Foreign Minister, 18 September 1926, pp. 1-15, SD 812.404/867½ (hereafter cited as Lagarde Memorandum).

5. "Calles, despite his realism and coldness, gave me the impression that he approached the religious question in an apocalyptical and mystical spirit . . . the conflict was, in his mind, a battle without quarter between religious and lay ideas, between reaction and progress, between light and shade, a battle in which he was supported not only by the majority of the Mexican people, but in addition by all liberals abroad" (Lagarde Memorandum, p. 65).

6. The most comprehensive account of the Cristiada is by Jean Meyer, in the three-volume *La Cristiada* (México, 1974). Other useful general summaries are David C. Bailey, *Viva Cristo Rey: The Cristero Rebellion and the Church-State Conflict in Mexico* (Austin, Tex., 1974); and Alicia Olivera Sedano, *Aspectos del conflicto religioso de 1926, sus antecedentes y consecuencias* (México, 1966).

7. Ernest Gruening, *Mexico and Its Heritage* (New York, 1928), 220-27,275-85, and 324-28; Esmond Ovey, the British Minister in Mexico City, to Sir Austen Chamberlain, the British Foreign Secretary, 12 August 1926; and David Kelley, the British chargé d'affaires in Mexico City, to Chamberlain, 20 April 1927 and 1 June 1927, FO 371/11148 (A4777/48/26) and /12001 (A2793/52/26) and (A3690/52/26); Ovey to Lord Cushendon, Acting Secretary of State at the Foreign Office, 15 August 1928, FO 371/12776 (A6164/185/26); Ian Jacobs, *Ranchero Revolt: The Mexican Revolution in Guerrero* (Austin, Tex., 1982), 126.

8. Meyer, *La Cristiada*, 3:85; *El Machete*, 24 December 1927; 10 March; 1 May; and 2, 9, and 23 June 1928; Ambassador James Sheffield to the Secretary of State, 20 January 1927, SD 812.00/28201.

9. Muñiz Silva, "Saturnino Cedillo," 26 September 1954.

10. Meyer, *La Cristiada*, 2:243, 252; *Excélsior*, 13 March 1927; Muñiz Silva, "Saturnino Cedillo," 4 and 11 July 1954; Ovey to Chamberlain, 22 March 1926, FO 371/11146 (A1947/48/26); Consul General Alexander Weddell to the Secretary of State, 20 March 1926, Mexico City; and Consul William W. Early to the Secretary of State, 25 March 1926, San Luis Potosí, SD 812.404/399 and 409.

11. "The rebels are in no way to be considered as bandits. . . . They never attacked the property of peons but robbed the establishments of the rich hacendados when they got a chance" (Edward J. Bumstead, Manager of the Álvarez Mining Company, Ixtlán del Río, Nayarit, statement to British officials, 24 September 1928, following his release from captivity with a band of Cristeros). Bumstead's views on the rebels were endorsed by British Vice-Consul Percy Holms in Guadalajara; Holms had negotiated Bumstead's ransom and had several such contacts with Cristeros in the field. The documentation of this case is in FO 371/12783 (A7148/5470/26).

12. Meyer, *La Cristiada*, 1:21, 136, and 137; *Excélsior*, 5 March 1927; *New York Times*, 6 March 1927, p. 14. The Anzanza Gordoa family owned the property rented by Cedillo for a military sports center he had founded in the state capital (Muñiz Silva, "Saturnino Cedillo," 21 and 28 November; 5 December 1954).

13. *New York Times*, 6 March 1927, p. 14; and 8 March 1927, p. 2; Muñiz Silva, "Saturnino Cedillo," 26 September 1954 and 3 April 1955.

14. "Arvide," pp. 182-84.

15. Ibid., pp. 185-89; Meyer, *La Cristiada*, 1:113, 160, and 179-81. According to the British chargé d'affaires, "the collapse of the Catholic armed movement—which without any doubt reached proportions very alarming for the Government in April—is due

first to the skillful strategic concentration by the Federal Government of their whole available forces assisted by auxiliary bodies of agrarians" (Kelley to Chamberlain, 1 June 1927, FO 371/12001 [A3690/52/26]).

16. Meyer, *La Cristiada*, 1:136; Muñiz Silva, "Saturnino Cedillo," 23 January 1955. Manuel Lárraga was imprisoned in San Luis Potosí but immediately released at the instigation of the then military commander of the Huasteca region, General Lázaro Cárdenas, a fact which calls into question the truth of the charge against the two brothers (Manuel Lárraga to Enrique del Llano, the editor of *La Prensa* in Mexico City, 7 November 1935, AGN, Ramo presidentes, Cárdenas, legajo 559.1/45).

17. Memorandum by the Departamento de Estado Mayor, 2 July 1927, SDN XI/III/1-244, vol. 2; Muñiz Silva, "Saturnino Cedillo," 2 January 1955.

18. Ovey to Chamberlain, 18 July 1928, FO 371/12768 (A5472/31/26).

19. *Excélsior*, 14 March 1928; Rafael Montejano y Aguiñaga, *El Valle de Santa Isabel del Armadillo* (San Luis Potosí, 1964), 215-19.

20. *Excélsior*, 16 August 1928; "Arvide," p. 198; Consul Early to the Secretary of State, 17 July 1928, San Luis Potosí, SD 812.00/San Luis Potosí.

21. *Excélsior*, 16 August 1928; Consul Early to the Secretary of State, 14, 16, and 21 August, 5 September, and 20 October 1928, SD 812.00/San Luis Potosí. One of the two local sympathizers of the Cristeros shot with Sánchez was Fidel Muro, who had continued to work for the rebels after his release. As Early commented, "the military authorities in San Luis Potosí are determined to suppress all rebellious movements with an iron hand" (*Excélsior*, 16 August 1928).

22. Meyer, *La Cristiada*, 1:199, 200, 248, and 280.

23. Ovey to Chamberlain, 19 July and 4 December 1928 and 30 April 1929, FO 371/12776 (A4978/185/26), /12778 (A8876/185/26), and /13489 (A3461/39/26).

24. *Excélsior*, 12 February 1929; Ovey to Chamberlain, 12 April 1929, FO 371/13489 (A2960/39/26).

25. Emilio Portes Gil, *Quince años de política Mexicana* (México, 1941), 35-36; Ovey to Chamberlain, 6 March 1929, FO 371/13489 (A2204/39/26); *El Machete*, 26 January 1929. Reports to the Secretary of State from the U.S. consuls James Powell (Torreón, 5 March 1929), William Blocker (Mazatlán, 8 March 1929), Lynn Franklin (Saltillo, 13 March 1929), and Edward Maney (Tampico, 19 March 1929), SD 812.00/Sonora etc.

26. James W. Wilkie and Edna Monzón de Wilkie, *México visto en el siglo XX: entrevistas de historia oral* (México, 1969), 542; Ovey to Chamberlain, 22 March 1929, FO 371/13489 (A2428/39/26); *El Azteca*, 31 March 1929.

27. Portes Gil, *Quince años*, pp. 280-81; Julio Cuadros Caldas, *El comunismo criollo* (Puebla, 1930), 13-17; *El Machete*, 18 May 1929; Jorge Prieto Laurens, *Anécdotas históricas* (México, 1977), 161. For an amusing and perceptive parody of the 1929 rebellion, see Jorge Ibarguengoitia, *Los relámpagos de agosto* (México, 1965).

28. "La ruta de Cedillo," *El Heraldo de San Luis Potosí*, 16 January 1954; Meyer, *La Cristiada*, 1:302-5; "Arvide," p. 226; Bailey, *Viva Cristo Rey*, pp. 250-51.

29. "Cedillo's campaign was of a type the cristeros had never experienced. The general took great pains to assure both the armed enemy and the civilian populace that he bore no animosity and that he believed in the possibility of a peaceful settlement of the religious question. He ended 'reconcentration' of the population, restrained his troops from molesting non-combatants, stopped the execution of captured cristeros and offered generous amnesties" (Bailey, *Viva Cristo Rey*, p. 251). "Arvide" relates how Cedillo once forced an angry Gonzalo Santos, one of his troop commanders, to return

some mules which he had "requisitioned" from local farmers (p. 225). See also Meyer, *La Cristiada,* 1:306; "La ruta de Cedillo," *El Heraldo de San Luis Potosí,* 19 January 1954; and *New York Times,* 29 July 1929, p. 34.

30. In 1929 15,000 hectares of land in San Luis Potosí were distributed to 482 heads of families in 10 grants of *ejidos* on a provisional basis, and 116,695 hectares of land were distributed to 4,278 heads of families in 40 grants of ejidos on a definite basis (*Informe rendido por el C. General de División Saturnino Cedillo, Gobernador Constitucional del Estado ante la H. XXXI legislatura del mismo, en la apertura del primer período de sesiones ordinarias correspondiente al primer año de su ejercicio legal* [15 September 1929]). FO 371/13499 contains an account of the negotiations prior to the peace agreement. For the death of Gorostieta and the end of the war in the field, see Bailey, *Viva Cristo Rey,* pp. 264-73. The demobilization of Cedillo's forces is described by U.S. Consul Early to the Secretary of State, 25 June 1929, San Luis Potosí, SD 812.00/San Luis Potosí.

31. "Arvide," pp. 222-34; *New York Times,* 29 July 1929, p. 34; Meyer, *La Cristiada,* 1:344-45. Among the Cristeros who settled in San Luis Potosí were Rodolfo Lozamárquez, J. Guadalupe Valdez, A. Sánchez Pérez, Refugio Huerta, E. Zermaño, and E. Garmendía ("Arvide," pp. 233-34).

32. Consul Bonney to the Secretary of State, 3 April 1929, Durango, SD 812.00/29434; *New York Times,* 3 August 1929, p. 5; Ovey to Chamberlain, 6 March 1929, FO 371/13489 (A2204/39/26); Cuadros Caldas, *El comunismo criollo,* pp. 11-20.

33. Ovey to Arthur Henderson, the British Foreign Secretary, 27 June 1929, FO 371/13479 (A4712/220/26); U.S. chargé d'affaires H. F. Arthur Schoenfeld to the Secretary of State, 28 January 1929, SD 812.52/Tierras. Portes Gil's Agrarian Code differed little from previous legislation on the subject. *Peones acasillados,* for example, defined in the *Diario official* as "those persons receiving day wages or rations and day wages, who lend their services in a permanent way on rural properties, occupying houses which are the property of the owner of the land without paying rent," were still excluded from the right to petition for land (13 February 1929).

NOTES TO CHAPTER 6

1. For a general history of the Maximato see Lorenzo Meyer, *Historia de la Revolución Mexicana. Periodo 1928-1934* (México, 1978). In his annual report for 1932 the British minister in Mexico commented, "It is well known that no single decision of any importance is taken without first consulting General Calles, and in more than one case he is known to have imposed his veto on some action contemplated by the government" (Edmond Monson to Sir John Simon, the British Foreign Secretary, 19 January 1933, FO 371/16582 [A1245/1245/26]).

2. Heather Fowler Salamini, *Agrarian Radicalism in Veracruz, 1920-1938* (Lincoln, Neb., 1978), 33-37, 65-67; Emilio Portes Gil, *Raigambre de la Revolución en Tamaulipas. Autobiografía en acción* (México, 1972), 87-303; Alan M. Kirshner, *Tomás Garrido Canabal y el movimiento de las Camisas Rojas* (México, 1977); Carlos Martínez Assad, *El laboratorio de la Revolución. El Tabasco Garridista* (México, 1979).

3. Graham Greene, *The Lawless Roads* (London, 1971), 42-61; Juan Muñiz Silva, "Saturnino Cedillo," *El Sol de San Luis Potosí,* 9 January 1955; Rafael Montejano y Aguiñaga, *Cárdenas S.L.P. Historia y Geografía* (San Luis Potosí, 1973), 40-41; Manuel Fernández Boyoli and Eustaqui Marrón de Angelis, *Lo que no se sabe de la rebelión Cedillista* (México, 1938), 152; Emilio Portes Gil, interview with author, 6 June 1974; and Jorge Prieto Laurens, interview with author, 20 August 1974.

4. Consul Geo. P. Shaw to the Secretary of State, 18 February 1931, San Luis Potosí, SD 812.00/San Luis Potosí.

5. Shaw to the Secretary of State, 20 July 1930, 18 February 1931, 31 January 1932, and 31 October 1933, SD 812.00/San Luis Potosí; Fernández Boyoli and Marrón de Angelis, *Lo que no se sabe,* pp. 145–95; "Arvide," p. 153; Carlos Purata Gómez, "Integrantes del poder legislativo de San Luis Potosí del constituyente de 1824 a la fecha," *Boletín* no. 5 of the Escuela de Jurisprudencia de la Universidad Autónoma de San Luis Potosí (August, 1965), 21–24. As far as I have been able to ascertain, Luis Lárraga was not related to the influential Huasteca family of the same name, whose leading member at this time, Manuel Lárraga, was a sworn enemy of Cedillo and his associates.

6. "Arvide," pp. 41, 146, and 222; Juana Villalón de Turrubiartes to the Mixed Agrarian Commission, 18 December 1941, DAAC 23/9137; Shaw to the Secretary of State, 31 January 1932, SD 812.00/San Luis Potosí.

7. "Arvide," pp. 119, 225; Monson to the Marquess of Reading, the British Foreign Secretary, 28 August 1931, FO 420/282 (A5568/49/26). Manuel Lárraga, an avowed opponent of Gonzalo Santos, once accused him of dismembering a political adversary and having twenty others shot in retaliation for the 1931 murder of his relative, Francisco Santos (Manuel Lárraga to Enrique del Llano [the editor of *La Prensa*], 7 November 1935, AGN, Ramo presidentes, Cárdenas, legajo 559.1/45).

8. *El Machete,* 6 February 1937 and 1 June 1938; Francisco Belloc to Cárdenas, 29 June 1937, AGN, Ramo presidentes, legajo 544.4/23; Fernández Boyoli and Marrón de Angelis, *Lo que no se sabe,* p. 194; anonymous letter to the Jefe del Estado Mayor, 29 July 1937, SDN XI/III/I-244, vol. 3; "La ruta de Cedillo," *El Heraldo de San Luis Potosí,* 2 February 1954; Consul Edmond B. Montgomery to the Secretary of State, San Luis Potosí, 9 August 1938, SD 812.00/San Luis Potosí. Romana Falcón's "The Rise and Fall of Military *Caciquismo* in Revolutionary Mexico: The Case of San Luis Potosí" (Ph.D. diss., Oxford University, 1983) provides a very good analysis of Cedillo's regime (see p. 220 for the opening of this discussion).

9. Fernández Boyoli and Marrón de Angelis, *Lo que no se sabe,* pp. 153–57. For Almazán see Virginia Prewett, *Reportage on Mexico* (New York, 1941), 200. For Rodríguez see J. H. Plenn, *Mexico Marches* (New York, 1939), 120–21.

10. Alfonso Taracena, *La Revolución desvirtuada* (México, 1966), 5:207–8; Martínez Assad, *El laboratorio de la Revolución,* p. 220; Kirshner, *Tomás Garrido Canabal y las Camisas Rojas,* pp. 61–74; Shaw to the Secretary of State, 20 July 1930 and 16 July 1932, SD 812.00/San Luis Potosí. Colonel José Arvide has in his possession a number of receipts for payments Cedillo made to various dependents during his time as minister of agriculture. For corruption during the Cárdenas period generally, see F. Z. Kluckhohn, *The Mexican Challenge* (New York, 1939), 153–54.

11. *El Universal,* 25 August 1931; Secretaría de Economía Nacional, Dirección General de Estadística, *Anuario estadístico, 1938,* 204–5; Arnaldo Córdova, *La clase obrera en la historia de México. En una época de crisis (1928–1934)* (México, 1980), 84.

12. *El Universal,* 23–24 November 1931. The officials involved in the kidnapping included three members of the state congress, Efrén González, Juan Luna, and Luis Lárraga, and the Municipal President of San Luis Potosí, Vicente Segura.

13. *El Universal,* 25–30 November and 4–6 December 1931; David L. Raby, *Educación y revolución social en México* (México, 1974), 166–67; Shaw to the Secretary of State, 31 January 1932, in SD 812.00/San Luis Potosí.

14. Muñiz Silva, "Saturnino Cedillo," 16 January 1955; George Ogilvie-Forbes, the British chargé d'affaires, to Sir Austen Chamberlain, the British Foreign Secretary, 14 December 1928, FO 371/13488 (39/39/26); Secretaría de Economía Nacional, Dirección

General de Estadística, *Compendio estadístico, 1941*, pp. 13-14; Córdova, *En una época de crisis*, pp. 80-87.

15. Partido Nacional Revolucionario, *La cuestión agraria* (México, 1934), 81; Eyler N. Simpson, *The Ejido: Mexico's Way Out* (Chapel Hill, N.C., 1937), 627, 654. Compare the comment of the American consul: "The Governor [Cedillo] is supported by the peon-agrarian group, and he has favored this group to the extent that nearly all of them that by any stretch of the imagination can claim lands have gotten them" (Shaw to the Secretary of State, 20 July 1930, SD 812.00/San Luis Potosí).

16. "Arvide," p. 283; Mauricio Durán, "En San Luis Potosí no hay Problema Agrario," *La Esfera* (January 1938), pp. 12-13; Martín Paz, "El General Cedillo en su Retiro de Palomas," *La Esfera* (January 1938), pp. 9, 34, and 35.

17. According to the figures provided by Cedillo and Turrubiartes in their annual reviews to congress for the years 1929 to 1934, land redistribution in San Luis Potosí was as listed below. No land was distributed in the state in the September 1930–September 1931 year. In his speech on 15 September 1931 Cedillo explained that "the beneficial work of agrarianism has ended."

Year (from September to September)	Provisional Grants of Land (in hectares)	Definitive Grants of Land (in hectares)
1928-1929	15,000	116,695
1929-1930	48,625	101,513
1930-1931	0	0
1931-1932	17,227	17,891
1932-1933	28,280	5,482
1933-1934	16,945	28,740

18. Octaviano Cabrera Ipiña, *Archivo Histórico de una hacienda* (Bledos, 1958), 157.

19. For wages, prices, and the conditions for renters and sharecroppers at this time, see the reports of the agrarian officials in San Luis Potosí. The usual price of maize was the same as in 1910, 5.00 pesos the hectoliter, although it was as low as 3.00 in some districts at certain times of the year. Wages, at between 0.50 and 1.00, were between 50% and 100% higher than in 1910 (DAAC 23/4208, 4275, 4279, 4362, 4548, 11442, 15699, and 20222).

20. Ing. J. Olivera Moreno to the CNA, 17 July 1929, DAAC 23/4548.

21. Ing. J. Olivera Moreno to the CNA, 22 June 1932, DAAC 23/11442.

22. "But above all, the rock which has blocked every path, the pervasive and omnipresent force which has debilitated almost every action and perverted practically every good intention, has been, and is, politics" (Simpson, *The Ejido*, p. 348). See also Marjorie Ruth Clark, *Organized Labor in Mexico* (Chapel Hill, N.C., 1934), 160. Some of the more glaring defects in the agrarian reform as practiced during this period are outlined in the memorandum sent to Cárdenas by the Confederación de Campesinos Mexicanos shortly after he assumed office as president; in *Excélsior*, 4 December 1934; and in the comments of the delegates to the second congress of the League of Agrarian Communities of Tamaulipas in 1929. (*Liga de Comunidades Agrarias y Sindicatos Campesinos del Estado. Segunda y Tercera Convención* [México, 1930], 117-29). Compare also the remarks of the British chargé d'affaires in his annual review for 1931 (Courtenay Forbes to Simon, 29 December 1931, FO 371/15844 [A337/337/26]):

> An attempt was at last made to do away with the political and other abuses to which the policy of expropriation had given rise. Complaints had become very frequent, for not only had the "hacendados" been freely robbed in defiance of the provisions of the law, but the

peasants themselves had in many cases been prevented from entering into the rights alleged to have been won for them by the revolution. The local "politicos" and members of the local commissions usually contented themselves with putting up dummy claimants and taking the land themselves, but there were even cases where, the land having been legally granted to the peons, attempts were made to make them hand it over by creating for them an untenable position. The feeling amongst the peasants became very strong, and found an outlet *inter alia* at an Agrarian Congress in the State of Puebla, which asked that no "político" or soldier be permitted to become a member of the League of Agrarian Communities. On the occasion of this congress the representative of the Ministry of Agriculture produced the interesting information that no less than eleven commissioners had been arrested for irregularities in one week.

It is perhaps worth noting that Forbes was sympathetic to the agrarian reform in principle.

23. "The real problem, that of giving confidence to land owners both small and large, has not yet been faced, no man knows whether his land is to be attacked and, if so, when" (Monson to Simon, 19 January 1933, FO 371/16582 [A1245/1245/26]); Sindicato de Agricultores de Jalisco, *En Defensa de la Agricultura Nacional* (Guadalajara, 1921).

24. *El Universal*, 23 June 1930, in which Calles stated that "the agrarian reform, as we have understood and practiced it up until now, has been a complete failure." See also Esmond Ovey, the British Minister in Mexico City, to Sir Austen Chamberlain, 30 April and 16 May 1929, FO 371/13489 (A3461/39/26) and /13496 (A3745/220/26); and Monson to Arthur Henderson, the British Foreign Secretary, 2 and 18 June, FO 371/14244 (A4362/1212/26) and /14240 (A4673/192/26).

25. San Luis Potosí, *Informe rendido por el C. General de División Saturnino Cedillo, Gobernador Constitucional del estado, ante la H. XXXI legislatura del mismo, en la apertura del primer período de sesiones ordinarias correspondiente al segundo año de su ejercicio legal* (San Luis Potosí, 1930); Shaw to the Secretary of State, 18 February 1931, SD 812.00/San Luis Potosí.

26. John W. F. Dulles, *Yesterday in Mexico: A Chronicle of the Revolution, 1919–1936* (Austin, Tex., 1967), 484–87; Emilio Portes Gil, *Quince años de política mexicana* (México, 1941), 402, 410–15. For Cedillo's close relationship with Calles at this time see Forbes to Simon, 20 January 1932, FO 371/15844 (A339/339/26). Both Flores's parents were detained for questioning, and his mother died shortly after their release. Some time later his two brothers were murdered, apparently on the orders of Alberto Araujo, the political boss of Charcas. His father died soon afterward ("La ruta de Cedillo," *El Heraldo de San Luis Potosí*, 21, 22, and 23 January 1954).

27. "Arvide," p. 238; Shaw to the Secretary of State, 20 July 1930, SD 812.00/San Luis Potosí.

28. Monson to Reading, 28 August 1931, FO 420/282 (A5568/49/26); and Forbes to Simon, 29 December 1931, FO 371/15844 (A337/337/26); "Arvide," pp. 253–54; "La ruta de Cedillo," *El Heraldo de San Luis Potosí*, 25 January 1954.

29. Shaw to the Secretary of State, 16 July 1932, SD 812.00/San Luis Potosí; Octaviano Cabrera Ipiña, *San Luis Potosí. Monografía del Estado* (San Luis Potosí, n.d.), p. 187.

30. Harold Farquhar, the British chargé d'affaires in Mexico City, to Simon, 24 January 1935, FO 371/18705 (A1338/363/26). For socialist education see Josefina Vázquez de Knauth, *El nacionalismo y la educación en México* (México, 1970), 151–61; and Raby, *Educación y revolución social en México*, 35–41.

31. C. S. McFarland said that Cedillo "takes little or no stock in socialistic teaching, regarding it as a sort of fad" (*Chaos in Mexico: The Conflict of Church and State* [London,

1935], 209-10). Primo Feliciano Velázquez, *Historia de San Luis Potosí* (México, 1946), 4:325; Raby, *Educación y Revolución en México,* pp. 147-97. For the widespread popular opposition to socialist education where it was implemented, see Monson to Simon, 9 and 18 October 1934, FO 371/17533 (A8495/274/26) and /17530 (A8764/130/26); and Hugh G. Campbell, *La Derecha Radical en México (1920-1940)* (México, 1976), 34-46. For the kind of violence inflicted against teachers by religious extremists, see *El Machete,* 8 January 1938.

32. Monson to Simon, 1 September 1932, FO 371/15842 (A6257/56/26).

33. Forbes to Simon, 29 December 1931, FO 371/15844 (A337/337/26); J. E. Sterrett and J. S. Davis, *The Fiscal and Economic Condition of Mexico: Report Submitted to the International Committee of Bankers on Mexico, May 25, 1928,* FO 371/12780; Clark W. Reynolds, *The Mexican Economy, Twentieth-Century Structure and Growth* (New Haven, Conn., 1970), 32; Secretaría de Economía Nacional, Dirección General de Estadística, *Anuario estadístico, 1938,* pp. 204-5, 280-81; Dulles, *Yesterday in Mexico,* p. 510.

34. The general manager of the Aguila Oil Company reported to the company board in London, "For some time there has been crystalizing a new junior school of politicians who profess the most forthright nationalistic views, and this party seems to have gained strength enormously in the last six months" (J. A. Assheton to Board of Directors, México, 20 October 1933, FO 371/16580 [A8208/1/26]).

35. Farquhar to Simon, 28 July 1933, FO 371/16580 (A3244/1/26). Rodríguez's ruling was not relevant to San Luis Potosí, where, in spite of Cedillo's earlier official acceptance of the end of land redistribution, the state agrarian commission had never ceased to exist and had even continued to process certain petitions for *ejidos.*

36. Simpson, *The Ejido,* pp. 759-808; Gilberto Bosques, *The National Revolutionary Party of Mexico and the Six Year Plan* (México, 1937); Monson to Simon, 21 December 1933, FO 371/17533 (A273/273/26).

37. Virginia Prewett, *Reportage on Mexico,* p. 81; Lázaro Cárdenas, *Apuntes 1913-1940,* vol. 1 of *Obras* (México, 1972-1974), 220-26; Nathaniel and Sylvia Weyl, *The Reconquest of Mexico: The Years of Lázaro Cárdenas* (New York, 1939), 105-8; Dulles, *Yesterday in Mexico,* pp. 566-77; Emilio Portes Gil, quoted in James W. Wilkie and Edna Monzón de Wilkie, *México visto en el siglo XX: entrevistas de historia oral* (México, 1969), 542.

38. Monson to Simon, 24 January 1934, FO 371/17535 (A2137/2137/26); Fowler Salamini, *Agrarian Radicalism in Veracruz,* pp. 35, 109; "La ruta de Cedillo," *El Heraldo de San Luis Potosí,* 26 January 1954.

39. Prewett, *Reportage on Mexico,* p. 81; Weyl and Weyl, *The Reconquest of Mexico,* p. 108; Dulles, *Yesterday in Mexico,* pp. 570-73; Saturnino Cedillo to Miguel Aranda Díaz, 4 May 1932, copy in the possession of Colonel José Arvide. According to "La ruta de Cedillo," Calles offered to Cedillo to support the latter's own candidacy, believing that he would be easier to manipulate than Cárdenas. But Cedillo refused and explained that he wished to remain in San Luis Potosí (*El Heraldo de San Luis Potosí,* 26 January 1954).

40. Monson to Simon, 7 June 1934, FO 371/17530 (A5082/130/26). For Cárdenas's campaign tour, see Weyl and Weyl, *The Reconquest of Mexico,* p. 125.

41. Monson to Simon, 5 July 1934, FO 371/17530 (A5939/130/26).

NOTES TO CHAPTER 7

1. Secretaría de Economía Nacional, Dirección General de Estadística, *Anuario Estadístico, 1938,* pp. 204-5; Memorandum on the Mexican Economy, H. M. Department of Overseas Trade, 18 July 1934, FO 371/17532 (A5822/267/26); Courtenay Forbes, the

British chargé d'affaires in Mexico City, to Sir John Simon, the British Foreign Secretary, 29 December 1931, FO 371/15844 (A337/337/26).

2. Partido Nacional Revolucionario, *La Cuestión Agraria* (México, 1934), 84–85; Siegfried Askinasy, *El problema agrario en Yucatán* (México, 1936), 63, 102; Moisés González Navarro, "Efectos sociales de la crisis de 1929," *Historia Mexicana* 19 (April–June 1970): 539–43; Romana Falcón, "El surgimiento del agrarismo Cardenista—Una revisión de las tesis populistas," *Historia Mexicana* 27 (January–March 1978): 333–86.

3. Forbes to Simon, 28 May 1932, and Edmond Monson, the British Minister in Mexico City, to Simon, 7 June and 15 November 1934, FO 371/15842 (A3877/56/26) and /17530 (A5082/130/26) and (A9590/130/26); Wayne A. Cornelius, Jr., "Crisis, Coalition-Building, and Political Entrepreneurship in the Mexican Revolution: The Politics of Social Reform under Lázaro Cárdenas" (unpublished research paper, Stanford University, 1969), pp. 26–30. A copy of the Cornelius paper can be found in the library of the Colegio de México, Mexico City.

4. "The key positions in the cabinet are in the hands of men on whom General Calles can rely. . . . General Cárdenas has been allowed to fill some of the minor appointments with his own nominees" (Monson to Simon, 3 December 1934, FO 371/17530 [A10324/130/26]).

5. On the CGOCM, see Joe C. Ashby, *Organized Labor and the Mexican Revolution under Lázaro Cárdenas* (Chapel Hill, N.C., 1963), 18; Anatol Shulgovski, *México en la encrucijada de su historia* (México, 1972), 273; and Arnaldo Córdova, *La clase obrera en la historia de México. En una época de crisis* (México, 1980), 164.

6. Victoria Prewett, *Reportage on Mexico* (New York, 1941), 93–94; John Murray, the British Minister in Mexico City, to Simon, 15 February 1935, FO 371/18705 (A2058/363/26).

7. Cárdenas wrote in his diary entry of 14 January 1935, "General Múgica, Minister of Economy, left today for Palomas, S.L.P., to interview General Saturnino Cedillo, and tell him that his attitude of discontent is serving to support the clergy and other reactionary elements in the seditious work which they are developing both inside and outside the country. General Cedillo's discontent is due to various causes, among which is the "singing" of his friends who are opposed to the present administration," *Apuntes 1913–1940*, vol. 1 of *Obras* (México, 1972–1974), 312.

8. Murray to Simon, 20 February 1935, FO 371/18705 (A2338/363/26). In spite of Cedillo's offer to Cárdenas to help him against Calles, the president remained concerned about his loyalty. In an entry in his diary on 15 March, Cárdenas wrote that he had been informed that Cedillo was disenchanted with the Cárdenas government, largely because he had not been offered a cabinet post. Cárdenas criticized Cedillo's "conservative way of thinking" but commented that if Cedillo's dissatisfaction continued, he would be brought into the cabinet. Cárdenas added that he had been reliably informed that Cedillo was plotting a rebellion, for which he had been offered half a million U.S. dollars from the El Aguila Oil Company through a member of the Braniff family. However, in view of Cedillo's support for Cárdenas in his confrontation with Calles three months later, and in the absence of any supporting evidence for the information, it is hard to believe this report. Even if El Aguila's directors had decided as early as March 1935 that they would not be able to reach an accommodation with the Cárdenas administration and that they were prepared to spend such a sum on promoting a coup d'état, they could have found a more suitable recipient for their funds at that time (Cárdenas, *Obras*, 1:316–17).

9. Victoriano Anguiano Equihua, *Lázaro Cárdenas. Su feudo y la política nacional* (México, 1951), 186–89.

10. Ashby, *Organized Labor,* p. 25. "There appears to be little justification for this latest outbreak [of strikes] which seems rather to form part of a deliberate policy of fomenting labour unrest" (Murray to Simon, 11 April 1935, FO 371/18710 [A3922/1455/26]); see also Murray to Simon, 24 April 1935, FO 371/18710 (A4311/1455/26).

11. "The great majority of both the Senate and Chamber and of the party itself were originally Callista in sympathy. Within the last few days the executive committee of the National Revolutionary Party has endeavoured with but scant success to drape with a cloak of constitutional respectability the not very edifying spectacle of the passage of this majority to the so-called left wing pledged to the support of President Cárdenas and his policy. The original right wing, or Majority Block, to give it its official designation, has simultaneously pronounced its own dissolution" (Murray to Sir Samuel Hoare, the British Foreign Secretary, 15 August 1935, FO 371/18706 [A7630/363/26]). See also Anguiano Equihua, *Lázaro Cárdenas,* pp. 204–19; *New York Times,* 15 June 1935, p. 1; 16 June 1935, p. 3; 17 June 1935, p. 1; 18 June 1935, p. 1; 19 June 1935, p. 14; 20 June 1935, p. 8; 23 June 1935, sec. 4, p. 1; *Excélsior,* 12–17 June 1935; Emilio Portes Gil, *Autobiografía de la Revolución Mexicana* (México, 1964), 691–701; Murray to Hoare, 12 June 1935, FO 371/18706 (A6022/363/26); Carlos Martínez Assad, *El laboratorio de la Revolución. El Tabasco Garridista* (México, 1979), 226.

12. "In the crisis of June 1935 the fact that he [Cedillo] sided with President Cárdenas probably accounted for the latter's success" (Murray to Anthony Eden, the British Foreign Secretary, 31 December 1936, FO 371/20640 [A1206/1206/26]). See also Nathaniel and Sylvia Weyl, *The Reconquest of Mexico: The Years of Lázaro Cárdenas* (New York, 1939), 163.

13. Murray to Hoare, 24 June and 3 July 1935, FO 371/18706 (A6157/363/26 and A6419/363/26).

14. Murray to Hoare, 11 August and 13 September 1935, FO 371/18706 (A7626/363/26) and (A8481/363/26). The removal of governors continued at least until 1937. "Since 1935 there has continued unobtrusively the gradual elimination of governors of states whose political sympathies and activities do not recommend themselves to the President" (Murray to Eden, 23 February 1937, FO 371/20639 [A1872/527/26]).

15. George Ogilvie-Forbes, the British chargé d'affaires in Mexico City, to Simon, 7 April 1932, FO 371/15842 (A2529/56/26); Consul Robert Pulford to Murray, Tampico, 25 July 1935, FO 371/18706 (A7195/363/26); *New York Times,* 24 July 1935, p. 6; 25 July 1935, p. 12; 26 July 1935, p. 10; 27 July 1935, p. 14; *El Universal,* 12 July 1935, 24 January, 8 March, and 17 December 1936; *El Machete,* 10 October 1935; "Arvide," p. 254; Alfonso Taracena, *La Verdadera Revolución Mexicana* (México, 1960–65), 18:107.

16. John W. F. Dulles, *Yesterday in Mexico: A Chronicle of the Revolution, 1919–1936* (Austin, Tex., 1967), 650–58; *El Universal,* 3 August 1935; Murray to Hoare, 16 July 1935, FO 371/18706 (A6866/363/26). Alan M. Kirshner, *Tomás Garrido Canabal y el movimiento de las Camisas Rojas* (México, 1977), 124–59; Carlos Martínez Assad, *El laboratorio de la Revolucion,* pp. 219–37.

17. Tzvi Medin, *Ideología y praxis política de Lázaro Cárdenas* (México, 1972), 71; Murray to Hoare, 15 December 1935, FO 371/18707 (A10571/363/26); *New York Times,* 17 December 1935, p. 1. "The summary dismissal of General Amaro, by common consent the best Mexican general, and of General Madinabeytia, the Commander of the Federal District, as well as the Commander of the Military School, the Director General of Supplies and the colonel of the 5th Cavalry Regiment, this last named General Amaro's brother, appears to have been taken by the army with a disciplined resignation which must have been as gratifying to the President as it was disappointing to his opponents.

It is the irony of fate that it is to General Amaro more than to any other individual that the credit for this improved discipline must be ascribed" (Murray to Hoare, 17 December 1935, FO 371/19791 [A199/196/26]).

18. Calles took with him a copy of Hitler's *Mein Kampf* to read on the aircraft that carried him into exile (Murray to Eden, 15 April 1936, FO 371/19792 [A3887/196/26]).

19. Murray to Eden, 27 February 1936, FO 371/19792 (A2055/196/26); Shulgovski, *México en la encrucijada de su historia,* pp. 279–80.

20. Rodney Gallop, the British chargé d'affaires in Mexico City, to Eden, 27 August 1936, FO 371/19792 (A7296/196/26). Cárdenas's apparent evenhandedness during the August crisis was largely tactical. Unlike Portes Gil, the latter's opponents soon returned to positions of power (Weyl and Weyl, *The Reconquest of Mexico,* p. 190; Gallop to Eden, 7 September 1937, FO 371/19792 [A7649/196/26]).

21. Murray to Eden, 6 February 1936, FO 371/19791 (A1532/196/26). Virginia Prewett, in *Reportage on Mexico,* calculated that Almazán's business interests were worth 30 million pesos in 1940, or approximately 5.5 million U.S. dollars (p. 199). See also Ogilvie-Forbes to Simon, 20 January 1932, FO 371/15844 (A339/339/26).

22. Murray to Eden, 12 December 1935 and 6 February 1936, FO 371/19791 (A196/196/26 and A1532/196/26).

23. "La ruta de Cedillo," *El Heraldo de San Luis Potosí,* 29 January 1954; U.S. Consul Edmond B. Montgomery to the Secretary of State, San Luis Potosí, 1 October 1936 and 9 January 1937, SD 812.00/San Luis Potosí.

24. C. S. MacFarland gives a total of 230 priests for the whole country (as compared with 4,493 in 1926), of whom 56 lived in San Luis Potosí *(Chaos in Mexico. The Conflict of Church and State* [London, 1935], 70). See also Murray to Hoare, 27 September 1935, FO 371/18706 (A8526/363/26).

25. MacFarland, *Chaos in Mexico,* p. 210.

26. Monson to Simon, 31 December 1934, FO 371/18707 (A664/659/26). Murray to Eden, 5 March 1936, FO 371/19792 (A2307/296/26).

27. Cárdenas, *Apuntes 1913–1940,* p. 247. For rural living standards, compare the remarks of the British vice-consul in Torreón in a report of April 1936: "Without wishing to be accused of ultra-radical views and appreciating the good intentions of the majority of the farmers, the living conditions of the majority of the peasants and labourers is such that no self-respecting orang utang would tolerate. From the mud floor on which they are born to the mud in which they rest when they die, they have no hope. If they eked out their lives far from civilization and had never heard of or seen better things, they would be less worthy of sympathy, but here they are on the very fringe of a prosperous town, the prosperity of which they do not share, although in great measure it is to they themselves that such prosperity is due" (Vice-Consul Stanley Dutton Pegram, Torreón, quoted by Murray to Eden, 21 April 1936, FO 371/19792 [A3895/196/26]).

28. Lázaro Cárdenas, *Palabras y documentos públicos* (México, 1978–1979), 1:226–28.

29. James W. Wilkie, *The Mexican Revolution: Federal Expenditure and Social Change since 1910* (Berkeley, Calif., 1970), 188, 194; Clark W. Reynolds, *The Mexican Economy: Twentieth-Century Structure and Growth* (New Haven, Conn., 1970), 139.

30. "The tendency becomes increasingly evident to give the ejido the character of a cooperative farm, and to make the state in practice, if not in theory, a vast monopolistic landowner" (Gallop to Eden, 11 September 1937, FO 371/20638 [A7240/213/26]). For Cárdenas's agrarian policy see Arnaldo Córdova, *La política de masas del Cardenismo* (México, 1974), 107–11; Partido Revolucionario Nacional, *El ideario agrarista del General Lázaro Cárdenas* (México, 1935). For the *ejidos* in the Laguna, see Clarence O. Senior,

Land Reform and Democracy (Gainesville, Fla., 1958); FO 371/19790; and Medin, *Ideología y praxis política de Lázaro Cárdenas*, pp. 169-72.

31. The report of the Dirección General de Estadística, *El Universal*, 2 January 1936; Prewett, *Reportage on Mexico*, pp. 145-49; Weyl and Weyl, *The Reconquest of Mexico*, pp. 186-87. For the prices and production of the leading agricultural crops during the presidency of Cárdenas, see Appendices 4 and 6.

32. Murray to Eden, 31 December 1935, FO 371/19794 (A1331/1331/26).

33. *Excélsior*, 6 and 7 February 1937. Naturally enough, the DAAC disputed Ayala's claims and the Ejidal Department he recommended was never set up. However, in a similar vein to Ayala, Ramón Beteta, the under-secretary in the Finance Ministry, admitted to the British minister that "Insecurity of tenure was widespread among both agrarians and hacendados, agrarian engineers were busy grinding their own axes and lining their own pockets at the expense of the Indian, and politics intruded into everything" (Murray to Eden, 18 March 1937, FO 371/20637 [A2394/213/26]).

34. For the corruption in the agrarian bureaucracy, both in the Laguna and elsewhere, see J. H. Plenn, *Mexico Marches* (Indianapolis, Ind., 1939), 248; Prewett, *Reportage on Mexico*, p. 148; Weyl and Weyl, *The Reconquest of Mexico*, pp. 180 and 218-27; and Consul General Eric Cleugh to Lord Halifax, the British Foreign Secretary, 18 October and 12 November 1938, FO 371/21481 (A8518/491/26 and A8520/491/26). In May 1937 even an official spokesman for the normally pro-government CTM accused the Banco de Crédito Ejidal of being as tyrannical an employer in the Laguna as the former landowners (Gallop to Eden, 11 May 1937, FO 371/20637 [A3798/213/26]).

35. Prewett, *Reportage on Mexico*, pp. 103-4, 145-148; Mario Gill, *Sinarquismo: su origen, su esencia, su misión* (México, 1944), 42-69; Unión de Revolucionarios Zapatistas del estado de Morelos to the Editor of *El Universal*, 10 June 1937; Thirty-nine *peones acasillados* of Bledos *hacienda* to the Governor of San Luis Potosí, 26 September 1937, DAAC 23/25696 (724.3); Alfonso Taracena, *La Revolución desvirtuada* (México, 1966) 5:179; Cárdenas, *Palabras y documentos públicos*, 1:169; Ian Jacobs, *Ranchero Revolt: The Mexican Revolution in Guerrero* (Austin, Tex., 1982), 159-161; Arturo Warman, *"We come to object." The Peasants of Morelos and the National State*, trans. Stephen K. Ault (Baltimore, 1980), 186-92.

36. Gallop to Eden, 11 May 1937, FO 371/20637 (A3798/213/26).

37. Prewett, *Reportage on Mexico*, pp. 173-75; Roger D. Hansen, *La Política del desarrollo Mexicano* (México, 1979), 153-59; Reynolds, *The Mexican Economy*, pp. 175-80. Speaking in 1940, General Joaquín Amaro, who had been born in a peon family before the Revolution, claimed that the Agrarian Reform had led to " 'a new form of slavery with an omnipotent landlord' " (quoted by Prewett, *Reportage on Mexico*, p. 184).

38. "Arvide," p. 283. Compare Murray's remarks: "General Cedillo is outspoken in his condemnation of the system of communal smallholdings which he regards as disastrous not merely for its effect on crops but even more on the live-stock industry" (Murray to Eden, 6 March 1937, FO 371/20637 [A2302/213/26]).

39. Murray to Simon, 30 April 1935, FO 371/18710 (A4573/1455/26); and Murray to Eden, 6 March 1937, FO 371/20637 (A2302/213/26); Cárdenas, *Palabras y documentos públicos*, 1:227-32, 297. For a public example of support for Cedillo's views, see the letter from the Unión de Revolucionarios Zapatistas del estado de Morelos in *El Universal*, 10 June 1937. For Cárdenas's awareness of the privations suffered by many smallholders as a result of the agrarian reform and the need to offer them guarantees, see Cárdenas, *Palabras y documentos públicos*, 1:224; and the statement he made to a delegation from the Confederación Campesina Mexicana when he became president (*Excélsior*, 4 December 1934). In March 1938, in the midst of the political tension following the oil expropria-

tion, Cárdenas convened a meeting of all state governors to discuss what further measures could be taken to offer smallholders adequate protection—an admission that their legal rights were being commonly ignored in the land redistribution program (Owen O'Malley, the British Minister in Mexico City, to Halifax, 30 March 1938, FO 371/21479 [A3277/239/26]).

40. *El Machete*, 11 July 1937; Gallop to Eden, 4 May 1937, FO 371/20637 (A3552/213/26).

41. Gallop to Eden, 4 May 1937, FO 371/20637 (A3552/213/26). For other examples of Cedillo's support of the creation of agricultural colonies rather than *ejidos* as the solution to an agrarian dispute (in Guanajuato and Sonora), see *El Universal*, 1 January 1936; and Pascual V. Ayan, President of the *Ejidal* Committee of El Yaqui, Cájeme, to Cárdenas, 12 January 1937, AGN, Ramo presidentes, Cárdenas, legajo 559.1/53.

42. *El Nacional*, 3 June 1933.

43. *Excélsior*, 2 and 4 December 1934, and 8 September 1935; Moisés González Navarro, *La Confederación Nacional Campesina, un grupo de presión en la revolución mexicana* (México, 1968), 131–36.

44. Lázaro Cárdenas, *La unificación campesina* (México, 1936), 8–9.

45. *El Universal*, 25 June 1937; Roberto Monsivais, "Obreros y patronos," *La Esfera* (January 1938), p. 22.

46. *El Machete*, 17 August 1935 and 14 September 1935.

47. *El Machete*, 31 August 1935 and 14 September 1935; *El Universal*, 3, 6, and 13 January 1936.

48. *El Universal*, 4 March, 14 November, and 23 December 1936; *Excélsior*, 18 January 1938. Prewett suggests in *Reportage on Mexico* that many government arbitration awards in industrial disputes at about this time were designed to force the owners of the factory in question to hand it over to their workers (p. 100).

49. As part of the settlement, the company agreed to pay the workers 10% of their wages for the three months of the strike, which amounted to 320,000 pesos, and a further 10,000 pesos toward the cost of the strike (*El Universal*, 28 November and 3 December 1936).

50. Murray to Eden, 12 November 1936, FO 371/19793 (A9531/196/26); Colonel Manuel Fuentes, a member of Cedillo's personal staff from 1931 to 1939, interview with author, 2 February 1974.

51. *El Universal*, 11 November 1936.

52. Murray to Eden, 12 November 1936, FO 371/19793 (A9531/196/26).

53. *El Universal*, 13 November 1936; Montgomery to the Secretary of State, 9 January 1937, San Luis Potosí, SD 812.00/San Luis Potosí. According to Montgomery, the banquet was "made still more interesting by the pearl-handled, silver-mounted side arms of high caliber which were in evidence on practically all sides."

54. *El Universal*, 22 and 27 June 1937; Francisco Ramírez, Secretary General of the Regional Committee of *campesino* organizations in Tamazunchale to Cárdenas, 3 April 1937, AGN, Ramo presidentes, Cárdenas, legajo 559.1/53. Ramírez claimed that Manrique's attacks upon Cedillo were designed to "sow dissention among the peasants and workers of the state who support General Cedillo in his patriotic and revolutionary work."

55. *El Machete*, 24 March 1937; *Excélsior*, 23 March 1937; *El Universal*, 1 July 1937. The official report on the investigation into Armendáriz's death by Manuel Rodríguez Martínez, the procurator general of San Luis Potosí, dated 24 March 1937, is in AGN, Ramo presidentes, Cárdenas, legajo 559.1/53. According to Rodríguez, Armendariz's death was accidental.

56. *El Machete*, 26 June 1937; *El Universal*, 22 June 1937. There is a discrepancy be-

tween these two sources over Manrique's figures for the cost of the dam; *El Machete* claimed that he said it cost 600,000 pesos, *El Universal,* 250,000. Manuel Fernández Boyoli and Eustaqui Marrón de Angelis provide the most authoritative account of this scandal in *Lo que no se sabe de la rebelión Cedillista* (México, 1938), 158–59, 290–92, supporting their presentation with documentary evidence. According to them, the construction of the dam cost the federal government and state authorities of San Luis Potosí 740,000 pesos. Cedillo and Carrera Torres later acquired the dam for—on paper, at least—220,000 pesos. However, the two men purchased it with bonds that the state government issued for use in paying its civil servants when it lacked sufficient hard currency. These bonds were often traded locally at well below their face value, and Cedillo and Carrera Torres bought the bonds that they needed to pay for the dam at a 90% discount. In real terms, therefore, the dam cost them only 22,000 pesos. Carrera Torres's business activities had been used by Cedillo's opponents as an issue over which to attack him from the beginning of the campaign; see Dr. Abundio Estrada to President Cárdenas, 15 March 1937, AGN, Ramo presidentes, Cárdenas, legajo 559.1/53.

57. *El Universal,* 22 June 1937. For instances of corruption in other states and in the federal government, see Prewett, *Reportage on Mexico,* p. 199; Cleugh to Halifax, 18 October 1938, FO 371/21481 (A8518/491/26); and Murray to Eden, 6 February 1937, FO 371/20639 (A1623/527/26).

58. *El Universal,* 25 June 1937. The local government employees' claim that they were not paid in bonds lacked credibility since the state authorities had admitted to the practice six months before *(El Universal,* 4 December 1936). For León García's earlier career in agrarian politics, see Heather Fowler Salamini, *Agrarian Radicalism in Veracruz, 1920–1938* (Lincoln, Neb., 1978), 120; and González Navarro, *La Confederación Nacional Campesina,* p. 136.

59. Consul Montgomery to the Secretary of State, 30 April 1937, San Luis Potosí, SD 812.00/San Luis Potosí; *Excélsior,* 3 April 1937; *El Universal,* 1 and 7 July 1937. See also María de los Angeles Parra, Vda. de González to Dr. José Siurob, Director of the Public Health Department, 8 December 1937, AGN, Ramo presidentes, Cárdenas, legajo 544.4/23, in which she claims that her husband was killed by Cedillista gunmen in June 1937 for having worked as a driver for Manrique's publicity agents.

60. *El Universal,* 12 June 1937.

61. *Excélsior,* 26 May 1937; *El Universal,* 5 July 1937; U.S. Consul Montgomery to the Secretary of State, 3 June and 2 July 1937, SD 812.00/San Luis Potosí; Cedillo to Cárdenas, 11 and 13 May 1937, and Cárdenas to Cedillo, 12 May 1937, AGN, Ramo presidentes, Cárdenas, legajo 544.4/23. For Belloc's hostility to Cedillo, his friendship with Cárdenas, and the implication that his candidacy enjoyed the president's patronage, see his letter to Cárdenas, 30 June 1937, AGN, Ramo presidentes, Cárdenas, legajo 544.4/23. Belloc's victory does not seem to have been particularly popular in his constituency. In a letter to Cárdenas, 19 May 1937, the *ejidal* committee of Villa de la Paz protested that Belloc was "unknown" in the district and accused the national PNR committee of imposing him (AGN, Ramo presidentes, Cárdenas, legajo 544.4/23).

62. Manrique's position as director of the National Library made him susceptible to official pressure, but Cárdenas made no apparent attempt to prevent his campaigning *(El Universal,* 22 June 1937). On government control of the press see Frank L. Kluckhohn, *The Mexican Challenge* (New York, 1939), 256.

63. *El Universal,* 20–26 July 1937; *El Nacional,* 15 and 17 August 1937; *New York Times,*

17 August 1937, p. 1; "Arvide," pp. 293-96; "La ruta de Cedillo," *El Heraldo de San Luis Potosí*, 1 February 1954; Colonel Manuel Fuentes, interview with author, 2 February 1975. Colonel Fuentes was Cedillo's telegraphist at the time and was with him during his exchange of telegrams with Cárdenas.

NOTES TO CHAPTER 8

1. Félix Cura, "La rebelión del General Cedillo, una incógnita de la historia," *El Heraldo de San Luis Potosí*, 8 November 1961; Sergeant Alejandro Peña to General Antonio Guerrero, 15 October 1937, SDN XI/III/I-244, vol. 3; "La ruta de Cedillo," *El Heraldo de San Luis Potosí*, 2 and 3 February 1954.

2. Owen O'Malley, the British Minister in Mexico City, to Anthony Eden, the Foreign Secretary, 19 January 1938, FO 371/21482 (A1975/1975/26).

3. For the rise of the CTM and army discontent, see Frank L. Kluckhohn, *The Mexican Challenge* (New York, 1939), 215-28; and Rodney Gallop,the British chargé d'affaires in Mexico City, to Eden, 12 August and 7 October 1937, FO 371/20639 (A6201/527/26 and A7551/973/26). In the second of these dispatches Gallop commented, "Of the dissatisfaction prevailing in the army I have received many indications. It is, for instance, notorious that the bulk of the officers sympathize with the insurgent cause in Spain and dislike the radical policy of the Mexican Government at home." On the rise in the cost of living at this time, see Virginia Prewett, *Reportage on Mexico* (New York, 1941), 151; Secretaría de Economía Nacional, Dirección General de Estadística, *Compendio estadístico 1941*, 860-79.

4. Gallop to Eden, 1 September 1937, FO 371/20639 (A6646/527/26). Furber added that the rebels used the latest ammunition available in Mexico and had sufficient funds for the rank and file to be paid two pesos a day. This led Gallop to speculate that apart from the product of pillage and the levies they exacted from local land owners such as Furber, the insurgents in Guanajuato might be receiving help from neighboring San Luis Potosí. He did not, however, produce any evidence in support of this suggestion other than the fact that the two states bordered on one another. For the armed opposition to the government elsewhere in the Bajío, see *El Universal*, 27 April and 11 June 1936; *Excélsior*, 4 March 1937; and the *New York Times*, 7 June 1936, p. 24.

5. J. H. Plenn, *Mexico Marches* (Indianapolis, Ind., 1939), 236-38; Gallop to Eden, 2 September 1937, FO 371/20639 (A6913/527/26); O'Malley to Eden, 19 January 1938, FO 371/21482 (A1975/1975/26); *El Universal*, 5-6 November and 17 December 1936; *Excélsior*, 23 May 1937; *El Machete*, 6 February and 6 and 13 June 1937; Jean Meyer, *La Cristiada* (México, 1974), 1:375.

6. Mario Gill, *Sinarquismo: su origen, su esencia, su misión* (México, 1944), 22-27; Manuel Fernández Boyoli and Eustaqui Marrón de Angelis, *Lo que no se sabe de la rebelión Cedillista* (México, 1938), 12-70; Hugh G. Campbell, *La Derecha Radical en México 1929-1949* (México, 1976), 50-51. The ARM were popularly known as the Gold Shirts, for the most distinctive feature of their uniform.

7. Fernández Boyoli and Marrón de Angelis, *Lo que no se sabe*, pp. 12, 27, and 38. Only the last-named group survived more than a few years; it is now the country's leading opposition to the ruling Partido Revolucionario Institucional.

8. *El Universal*, 21 June 1936.

9. John Murray, the British Minister in Mexico City, to Sir Samuel Hoare, the Brit-

ish Foreign Secretary, 21 November 1935, and O'Malley to Jack Balfour, British Foreign Office, American Department, 8 February 1938, FO 371/18707 (A10388/363/26) and /21480 (A1538/491/26): Hugh G. Campbell, *La Derecha Radical*, pp. 50–55, 64 and 72.

10. "Arvide," p. 289; Fernández Boyoli and Marrón de Angelis, *Lo que no se sabe*, p. 16; Jorge Prieto Laurens, interview with author, 20 August 1974.

11. *Daily Worker*, 2 January 1936. *El Machete*, 11 November 1937, described Cedillo as "a lackey of the imperialists" and from late 1937 onward frequently alleged that he was implicated in a fascist conspiracy to overthrow the government.

12. For Lombardo Toledano's denunciation of the UNVR's "fascist plot" and Cárdenas's reaction to it, see Gallop to Eden, 5 and 11 August 1937, FO 371/20639 (A5928/527/26 and A6194/527/26). For Cedillo's interview with the Italian ambassador and the member of the German legation in February 1937, see Murray to Eden, 24 February 1937, FO 371/20639 (A1873/527/26). British officials concluded that there was nothing particularly sinister in this meeting, Cedillo's first with the ambassador.

13. Graham Greene, *The Lawless Roads* (London, 1971), 58.

14. Peña to Guerrero, 15 October 1937, SDN XI/III/I-244, vol. 3.

15. "Fascism scarcely exists in Mexico, and could hardly be taken seriously as a menace to the government, although the press, and particularly the American press, would have it that General Cedillo is tarred with its brush" (British Consul-General James Dalton Murray to Lord Halifax, the British Foreign Secretary, 6 June 1938, FO 371/21480 [A4865/491/26]).

16. Consul Charles Powell to the Secretary of State, 5 March 1929, Torreón, SD 812.00/Sonora etc.; Murray to Eden, 1 March 1937, FO 371/20637 (A2047/213/26); Gallop to Eden, 16 April and 16 July 1937, FO 371/20639 (A3094/527/26 and A5738/527/26);/ Thomas Ifor Rees, Consul-General in Mexico City, to Halifax, 3 July 1939, FO 371/22780 (A5026/5026/26); *El Machete*, 20 March 1937; Fernández Boyoli and Marrón de Angelis, *Lo que no se sabe*, p. 12; Nathaniel and Sylvia Weyl, *The Reconquest of Mexico: The Years of Lázaro Cárdenas* (New York, 1939), 239.

17. *El Machete*, 12 March 1938; Gallop to Eden, 7 October 1937, FO 371/20639 (A7551/527/26); "La ruta de Cedillo," *El Heraldo de San Luis Potosí*, 3 February 1954; Peña to Guerrero, 15 October 1937, SD XI/III/I-244, vol. 3; "Arvide," p. 364; *El Universal*, 29 October 1937.

18. "Arvide," p. 333; Gallop to Eden, 9 September 1937, FO 371/20639 (A6912/527/26); The total cost of the new planes purchased by Cedillo was $49,000 U.S., of which the majority came from the municipalities (Fernández Boyoli and Marrón de Angelis, *Lo que no se sabe*, pp. 182–83).

19. Peña to Guerrero, 15 October 1937, SDN XI/III/I-244, vol. 3; Gallop to Eden, 7 October 1937, FO 371/20639 (A7551/527/26). Consul Edmond B. Montgomery to the Secretary of State, 1 October 1937, San Luis Potosí, SD 812.00/San Luis Potosí.

20. *El Universal*, 15 and 20 September and 6 October 1937. The league appears to have followed up its defense of Cedillo by mobilizing declarations of support for him from local *ejidatarios*. At least twenty-three *ejidal* committees sent telegrams to Cárdenas between 7 and 12 November 1937, protesting against attacks upon Cedillo in the press (AGN, Ramo presidentes, Cárdenas, legajo 559.1/53).

21. *Excélsior*, 14 October 1937. For the size of Illescas see Appendix I, note d.

22. Cedillo's interest in granting the *ejido* was reflected in the unusual speed with which the petition was processed. It was first lodged on 9 April 1936, and provisional possession was given on the following 17 October. Papers relating to the *ejido* are in DAAC 23/23709.

23. Murray to Eden, 27 October 1936, FO 371/19790 (A9081/194/26).

24. *El Nacional,* 2 October 1937.

25. *El Nacional,* 2 October 1937. The numbers of those employed in agriculture in San Luis Potosí rose from 130,800 in 1930 to 139,209 in 1940. The 59,189 persons who had received *ejidos* up to September 1937 or their heirs would therefore represent approximately half the agricultural work force. (Secretaría de Economía Nacional, Departmento de Estadística, *Anuario estadístico, 1940,* p. 60; and *1943-1945,* p. 27.

26. *New York Times,* 28 November 1937, sec. 3, p. 7. For examples of *ejidatarios* who were confirmed in their titles to land they already possessed provisionally, see the papers relating to the *ejidos* of El Platanito and La Lagunita, both in the municipality of Ciudad del Maíz, DAAC 23/20218 (724.1) and 23/18053 (724.3).

27. See the report on La Labor *ejido* of 8 February 1940 by Ing. S. Teuffer, DAAC 9296/Colonias. According to the 1938 *Anuario estadístico,* 1,738,011 hectares of land had been distributed as *ejidos* by the end of 1937, or 372,011 hectares more than the 1,366,000 hectares which Vázquez admitted were covered by *ejidos* when he arrived in the state (p. 192). *El Nacional,* 2 October 1937.

28. In September 1937 the peons on Bledos *hacienda* petitioned for an *ejido.* In November, however, some of them wrote to the Agrarian Department claiming that the petition was a fraud, that their names had been added to the list of petitioners against their wishes, and that they didn't want any land. Their letter was unanswered, and at a meeting of all the *hacienda* peons, a department engineer informed those present that, whatever their views, the *hacienda* was to become an *ejido.* Shortly afterward, 3,478 hectares of the *hacienda* were awarded to the neighboring *ejido* of San Francisco, and 22,066 hectares were converted into a new *ejido* for the *hacienda*'s work force. The owners, the Ipiña family, kept 173 hectares and the main house. In 1945 some of the *ejidatarios* wrote to the Agrarian Department complaining that the president of the *ejidal* committee was a petty tyrant *(cacique)* and that in eight years they had not received credit from any government agency. Apparently the fears of the more reluctant *ejidatarios* had been justified. Documentation of the case is in DAAC 23/25696 (724.3). See also Jan Bazant, *Cinco haciendas Potosinas. Tres siglos de vida rural en San Luis Potosí (1600-1910)* (México, 1975), 188; and Ernesto Cabrera Ipiña, interview with author, 4 August 1974. In 1974 the *ejidatarios* still lived at little more than subsistence level, and the *hacienda*'s former industries, such as a fruit-canning factory and a wine press, were in ruins.

29. "Decreto por el cual se ordena la inmediata titulación de los terrenos de diversas colonias ubicadas en los Estados de San Luis Potosí, Nuevo León y Tamaulipas," *Diario Oficial,* 2 November 1937.

30. For examples of the mounting political violence before the election campaign, see Herminio Salas to Cárdenas, 30 January and 10 February 1937, AGN, Ramo presidentes, Cárdenas, legajo 559.1/53; *El Machete,* 20 February 1937; and *El Universal,* 20 March 1937. Political violence was, however, probably no worse in San Luis Potosí at this time than in many other states and less than in such areas of lingering Cristero unrest as Jalisco and Guanajuato. On Torres, see *La Prensa,* 5 October 1937.

31. *Excélsior,* 4-6 October 1937; *La Prensa,* 5-6 October 1937.

32. *Excélsior,* 6 October 1937; Fernández Boyoli and Marrón de Angelis, *Lo que no se sabe,* p. 178; Tomás Oliva to Cárdenas, 4 October 1937; Mateo Hernández Netro to Cárdenas, 4 October 1937; Arellano Belloc to Cárdenas, 4 October 1937; Diputados Juan Soria Urias, J. Pilar García, and Genaro Morales to Cárdenas, 6 October 1937; the four preceding references are in AGN, Ramo presidentes, Cárdenas, legajo 559.1/53.

33. *New York Times,* 10 October 1937, p. 35; Montgomery to the Secretary of State, 8

October 1937, SD 812.00/San Luis Potosí; José Isabel Martínez, interview with author, 10 August 1974. (Señor Martínez worked closely with Tapia in the state agrarian league from 1929 until Tapia's death in 1937.)

34. *El Universal,* 9 October 1937; *Excélsior,* 8 and 9 October 1937; M. Hernández Netro to Cárdenas, 8 October 1937; Diputados Arnulfo Hernández, Epifanio Castillo, Josué Escobedo, Alfonso Salazar, and José Santos Alonso to Cárdenas, 8 October 1937; and Herminia R., viuda de Tapia, to Cárdenas, 23 October 1937. Señora Tapia claimed that her husband had previously expressed fears that the Leija brothers might kill him because he had criticized their poor treatment of the local *campesinos.* See also Ruíz Pecho, J. Guadalupe Zuñiga, and Luis Nuñez to Cárdenas, 8 October 1937; these three were witnesses to Tapia's murder. According to their document, one of Tapia's murderers had stated that Arturo Leija had obtained Cedillo's prior agreement to Tapia's assassination; but there is no independent evidence for this claim, nor was it taken up by Cedillo's enemies in the press. The cited documentation of the case is in AGN, Ramo presidentes, Cárdenas, legajo 559.1/53.

35. Graham Greene, following his visit to San Luis Potosí in early 1938, wrote "You notice only that your tap doesn't run when you go to bed at night. Later you learn that there's not enough water to go round" (*The Lawless Roads,* p. 43); *Excélsior,* 23–27 November 1937; Valentín Narváez, Secretary General, Federación Regional de Obreros y Campesinos (FROC), to Cárdenas, 1 November 1937; the Federación was the local labor organization in San Luis Potosí. Narváez wrote to protest about CTM criticism of Saturnino Cedillo, who he claimed, somewhat impausibly, "is completely divorced from any involvement in state politics" (AGN, Ramo presidentes, Cárdenas, legajo 559.1/53).

36. *Excélsior,* 30 November–3 December 1937; Diputados Juan Soria Urias and J. Pilar García to Cárdenas, 5 December 1937, AGN, Ramo presidentes, Cárdenas, legajo 559.1/53.

37. *Excélsior,* 13 February 1938; *El Universal,* 2 and 4 March 1938; *El Machete,* 12 March 1938; Arellano Belloc to Cárdenas, 10 January 1938; and ten *Ejidos* in the municipality of Villa de Arriaga to Cárdenas, 6 January 1938. The Belloc and *ejidal* references are in AGN, Ramo presidentes, Cárdenas, legajo 559.1/53.

38. *Excélsior,* 13, 24, and 27 January 1938.

39. *El Universal,* 6 March 1938.

40. Peña to Guerrero, 15 October 1937, SDN XI/III/I-224, vol. 3.

41. Fernández Boyoli and Marrón de Angelis, *Lo que no se sabe,* pp. 84, 86, 93, 111, and 182–85. Cedillo had been importing munitions into San Luis Potosí since 1936, but the flow of armaments increased in late 1937 as he prepared for a possible revolt. Sindicato Gremial de Albañiles y Similares "Mártires de Chicago" to Cárdenas, 2 December 1936; Dr. Abundio Estrada to General Francisco Múgica, 23 October 1936 and 14 November 1936; and Consul A. Cano del Castillo to the Foreign Ministry, 23 March 1938, Galveston, AGN, Ramo presidentes, Cárdenas, legajo 559.1/53.

42. Peña to Guerrero, 15 October 1937, SDN XI/III/I-244, vol. 3; Kluckhohn, *The Mexican Challenge,* p. 209; Luis Flores to President Cárdenas, 20 February 1938, Hidalgo, SDN XI/III/I-244, vol. 2. Flores was the representative of the *ejidatarios* of Pisaflores. According to Frank Kluckhohn, General Andreu Almazán had the reputation of "never starting a revolution and never joining the losing side after one begins" (*New York Times,* 11 August 1938, p. 6).

43. O'Malley to Eden, 19 January 1938, FO 371/21482 (A1975/1975/26).

44. *El Machete,* 5, 12, and 19 February 1938; Fernández Boyoli and Marrón de Angelis, *Lo que no se sabe,* p. 109; O'Malley to Balfour, 8 February 1938, FO 371/21480 (A1538/491/26).

45. Fernández Boyoli and Marrón de Angelis, *Lo que no se sabe,* pp. 160-61.

46. Ibid., pp. 163-64. Even after Cárdenas expropriated the foreign-owned oil companies in Mexico in March 1938, there is no hard evidence for the widespread accusations on the Left that the oil companies' directors provided Cedillo with finance for a revolt. See *Foreign Relations of the United States. Diplomatic Papers 1938* (Washington, D.C., 1956), 754, for an account of a meeting between the directors of the leading U.S. oil companies and the Secretary of State in June 1938. See also E. David Cronon, *Josephus Daniels in Mexico* (Madison, Wisc., 1960), 212; Luis Noyola Barragán, *Como murieron los Generales Magdaleno y Saturnino Cedillo* (San Luis Potosí, 1964), 45; and Lorenzo Meyer, *México y Estados Unidos en el conflicto petrolero (1917-1942)* (México, 1972), who states (p. 363) that "there is no conclusive proof" concerning what help—if any—Cedillo received from the oil companies. For the accusations, see Anatol Shulgovski, *México en la encrucijada de su historia* (México, 1972), 374-75.

47. Fernández Boyoli and Marrón de Angelis, *Lo que no se sabe,* pp. 163-68; Primo Feliciano Velázquez, *Historia de San Luis Potosí* (México, 1946), 4:329, and the *New York Times,* 22 November 1938, p. 27.

48. Meyer, *México y Estados Unidos en el conflicto petrolero,* p. 347; Virginia Prewett, *Reportage,* pp. 166-67; Robert E. Scott, *Mexican Government in Transition* (Urbana, Ill., 1964), 130-31.

49. Magaña's published account of this interview naturally omits any reference to his own participation in a revolt; see Fernando Muñoz Moreno and Ramón Suárez de la Lastra, *El ocaso de un régimen* (San Luis Potosí, 1938), 129. But the same authors (pp. 123, 126); "Arvide," p. 364; and "La ruta de Cedillo," *(El Heraldo de San Luis Potosí,* 5 February 1954) all state or imply that Magaña was sympathetic to Cedillo's plotting in the winter of 1937-1938 and that he thought seriously of joining Cedillo if he decided to launch a rebellion.

50. *Excélsior,* 2 April 1938; Muñoz Moreno and Suárez de la Lastra, *El ocaso,* p. 129; "La ruta de Cedillo," 13 February 1954.

51. *El Machete,* 19 March 1938; Greene, *The Lawless Roads,* p. 59; "La ruta de Cedillo," 5 February 1954. When Rivas Guillén was wounded in a skirmish with Cristero rebels in 1937, Cedillo had him flown to Mexico City and cared for in the French hospital at his own expense ("Arvide," p. 299).

52. *New York Times,* 12 September 1937, p. 38; General Manuel Ávila Camacho to the General de Brigada Director de Armas, 31 March 1938, SDN XI/III/I-224, vol. 3; Fernández Boyoli and Marrón de Angelis, *Lo que no se sabe,* p. 190; Kluckhohn, *The Mexican Challenge,* p. 3.

53. Cedillo to Ávila Camacho, 1 April 1938; Rivas Guillén to the Secretaría de Guerra, 31 March 1938; Subdirección de infantería, untitled circular, 8 April 1938; Ávila Camacho to Cedillo, 4 April 1938; these four sources are in SDN XI/III/I-244, vol. 3. See also Cedillo to the Secretaría de Guerra, 7 April 1938; and the untitled medical report of Dr. Ignacio Morones Prieto, 1 April 1938, both in SDN XI/III/I-244, vol. 4.

54. *New York Times,* 21 May 1938, p. 1; Murray to Eden, 31 December 1936, FO 371/20640 (A1206/1206/26).

55. Fernández Boyoli and Marrón de Angelis, *Lo que no se sabe,* pp. 181, 191, and 196; Rogelio Sánchez C. to Cedillo, 27 April 1938, AGN, Ramo presidentes, Cárdenas, le-

gajo 559.1/53-3. Sánchez was one of Cedillo's agents in Aguascalientes and Zacatecas, and his letter is a report on the preparations for a revolt there.

56. Luis Noyola Barragán, *Como murieron los generales Magdaleno y Saturnino Cedillo*, p. 28; Fernández Boyoli and Marrón de Angelis, *Lo que no se sabe*, p. 193.

57. Cedillo to Avila Camacho, 8 May 1938, SDN XI/III/I-244, vol. 3; "Arvide," pp. 308-10; "La ruta de Cedillo," 6 February 1954.

58. "Arvide," pp. 310-11.

59. A copy of this memorandum is in the possession of Colonel José Arvide.

60. "Arvide," p. 314.

61. Fernández Boyoli and Marrón de Angelis, *Lo que no se sabe*, p. 162.

62. Ibid., p. 197.

63. Noyola Barragán, *Como murieron los generales Magdaleno y Saturnino Cedillo*, pp. 28-32; "Arvide," pp. 313, 338; *New York Times*, 18 May 1938, p. 5.

64. Gallop to Halifax, 21 April 1938; and British Consul-General James Dalton Murray in Mexico City to Halifax, 6 June 1938; the sources are FO 371/21479 (A3656/239/26) and /21480 (A4865/491/26); Kluckhohn, *The Mexican Challenge*, pp. 209-14; Weyl and Weyl, *The Reconquest of Mexico*, p. 239; *New York Times*, 25 July 1938, p. 7.

65. Rubén Rodríguez Lozano, *San Luis Potosí en su lucha por la libertad* (México, 1938), p. 21. Fernández Boyoli and Marrón de Angelis, *Lo que no se sabe*, p. 197. I am grateful to Romana Falcón for the observation that Cedillo tended to personalize his differences with Cárdenas.

66. *New York Times*, 19 May 1938, p. 1; Eduardo J. Correa, *El Balance del Cardenismo* (México, 1941), 408; Fernández Boyoli and Marrón de Angelis, *Lo que no se sabe*, pp. 197 and especially 325-28, which contain the text of Cárdenas's speech in San Luis Potosí.

67. Weyl and Weyl, *The Reconquest of Mexico*, p. 301; Rodríguez Lozano, *San Luis Potosí en su lucha*, p. 42; *New York Times*, 21 and 22 May 1938, p. 1; "Arvide," p. 321.

68. Noyola Barragán, *Como murieron los generales Magdaleno y Saturnino Cedillo*, p. 43; Fernández Boyoli and Marrón de Angelis, *Lo que no se sabe*, p. 202. Muñoz Moreno and Suárez de la Lastra, *El ocaso*, pp. 89-103, give a list of the various bands of rebels and when they surrendered.

69. *New York Times*, 23-27 May 1938; *El Machete*, 31 May and 5-7 June 1938; *Excélsior*, 19-22 May 1938; Muñoz Moreno and Suárez de la Lastra, *El ocaso*, pp. 91-103; Noyola Barragán, *Como murieron los generales Magdaleno y Saturnino Cedillo*, pp. 40, 43; Fernández Boyoli and Marrón de Angelis, *Lo que no se sabe*, p. 199; "La ruta de Cedillo," 9 February 1954; Gallop to Halifax, 24, 27, and 31 May 1938, FO 371/21480 (A4048/491/26, A4240/491/26 and A4312/491/26); Montgomery to the Secretary of State, 9 August and 3 November 1938, SD 812.00/San Luis Potosí.

70. "Arvide," pp. 326 and 331; Muñoz Moreno and Suárez de la Lastra, *El ocaso*, p. 93.

71. *Excélsior*, 22 May 1938; "La ruta de Cedillo," 13 February 1954. The two pilots, José Martínez and Rafael Rico, subsequently moved their aircraft to Zezontle, where they were captured by federal troops on 26 May (Fernández Boyoli and Marrón de Angelis, *Lo que no se sabe*, p. 201).

72. *El Machete*, 31 May 1938; "Arvide," p. 299; "La ruta de Cedillo," 15 February 1954; Fernández Boyoli and Marrón de Angelis, *Lo que no se sabe*, p. 202.

73. *El Machete*, 2 and 5 June 1938; Muñoz Moreno and Suárez de la Lastra, *El ocaso*, p. 96. Complaints about the tyranny of local government during Cedillo's rule may be found in letters to Cárdenas, some of them anonymous, from villagers in the munici-

palities of Mexquitic (29 July 1937), Villa Unión (17 July 1935), Tanquían (28 December 1937), and Pisaflores (20 February 1938), SDN XI/III/I-244, vol. 3.

74. Muñoz Moreno and Suárez de la Lastra, *El ocaso,* pp. 95–96; Catarina Gómez and Eusebia Ramírez to Cárdenas, 5 September 1938; Mateo Hernández Netro and Eustolio Méndez to Cárdenas, 15 March 1939, AGN, Ramo presidentes, Cárdenas, legajo 559.1/53.3. Cedillo's own family, however, lost much of their property and their business interests were confiscated (Higinia Cedillo, viuda de González, to Cárdenas, 3 March 1939; and Elena Cedillo to Cárdenas, 10 October 1938; both are in AGN, Ramo presidentes, Cárdenas, legajo 559.1/53-3).

75. *New York Times,* 23–24 May 1938, p. 1 of each issue; Muñoz Moreno and Suárez de la Lastra, *El ocaso,* pp. 100–102; Fernández Boyoli and Marrón de Angelis, *Lo que no se sabe,* p. 203; Gallop to Halifax, 27 May 1938, FO 371/21480 (A4240/491/26). As Frank Kluckhohn commented, "It appears that the San Luis Potosí conflict is an entirely local affair, although every effort is being made by the officially controlled press here [in Mexico] to make the Cedillo-Cárdenas clash appear as a fascist-leftist struggle with nation-wide ramifications" *(New York Times,* 25 May 1938, p. 15).

76. Fernández Boyoli and Marrón de Angelis, *Lo que no se sabe,* pp. 101–2; Colonel Manuel Fuentes Jiménez, interview with author, 2 February 1975. Colonel Fuentes Jiménez remained with Cedillo until his death. In late May, General Ávila Camacho set up a task force to hunt for Cedillo under General Miguel Z. Martínez. Presumably the defense minister hoped that Martínez would be more fortunate than when he had conducted a similar—and unsuccessful—operation as a colonel in the Constitutionalist army twenty years previously *(New York Times,* 25 May 1938, p. 15). See chap. 3, p. 84, for Martínez's earlier efforts to catch Cedillo.

77. A copy of this manifesto, which is undated but appears to have been issued soon after Cedillo disbanded most of his followers, can be found in AGN, Ramo presidentes, Cárdenas, legajo 559.1/53-7. It is translated in Appendix 7.

78. *Hoy,* 23 July 1938. The photograph of Cedillo accompanies the article. According to "Arvide," p. 340, Cedillo lost more than forty pounds in weight during his first few months on the run.

79. Ibid., p. 370; "La ruta de Cedillo," 22 and 23 February 1954.

80. "La ruta de Cedillo," 24–26 February and 1 March 1954; Lázaro Cárdenas, *Apuntes 1913–1940,* vol. 1 of *Obras* (México, 1971–1974), p. 406. Blas Ruíz was well rewarded for betraying Cedillo and shortly afterward had a fine house built in Guadalcázar. However, he did not enjoy the fruits of his treachery for long. A few months later he was found murdered in the spot where Cedillo himself had died (Velázquez, *Historia,* 4:341). Cedillo's family fled to the United States when he revolted but were permitted to return after his death. A short time later his sister, Higinia, was murdered by gunmen working for Reynaldo Pérez Gallardo, then state governor. General Manuel Ávila Camacho to the Commander of the Laredo Garrison, 13 January 1939, SDN XI/III/I-244, vol. 3; Higinia Cedillo de González in Mission, Texas, to Sir Ronald Lindsay, the British Ambassador in Washington, 5 September 1938, FO 371/21481 (A7284/491/26); Rafael Montejano y Aguiñaga, *El Valle de Maíz S.L.P.* (Ciudad del Maíz, 1967), 370.

BIBLIOGRAPHY

Anyone wishing to study the history of early twentieth-century Mexico will find that rich and varied archival sources are available. Outside Mexico there are the diplomatic papers of the United States and of several European governments. Within Mexico itself there are both national and state archives, as well as a number of semi-official or private collections of documents or other papers of value. Much of this Mexican material has only recently begun to be properly catalogued and access to certain archives is limited, but there is nevertheless more than enough to whet the researcher's appetite.

My main sources for the general history of the period were the Mexican press, the United States consular reports on Mexico for the years 1910–1929, the British Foreign Office correspondence on Mexico for 1910 to 1938, and the national archive in Mexico City, the Archivo de la Nación. With the exception of the most troubled years, such as 1915, the Mexican press provides a full and useful account of the period. Most of the national papers were conservative in outlook, but for the 1920s and also for the thirties their viewpoint was balanced by those of two other publications. These were the Communist party paper, *El Machete,* of which copies survive only for certain years, and the official governing party paper, *El Nacional,* founded in 1929, whose position under Cárdenas was more radical than that of most other Mexican papers, even if its perspective was heavily distorted in the government's favor. The U.S. consular reports on Mexico for the years 1910–1929 (the 812.00/ series) are available on microfilm, and I consulted the set held by Cambridge University. This material is a well-known mine of information for historians of the period. The American government posted consular agents throughout the country, and a reading of their reports provides a detailed picture of the general situation there at any given time. Some consuls were obviously more conscientious than others. I was fortunate that two of the consuls posted to San Luis Potosí during the period covered by this book, Wilbert Bonney and Walter Boyle, were both particularly industrious and, in the former case, unusually perceptive. Since the relevant consular material after 1929 is not yet available on microfilm, I later visited the National Archive in Washington, where I consulted the reports from the consuls in San Luis Potosí for the years 1930–1938.

The British consular reports on Mexico for the period in question were more difficult to consult when I did my research; they were kept in store some distance from London, and one could request only a few files at a time. Since there was no means of knowing which files contained material on San Luis Potosí; and as the first few reports I consulted seemed to cover the same ground as their American counterparts, but in less detail, I abandoned this source. The British Foreign Office files on Mexico were, however, readily available at the Public Record Office in London, and with an excellent cataloguing system. These files contained a considerable amount of interesting information, including copies of the more significant consular reports. The British embassy's reporting during the presidency of Cárdenas is, I believe, particularly noteworthy. The Archivo de la Nación in Mexico City has suffered in the past from poor organization and theft, which made life difficult for researchers when I visited it in 1972 and 1974. However, profiting by Hans Werner Tobler's pioneer research there on the role of the military in agrarian reform during the years 1920–1940, I nevertheless found quite a lot of useful material. A subsequent visit in 1979 revealed that the archive had been reorganized and the cataloguing system greatly improved, enabling me to consult many documents relating to the last years of Cedillo's life that were of great assistance. Through the recommendation of the late former president, Emilio Portes Gil, I obtained access in 1974 to the archive of the Defense Ministry in Mexico City, where I was permitted to consult the personal file of Saturnino Cedillo. Though my request to see other files was courteously refused, what I saw proved very useful. These sources were supported by official publications, the memoirs of politicians, and a number of other contemporary works, of which the most useful were Ernest Gruening's *Mexico and Its Heritage,* Eyler N. Simpson's *The Ejido: Mexico's Way Out,* and Virginia Prewett's *Reportage on Mexico.*

In San Luis Potosí the situation is checkered. Whereas there are several good local primary sources on the Porfiriato, this is not the case for the years 1920–1938. For the Porfiriato I consulted the local newspaper, *El Estandarte,* which ran from 1892 until 1912; the state archive, which contains selected editions of a number of contemporary publications as well as the government's *Periódico Oficial;* and the archive of Señor Octaviano Cabrera Ipiña, whose grandfather, José Encarnación Ipiña, was a prominent local landowner and businessman. This archive, which is in Octaviano Cabrera Ipiña's personal library, contains the records of several *haciendas* dating back to the seventeenth century, as well as forty volumes of José Encarnación Ipiña's correspondence. Octaviano Cabrera Ipiña, a noted local historian, kindly gave me a number of monographs he has written as well as an interesting verbal account of his experiences as a landowner under Cedillo's regime. Another distinguished local historian whose personal reminiscences and written works proved particularly illuminating was the late Nereo Rodríguez Barragán, with whom I held several long and valuable conversations.

For the 1920s and 1930s much less written material is available in San Luis Potosí. Very few editions of the local newspapers for the years 1912–1940 have survived, and in the state archive I found only copies of documents which had appeared in the *Periódico Oficial.* Therefore, I had to rely upon the archives mentioned above, supplemented by the archive of the former Agrarian Department (Departamento de Asuntos Agrarios y Colonización), now the Secretaría de la Reforma Agraria. This bureau has files on every *ejido* in the country, some of the most perfunctory nature but others containing very valuable material on the period. This archive also holds files on Cedillo's agrarian-military colonies. Although I was eventually allowed to consult these usually restricted files, they proved disappointing, since most of the papers they contained related to the years after 1940. However, the few documents there from the pre-1940 period were most informative.

Apart from archival material, I found of great help a manuscript biography of Saturnino Cedillo written by his former secretary, Colonel José Arvide. He worked with Cedillo for over twenty years; and his manuscript revealed much about Cedillo's character, as well as his participation in national politics. Colonel Arvide broke with Cedillo at the time of the Cedillista revolt, a decision which cost him the friendship of many of his former comrades. However, most of Cedillo's other surviving followers remain in touch with each other and meet on a regular basis. I interviewed several of them, of whom the most interesting were Salvador Muñiz, the head of the local industrial arbitration board in 1938, and Colonel Manuel Fuentes, another of Cedillo's secretaries who remained with him until he died. I also found helpful a number of articles on Cedillo which appeared in the local press fifteen years after his death. These included two series, "La ruta de Cedillo," an account of Cedillo's life written by staff journalists of a local newspaper and based on interviews with anonymous friends and associates, and "Saturnino Cedillo," by a local historian, Juan Muñiz Silva.

Secondary sources are like the primary sources, better on the Porfiriato than on the later period. Primo Feliciano Velázquez's four-volume history of San Luis Potosí, published in 1946, is a thorough work by the best-known local historian. Two other notable books dealing with the Porfiriato are James D. Cockroft's *Intellectual Precursors of the Mexican Revolution* and Jan Bazant's *Cinco Haciendas Potosinas.* The former is a mine of information on San Luis Potosí for the years 1876 to 1910. Bazant's book, which is largely based upon research in Octaviano Cabrera Ipiña's archive and the archive of Bocas *hacienda,* deals with the economic history of five *haciendas* in the state from their foundation until their expropriation between 1920 and 1938. There is no significant published work which deals specifically with the period from 1920 to 1940 in San Luis Potosí. A number of articles, however, have appeared in the press or in journals such as *Historia Mexicana,* and I also found useful the concluding chapters of several local histories. Of the latter, the most interesting were the chronicles of several municipalities in the state, compiled by Fr. Rafael Montejano y Aguiñaga. Romana Falcón's unpublished dissertation on Cedillo's regime became available in April 1983, while I was completing·the final draft of this book. Although I believe she somewhat underestimates the agrarian content in Cedillo's initial movement—and thus his subsequent local importance and popularity as an agrarian reformer—her work nevertheless makes stimulating and informative reading for anyone interested in Cedillo's later career.

To all the historians of modern Mexico whose work I have consulted, as well as to those who have contributed to the formation and maintenance of the archives I have mentioned, I am greatly indebted. Without their labors, it would have been impossible to write this book. One hopes that in due course more material will come to light on the recent history of San Luis Potosí. This illumination was certainly the purpose of Fr. Montejano y Aguiñaga and his team of researchers, who were renovating several local archives when I was last there. If their efforts are rewarded, future historians will have the opportunity to re-examine the period covered by this book in greater detail and thus add to our knowledge and understanding of perhaps the most turbulent epoch in the state's history.

ARCHIVAL SOURCES

Mexico City
    Archivo General de la Nación.
    Hemeroteca Nacional.
    Archivo de la Secretaría de Defensa Nacional.
    Archivo de la Secretaría de la Reforma Agraria.
    Oficina de Estadística de la Secretaría de la Reforma Agraria.
    Biblioteca de la Secretaría de Economía Nacional, Departamento de Estadística.
San Luis Potosí
    Archivo General del Gobierno del Estado de San Luis Potosí.
    Archivo de la Universidad Autónoma de San Luis Potosí.
    Archivo de la Secretaría de la Reforma Agraria.
    Archivo del Señor Octaviano Cabrera Ipiña.
London
    The Public Record Office.
Washington, D.C.
    The National Archive of the United States.

OFFICIAL PUBLICATIONS

The Mexican Government. (The official publications of the Mexican government are listed chronologically by date of publication under the various ministries or departments that sponsored them.)
Banco Nacional de México. *Algunos aspectos de nuestra economía al finalizar 1925.* México, 1925.
El Colegio de México. Seminario de Historia Moderna de México. *Estadísticas económicas del Porfiriato. Fuerza de trabajo y actividad económica por sectores.* México, no date of publication.

Comisión Nacional Agraria. *Estadística 1915–1927*. México, 1928.

Comisión Nacional para la Celebración del Sesquicentenario de la Proclamación de la Independencia Nacional y del Cincuentenario de la Revolución Mexicana. *Diario de los debates del Congreso Constituyente 1916–1917*. 2 vols. México, 1960.

Comisión Nacional del Salario Mínimo. *Memoria*. México, 1934.

Departamento Agrario. *Ideario agrarista del General de División Lázaro Cárdenas*. México, 1935.

Departamento de Trabajo. *Memoria 1936–1937* and *1937–1938*. México, 1937, 1939.

Ministerio de Fomento. *Estadística de la República Mexicana. Resumen y análisis de los informes rendidos a la Secretaría de Hacienda por Emiliano Bustos*. 2 vols. México, 1880.

————. *Anales*. 7 vols. México, 1881.

————. *Dirección General de Estadística. Boletín Semestral 1892*. México, 1893.

————. *Dirección General de Estadística. Censo general de la República Mexicana. 1895*. México, 1899.

National Financiera. *Statistics on the Mexican Economy*. México, 1966.

Secretaría de Economía Nacional. Dirección General de Estadística. *Aspectos estadísticos de un quinquenio 1921–1925*. México, 1927.

————. *Censo de población 1930. Estado de San Luis Potosí*. México, 1935.

————. *La reforma agraria en México*. México, 1937.

————.*Anuario estadístico* or *Compendio estadístico* for the years *1938, 1939, 1940, 1941* and *1942*. México, various dates of publication.

————. *Censo Ejidal 1940*. México, 1949.

————. *Estadísticas Sociales del Porfiriato 1877–1910*. México, 1956.

Secretaría de Educación Pública. *Boletín Mensual*. September 1922 to September 1925.

————. *La educación pública en México a través de los mensajes presidenciales desde la independencia hasta nuestros días*. México, 1926.

Secretaría de Fomento, Colonización e Industria. *Anuario Estadístico 1896, 1898, 1900, 1902, 1903, 1904, 1905* and *1906*. México, various dates of publication.

————. *Censo general de la República Mexicana. Estado de San Luis Potosí 1900*. México, 1903.

————. *División Territorial de la República Mexicana formada con los datos del censo de 1900*. México, 1904.

Secretaría de Gobernación. *Diario Oficial 1920–1938*. México, published annually.

————. *Diario de los debates de la Cámara de Diputados del Congreso de los Estados Unidos Mexicanos July 1937–July 1938*. México, 1938.

————. *Seis años de gobierno al servicio de México*. México, 1940.

Secretaría de Hacienda. Dirección General de Estadística. *Tercer censo de población de los Estados Unidos Mexicanos verificado el 27 Octubre 1910*. México, 1918.

————. *División Territorial de los Estados Unidos Mexicanos correspondiente al censo de 1910. Estado de San Luis Potosí*. México, 1918.

Government of San Luis Potosí.

Periódico Oficial 1920–1938. San Luis Potosí, published annually.

_____. *Informe leído por el C. Gobernador del estado José María Espinosa y Cuevas en la apertura del tercer período de sesiones del XXII Congreso Constitucional la noche del 15 de Septiembre de 1908. 1908.*

_____. *Informe leído por el C. C. Aurelio Manrique Jr., Gobernador Constitucional del estado de San Luis Potosí, en la instalación de la XXIX legislatura del mismo. 1925.*

_____. *Informe leído por el C. Dr. Abel Cano, Gobernador Constitucional del estado de San Luis Potosí en la inauguración del segundo período de sesiones de la XXIX legislatura del mismo. 1926.*

_____. *Informe leído por el C. Dr. Abel Cano, Gobernador Constitucional del estado de San Luis Potosí en la inauguración del primer período de sesiones de la XXX legislatura del mismo. 1927.*

_____. *Informe rendido por el C. General de División Saturnino Cedillo, Gobernador Constitucional del estado, ante la H. XXX legislatura del mismo en la apertura del primer período de sesiones ordinarias correspondiente al segundo año de su ejercicio legal. 1928.*

_____. *Informe rendido por el C. General de División Saturnino Cedillo, Gobernador Constitucional del estado, ante la H. XXXI legislatura del mismo, en la apertura del primer período de sesiones ordinarias correspondiente al primer año de su ejercicio legal. 1929.*

_____. *Informe rendido por el C. General de División Saturnino Cedillo, Gobernador Constitucional del estado, ante la H. XXXI legislatura del mismo, en la apertura del primer período de sesiones ordinarias correspondiente al segundo año de su ejercicio legal. 1930.*

_____. *Informe rendido por el C. Gobernador del estado en la apertura del primer período ordinario de sesiones de la H. XXXII legislatura del mismo. 1931.*

_____. *Informe que rinde el C. General Brigadier Ildefonso Turrubiartes, Gobernador Constitucional del estado, ante la XXXII legislatura del mismo, en la apertura del primer período de sesiones ordinarias correspondiente al segundo año de su ejercicio legal. 1932.*

_____. *Informe que rinde el C. General Brigadier Ildefonso Turrubiartes, Gobernador Constitucional del estado, ante la XXXIII legislatura del mismo, en la apertura del primer período de sesiones ordinarias correspondiente al primer año de su ejercicio legal. 1933.*

_____. *Informe rendido por el C. Gobernador del Estado, General Ildefonso Turrubiartes ante la H. XXXIII legislatura del estado el día 15 de Septiembre de 1934. 1934.*

_____. *Informe rendido por el C. Gobernador General Ildefonso Turrubiartes ante la H. XXXIV legislatura del estado, el día 15 de Septiembre de 1935. 1935.*

_____. *Informe de la gestión administrativa que rinde el C. Col. Mateo Hernández Netro, Gobernador Constitucional del estado a la H. XXXIV legislatura del mismo, correspondiente al período comprendido del 1 de Septiembre de 1935 al 31 de Agosto de 1936. 1936.*

_____. *Informe que rinde el C. Col. Mateo Hernández Netro de su gestión administrativa como gobernador constitucional del estado de San Luis Potosí, a la XXXV le-*

gislatura del mismo, correspondiente al período del 1 de Septiembre de 1936 al 31 de Agosto de 1937. 1937.

United Kingdom.

Department of Overseas Trade. *Report on the Economic and Financial Conditions in Mexico*. London, 1921, 1923, 1924, and 1928.

U.S. Department of State.

Papers Relating to the Foreign Relations of the United States. Washington D.C. Various dates between 1910 and 1940.

CONTEMPORARY SOURCES: PAMPHLETS.

Bustamante, Luis F. *Quién es el Coronel Juan B. Barragán?* San Luis Potosí, 1917.
Cárdenas, Lázaro. *La Unificación Campesina*. México, 1936.
Compañía Anónima de la Empresa de Aguas de la Ciudad de San Luis Potosí. *Estatutos*. San Luis Potosí, 1904.
Compañía Anónima Restauradora del Mineral de Ramos, San Luis Potosí. *Estatutos*. San Luis Potosí, 1887.
Compañía Minera de San Pedro el Alto y anexas. *Estatutos*. San Luis Potosí, 1879.
Confederación Patronal de la República Mexicana. *Directorio general de socios*. San Luis Potosí, 1936.
Empresa de Aguas de San Luis Potosí. *Contrato celebrado entre el gobierno del estado y la Empresa de Aguas de San Luis Potosí prorrogado el día de fecha 20 de Julio de 1895*. San Luis Potosí, 1904.
Grimaldo, Isaac. *Gobernantes Potosinos*. San Luis Potosí, 1939.
_____. *Rasgos biográficos del Dr. Rafael Cepeda*. San Luis Potosí, 1912.
_____. *Vida del G. Divisionario Saturnino Cedillo*. San Luis Potosí, 1935.
Guardiola, B. *El estado de San Luis Potosí. Cartilla explicativa del mapa editado por esta casa*. San Luis Potosí, 1913.
Hacienda de Bocas. *Condiciones con que se dan a partido algunas de las tierras de la Hacienda de San Antonio de Bocas, en el año de 1875*. San Luis Potosí, 1883.
Hernández, F., and A. Flores. *Amparo Espinosa y Cuevas. Apuntes de alegato que ante la Corte Suprema de Justicia de la Nación y en favor de los quejosos presentan los licenciados F. Hernández y A. Flores*. San Luis Potosí, 1913.
Laborde, Hernán. *La unidad a toda costa*. México, 1937.
Nieto, Rafael. *Exposición de los motivos que el ejecutivo del estado tuvo para pedir al H. Congreso la expedición de la ley agraria*. San Luis Potosí, 1921.
Orozco, Wistano Luis. *Los negocios sobre terrenos baldíos. Resoluciones judiciales y estudios del Lic. Wistano Luis Orozco en el caso especial de Agustín R. Ortiz contra los Moctezumas*. San Luis Potosí, 1902.
Partido de la Revolución Mexicana. *Contra la traición*. México, 1938.

Representación que elevan a su majestad el emperador algunos propietarios del departamento de San Luis Potosí pidiendo respetuosamente sean modificadas las leyes de 26 de Mayo y 9 de Junio de 1866 sobre propiedad raíz. México, 1866.

Ruíz, M. N. *Errores económicos del socialismo.* Comitán, 1921.

San Luis Potosí. *Bases a las que deberá sujetarse la tercera exposición agrícola, ganadera e industrial de San Luis Potosí.* San Luis Potosí, 1934.

San Luis Potosí. *Directorio gobernativo, profesional y comercial.* San Luis Potosí, 1931.

San Luis Potosí. Liga de Comunidades Agrarias. *Tierra, libertad y justicia. Estatutos de la Liga de Comunidades Agrarias de San Luis Potosí.* San Luis Potosí, 1930.

Sustaita, A., and M. González Pérez. *Homenaje al General Carlos Díez Gutiérrez.* San Luis Potosí, 1897.

Villaurrutia, Agustín. *La Hacienda de La Pila.* San Luis Potosí, 1881.

CONTEMPORARY SOURCES: ARTICLES

Beals, Carleton. "Mexico and the Communists." *New Republic,* 19 February 1930, pp. 10–12.

———. "The Obregón Regime." *Survey Graphic* 5, no. 2 (May 1924): 135–37, 188–89.

De Negri, Ramón P. "The Agrarian Problem." *Survey Graphic* 5, no. 2 (May 1924): 149–52.

Díaz Soto y Gama, Antonio. "Los Hermanos Cedillo, destacados agraristas." *El Sol de San Luis Potosí,* 7 July 1953.

Durán, Mauricio. "En San Luis Potosí no hay problema agrario." *La Esfera,* January 1938, pp. 12–13.

Haberman, Robert. "Bandit Colonies." *Survey Graphic* 5, no. 2 (May 1924): 147–48, and 196.

Lombardo Toledano, Vicente. "The Labor Movement." *Annals of the American Academy of Political and Social Science* 208 (March 1940): 48–54.

Melgarejo, Luis R. "Por que salió del Gabinete Cardenista el Gral. Cedillo." *La Esfera,* January 1938, pp. 7, 31.

Monsivais, Roberto. "Obreros y Patronos." *La Esfera,* January 1938, p. 22.

Parkes, Henry Bamford. "Political Leadership in Mexico." *Annals of the American Academy of Political and Social Science* 208 (March 1940): 12–22.

Paz, Martín. "El General Cedillo en su Retiro de Palomas." *La Esfera,* January 1938, pp. 9, 34, 35.

Prendergast, L. P. "Behind the Overthrow of Calles." *Nation* 142 (17 June 1935): 67–69.

Prewett, Virginia. "The Mexican Army." *Foreign Affairs,* April 1941, pp. 609–620.

Tannenbaum, Frank. "Mexico—A Compromise." *Survey Graphic* 5, no. 2 (May 1924): 129–32.

CONTEMPORARY SOURCES: BOOKS

Askinasy, Siegfried. *El problema agrario de Yucatán.* México, 1936.

Baerlein, Henry. *Mexico, The Land of Unrest.* London, 1914.

Barragán Rodríguez, Juan. *Historia del ejercito y de la Revolución Constitucionalista.* 2 vols. México, 1946.

Beals, Carleton. *Mexico: An Interpretation.* New York, 1923.

_____. *Porfirio Díaz: Dictator of Mexico.* Philadelphia, 1932.

Beteta, Ramón. *Programa económico y social de México.* México, 1935.

Blasco Ibañez, Vicente. *El militarismo Méjicano.* Valencia, 1920.

Bórquez, Djed. [Juan de Dios Bojórquez, pseud.] *Obregón. Apuntes biográficos.* México, 1929.

Bosques, Gilberto. *The National Revolutionary Party of Mexico and the Six Year Plan.* México, 1937.

Brantz, Mayer. *Mexico: Aztec, Spanish and Republican.* Hartford, Conn., 1853.

Brocklehurst, T. K. *Mexico Today: A Country with a Great Future and a Glance at the Prehistoric Remains and Antiquities of the Montezumas.* London, 1883.

Bulnes, Francisco. *El verdadero Díaz y la Revolución.* México, 1920.

_____. *The Whole Truth about Mexico—President Wilson's Responsibility.* New York, 1916.

Bustamante, Luis F. *Perfiles y bocetos revolucionarios.* México, 1917.

Cabrera, Luis. *El balance de la Revolución.* México, 1931.

_____. *Obras completas.* 4 vols. México, 1975.

_____. *Veinte años después.* México, 1938.

Calles, Plutarco Elías. *Méjico ante el mundo.* Barcelona, 1927.

Cárdenas, Lázaro. *Apuntes 1913–1940.* Vol. 1 of *Obras.* 4 vols. México, 1972–1974.

_____. *Palabras y documentos públicos de Lázaro Cárdenas.* 3 vols. México, 1978–1979.

Carson, W. E. *Mexico: The Wonderland of the South.* New York, 1909.

Clark, Marjorie Ruth. *Organized Labor in Mexico.* Chapel Hill, N.C., 1934.

Correa, Eduardo J. *El balance del Cardenismo.* México, 1941.

Cossio, José L. *Monopolio y fraccionamiento de la propiedad en México.* México, 1914.

Daniels, Josephus. *Shirt-Sleeve Diplomat.* Chapel Hill, N.C., 1947.

Denny, Ludwell. *We Fight for Oil.* New York, 1928.

Díaz Leal, José. *Legislación y guía de terrenos baldíos.* México, 1878.

Dillon, E. J. *Mexico on the Verge.* London, 1922.

Fabila, Manuel. *Cinco siglos de legislación agraria en México.* México, 1941.

Feller, A. H. *The Mexican Claims Commission, 1923–1934.* New York, 1935.

Fernández, R. D. *Los gobernantes de México desde Agustín de Iturbide a General don Plutarco Elías Calles.* Sabinas, 1931.

Fernández Boyoli, Manuel, and Eustaqui Marrón de Angelis. *Lo que no se sabe de la rebelión Cedillista.* México, 1938.

Fyfe, Henry Hamilton. *The Real Mexico: A Study on the Spot.* New York, 1914.

Gill, Mario. *El Sinarquismo. Su origen, su esencia, su misión.* México, 1944.

González Ramírez, Manuel, ed. *Planes políticos y otros documentos.* México, 1954.

González Roa, Fernando. *El aspecto agrario de la Revolución Mexicana.* México, 1919.

Greene, Graham. *The Lawless Roads.* London, 1939.

Gruening, Ernest. *Mexico and Its Heritage.* New York, 1928.

Gutiérrez de Lara, Lázaro, and Edgcumb Pinchón. *The Mexican People: Their Struggle for Freedom.* New York, 1914.

Guzmán, Martín Luis. *Memorias de Pancho Villa.* México, 1951.

Guzmán Esparza, Roberto E. *Memorias de don Adolfo de la Huerta, según su propio dictado: transcripción y comentarios de Lic. Roberto Guzmán Esparza.* México, 1957.

Herring, Hubert, and Herbert Weinstock, eds. *Renascent Mexico.* New York, 1935.

Kelly, Sir David. *The Ruling Few.* London, 1952.

King, Rosa E. *Tempest over Mexico.* Boston, 1935.

Kirk, Betty. *Covering the Mexican Front.* Norman, Okla., 1942.

Kluckhohn, Frank L. *The Mexican Challenge.* New York, 1939.

McBride, George McCutcheon. *The Land Systems of Mexico.* New York, 1923.

McFarland, Charles S. *Chaos in Mexico: The Conflict of Church and State.* London, 1935.

Madero, Francisco I. *La sucesión presidencial en 1910.* México, 1909.

Magaña, Gildardo, and Carlos Pérez Guerrero. *Emiliano Zapata y el agrarismo en México.* 5 vols. México, 1951–1952.

Marrott, Robert H. K. *An Eye-Witness of Mexico.* London, 1939.

Mendoza Vargas, Eutiquio. *Gotitas de placer y chubascos de amargura: memorias de la Revolución Mexicana en la Huasteca.* México, 1960.

Millan, Verna C. *Mexico Reborn.* Boston, 1939.

Molina Enríquez, Andrés. *Los grandes problemas nacionales.* México, 1909.

Monroy Durán, Luis. *El último caudillo.* México, 1924.

Muñoz Moreno, Fernando, and Ramón Suárez de la Lastra. *El ocaso de un régimen.* San Luis Potosí, 1938.

Muro, Manuel. *Historia de San Luis Potosí.* 3 vols. San Luis Potosí, 1910.

Nicolson, Harold. *Dwight Morrow.* London, 1935.

Obregón, Álvaro. *Ocho mil kilómetros de campaña. Relación de las acciones de armas efectuadas en más de veinte estados de la República durante un período de cuatro años.* México, 1917.

O'Hea, Patrick. *Reminiscences of the Mexican Revolution.* México, 1966.

Orozco, Wistano Luis. *La cuestión agraria.* Guadalajara, 1911.

————. *Los ejidos de los pueblos. Con prólogo de Elena Sánchez Orozco.* México, 1975.

————. *Los negocios sobre terrenos baldíos. Resoluciones judiciales y estudios de Licenciado Wistano Luis Orozco en el caso especial de Agustín R. de Ortiz contra los Moctezumas.* San Luis Potosí, 1902.

O'Shaughnessy, Edith. *A Diplomat's Wife in Mexico.* New York, 1916.

Palavicini, Félix F. *Mi vida revolucionaria.* México, 1937.

Pani, Alberto J. *Apuntes autobiográficos.* 2 vols, México, 1950.

————. *El camino hacia la democracia*. México, 1918.

Partido de la Revolución Mexicana. *¡Cárdenas habla!* México, 1940.

Parsons, Wilfred. *Mexican Martyrdom*. New York, 1936.

Pettus, Daisy Caden. *The Rosalie Evans Letters from Mexico*. Indianapolis, Ind., 1926.

Plenn, J. H. *Mexico Marches*. Indianapolis, Ind., 1939.

Portes Gil, Emilio. *Autobiografía de la Revolución Mexicana*. México, 1964.

————. *La lucha entre el poder civil y el clero*. México, 1934.

————. *Quince años de política Mexicana*. México, 1941.

————. *Raigambre de la Revolución en Tamaulipas*. México, 1972.

Prewett, Virginia. *Reportage on Mexico*. New York, 1941.

Prieto Laurens, Jorge. *Anécdotas históricas*. México, 1977.

————. *Cincuenta años de política Mexicana. Memorias políticas*. México, 1968.

Ramos, Samuel. *Veinte años de educación en México*. México, 1941.

Ramos Pedrueza, Rafael. *La lucha de clases a través de la historia de México. Revolución democraticoburguesa*. México, 1934.

Reed, John. *Insurgent Mexico*. New York, 1969.

Rippy, J. Fred, José Vasconcelos, and Guy Stevens. *Mexico*. Chicago, 1928.

Rodríguez Lozano, Rubén. *San Luis Potosí en su lucha por la libertad*. México, 1938.

Sánchez, George I. *Mexico: A Revolution by Education*. New York, 1936.

Silva Herzog, Jesús. *Una vida en la vida de México*. México, 1972.

Silva Herzog, Jesús, ed. *La Cuestión de la Tierra. Colección de folletos para la historia mexicana dirigida por Jesús Silva Herzog*. 4 vols. México, 1960.

Simpson, Eyler Newton. *The Ejido: Mexico's Way Out*. Chapel Hill, N.C., 1937.

Salazar, Rosendo, and José G. Escobedo. *Las pugnas de la gleba 1907–1922*. México, 1923.

Sindicato de Agricultores de Jalisco. *En defensa de la agricultura nacional*. Guadalajara, 1921.

Sterrett, Joseph E., and Joseph S. Davis. *The Fiscal and Economic Condition of Mexico*. New York, 1928.

Tamaulipas. *Liga de comunidades agrarias y sindicatos campesinos del estado. Segunda y tercera convención*. México, 1930.

Tannenbaum, Frank. *The Mexican Agrarian Revolution*. Washington, D.C., 1930.

————. *Peace by Revolution: An Interpretation of Mexico*. New York, 1933.

Toro, Alfonso. *La iglesia y el estado en México*. México, 1927.

Tovar, Mariano. *Síntesis y antítesis revolucionarias. Cárdenas, Calles, Canabal, Cedillo*. México, 1935.

Turner, John Kenneth. *Barbarous Mexico*. Chicago, 1911.

Tweedie, Mrs. Alec. *Mexico as I Saw It*. London, 1911.

Vasconcelos, José. *Obras completas*. 4 vols. México, 1961.

Vera Estañol, Jorge. *La Revolución Mexicana. Orígenes y resultados*. México, 1957.

Ward, H. G. *Mexico*. 2 vols. London, 1829.

Weyl, Nathaniel, and Sylvia Weyl. *The Reconquest of Mexico: The Years of Lázaro Cárdenas*. New York, 1939.

SECONDARY SOURCES: ARTICLES

Aguilar Camín, Héctor. "The Relevant Tradition: Sonoran Leaders in the Revolution." In *Caudillo and Peasant in the Mexican Revolution.* Edited by D. A. Brading, 92–123. Cambridge, 1980.

Alcocer Andalón, Alberto. "El General y Profesor Alberto Carrera Torres." *Archivos de Historia Potosina*, no. 1 (July–September 1969): 32–48.

Anderson, Bo, and James D. Cockroft. "Control and Cooptation in Mexican Politics." In *Dependence and Underdevelopment: Latin America's Political Economy.* Edited by James D. Cockroft, André Gunder Frank, and Dale L. Johnson, 219–45. New York, 1972.

Boorstan Couturier, E. "Modernización y tradición en una hacienda (San Juan de Hueyapan 1902–1911)." *Historia Mexicana* 18 (July–September 1968): 35–40.

Britton, John A. "Teacher Unionization and the Corporate State in Mexico 1931–45." *Hispanic American Historical Review* 59, no 4 (November 1979): 674–90.

Buve, Raymond Th. "Patronaje en las zonas rurales de México." *Boletín de Estudios Latinoamericanos y del Caribe* 16 (June 1974): 3–15.

———. "Peasant Movements, Caudillos and Land Reform during the Revolution (1910–1917) in Tlaxcala, Mexico." *Boletín de Estudios Latinoamericanos y del Caribe* 18 (June 1975): 112–52.

Calderón, Francisco. "Los Ferrocarriles." In *Historia moderna de México. El Porfiriato. La vida económica.* Edited by Daniel Cosío Villegas, 483–634. México, 1965.

Carr, Barry. "Organised Labour and the Mexican Revolution 1914–1928." *Occasional Papers*, no. 2. Oxford: The Latin American Centre, St. Antony's College, 1972.

———. "The Peculiarities of the Mexican North 1880–1928: An Essay in Interpretation." *Occasional Papers,* no. 4. Glasgow: University of Glasgow, Institute of Latin American Studies, 1971.

Carr, Raymond. "Mexican Agrarian Reform 1910–1960." In *Agrarian Change and Economic Development.* Edited by E. L. Jones and S. J. Woolf, 152–63. London, 1969.

Chevalier, François. "The Ejido and Political Stability in Mexico." In *The Politics of Conformity in Latin America.* Edited by Claudio Veliz, 158–91. London, 1967.

Coatsworth, John. "Railroads, Landholding, and Agrarian Protest in the Early Porfiriato." *Hispanic American Historical Review* 54, no. 1 (February 1974): 48–71.

Cockroft, James D. "El maestro de primaria en la Revolución Mexicana." *Historia Mexicana* 16 (April–June 1967): 565–87.

Cura, Félix. R. "La rebelión del General Cedillo, una incógnita de la historia." *El Heraldo de San Luis Potosí*, 8 November 1961.

Falcón, Romana. "¿Los orígenes populares de la revolución de 1910?—El caso de San Luis Potosí." *Historia Mexicana* 29 (July 1979–June 1980): 197–240.

————. "El surgimiento del agrarismo Cardenista—una revisión de las tesis populistas." *Historia Mexicana* 27 (January–March 1978): 333–86.

Feder, Ernest. "Land Reform: A Twentieth Century World Issue." *América Latina* 10, no. 1 (January–March 1967): 96–136.

Fowler Salamini, Heather. "Revolutionary caudillos in the 1920's: Francisco Múgica and Adalberto Tejeda." In *Caudillo and Peasant in the Mexican Revolution*. Edited by D. A. Brading, 169–92. Cambridge, 1980.

González Navarro, Moisés. "Le développement économique et social du Mexique." *Annales, économies, sociétés, civilisations* 21 (July–August 1966): 842–58.

————. "Efectos sociales de la crisis de 1929." *Historia Mexicana* 19 (April–June 1970): 536–58.

————. "La ideología de la Revolución Mexicana." *Historia Mexicana* 10 (April–June 1961): 628–36.

————. "Social Aspects of the Mexican Revolution." *Cahiers d'histoire mondiale* 8 (1964): 281–89.

Gutiérrez, Hermenegildo. "Que Cárdenas no provocó la muerte de Saturnino Cedillo." *El Heraldo de San Luis Potosí*, 2 July 1952.

Hall, Linda B. "Alvaro Obregón and the Agrarian Movement 1912–1920." In *Caudillo and Peasant in the Mexican Revolution*. Edited by D. A. Brading, 124–39. Cambridge, 1980.

————. "Alvaro Obregón and the Politics of Mexican Land Reform 1920–1924." *Hispanic American Historical Review* 60, no. 2 (May 1980): 213–38.

El Heraldo de San Luis Potosí. "La ruta de Cedillo." Series dated from 5 January 1954 and 1 March 1954, intermittent dates.

Himes, J. R. "La formación de capital en México." *El Trimestre Económico* 32, no. 125 (January–March 1965): 153–79.

Jacobs, Ian. "Rancheros of Guerrero: The Figueroa Brothers and the Revolution." In *Caudillo and Peasant in the Mexican Revolution*. Edited by D. A. Brading, 76–91. Cambridge, 1980.

Joseph, Gilbert M. "Caciquismo and the Revolution: Carrillo Puerto in Yucatán." In *Caudillo and Peasant in the Mexican Revolution*. Edited by D. A. Brading, 193–221. Cambridge, 1980.

Katz, Friedrich. "Labor Conditions on Haciendas in Porfirian Mexico: Some Trends and Tendencies." *Hispanic American Historical Review* 54, no. 1 (February 1974): 1–47.

————. "Pancho Villa, Peasant Movements and Agrarian Reform in Northern Mexico." In *Caudillo and Peasant in the Mexican Revolution*. Edited by D. A. Brading, 59–75. Cambridge, 1980.

Keesing, Donald B. "Structural Change Early in Development: Mexico's Changing Industrial and Occupational Structure from 1895 to 1950." *Journal of Economic History* 29 (December 1969), 716–38.

Kerblay, Basile. "Chayanov and the Theory of Peasantry as a Specific Type of Economy." In *Peasants and Peasant Societies*. Edited by Teodor Shanin, 150–61. London, 1971.

Kitchens, J. W. "Some Considerations on the *rurales* of Porfirian Mexico." *Journal of Inter-American Studies* 9, no. 3 (July 1967): 441–55.

Knight, Alan. "Peasant and Caudillo in Revolutionary Mexico 1910–17." In *Caudillo and Peasant in the Mexican Revolution*. Edited by D. A. Brading, 17–58. Cambridge, 1980.

Lerner, Victoria. "Los fundamentos socioeconómicos del cacicazgo en el México postrevolucionario—el caso de Saturnino Cedillo." *Historia Mexicana* 29 (July 1979–June 1980): 375–446.

Lozoya, J. A. "Breve historia del ejercito Mexicano." *Aportes*, no. 20 (April 1971): 113–31.

Meyers, William K. "Politics, Vested Rights, and Economic Growth in Porfirian Mexico: The Company Tlahualilo in the Comarca Lagunera 1885–1911." *Hispanic American Historical Review* 57, no. 3 (August 1977): 425–54.

Michaels, Albert L. "El nacionalismo conservador Mexicano desde la revolución hasta 1949." *Historia Mexicana* 16 (October–December 1966): 213–38.

Muñiz Silva, Juan. "Saturnino Cedillo." *El Sol de San Luis Potosí*. Series published from 3 January 1954 to 3 April 1955, intermittent dates.

Nava Oteo, Guadalupe. "La Minería." In *Historia moderna de México. El Porfiriato. La vida económica*. Edited by Daniel Cosío Villegas, 179–310. México, 1965.

Purata Gómez, Carlos. "Integrantes del poder legislativo de San Luis Potosí del Constituyente de 1824 a la fecha." *Boletín de la Escuela de Jurisprudencia de la Universidad Autónoma de San Luis Potosí*, no. 5 (August 1965): 1–27.

Richmond, Douglas W. "Factional Strife in Coahuila 1910–1920." *Hispanic American Historical Review* 60, no. 1 (February 1980): 49–68.

Rosenzweig Hernández, Fernando. "El desarrollo económico de México de 1877 a 1911." *El Trimestre Económico* 32, no. 127 (July–September 1965): 405–54.

———. "La industria." In *Historia moderna de México. El Porfiriato. La vida económica*. Edited by Daniel Cosío Villegas, 311–481. México, 1965.

Stavenhagen, Rodolfo. "Seven Erroneous Theses about Latin America." In *Latin American Radicalism*. Edited by Irving Louis Horowitz, Josué de Castro, and John Gerassi, 102–17. London, 1969.

Tobler, Hans-Werner. "Las paradojas del ejercito revolucionario: su papel en la reforma agraria 1920–1935." *Historia Mexicana* 21 (July–September 1971): 38–79.

Vanderwood, Paul J. "Response to Revolt: The Counter-Guerrilla Strategy of Porfirio Díaz." *Hispanic American Historical Review* 56, no. 4 (November 1976): 551–79.

Wells, Allen. "Family Elites in a Boom-and-Bust Economy: The Molinas and Peóns of Porfirian Yucatán." *Hispanic American Historical Review* 62, no. 2 (May 1982): 224–53.

Wolf, Eric R. "Aspects of Group Relations in a Complex Society: Mexico."

In *Peasants and Peasant Societies*. Edited by Teodor Shanin, 50–68. London, 1971.

SECONDARY SOURCES: BOOKS

Aguilar Camín, Héctor. *La frontera nómada: Sonora y la Revolución Mexicana.* México, 1977.

Alba, Victor. *Historia del Frente Popular: análisis de una táctica política.* México, 1959.

———. *The Mexicans: The Making of a Nation.* New York, 1967.

Amaya, Juan Gualberto. *Los gobiernos de Obregón, Calles y regímenes "peleles" derivados del Callismo.* México, 1947.

Anguiano Equihua, Victor. *Lázaro Cárdenas: su feudo y la política nacional.* México, 1951.

Ashby, Joe C. *Organized Labor and the Mexican Revolution under Lázaro Cárdenas.* Chapel Hill, N.C., 1963.

Atkin, Ronald. *Revolution! Mexico 1910–20.* London, 1969.

Bailey, David C. *Viva Cristo Rey: The Cristero Rebellion and the Church-State Conflict in Mexico.* Austin, Tex., 1974.

Barba González, Silvano. *La rebelión de los cristeros.* México, 1967.

Bassols Batalla, Narciso. *El pensamiento político de Obregón.* México, 1967.

Bazant, Jan. *Alienation of Church Wealth in Mexico: Social and Economic Aspects of the Liberal Revolution 1856–1875.* Cambridge, 1971.

———. *Cinco haciendas Mexicanas. Tres siglos de vida rural en San Luis Potosí (1600–1910).* México, 1975.

———. *Historia de la deuda exterior de México (1823–1946).* México, 1968.

Beezley, William H. *Insurgent Governor: Abraham González and the Mexican Revolution in Chihuahua.* Lincoln, Neb., 1973.

Benítez, Fernando. *Lázaro Cárdenas y la Revolución Mexicana.* 3 vols. México, 1977–1978.

Blaisdell, Lowell L. *The Desert Revolution: Baja California, 1911.* Madison, Wis., 1962.

Blanco Moheno, Roberto. *Crónica de la Revolución Mexicana.* 3 vols. México, 1967.

Braddy, Haldeen. *Cock of the Walk: Qui-qui-ri-qui: The Legend of Pancho Villa.* Albuquerque, N.M., 1955.

Brading, D. A. *Haciendas and Ranchos in the Mexican Bajío, 1700–1860.* Cambridge, 1978.

———. *Miners and Merchants in Bourbon Mexico 1763–1810.* Cambridge, 1971.

———. *Los orígenes del nacionalismo Mexicano.* México, 1980.

Brading, D. A., ed. *Caudillo and Peasant in the Mexican Revolution.* Cambridge, 1980.

Brandenburg, Frank. *The Making of Modern Mexico.* Englewood Cliffs, N.J., 1964.

Brenner, Anita, and George R. Leighton. *The Wind That Swept Mexico.* New York, 1943.

Cabrera Ipiña, Octaviano. *Archivo histórico de una hacienda.* Bledos, San Luis Potosí, 1958.

————. *San Luis Potosí. Monografía de un estado.* San Luis Potosí, n.d.

Cabrera Ipiña de Corsi, Matilde. *Cuatro grandes dinastías Mexicanas en los descendientes de los hermanos Fernández de Lima y Barragán.* San Luis Potosí, 1956.

Calvert, Peter. *The Mexican Revolution, 1910-1914: The Diplomacy of Anglo-American Conflict.* Cambridge, 1968.

Campbell, Hugh G. *La derecha radical en México (1929-1949).* México, 1976.

Carpizo, Jorge. *La Constitución Mexicana de 1917.* México, 1969.

Carr, Barry. *El movimiento obrero y la política en México 1910-1929.* 2 vols. México, 1976.

Castillo, Isidro. *México y su revolución educativa.* México, 1965.

Chevalier, François. *Land and Society in Colonial Mexico: The Great Hacienda.* Berkeley, Calif., 1963.

Chowell, Martín. *Luis Navarro Origel, el primer cristero.* México, 1959.

Cline, Howard. *The United States and Mexico.* New York, 1963.

Coatsworth, John H. *Growth against Development: The Economic Impact of Railroads in Porfirian Mexico.* DeKalb, Ill., 1981.

Cockroft, James D. *Intellectual Precursors of the Mexican Revolution.* Austin, Tex., 1968.

Cockroft, James D., André Gunder Frank, and Dale L. Johnson. *Dependence and Underdevelopment: Latin America's Political Economy.* New York, 1972.

Córdova, Arnaldo. *La clase obrera en la historia de México. En una época de crisis (1928-1934).* México, 1980.

————. *La ideología de la Revolución Mexicana.* México, 1973.

————. *La política de masas del Cardenismo.* México, 1974.

Cosío Villegas, Daniel. *Historia moderna de México: El Porfiriato.* 10 vols. México, 1956-1972.

Costeloe, Michael P. *Church Wealth in Mexico: A Study of the "Juzgado de Capellanías" in the Archbishopric of Mexico, 1800-1856.* Cambridge, 1966.

Cumberland, Charles Curtis. *Mexican Revolution: The Constitutionalist Years.* Austin, Tex., 1972.

————. *Mexican Revolution: Genesis under Madero.* Austin, Tex., 1952.

————. *Mexico: The Struggle for Modernity.* New York, 1968.

Custodio, Alvaro. *El corrido popular Mexicano.* Madrid, 1976.

Diccionario Porrúa de historia, biografía y geografía de México. México, 1964.

Dulles, John W. F. *Yesterday in Mexico: A Chronicle of the Revolution, 1919-1936.* Austin, Tex., 1961.

Estrada, Antonio M. *La grieta en el yugo.* San Luis Potosí, 1963.

Falcón, Romana. *El agrarismo en Veracruz. La etapa radical (1928-1935).* México 1977.

Foix, Pere. *Cárdenas.* México, 1971.

Fowler Salamini, Heather. *Agrarian Radicalism in Veracruz, 1920-1938.* Lincoln, Neb., 1978.

Frank, André Gunder. *Capitalism and Underdevelopment in Latin America.* New York, 1967.

Friedrich, Paul. *Agrarian Revolt in a Mexican Village*. Chicago, 1977.

Fuentes Mares, Juan. *México se refugió en el desierto*. México, 1954.

Gilly, Adolfo. *La Revolución Interrumpida*. México, 1972.

Glade, William P., and Charles W. Anderson. *The Political Economy of Mexico*. Madison, Wis., 1963.

González, Luis. *Historia de la Revolución Mexicana. Los días del presidente Cárdenas*. México, 1981.

──────. *Pueblo en vilo: microhistoria de San José de Gracia*. México, 1968.

González Casanova, Pablo. *La democracia en México*. México, 1965.

González Casanova, Pablo, and Enrique Florescano. *México, hoy*. México, 1979.

González Navarro, Moisés. *La colonización en México 1877-1910*. México, 1960.

──────. *La Confederación Nacional Campesina, un grupo de presión en la Revolución Mexicana*. México, 1968.

──────. *El Porfiriato: La vida social*. Vol. 4 of *Historia moderna de México: El Porfiriato*, ed. Daniel Cosío Villegas. México, 1957.

González Ramírez, Manuel. *La revolución social de México*. 3 vols. México, 1960.

Hale, Charles A. *Mexican Liberalism in the Age of Mora, 1821-1853*. New Haven, Conn., 1968.

Hall, Linda B. *Álvaro Obregón: Power and Revolution in Mexico, 1911-1920*. College Station, Tex., 1981.

Hansen, Rodger D. *The Politics of Mexican Development*. London, 1971.

Hart, John M. *Anarchism and the Mexican Working Class, 1860-1931*. Austin, Tex., 1978.

Henderson, Peter V. N. *Félix Díaz, The Porfirians and the Mexican Revolution*. Lincoln, Neb., 1981.

Hicks, J. D. *Republican Ascendency, 1921-1933*. London, 1960.

Hill, Larry D. *Emissaries to a Revolution: Woodrow Wilson's Executive Agents in Mexico*. Baton Rouge, La., 1973.

Hobsbawm, E. J. *Bandits*. London, 1972.

Hodges, Donald, and Ross Gandy. *Mexico, 1910-1976: Reform or Revolution?* London, 1979.

Hughes, Lloyd H. *Las misiones culturales Mexicanas y su programa*. UNESCO, Paris, 1951.

Huizer, Gerrit. *La lucha campesina en México*. México, 1970.

──────. *Peasant Rebellion in Latin America*. London, 1973.

Islas Escárcega. L. *Diccionario rural de México*. México, 1961.

Jacobs, Ian. *Ranchero Revolt: The Mexican Revolution in Guerrero*. Austin, Tex., 1982.

Johnson, John J. *Political Change in Latin America: The Emergence of the Middle Sectors*. Stanford, Calif., 1958.

Joseph, G. M. *Revolution from Without: Yucatán, Mexico and the United States, 1880-1924*. Cambridge, 1982.

Katz, Friedrich. *The Secret War in Mexico: Europe, The United States and the Mexican Revolution*. Chicago, 1980.

Kirshner, Alan M. *Tomás Garrido Canabal y el movimiento de las Camisas Rojas*.

México, 1976.

Lewis, Oscar. *The Children of Sánchez.* New York, 1961.

———. *Five Families.* New York, 1959.

———. *Life in a Mexican Village: Tepoztlán Revisited.* Urbana, Ill. 1963.

———. *Pedro Martínez.* London, 1969.

Lieuwen, Edwin. *Mexican Militarism: The Political Rise and Fall of the Revolutionary Army, 1910–1940.* Albuquerque, N.M., 1968.

Martínez Assad, Carlos. *El laboratorio de la Revolución. El Tabasco Garridista.* México, 1979.

Martínez Nuñez, Eugenio. *La Revolución en el estado de San Luis Potosí.* México, 1964.

Meade, Joaquín. *Historia de Valles. Monografía de la Huasteca Potosina.* San Luis Potosí, 1970.

———. *Semblanza de don José Encarnación Ipiña.* San Luis Potosí, 1956.

———. *La Huasteca Veracruzana.* 2 vols. México, 1962.

Mecham, John Lloyd. *Church and State in Latin America: A History of Politico-Ecclesiastical Relations.* Chapel Hill, N.C., 1934.

Medin, Tzvi. *Ideología y praxis política de Lázaro Cárdenas.* México, 1977.

Mendieta y Nuñez, Lucio. *El problema agrario de México.* México, 1964.

Menéndez, Gabriel Antonio. *Doheny el cruel.* México, 1958.

Menéndez Peña, H. *La Huasteca y su evolución social.* México, 1955.

Meyer, Jean. *Le sinarquisme: un fascisme mexicain? 1937–1947.* Paris, 1977.

———. *La Cristiada.* 3 vols. México, 1974.

———. *Historia de la Revolución Mexicana. Período 1924–1928. Estado y sociedad con Calles.* México, 1977.

———. *Problemas campesinos y revueltas agrarias (1821–1910).* México, 1973.

Meyer, Lorenzo. *Historia de la Revolución Mexicana. Período 1928–1934. Los inicios de la institucionalización. La política del Maximato.* 2 vols. México, 1978.

———. *México y Estados Unidos en el conflicto petrolero (1917–1942).* México, 1972.

Meyer, Michael C. *Huerta—A Political Portrait.* Lincoln, Neb., 1972.

———. *Mexican Rebel: Pascual Orozco and the Mexican Revolution, 1910–1915.* Lincoln, Neb., 1967.

Millon, Robert Paul. *Mexican Marxist. Vicente Lombardo Toledano.* Chapel Hill, N.C., 1966.

Montejano y Aguiñaga, Rafael. *Cárdenas, S.L.P. Historia y Geografía.* San Luis Potosí, 1973.

———. *El Valle de Santa Isabel del Armadillo S.L.P.* San Luis Potosí, 1964.

———. *El Valle del Maíz, S.L.P.* San Luis Potosí, 1967.

Moore, Barrington, Jr. *Social Origins of Dictatorship and Democracy: Lord and Peasant in the Making of the Modern World.* London, 1973.

Muñoz, Ignacio. *Verdad y Mito de la Revolución Mexicana.* México, 1962.

Niemeyer, E. V. *Revolution at Querétaro: The Mexican Constitutional Convention of 1916–1917.* Austin, Tex., 1974.

Noyola Barragán, Luis. *Como murieron los Generales Magdaleno y Saturnino Cedillo.* San Luis Potosí, 1964.

Olivera Sedano, Alicia. *Aspectos del conflicto religioso de 1926 a 1929. Sus antecedentes y consecuencias.* México, 1966.

Parkes, Henry Bamford. *A History of Mexico.* Boston, 1969.

Perry, Laurens Ballard. *Juárez and Díaz: Machine Politics in Mexico.* DeKalb, Ill., 1978.

Pletcher, David M. *Rails, Mines and Progress: Seven American Promoters in Mexico, 1867-1911.* New York, 1958.

Powell, Philip Wayne. *Capitán Mestizo: Miguel Caldera y la frontera norteña. La pacificación de los Chichimecas (1548-1597).* México, 1980.

Powell, T. G. *El liberalismo y el campesinado en el centro de México (1850 a 1876).* México, 1974.

Quirk, Robert E. *An Affair of Honor: Woodrow Wilson and the Occupation of Veracruz.* New York, 1968.

_____. *The Mexican Revolution and the Catholic Church, 1910-1929.* Bloomington, Ind., 1973.

_____. *The Mexican Revolution, 1914-1915: The Convention of Aguascalientes.* Bloomington, Ind., 1960.

_____. *Mexico.* Englewood Cliffs, N.J., 1971.

Raby, David L. *Educación y revolución en México.* México, 1974.

Reed, Nelson. *The Caste War of Yucatán.* Stanford, Calif., 1964.

Reina, Leticia. *Las rebeliones campesinas en México (1819-1906).* México, 1980.

Reyes Heroles, Jesús. *El liberalismo Mexicano.* 3 vols. México, 1957-1961.

Reynolds, Clark W. *The Mexican Economy: Twentieth-Century Structure and Growth.* New Haven, Conn., 1970.

Rius Facius, Antonio. *Méjico cristero, historia de la ACJM, 1925-1931.* México, 1960.

Rivera Marín, Guadalupe. *El mercado de trabajo. Relaciones obrero-patronales.* México, 1955.

Rodríguez Barragán, Nereo. *Biografías Potosinas.* San Luis Potosí, 1976.

_____. *El canónigo Mauricio Zavala, apóstol del agrarismo en el Valle del Maíz.* San Luis Potosí, 1972.

_____. *Historia y Geografía del Municipio de Rayón.* San Luis Potosí, 1972.

Ross, Stanley R. *Francisco I. Madero: Apostle of Mexican Democracy.* New York, 1955.

Rouaix, Pastor. *Diccionario geográfico, histórico y biográfico del estado de Durango.* México, 1960.

_____. *Génesis de los artículos 27 y 123 de la Constitución Política de 1917.* México, 1959.

Ruíz, Ramón Eduardo. *The Great Rebellion: Mexico, 1905-1924.* New York, 1980.

_____. *Mexico: The Challenge of Poverty and Illiteracy.* San Marino, Calif., 1963.

_____. *Labor and the Ambivalent Revolutionaries: Mexico, 1911-1923.* Baltimore, 1976.

Schmitt, Karl M. *Communism in Mexico: A Study in Political Frustration.* Austin, Tex., 1965.

Schryer, Frans J. *The Rancheros of Pisaflores: The History of a Peasant Bourgeoisie in*

Twentieth Century Mexico. Toronto, 1980.

Scott, Robert E. *Mexican Government in Transition.* Urbana, Ill., 1964.

Senior, Clarence. *Land Reform and Democracy.* Gainesville, Fla., 1958.

Shanin, Teodor, ed. *Peasants and Peasant Societies.* London, 1971.

Shulgovski, Anatol. *México en la encrucijada de su historia.* México, 1972.

Silva Herzog, Jesús. *El agrarismo Mexicano y la reforma agraria. Exposición y crítica.* México, 1959.

———. *Breve historia de la Revolución Mexicana.* 2 vols. México, 1960.

———. *Una vida en la vida de México.* México, 1972.

Simpson, Lesley Byrd. *Many Mexicos.* Berkeley, 1966.

Sinkin, Richard N. *The Mexican Reform, 1855-1876: A Study in Liberal Nation-Building.* Austin, Tex., 1979.

Spectator [pseud. Enrique de Jesús Ochoa]. *Los cristeros del volcán de Colima.* 2 vols. México, 1961.

Spender, J. A. *Weetman Pearson. First Viscount Cowdray.* London, 1930.

Stein, Stanley J., and Barbara H. Stein. *The Colonial Heritage of Latin America.* New York, 1970.

Taracena, Alfonso. *La Revolución desvirtuada.* 7 vols. México, 1966–1970.

———. *La verdadera Revolución Mexicana.* 18 vols. México, 1960–1965.

Tischendorf, Alfred. *Great Britain and Mexico in the Era of Porfirio Díaz.* Durham, N.C., 1961.

Townsend, William C. *Lázaro Cárdenas. Demócrata Mexicano.* México, 1954.

Tuchman, Barbara W. *The Zimmerman Telegram.* New York, 1979.

Turner, Frederick C. *The Dynamics of Mexican Nationalism.* Chapel Hill, N.C., 1968.

Urquizo, Francisco L. *Origen del ejercito constitucionalista.* México, 1964.

Valadés, José C. *Historia de la Revolución Mexicana.* 10 vols. México, 1963–1967.

———. *Imaginación y realidad de Francisco I. Madero.* México, 1960.

———. *Orígenes de la república mexicana. La aurora constitucional.* México, 1972.

Vanderwood, Paul J. *Disorder and Progress: Bandits, Police and Mexican Development.* Lincoln, Neb., 1981.

Velázquez, Primo Feliciano. *Historia de San Luis Potosí.* 4 vols. México, 1946.

Veliz, Claudio, ed. *The Politics of Conformity in Latin America.* London, 1967.

Vernon, Raymond. *The Dilemma of Mexico's Development: The Roles of the Private and Public Sectors.* Cambridge, 1963.

Warman, Arturo. *"We Come to Object." The Peasants of Morelos and the National State.* Translated by Stephen K. Ault. Baltimore, 1980.

Weber, Max. *General Economic History.* Translated by Frank H. Knight. New York, 1966.

Whetton, Nathan L. *Rural Mexico.* Chicago, 1948.

Wilkie, James W. *The Mexican Revolution: Federal Expenditure and Social Change since 1910.* Berkeley, 1970.

Wilkie, James W., and Edna Monzón de Wilkie. *México visto en el siglo XX: entrevistas de historia oral.* México, 1969.

Wolf, Eric R. *Peasant Wars in the Twentieth Century.* New York, 1968.

Wolfskill, George, and Douglas W. Richmond, eds. *Essays on the Mexican Revo-*

lution: Revisionist Views of the Leaders. Arlington, Tex., 1979.
Womack, John, Jr. *Zapata and the Mexican Revolution.* London, 1972.
Zalce y Rodríguez, Luis J. *Apuntes para la historia de la masonería en México.* 2 vols. México, 1950.

SECONDARY WORKS: UNPUBLISHED MATERIAL

Ankerson, Dudley Charles. "Saturnino Cedillo and the Mexican Revolution in San Luis Potosí 1890–1940." Ph.D diss., Cambridge University, 1981.
Arvide, José. "General de División Saturnino Cedillo." Unpublished manuscript made available to me by Colonel José Arvide, San Luis Potosí.
Beezley, William Howard. "Revolutionary Governor: Abraham González and the Revolution in Chihuahua 1909–1913." Ph.D diss., University of Nebraska, 1969.
Cornelius, Wayne A., Jr. "Crisis, Coalition-Building, and Political Entrepreneurship in the Mexican Revolution: The Politics of Social Reform under Lázaro Cárdenas." Unpublished manuscript, Stanford University, July 1969.
Falcón, Romana. "The Rise and Fall of Military Caciquismo in Revolutionary Mexico: The Case of San Luis Potosí." D.Phil. diss., Oxford University, 1983.
Fowler Salamini, Heather. "The Agrarian Revolution in the State of Veracruz 1920–1940: The Role of the Peasant Organizations." Ph.D diss., American University, 1970.
Watkins, Holland Dempsey. "Plutarco Elías Calles: El Jefe Máximo of Mexico." Ph.D diss., Texas Technical College, 1968.

NEWSPAPERS

El Estandarte, San Luis Potosí	1892–1911
Excélsior, Mexico City	1920–1938
El Nacional, Mexico City	1930–1938
El Universal, Mexico City	1920–1938
Times, London	1920–1938
New York Times, New York	1920–1938
El Agricultor Mexicano, Mexico City	1900–1910
El Demócrata, Mexico City	1915
El Machete, Mexico City	1926–1938
La Esfera, San Luis Potosí	1938
Daily Worker, London	1934–1936
El Azteca, San Luis Potosí	1929
Única, Mexico City	1967
Hoy, Mexico City	1938
El Diario de Yucatán, Mérida	1948
El Sol de San Luis Potosí, San Luis Potosí	1953–1955
El Heraldo de San Luis Potosí, San Luis Potosí	1952, 1954, and 1961

INTERVIEWS

Arvide, Colonel José. July–August 1974, San Luis Potosí. Arvide was Cedillo's secretary from 1920 to 1938.

Cabrera Ipiña, Ernesto. July–August 1974, Bledos *hacienda* and San Luis Potosí. Ernesto Cabrera Ipiña is the brother of Octaviano, with whom he administered the family estates during the decade prior to the expropriation of the Bledos *hacienda* in 1937.

Cabrera Ipiña, Octaviano. July–August 1974, San Luis Potosí. Octaviano Cabrera Ipiña is the grandson of José Encarnación Ipiña, whose archive he keeps in San Luis Potosí.

Espinosa y Pitman, Alejandro. 16 August 1974, San Luis Potosí. The son of Alejandro Espinosa y Cuevas, joint owner of Angostura until his death in 1914, Sr. Espinosa y Pitman retains what little remains of the family archive.

Fuentes, Colonel Manuel. 2 February 1975, Mexico City. One of Cedillo's secretaries and his personal telegraphist from 1931 to 1938, Colonel Fuentes remained with Cedillo until his death.

Martínez, José. 10 August 1974, San Luis Potosí. Martínez was a veteran of Cedillo's campaigns against the Cristeros.

Mata, Manuel, 31 July 1974, Mexquitic, San Luis Potosí. Mata was a veteran of Cedillo's campaigns against the Cristeros.

Muñiz Moreno, Salvador. 19 February 1975, San Luis Potosí. Muñiz Moreno was chairman of the Central Conciliation and Arbitration Board in San Luis Potosí in 1938.

Ochoa, Juan. July 1974, San Luis Potosí. A member of Cedillo's personal staff in 1938, Ochoa was in 1974 the Agrarian Department official in San Luis Potosí responsible for the management of the colonies Cedillo founded.

Perogordo y Lazo, José. 2 August 1974, San Luis Potosí. A local magistrate in Ciudad del Maíz in 1911, Perogordo y Lazo was defense lawyer for Saturnino Cedillo when Cedillo was accused of rebellion in 1913.

Portes Gil, Emilio. 6 June 1974, Mexico City. Portes Gil was president of the republic in 1929.

Prieto Laurens, Jorge. 20 August 1974, San Luis Potosí. Prieto Laurens was governor of San Luis Potosí from September through December of 1923.

Index

Acción Revolucionaria Mexicana (ARM), 167, 168, 170, 178
Acosta, Emilio, 185
Acosta, Miguel, 41–42, 46, 50, 185
Acosta, Ramón, 65
Acosta, Timoteo, 65
Administrador, defined, 219
Administradores de campo, 13
Agrarian Convention, in San Luis Potosí, 113–14, 115–16
Agrarian credit banks, 115, 153–54
Agrarian Department. See *Departamento de Asuntos Agrarios y Colonización* (DAAC)
Agrarian laws. *See* Land redistributions
Agraristas, xii–xiii, 139, 193, 219; in De la Huerta revolt, 108–9; of Cedillo, 110, 130, 134–35, 144, 151, 181–82, 184; disarmed, 110–11, 130; in Cristero revolt, 122–27, 129–30; in Escobar revolt, 128–29, 130
Agricultores, 13–14, 21; defined, 219
Agricultural School at Chapingo, 163
Agriculture, 1, 205–11; growth of, 4–7, 9–12; crisis of 1908–1909 in, 21–24; during revolutionary period, 68, 76–77, 86; during Great Depression, 146; and land reforms of Cárdenas, 154. *See also* Land redistributions
Agua Prieta movement, 90, 92, 97, 195
Aguascalientes, 8; Convention of, 71, 73
Aguilar, Cándido, 64, 65, 78
Aguilar, Higinio, 81
Aguilar, Severo, 135
Aguilar, Valentin, 100
Aguirre, General, 128
Ahumada (rancher), 41
Alamilla, Rutilio, 134, 136, 187
Alardín, Ismael, 65
Alatorre, Enrique, 182, 183
Aldape, Gonzalo, 65
Alexander, Knox, U.S. vice-consul, quoted, 241
Alger, William E., U.S. consul, quoted, 31

Almazán, General Andreu, 135, 142, 143, 147–48, 170, 178, 190, 196, 198; regime of, at Nuevo León, 151–52, 183
Alvarado, General Salvador, 77–78, 102, 108, 196
Álvarez, Herminio, 73
Amaro, General Joaquin, 122, 125, 129, 141–42, 150, 185, 196
American National Metallurgical Company, 9
American Smelting and Refining Company (ASRC), 86, 112–13, 117, 158–61
Amparo, defined, 219
Anaya, Aureliano, 187
Anaya, Rafael, 135
Angostura, *hacienda* of, 9–10, 21, 22, 55; conflicts of, with smallholders, 17–20; and Cedillo family, 28, 29; raids by Cedillo on, 57, 66–67; land of, redistributed, 97
Antejos colony, 139
Anticlericalism. *See* Roman Catholic Church
Anti-Reelectionist Party, 167
Anti-reelectionists, and Madero 32–35
Aranda Díaz, Miguel, 182
Arango, General, 178
Araujo, Alberto, 135, 161, 187
Arbitration and Conciliation Board, 112, 158–59
Arguinzóniz, Joaquin, 18
Arguinzóniz, Mariano, 18
Arguinzóniz family, 14, 29, 40, 194
Argumedo, Benjamín, 52, 56, 57, 62, 77
ARM. See *Acción Revolucionaria Mexicana*
Armendáriz, Rafael, 161
Army, 32; and Madero, 40, 44, 47, 48; and Huerta, 59; Agua Prieta movement in, 90, 92, 97, 195; De la Huerta revolt in, 108–11, 124, 127, 134, 196; campaign against *agraristas* by, 111, 130; Escobar revolt in, 128–30, 139, 170, 196; and Cárdenas, 166. *See also* Constitutionalists

Arrendatario, defined, 219
Arriaga, Camilo, 24-25
Arrieta, Domingo, 38, 60
Arrieta, Mariano, 60
Arroba, defined, 219
Arvide, José, 134
ASRC. *See* American Smelting and Refining Company
Ataturk, Kemal, 141
Atlas factory, 159
Avendaño, General, 189
Ávila Camacho, General Manuel, 171, 181, 185, 186
Ayala, David, 155
Ayana, Manuel, 158

Bailey, David C., quoted, 249
Banco de Crédito Ejidal, 115, 172
Banco de San Luis Potosí, 10-11
Banco Ixtlero, 135-36
Banco Nacional de Crédito Agrícola, 115
Bañuelos, General, 170-71, 180, 188, 189
Barba González, Silvano, 147, 148
Barbosa, General, 178
Barragán, Juan, 82-83, 85-88, 103-4
Barragán, Juanita, 100, 120
Barragán, Pablo, 100
Barragán family, 14, 18, 120
Barrenechea, Arturo Mayo, 71
Barrenechea, Pedro, 36, 49-50
Barrenechea family, 14
Barrientos, Gabriel, 135
Barrón, Adelardo, 187
Bassols, Narciso, 142
Bazant, Jan, 21
Becerra, Daniel, 50, 56, 70
Belloc, Arellano, 162, 172, 175-76
Beltrán, José, 186
Benavides, General Eugenio Aguirre, 75
Black Shirts, 167
Bledos, *hacienda* of, 78, 205-8
Blocker, William, U.S. consul, 80
Bojórquez, Juan de Dios, 147, 159
Bonillas, Ignacio, 89-90
Bonney, Wilbert E., U.S. consul, 39, 42, 50, 64, 69, 77, 80; quoted, 45, 51-53, 60, 63, 233-36
Boyle, Walter F., U.S. consul, 112;
quoted, 92, 109, 116, 246, 247
Brena, General, 189
Brito Foucher, Rodolfo, 161
Buentello, Manuel, 55-57
Burlingham, Lloyd, U.S. consul, quoted, 241

Caballero, General Luis, 82-84
Cabrera, Luis, 47
Cabrera family, 14, 25
Caciques, 11, 135, 155, 191, 196; defined, 219
Caciquismo, defined, 219
Calles, Plutarcho Elías, 125, 128-30, 135, 137, 170, 193, 196-97; as presidential candidate, 100, 102-8; elected president, 114-15; relationship with Manrique, 114-19; quoted, 120; anticlerical policy of, 121-23; Portes Gil succeeds, 127; dominates Mexican politics, 132; land reforms of, 115, 122, 139-40
Calles, Rodolfo, 147
Campesino, defined, 219
Campos, Cheche, 60
Canada, William, U.S. consul, quoted, 60-61
Cano, Dr. Abel, 106, 133; as governor of San Luis Potosí, 118, 121-22
Cantú, Esteban, 89-91
Carbajal, Francisco, 70
Cárdenas, *hacienda of,* 8, 18, 24, 97
Cárdenas, Lazaro, 142, 193, 197-98; assumes presidency, 143-44; quoted, on Cedillo, 146, 255; reforms under, 146-47, 153-58, 166-67; victorious over Calles, 147-50; victorious over Portes Gil, 150-51: nationalizes Atlas factory, 159; and 1937 elections, 162-63; forces Cedillo to resign as minister of agriculture, 163-64; right-wing opposition to, 167-69; tries to weaken Cedillo, 171-78; expropriates oil companies, 180; orders Cedillo to Michoacán, 181; memoranda by Cedillo to, 183-84, 189; attacked, 187-88
Carmona, General, 178
Carranza, General, 178
Carranza, Jesús, 69

Carranza, Venustiano, 33–34, 49, 100, 114, 121, 125, 192, 194, 195; leads Constitutionalists against Huerta, 59–70; opposes Villa, 69–70, 71–89, 91; land reform decree of, 73–75, 80, 81, 88, 102; and 1917 constitution, 80–82; backs Barragán in San Luis Potosí 82–83, 85; confronted with labor unrest, 86–87; and presidential election of 1920, 89–90; death of, 90

Carreño, Hermilo, 104

Carrera, Pedro, 65

Carrera Torres, Alberto, 36, 38, 42–43, 60, 64, 65, 73, 75, 76; land reform plan of, 62–63, 67, 73, 87; death of, 83

Carrera Torres, General Francisco, 63–65, 73, 129, 130, 134–37, 177, 180, 197

Carson, W. E., quoted, 1, 224

Casa del Obrero Mundial, 48, 70, 86–87

Castillo, Epifanio, 106, 134

Castillo, Ignacio, 187

Castillo, José, 64, 134

Castillo, Julio, 65

Castillo, Zacarías, 65

Castrejón, Captain, 190

Castro, Agustín, 38

Castro, Cesario, 38

Castro, J. A., 65

Castro, José Rodríguez, 62

Catorce, town of, 34, 63; mining strike at, 44, 103

Caudillismo, defined, 219

Caudillos, 3, 7, 8, 72, 110; defined, 219

Cavazos, Marcial, 84, 110

CCM. See Confederación Campesina Mexicana; Confederación de Clase Media

Cedillo, Amado, 27–29, 55

Cedillo, Cleofas, 27, 28, 65; in revolt against Cepeda, 53–57; in revolt against Huerta, 60, 62; in revolt against Carranza, 73–75; death of, 75

Cedillo, Elodio, 190

Cedillo, Engracia, 27

Cedillo, Higinia, 27, 136

Cedillo, Hipólito, 134, 186

Cedillo, Homobono, 27, 84

Cedillo, Magdaleno, 27–28, 36, 65, 142; in revolt against Cepeda, 53–57; in

revolt against Huerta, 60, 62–67, 70; in revolt against Carranza, 73–84: death of, 84, 195

Cedillo, Saturnino, xi–xiv, 16, 193–99; background of, 27; defends Palomas workers, 29; visits Madero in prison, 35–36; in revolt against Cepeda, 53–57; imprisoned, 57, 62; opposes Huerta, 66–67, 70; and death of J. Espinosa y Cuevas, 71; opposes Carranza, 73–89; land reforms under, 87, 95–100, 111–12, 138–41, 172–74, 197; joins Agua Prieta movement, 90–91; backs Manrique, 103–11; relationship with Manrique deteriorates, 116–19; second marriage of, 120; moves against Cristeros, 123–27; elected governor of San Luis Potosí, 125; moves against Escobar revolt, 128–29: retains power of agraristas, 130–31; at high point as ruler of San Luis Potosí, 132–35, 142, 144–45; financial mismanagement by, 135–36; tours Europe, 136, 141; becomes minister of agriculture, 136, 142, 146, 152; backs Cárdenas, 143–44, 147–49; religious tolerance under, 149, 152–53; opposes land reforms of Cárdenas, 153–58; threatened by labor unrest, 158–60; and 1937 elections, 160–63; resigns as minister of agriculture, 163–64; tries to form antigovernment alliance, 165–71; government campaign to weaken, 171–78; seeks loans from U.S., 179; ordered to Michoacán, 181–82; contemplates revolt, 181–86; manifestos by, 185, 189, 212–17 (reproduced); revolt against Cárdenas by, 186–89; in hiding, 189–90; death of, 190–91

Cedillo, Vicente, 16

Cedillo family, 17–18, 20, 23; history of, 27–30; and anti-reelectionists, 35–36; and Maderistas, 42–43

Ceniceros, Severiano, 38

Centro Industrial y Agrícola Potosino, 14–15, 22

Centro Patronal de San Luis Potosí, 158–59, 178

Cepeda, Gustavo, 35

Cepeda, Dr. Rafael, 34, 35, 41, 42; as governor of San Luis Potosí, 45-46, 49-58, 61-63
Cerritos district, 7
Cerro Prieto, hacienda of, 21-22, 51
Cervantes, Justina, 65
CGOCM. See Confederación General de Obreros y Campesinos de México
Chao, General Manuel, 38, 60, 75
Chapingo, Agricultural School at, 163
Charles III of Spain, 3
Chase National Bank, 179
Chichimecas, 4
Chihuahua, state of, 11-12, 37-38, 39, 48
Científicos, 32; defined, 219
Cinco Estrellas Mining Company, 50
Ciudad del Maíz, 4, 26, 53, 75-76, 138, 194; unrest in, during Porfiriato, 15, 16, 20; Cedillo family in, 20, 27, 39; attack on, by Cedillos, 56-57; renamed "Magdaleno Cedillo," 142, 198
Civic Action Party of the Middle Class, 167
Clevenger, Lloyd, 179
CNA. See Comisión Nacional Agraria
CNC. See Confederación Nacional Campesina
CNOM. See Confederación Nacional de Organizaciones Magisteriales
Coahuila, state of, 32, 33-34, 59, 82
Coatsworth, John, 7
Cobb, Zachary, 69
Collado, Florencio, 187
Colonization Law, 12
Colorado River Land Company, 156-57
Comisión Nacional Agraria (CNA), 95, 99, 100, 106, 115, 139, 143
Comité Popular de Acción Revolucionaria, 174
Communist party, 152, 166, 167, 171
Compañía Deslindadora de Tierras Baldías, 17
Compañía Deslindadora Eisman Urista, 17

Compañía Metalúrgica Mexicana, 9
Compañía Nacional Ixtlera, La, 135-36
Composiciones hechas, 12
Condueñazgo, 18; defined, 219
Confederación Campesina Mexicana (CCM), 157, 161-62, 171-72, 176
Confederación de la Clase Media (CCM), 167-68, 169
Confederación de Trabajadores de México (CTM), 150, 159, 160-61, 166, 174, 176-77, 179, 185
Confederación General de Obreros y Campesinos de México (CGOCM), 147, 150
Confederación Nacional Campesina (CNC), 157-58, 161-62
Confederación Nacional de Organizaciones Magisteriales (CNOM), 137
Confederación Patronal de la República Mexicana (CPRM), 166
Confederación Regional de Obreros Mexicanos (CROM), 87, 89, 101-5, 114, 122, 137-38, 147, 150
Confederation of Independent Parties, 167
Confederation of the Middle Class. See Confederación de la Clase Media (CCM)
Conscription law, 63-64
Constitutions: of 1857, 11, 16, 24-25, 80; of 1917, 80-81, 82, 88, 111, 112, 123, 142
Constitutionalist Democratic Party, 168-69
Constitutionalists: organized, 59-61; in campaign against Huerta, 61-70; victorious in San Luis Potosí, 70-71; in campaign against Villa, 71-73; as army of occupation, 77-85
Contreras, Calixto, 20, 38-39, 45, 60, 68, 77, 82, 91
Contreras, Jesús, 65
Córdova, General, 178
Coronado, Ramón, 65
Corral, Ramón, 32, 33, 35
Cortina, Felipe, 16
Cosío Robledo, Francisco, 65
CPRM. See Confederación Patronal de la República Mexicana
Creel, Enrique, 37

Cristiada, 122; defined, 219. *See also* Cristero revolt

Cristero revolt, xiii, 122–29, 134, 135, 144, 147, 152, 193, 196, 219; resurgence of, 167, 178, 182

CROM. See *Confederación Regional de Obreros Mexicanos*

Cruces, *hacienda* of, 106

Cruz, General, 128

CTM. See *Confederación de Trabajadores de México*

Cuellar, General Ignacio, 134, 189

Cura, Félix, 187

Curiel, Ignacio, 135–36

DAAC. See *Departamento de Asuntos Agrarios y Colonización*

Daily Worker, The, 169

Dávila, Alberto, 65, 66

Dávila, José Maria, 110

Dávila, Jesús Sánchez, 65

Dávila, Vicente, 79–80

Dawson, Claude, U.S. consul, quoted, 59, 238, 240

De la Huerta, Adolfo, 90, 102, 107; revolt of, 108–11, 124, 127, 134, 196

De la Maza, Refugio, 123

De la Maza family, 14

De la Mora, Monsignor Miguel, 123, 124

De la O, Genovevo, 91, 193

De la Torre, Genaro, 18, 20, 29

De la Torre family, 18

De los Santos, Pedro Antonio, 35, 43, 45–46, 62, 64, 75

De los Santos, Samuel, 75, 79, 103–5

Del Pozo, Jesús, 71

De Negri, Ramón, 95

Denunciations. See *Tierras baldías,* denunciations of

Departamento de Asuntos Agarios y Colonización (DAAC), 143, 147, 150, 153, 155, 156, 173, 174

Depressions: during Porfiriato, 14, 24, 37, 49; Great, 136–37, 143, 146

Díaz, Félix, 20, 49, 81, 82, 89, 90

Díaz, Porfirio, xii, 20, 22, 31, 49, 52, 53, 58, 62, 124, 129, 192, 194; assumes presidency, 3–4, 14; and railroad

building, 7; agrarian laws of, 11–12, opposition to, growth of, 15–16, 24–26; 1910 reelection of, 32–35; revolt against, 35–43; resignation from presidency, 43

Díaz Soto y Gama, Antonio, 83, 103, 114, 138, 162

Diéguez, General Manuel, 76, 83–84, 108, 196

Díez Gutiérrez, Carlos, 8, 18, 42

Díez Gutiérrez, colony of, 57

Díez Gutiérrez, Pedro, 16

Díez Gutiérrez family, 14

División de Centro, 128

Doheny, Edward, 10–11

Donación, defined, 219

Ejidal Patrimony, Law of, 115

Ejidatarios, xii–xiii; defined, 219. See also *Agraristas*

Ejidos, defined, 219; as communal land, 12, 47, 56, 74; petitioning for, *see* Land redistributions

Elizondo, Jerónimo, 159

Escandón, Pablo, 41–42

Escobar, General, 128

Escobar revolt, 128–30, 139, 170, 196

Escobedo, Colonel Josué, 134, 181, 182

Espejel Chavarría, General Enrique, 189

Espinosa Mireles, Gustavo, 79, 82

Espinosa y Cuevas, Alejandro, 17

Espinosa y Cuevas, Antonio, 17

Espinosa y Cuevas, Javier, 71

Espinosa y Cuevas, José María, 14–15, 17, 62, 67; as governor of San Luis Potosí, 20, 24, 26, 43

Espinosa y Cuevas family, 22, 29, 194; and Angostura *hacienda,* 9–10, 17–18, 22, 23, 53–55

Estancita, 27, defined, 219

Estandarte, El, 23, 25, 33–35, 37, 43; closed, 58; quoted, 25, 225, 231–32

Estrada, General Enrique, 108, 109, 196

Estrada, Roque, 35

Excélsior, 163

"Executive Law for Land

Redistribution, An" (manifesto by A. Carrera Torres), 63

Fascists, 167, 168–70, 178, 181
Federación Regional de Obreros y Campesinos (FROC), 158
Fiber production, 10, 27, 28, 55–56, 135–36, 151
Fierro, Rodolfo, 71
Figueroa, Ambrosio, 38
Figueroa, Francisco, 38
Figueroa, Rómolo, 38, 60
First Agrarian Junta, 63
Flores, Andrés, 41, 125
Flores, Daniel, 141
Flores, Mariano, 65
Flores, Nicolás, 65
Flores Magón, Ricardo, 25
Foodstuffs, prices of, 87, 209
Forbes, Courtenay, British chargé d'affaires, quoted, 252–53
Franco, Francisco, 166
Freemasons, 122
France, 121
Frente Único de Trabajadores, 159, 174
Frías, General, 178
Furber, Carlos, 166

Gallegos, Rodolfo, 125
Gallop, Rodney, quoted, 257, 261
Galván, Francisco, 18
Galván, Ignacio, 124
Galván, Úrsulo, 157
Ganaderos, 13; defined, 219
García, J. Guadalupe, 187
García, León, 112–15, 119, 161–62, 171–72, 176
García, Magdaleno, 135, 190
García, Paulino, 56–57
García, Pedro, 65
García Téllez, Ignacio, 142, 147, 185
García Vigil, Colonel Manuel, 73, 75
Garcinava, Fernando, 108
Garrido Canabal, Tomás, 132–33, 136, 147–53, 158, 177, 181
Gasca, Celestino, 105
Gavira, General Gabriel, 76, 79

Germany, 169, 170
Gogorrón, *hacienda* of, 51, 80, 106, 114
Gold Shirts, 169, 170, 178
Gómez, General Arnulfo, 124–25, 196
Gómez, Marte, 102, 157
González, Efrén, 134, 136
González, Félix, 100
González, Jesús, 16
González, Pablo, 61, 69–70
Gordoa, María Azanza, 124
Gordoa family, 14
Gorostieta, Enrique, 127, 129
Great Britain, 7, 169
Greene, Graham, quoted, 169–70, 264
Gruening, Ernest, quoted, 85, 93
Guanajuato, state of, 1, 4; Cristero revolt in, 122, 125–27; revolt against agrarian reform in, 166–67
Guggenheims (investors), 9
Gutiérrez, Eulalio, 64, 65, 70–71, 73, 75
Gutiérrez, Hermenegildo, 172
Gutiérrez, Ignacio, 38
Gutiérrez, General Luis, 82, 106, 109

Hacendados, xii–xiii, 91, 193–94; during economic development, 9–10, 14–15; and Díaz, 11–14, 33; struggle with smallholders, 11–12, 15–20, 26, 31, 53–55, 193–94; during 1908–1909 agricultural crisis, 21–24; and Cedillo family, 28–30, 55–56; and Madero uprising, 41–42; Madero's attempt to limit holdings of, 45; refusal to raise wages, 51, 55; and Huerta, 62; and Constitutionalist pillaging, 64, 66, 76–79; and Dávila, 80; and Cedillo, 97–99, 139–40, 172, 194–95; benefit from disarming of *agraristas,* 111; and Cárdenas, 154–55, 166; defined, 220
Haciendas, defined, 220. *See also* individual names, e.g., Angostura, Bledos, etc.
Hall, Linda, 93–94
Hamm, Theodore, U.S. consul, quoted, 234–35

Henequén, 9, 10
Henshaw, Enrique, 100, 117
Hermosillo, Hilario, 118
Hernández, Arnulfo, 184, 187
Hernández, Dionisio, 50
Hernández, Lamberto, 134–35
Hernández, General Noriega, 75
Hernández, Rafael, 55
Hernández Ceballos family, 14
Hernández Netro, Mateo, 134, 152; as
    governor of San Luis Potosí, 176–78,
    182, 185
Herrera, Rodolfo, 110
Hintze, Paul von (German
    ambassador), 48–49, 58
Hohler, Thomas, quoted, 230
Hoy, 189
Huasteca, 1–2, 12, 33, 62, 125, 135;
    described in 1871, 4–5; development
    of, 10–11; revolts in, 36–37, 40, 42, 46,
    50, 57
Huasteca Oil Company, 147, 179
Huerta, Refugio, 188
Huerta, General Victoriano, 44, 48, 71,
    84; seizes power, 49, 58; revolt
    against, 59–70; resignation from
    presidency, 70

Illescas, *hacienda* of, 41, 101, 172
Indians, 4, 15, 36, 38, 60–61, 135;
    Chichimeca, 4; Oqui, 38; Yaqui, 90,
    93, 126, 170–71, 193; Mayo, 93, 193. *See
    also* Mestizos
Infante, Juan, 161
Ipiña, José Encarnación, 10, 21, 22, 51,
    102; as governor of San Luis Potosí,
    43, 45–46
Ipiña, Roberto, 9
Ipiña family, 14, 194
Italy, 169, 170
Iturbe, General Ramón, 78, 85, 185
Ixtle. See Fiber production
Izaguirre, Pedro, 135, 187

Jabali, El, *hacienda* of, 41–42
Jacobs, Ian, 155
Jara, Heriberto, 85
Jara, Mariano, quoted, 239
Jaramillo, Antonio, 187

Jasso, Bruno, 187
Jefe Máximo (title), 132, 220
Jefes políticos, 20, 38, 41; created by
    Díaz, 3–4; hostility to, 26; abolished,
    49; restored, 62, 64; defined, 220
Jiménez, Eugenio, 117–18; 134, 182–84,
    187

Katz, Friedrich, 68, 72

Labor, La, *ejidos* of, 99, 173
Labor Department, 79, 159
Labor Party, 104
Laguna region, 38, 154, 155
Lagunillas, *hacienda* of, 18, 33, 41, 97
Land redistributions: by Díaz, 11–12; by
    Madero, 47, 55–56, 60; Carrera
    Torres plan for, 62–63, 67, 73, 87; and
    Carranza decree, 73–75; and *peones
    acasillados,* 74, 88, 95, 124, 138, 143; by
    Cedillo, 87, 95–100, 111–12, 138–41,
    172–74, 197; by Obregón, 93–95, 101,
    129; by Nieto, 101–2; and *agraristas,*
    110–11; by Calles, 115, 122, 139–40; by
    Cano, 121; divisive effects of, 122, 124;
    and political machines, 132–33; by
    Ortiz Rubio, 138–40; by Cárdenas,
    146–47, 153–59, 166–67, 193
Lárraga, Leopoldo, 37, 40, 41, 46, 125
Lárraga, Luis, 134, 175
Lárraga, Manuel, 40, 41, 65, 66, 75,
    79, 100, 125
Lárraga family, 33, 46
League for the Defense of Religious
    Liberty (LNDLR), 122–27, 178
Lechuguilla, 10, 205
Leija, Arturo, 176, 182, 187
Leija, José María, 176, 187
León, Luis, 102, 113–14, 150
León de la Barra, Francisco, 43, 44
Letcher, Marion, U.S. consul,
    quoted, 236
Liberal Party, 11, 24, 121. See also
    Partido Liberal Mexicano (PLM)
Liberal Republican Party, 104
Liga Católica Popular Potosina, 123–25
Liga Nacional Campesina (LNC), 130, 157
Limantour, José, 32
Lista de raya, defined, 220

Llano del Perro, *hacienda* of, 97
LNC. See *Liga Nacional Campesina*
LNDLR. *See* League for the Defense of Religious Liberty
Lombardo Toledano, Vicente, 147, 150–51, 159, 163–64, 169–71, 181
López de Lara, César, 75, 82
Loyola, Alfonso, 179
Loyola, Jacinto, 127
Luna, Melitón, 186
Luviano, Rentería, 84

McGoogan, G. B., quoted, 230–31
Machete, El, 152, 156–57, 169
Madero, Francisco, 20, 23–24, 29–30, 31, 55, 58, 129, 170, 192, 194; as presidential candidate, 32–35; imprisoned, 35–36; revolt by, 36–43; becomes president, 43–44; attempts reform, 43–49; death of, 49
Madero, Gustavo, 83
Madero, General Raúl, 102
Magallanes, Ponciano, 124
Magaña, General Gilgardo, 89, 170, 180, 181, 183–85, 189
Mange, General, 111
Manrique, Aurelio, Jr., 137, 138, 143, 158, 171; Cedillo backs, 103–11; as governor of San Luis Potosí, 111–18; overthrown, 118–19, 120–21, 125, 131, 133; visits Cedillo, 126; supports Escobar revolt, 128; assaulted by Cedillo forces, 161–62
Manufacturing, 7, 8, 24, 146
Manzo, General, 85, 128
Márquez brothers, 81
Martí, Arturo, 69
Martínez, Gregorio, 57
Martínez, Juan, 118, 119
Martínez, Miguel Z., 84
Martínez, Pantaleona, 27, 28
Martínez, Severino, 88–90
Martínez, Zeferino, 29, 56
Marxism, 142
Mata, Manuel, quoted, 120
Maximato, 132–45, 138, 139, 145, 196–97, 220
Maximilian, emperor of Mexico, 3, 17

Maycotte, General Fortunato, 108, 196
Mayo Indians, 93, 193
Maytorena, José Mariá, 38, 59–60, 72
Meade, Eduardo, 67, 135–36
Meade, Federico, 36
Meade family, 14
Medrano, Julian, 65
Meixuero, Guillermo, 81–82
Méndez, Sidronio, 56–57
Mendoza, Santana, 110, 135
Mestizos, 4, 122; defined, 220
Mexican Catholic Apostolic Church, 117, 122
Mexican Central Railroad, 7–8
Mexican Crude Rubber Company, 79
Mexican Light and Power Company, 112
Mexican Metallurgical Company, 40
Mexican Nationalist Youth, 167
Mexican National Railroad, 7–8
Mexican Revolution, xii, 31–58, 193–95, 198
Mexican Revolutionary Action. See *Acción Revolucionaria Mexicana* (ARM)
Mexican Telephone and Telegraph Company, 148
Mexican Tramway Company, 147
Mexico City, 10, 15, 44, 46, 102; anti-reelectionist congress in, 34; Cepeda's imprisonment in, 61; kidnapping of teachers in, 137; Zapatistas' occupation of, 109
Michoacán, 181–82
Middle class, 139, 194; rise of, 14, 25–26; opposition to Díaz, 32, 34, 37, 39, 49; opposition to Cárdenas, 166
Milpitas colony, 139
Mines, 49, 66, 68, 79, 86; during Porfiriato, 3, 4, 7–9, 24, 26, 31; strike against, at Catorce, 44, 103; closings of, 50, 76; affected by Cedillo's policies, 136, 137; during Great Depression, 138, 146
Ministry of Agriculture, 20, 47, 99; as headed by Cedillo, 136, 142, 146, 152, 156–57, 163–64
Ministry of Development, 17, 47–48, 53–55

Ministry of War, 93, 97, 99
Moctezuma, José, 17
Moctezuma, Mariano, 16
Moctezuma family, 23, 27, 28; disputes over property of, 18-20, 29, 53-55, 76, 99
Monson, Edmund, British minister, quoted, 132, 250, 255
Montebello, *hacienda* of, 10, 27, 56-57, 84, 205-8; profits of, 22, 208; and Cedillo family, 28, 29; colony on land of, 97
Monterrey, city of, 7, 32, 34, 55, 151, 152
Montoya, Pedro, 41, 42
Morales, Genaro, 187
Morales, Jesús, 38
Morelos, state of, 9, 11-12, 41; Zapatista revolt in, 20, 38-39, 61; Brigade of, 71
Moro, Fidel, 124, 125
Morones, Luis, 105, 114, 138, 150
Morrow, Dwight, U.S. ambassador, 115, 129, 140, 143
Moya, Luis, 38
Múgica, General Francisco, 77-78, 147, 150-52, 160, 163, 181
Murguía, General, 85, 100
Muriedas family, 14
Murray, John, quoted, 256-57
Mussolini, Benito, 141, 167

Nacional, El, 160
Najera, Feliciano, 187
Naranjo, El, colony of, 99
Natera, Pánfilo, 61
National Agrarian Commission. See *Comisión Nacional Agraria*
National Aviation School, 169, 171
National Civic Action, 167
National Committee in Defense of the Race, 167
National Labor Office, 47-48
National Union of Revolutionary Veterans. See *Unión Nacional de Veteranos de las Revolución*
Navarro, Cándido, 41-43, 50, 65
Navarro, Ponciano, 46, 50
Nieto, Lorenzo, 106, 109
Nieto, Rafael, 88; as governor of San

Luis Potosí, 100-102, 104, 138
Noriega López, Antonio, 65
Nuevo León, Almazán regime in, 151-52, 183

Obregón, Álvaro, 80, 86, 118, 121, 128, 143, 192, 193, 195-96; command of Constitutionalists, 61, 72; opposition to Villistas, 72-73, 75, 77; as entrepreneur, 85; as presidential candidate, 89-90; elected president, 90; land reforms of, 93-95, 101, 129; backing of Calles, 102; and election in San Luis Potosí, 104-8; De la Huerta revolt against, 108-10; visit to Cedillo, 125-26; death of, 127
Obregón, Álvaro, colony of, 99, 134
Ocay y Obregón, Ignacio Montes de, 36
O'Hea, Patrick, U.S. consul, quoted, 241
Oil companies, 10-11, 136; Cedillo seeks loan from, 179; Cárdenas expropriates, 180, 185
Oliva, Tomás, 174-75
Olivera, Práxedis, 106, 110
Olivo, Eugenio, 65
Oqui Indians, 38
Oriente Brigade, 71
Orozco, Pascual, 38, 39, 57
Orozco, Pascual, Jr., 48, 49, 52, 56, 60
Orozco, Wistano Luis, 20, 76
Orozquistas, 48, 61, 71
Ortega, Melchor, 150
Ortega, Toribio, 38
Ortiz, Agustín, 18-20
Ortiz, Emilio, 18
Ortiz Rubio, Pascual, 128, 148; as president, 132, 134, 137, 139-42
Osornio, Saturnino, 149-50
Oyarbide, Francisco, 65

Palma, 10, 205
Palomas, *estancita* of, 36, 55, 56, 165; Cedillo family in, 27-29; Cedillo regime in, 133-35
Pani, Alberto, 48
Parada, La, *hacienda* of, 106

Parente, Manuel, 41
Parker, Charles, 81-82
Parra, Leocadio, 77
Parres, Dr. José, 163
Partido Cooperatista Nacional (PCN), 102-3
Partido de la Revolución Mexicana (PRM), 180, 185
Partido Liberal Mexicano (PLM), 16, 24-25, 32
Partido Renovador Potosino, 161, 162
Partido Revolucionario Nacional (PRN) 127, 128, 130, 132, 135, 142-44, 147-75 passim, 180
Partidos, of San Luis Potosí, 4-5, 11; defined, 220
Party of National Action, 167
Pegram, Stanley Dutton, quoted, 257
Peláez, Manuel, 72, 77, 84, 89, 91
Peña, José, 15
Peones, 13-14; defined, 220
Peones acasillados, 14, 45, 62, 101, 194-95; and *ejidos,* 74, 88, 95, 124, 138, 143; defined, 220
Peones de campo, 14, 21
Peotillos, *hacienda* of, 106
Pequeña propiedad, defined, 220
Pequeño propietario, defined, 220
Pereyra, Orestes, 38
Pérez, Idelfonso, 65
Pérez Castro, José, 42, 50, 57, 71
Pérez Gallardo, Reynaldo, 188
Pérez Treviño, Manuel, 143, 144
Pesquera, Pedro, 50
Pilar García, J., 135
Pineda O., Alberto, 89-91
Pino Suárez, Jose Maria, 46
Plan of Agua Prieta, 90
Plan of Ayala, 48, 57, 73
Plan of Guadalupe, 58-59, 69
Plan of San Luis Potosí, 36-37, 44, 55-56
Plan of Veracruz, 108
PLM. See *Partido Liberal Mexicano*
PRN. See *Partido Revolucionario Nacional*
Poblado, defined, 220
Population, in San Luis Potosí, 4-5, 11, 12-13, 22, 223-24

Porfiriato, 3-43, 90, 120, 121, 156, 192-94, 198, 220
Portes Gil, Emilio, 95, 112, 143, 148, 149, 152, 157, 158; as president, 129-32, 137-38
Posadas, Jesús, 124
Posesión definitiva, 101, defined, 220
Posesión provisional, 101, defined, 220
Potosí Revolutionary Party, 104
Presidente municipal, defined, 220
Presidential elections: of 1910, 31-35; of 1920, 89-90; of 1924, 102-7; of 1940, 158, 165, 178, 190, 193
Prieto Laurens, Jorge, 102-7, 116-17, 124, 168-69
PRM. See *Partido de la Revolución Mexicana*
Puerto, Elvira Carrillo, 118

Querétaro, state of, 1, 125, 126, 128

Railroads, 76; constructed, 7-8, 15, 18; economy stimulated by, 8-10; strikes against, 24; rebel attacks on, 57-58, 63-64, 69, 79, 80, 83, 84
Ramos, Matías, 148
Rancheros, changes in numbers of, during Porfiriato, 12-14, 21; struggle with *hacendados,* 11-12, 15-20, 26, 31, 53-55, 193-94; during 1908-1909 agricultural crisis, 21-23; in Palomas, 28; support of Madero by, 32-33, 38; and Constitutionalist pillaging, 76-77, 79; and *ejidos,* 122, 124, 155; defined, 220
Rascón, *hacienda* of, 23, 66-67
Rascón family, 14
Red Batallions, 87
Red Shirts, 136, 153
Reformist Party, 104
Reglamento, defined, 220
Restitución, defined, 220
Reyes, General Bernardo, 15, 16, 32-34, 40, 46, 49, 50, 83
Reyes, Juan, 17
Reyes Vega, Father, 128
Rincón Gallardo, Santiago, 162
Rincón Terrenos, Miguel, 42

Ríos Zertuche, General, 170-71
Rivas Guillén, Genovevo, 180-82, 184, 188
Road Workers' Union. See *Frente Único de Trabajadores*
Robledo, Francisco, 39
Robles, José Isabel, 81-82
Rodríguez, General Abelardo, 135, 147-48; as president, 132, 142-43
Rodríguez, Conrado, 163
Rodríguez, Guadalupe, 130
Rodríguez, Luis, 150, 185
Rodríguez, Nicolas, 167, 168, 170, 178
Rodríguez, Wenceslao, 110, 128
Rodríguez Cabo, José, 62, 65
Rodríguez Cabo family, 14
Roman Catholic Church: and *Partido Liberal Mexicano,* 24-25; and E. Gutiérrez, 70; and Constitution of 1917, 80-81; and Nieto, 101; and Manrique, 117; and Cano, 121-22; and P. Calles, 121-23; and Cristero revolt, 122-27; and socialist education, 142; and Cárdenas, 149, 152-53, 166, 167, 197
Romero, General, 70
Rubio, Colonel García, 118, 123
Rubio, General, 178
Ruíz, Jose, 38
Ruíz Blas (of Agrarian League), 190
Rurales, 40, 48, 50, 52, 55, 58; created, 3-4; defined, 220

Sáenz, Aarón, 102, 128, 147
Sáinz, Gregorio, 33
Salas, Enrique, 64, 65, 73, 83, 84
Salas, Herminio, 174
Salas family, 27-28
Salinas Salt Company, 71
Sánchez, Fiacro, 127
Sánchez, Graciano, 106, 110-19, 143, 144, 147, 157, 171-72, 176, 198
Sánchez, General Guadalupe, 108, 196
Sánchez Gascón, Rubén, 182
San Diego, *hacienda* of, 10
Sandoval, Benigno, 134, 135
San José colony, 98-100
San Luis Potosí, city of, 3, 8. *See also*

San Luis Potosí, state of
San Luis Potosí, state of, 1-3; in early Porfiriato, 3-7; economic development of, 7-10, 14-15; and agrarian laws, 12-14; agrarian unrest in, 15-20; Espinosa y Cuevas regime in, 20, 24, 26, 43; during 1908-1909 agricultural crisis, 21-24; during Madero revolt, 32-33, 34-37, 39-43; Madero government and strikes in, 44-45; Cepeda regime in, 45-46, 49-58, 61-63; Constitutionalist movement in, 61-70; Gutiérrez regime in, 70-71; Carranza forces, victory in, 75-79; Dávila regime in, 79-80; Barragán regime in, 82-83, 85-88; Martínez regime in, 88-90; Nieto regime in, 101-2, 104, 138; 1921 election in, 103-11; Manrique regime in, 111-19; Cano regime in, 118, 121-22; and Cristero revolt, 123-25; Cedillo's assumption of governorship of, 125; Cedillo's dominance in, 132-38, 142, 144-45; teachers' strike in, 137, 144, 160; slowing of redistribution in, 138-40; religious tolerance in, 149, 152-53; Cedillo and labor unrest in, 158-60; elections of 1937 in, 160-63; Cedillo's retirement to, 165; Defense Ministry's action against, 171; attack on agrarian reforms of Cedillo in, 171-74; drought in, 177; Cárdenas speech in, 185-86; Rivas Guillén as governor of, 188
San Rafael, *hacienda* of, 56
San Rafael Paper Company, 147
Santa María de Río, *partido* of, 4, 12
Santiago, Juan, 15-16
Santos, Francisco, 65
Santos, Fulgencio, 65
Santos, Gonzalo, 104, 132, 135, 141-44, 176, 187, 197, 198
Santos, Samuel, 65
Santos, Trinidad, 65
Santos Alonso, Manuel, 65
Santos Coy, Ernesto, 63, 64, 65
Santos family, 46, 75
Sarabia, Juan, 82-83, 103-4

Schryer, Frans, 27; quoted, 228
Segura, Vicente, 161, 175, 182, 187, 188
Serdán, Aquiles, 37
Serrano, General, 196
Sharecroppers, 14, 23, 28, 55, 70, 77, 155
Shaw, George P., quoted, 132
Silver, 8–9
Sinarquismo, defined, 220
Sinarquista, defined, 220
Sindicato de Mineros, Metalúrgicos y Similares, 160
Sintora, General, 178
Siurob, Dr., 177
Six-Year Plan, 143
Smallholders. See Rancheros
Smelting, 8–9, 24, 44, 58, 136. See also American Smelting and Refining Company (ASRC)
Soberón, Agustín, 67
Soberón family, 14
Social Democrat Party, 167
Socialist education, 142, 152–53, 167, 197
Sonora, state of, 38, 59–61, 90, 192–93
Soviet Union, 167
Spaniards, 66
Spanish Anti-Communist and Anti-Jewish Association, 167
Stackpole (American trader), 78–79
Strikes, 44–45, 47, 147–48; mining, 44; American Smelting and Refining Company, 112, 159–60; teachers', 137, 144, 160; Mexican Telephone and Telegraph Company, 148; Atlas plant, 159; Confederación de Trabajadores de México, 177
Sucesión Presidencial en 1910, La (Madero), 32, 33
Survey companies, 11–12, 17

Tamaulipas, 82, 149; insurrection in, 178
Tamazunchale district, 33, 42; described, 5–6; disturbances in, 7, 15–16, 32
Tanguma, Captain, 126–27
Tapia, Catarino, 57
Tapia, Juan, 57

Tapia, Rafael, 38
Tapia, Tomás, 135, 157, 176
Teachers' strike, 137, 144, 160
Tejeda, Adalberto, xii, 95, 113, 118, 132–33, 143, 152
Téllez, Manuel, 137
Terrazas, Luis, 37
Tienda de raya, defined, 220
Tierras baldías, denunciations of, 11, 12, 17–20; defined, 220
Tierras demasiadas, defined, 221
Tierra temporal, defined, 221
Topete, General, 128
Toranzo, Luis, 22, 51
Toranzo family, 14
Torres, Antonio, 65
Torres, Juan, V., 174–76
Torres, Nicolás, 42
Torres, Simplicio, 65
Treviño, Jacinto B., 75
Turrubiartes, Apolonio, 57
Turrubiartes, Florencio, 187
Turrubiartes, General Ildefonso, 57, 110, 124, 125, 127, 130, 182, 183, 187; as governor of San Luis Potosí, 134, 137

Ugalde, Manuel, 40, 41
Unión Nacional de Veteranos de las Revolucion (UNVR), 167–70
United States, 32, 39, 41, 72, 127, 177; war with, 3; and railroads, 7, 24; ownership of industry by, 9–11, 23, 147; Madero's flight to, and Huerta, 59; occupation of Veracruz by, 68–69; repatriation of Mexican workers from, 146; Cedillo seeks help from, 178, 179
Universal, El, 161, 163, 171, 177
Unused Lands, Law of, 93–94
UNVR. See Unión Nacional de Veteranos de las Revolución
Urbina, Tomás, 75–76

Valadez, Macías, 12–13
Valles, town of, described, 5
Vanderwood, Paul J., 40
Vázquez, Gabino, 147, 173, 174, 176, 182

Vázquez, Juan Ocho, quoted, 165
Vázquez Gomez, Emilio, 46, 47
Vázquez Gomez, Francisco, 34, 36, 39, 46, 47
Vázquez Vela, Gonzalo, 185
Vega, Leopoldo, 33, 39
Veracruz, 60-61; U.S. occupation of, 68-69; Plan of, 108
Veral, Angel, 71
Verástegui, Isauro, 41-42
Verástegui, Ramón, 187
Verástegui family, 14
Vidal, General Carlos, 109
Villa, Francisco, 38, 102, 195; with Constitutionalist Army, 60, 61, 68; in conflict with Carranza, 69-70, 71-89, 91; joins Agua Prieta movement, 90
Villa de Arriaga, 23, 26, 40
Villa de Carbonera, 17
Villa de Reyes, 26, 41, 114
Villarreal, General Antonio, 94-95, 102, 149
Von Merck, Ernesto, 134, 137

Ward, H. G., 3
Waters Pierce Oil Company, 10
Wheeler, H. J. A., 80

Wilson, Henry Lane, U.S. ambassador, 31, 48-49; quoted, 25, 230
Wilson, Woodrow, 68
Wollemberg, Carmen, 120
Wollemberg, Federico, 120, 187

Yaqui Indians, 90, 93, 126, 170-71, 193
Yocupicio, General 170, 180, 188, 189

Zapata, Emiliano, xiv, 27, 30, 91, 104, 162, 193, 194; in revolt against Díaz, 39, 45; and Madero, 44, 45, 56; and Carranza, 82, 83, 85; death of, 89
Zapatismo, 193-94
Zapatistas, 20, 76, 82, 109, 192-94; break with Madero, 44, 56; Plan of Ayala of, 48, 57, 73; and Huerta, 60, 61; and Villa, 72; under Magaña, 89; and De la Huerta, 90
Zavala, Father Mauricio, 15-16
"Zavala, Padre," 39-40
Zúñiga, Marcelino, 134, 161, 175, 182, 186-87
Zuñiga, Mariano, 20, 42
Zuno, José, 95